Reconstructing Political Economy

Reconstructing Political Economy offers an original perspective on the questions the great economists have asked and looks at their significance for today's world. Written in a provocative and accessible style, it examines how the diverse traditions of political economy have conceptualized economic issues, events and theory. Going beyond the orthodoxies of mainstream economics, it shows the relevance of political economy to debates on the economic meaning today.

This book is a timely and thought provoking contribution to a political economy for our time. In this light, it offers fresh insights into such issues as modern theories of growth, the historic relations between state and market, and the significance of globalization for modern societies. *Reconstructing Political Economy* will be of great interest to economists, political scientists, and historians of economic thought.

William K. Tabb is Professor of Economics and Political Science at Queens College and the Graduate Center of the City University of New York. He is the author of *The Japanese System: Cultural Economy and Economic Transformation*; *The Political Economy of the Black Ghetto*; and co-editor of *Instability and Change in the World Economy*.

Contemporary Political Economy series

Edited by Jonathan Michie, Birkbeck College, Univer

Reconstructing Political Economy

The great divide in economic thought

William K. Tabb

London and New York

First published 1999
by Routledge
11 New Fetter Lane, London EC4P 4EE

Simultaneously published in the USA and Canada
by Routledge
29 West 35th Street, New York, NY 10001

Routledge is an imprint of the Taylor & Francis Group

Typeset in Baskerville by
M Rules
49, Southwark Street, London, SE1 1RU
Printed and bound in Great Britain by MPG Books Ltd, Bodmin

British Library Cataloguing in Publication Data
A catalogue record for this book is available from the British Library

Library of Congress Cataloguing in Publication Data
Tabb, William K.
  Reconstructing political economy: the great divide in economic
  thought/William K. Tabb.
  p. cm. – (Contemporary political economy series)
  Includes bibliographical references and index.
  ISBN 0–415–20762–2 (hardbound: alk. paper).–
  ISBN 0–415–20763–0 (pbk.: alk. paper)
  1. Economics. 2. Economics–History. I. Title. II. Series.
  HB171.5.T13 1999
  330–dc21   98-47961
                                                        CIP

ISBN 0–415–20762–2 (hbk)
ISBN 0–415–20763–0 (pbk)

The Econ tribe occupies a vast territory within the far North. Their land appears bleak and dismal to the outsider, and travelling through it makes rough sledding; but the Econ, through a long period of adoption, have learned to wrest a living of sorts from it. They are not without some genuine and sometimes even fierce attachment to their ancestral ground, and their young are brought up to feel contempt for the softer living in the warm lands of their neighbours, such as the Polscis and the Sociogs. Despite a common genetical heritage, relations with these tribes are strained – the distrust and contempt that the average Econ feels for these neighbours being heartily reciprocated by the latter – and social intercourse with them is inhibited by numerous taboos. The extreme clannishness, not to say xenophobia, of the Econ makes life among them difficult and perhaps even dangerous for the outsider. This probably accounts for the fact that the Econ have so far not been systematically studied.

(Leijonhufvud 1973: 347)

Contents

1 The two cultures in economics

[A]nalytic effort is of necessity preceded by a preanalytic cognitive act that supplies the raw material for the analytic effort . . . [T]his preanalytic cognitive act will be called Vision. It is interesting to note that vision of this kind not only must precede historically the emergence of analytic effort in any field but also must re-enter the history of every established science each time somebody teaches us to *see* things in a light of which the source is not to be found in the facts, methods, and results of the preexisting state of the science.

(Schumpeter 1954: 41)

Arjo Klamer (1990) has a way of describing what is peculiar about modern economics. He draws a square to stand for the rigid axiomatic method that dominates most journals in the field. The square, he points out, is the ideal shape of modernist architecture and painting, of Mondrian and Mies van der Rohe. Squares are about facts and logic. Show me the theorem. Then he draws a circle some distance from the square. Circles are about metaphor and story. Circle reasoning is the other half. Tell me your story. Since the seventeenth century, and especially during the mid-twentieth century the square and the circle have stood in nonoverlapping spheres, sneering at each other.

(McCloskey 1993:69)

One is tempted to say that there are two types of people, those who require determinacy and closure, and those who can tolerate ambiguity and open-endedness.

(Samuels 1992: 11)

The work of most economists consciously or not involves a characterization of their own time and place. For Adam Smith, it is the conflict between an old system of centralized authority in which the crown attempted to organize allocation of resources, and a new way of doing things in which individuals were to be trusted to know their own best interests; and, rather than these interests being only in conflict, Smith said that out of competition would come greater wealth for the nation (yet he did, as we shall see, support statist interventions in some circumstances). Within half a century, the business class had grown and the conflict between landlords and capitalists became the central issue. Thomas Malthus developed theories that supported the claims of the landlord class, whilst David Ricardo championed the manufacturers. These classical economists saw the period in which they lived as a transitional one of struggle for control over the future direction of society. Advocacy of competing claims brings out the creative talents of thinking individuals as they reconceptualize the world around them. In the Great Depression, John Maynard Keynes addressed the causes of unemployment by reinterpreting how capitalism functions. State intervention, which in Smith's time was often an exercise in monopoly power to extend privilege and economic rents to friends of the sovereign, becomes for Keynes, in an era of democratic governance, a vehicle that, if used wisely, could produce stability and generate growth.

By the end of the twentieth century, the cutting edge of economics was a new classical economics which, because of developments in the larger society, theorized state intervention as the problem and not the solution. Deregulation, privatization and market flexibility were once again the point of departure for innovative economics. I will suggest that after neoliberalism as a policy practice, and new classical economics as a theoretical stance, have run their course, the strength of the political economy approach will become more prominent within the profession. The reason is that the social structure of accumulation and regulatory regime that dominated the postwar period has eroded. This process of decomposition is one in which market forces do this work, or rather their undoing work. At a certain point, it is argued, this negative moment comes to have severe costs; it goes too far in a sense, and there is need to build a new stable, regulatory pattern. This argument will be more appealing to readers for whom the political economy approach to the institutional embeddedness of markets and concerns over the costs of social inefficiency are core parts of how they understand economics.

Material conditions and epochal change interact with people's *Weltanschauung*, world-view, pre-analytic vision, personal psychology and optimistic or pessimistic natures, and together contribute as much and perhaps more than their education and training to how they go about answering such questions. There are those who see order and stability underlying temporary dislocations; others see instability as the norm. The first group wants to explain permanence; the second studies the nature of evolution and change. The mainstream of economic science concerns itself with the first sort of project. This book is about understanding socio-economic transformation from the latter perspective, which I will call the mainline tradition. Our subject is how change in the political economy is experienced and theorized. We take a long view in examining how economists think and have thought over the last 200 years and more about the economy – how they make up the stories and ways of answering questions they label economic. This book explores how to think about our own time through a rereading of the history of economic thought. It is both an intervention in an ongoing conversation concerning what constitutes a usable economics and a reflection on the classical question of the nature and causes of the wealth and wellbeing of nations. It is written for those who are coming into this ongoing conversation with little knowledge of what has been said and are confused as a result. Of course, there are perhaps as many interpretations of what the conversation has been about as there are participants in the conversation, and so what follows, whilst it draws on a vast literature and on hundreds of opinions, is only one possible telling of the story.

Themes of a political economy for our time

Defining trends are hard to read as they unfold. That is part of the reason why economists line up on different sides of explanatory divides; but they also disagree for the reason Joseph Schumpeter suggests ―they begin with different ideas about the way the world works and should function. They have different pre-analytic visions. He believed that such vision is 'ideological almost by definition' (Schumpeter 1954: 42). Since, as Schumpeter thought, it is the 'preanalytic cognitive act that supplies the raw material for the analytic effort,' vision selects the topics and the approach to their study without which there is no economics. As a result, when we look at our subject from various angles, and when different people do the looking, the world can take on a multitude of shapes. Methodology has become a growth industry in economics, although we shall not comment on the many efforts to organize the topic (Khalil 1995; Dow 1997; Samuels 1997).

My account of how our time in economic history can be understood may tell something of my own approach. It stands at variance to the mainstream procedure that proposes economic science to be relevant to all times and places and its task to be building a system of logical order from given premises. Like much of the work in the mainline tradition, my account stresses historical specificity and institutional embeddedness, and builds generalized models from such awarenesses. The view taken is that the central process that characterizes our time is that of decomposition of the particular postwar technological foundation and the regulatory regime that went with it, and a recomposition based on a very different pattern of production and of spatial arrangement within the world system. I want to argue that seeing economics in this way, as a set of questions better described from the stance of the study of political economy, is a tradition of long standing in the history of economic thought. Seen in this way, contemporary approaches that fit this mainline approach need to be understood as a broad and historically influential methodology. The fact that mainstream economics has marginalized this approach, has weakened the profession in ways that will be discussed. This book is an effort to restore the holistic quality of economics or political economy as a *social* science. In periods in which the institutional givens and broader political economic context in which economists work are changing, this broader understanding of the discipline is especially essential.

The transformation of the late twentieth century is talked about in many ways. Some stories stress the importance of flexible and time-responsive innovation and niche marketing, a freeing of finance, a reordering of our industrial relations system, and of government as an actor in the political economy. Today we can speak of the world rushing headlong in two directions at the same time. The accelerated project of modernity, the efficiency driven reorganization and rationalization of commodity space, coexists with a renewed vitality of identity politics and its strong resistances based on notions of self-preservation and traditional understandings of fairness. Thus, on the one hand, there is the globalization of economies, a technological revolution in communication, a sweeping aside of traditional ways and the more secure accommodations of the past, and a forcing of a new stance on nations wanting access to leading technologies, lowest cost capital, and widest choice of products. Countries, corporations, and individuals are all being told that they need to get more competitive through privatization and balanced budgets.

On the inevitable other hand, this process which economists applaud – thinking it is better to 'get with' historic change than to try to stop 'progress' – has created many losers who are in pain, confused, and angry at being told that they 'don't have the right attitudes,' that they aren't showing proper 'flexibility.' The pressures have spawned freelance efforts to survive through work in the underground economy to individualized acts of violence. Politically, movements of collective resistance organize around local identities – nationalism, ethnicity, racial and religious – in an effort to forge an 'us' suitable for venting dissatisfaction, outrage, and anger over what is happening, and to change a future that seems to exclude the sort of life the various 'we' want, and were brought up to think possible, even likely. The world moves in one and the same historical conjuncture toward a hyper-modernism of economic integration and a post-modern fragmentation of localisms.

Many economists tend to be optimistic, believing that developments in technology, given freedom to play themselves out, will produce employment and raise living standards. Innovations in computational power, biotechnology, new material sciences, and all manner of capacities undreamed of in the philosophies of even a few years ago, are opening doors to a better future. A new 'industrial' revolution, based upon the power unleashed by the microprocessor, has the potential so far only hinted at to lighten work and produce a dazzling array of consumer products and business services. The combination of free markets, global mobility, and technological innovation will free humankind from age-old miseries, or so it is hoped. Others ask how widely these benefits will be enjoyed in a world where half the world's population has never even used a telephone – the dirt road of the information highway.

A globalized economy reemerged after a hiatus of two world wars, a great depression and postwar recoveries. It is built upon technological underpinnings that, as usual in periods of significant transition, are experienced most dramatically in innovations in communication and transportation. Mainstream economics is constrained in making sense of such discontinuous developments by its methodological privileging of marginal change, regularities and self-equilibrating tendencies. Viewing economic processes as part of the larger societal functioning is discouraged by the broader specialization among academic disciplines, and the focus on understanding economics-as-science leads to a technical framing of issues that diminishes the role of social choice and enforces an economic determinism.

For its first century (roughly from Adam Smith's *The Wealth of Nations* published in 1776 to the neoclassical revolution circa 1870), economics was called 'political economy' and reflected a continuity with its earliest origin in the management of the public household and in ethics. The separation of some of its broader concerns, with the division at the end of the nineteenth century into the academic disciplines of the social sciences, increased the analytic power of the specialized discourses but perforce narrowed the scope of what had been political economy. Social concerns were for the most part left to the 'soft' academic disciplines and as topics for religion and politics. Economics aspired to scientific status and the profession came to marginalize these older traditions.

Within economics, methodologists have gone through cycles of new ways of thinking about their field. Logical positivism, Popperian falsification, Kuhnian paradigm conflicts, Lakatos research programs, and McCloskey rhetoric projects have all grabbed their attention, until they tired of a particular way of talking about how economists communicate with each other and judge how they do what it is that they do (Blaug 1976; deMarchi and Blaug 1991). There are endless ways of thinking about the profession's subcultures as a collection of ideas, symbols and learned aspects that pattern thoughts and perception, which are taught to disciples and reinforced by peers and acknowledged gifted practitioners. There are indeed separate grammars and imageries, stories and approved modes of story telling among these separate discourses. The distinctions can be variously grouped and differences can be overdrawn, of course; but sometimes it seems that distinct groups of economists are part of different tribal groupings.

In truth, there are many possible taxonomical categorizations possible for setting apart the branches of economic thinking. I am drawn to a simplifying strategy that is inspired by C.P. Snow's idea of 'the two cultures.' The contrasting cultures that C.P. Snow saw, looking at the humanities and the sciences, have I think a parallel in a division between two cultures within economics that has always been present since economics was first understood as a separate intellectual undertaking. It is not surprising that economics, which has roots in moral philosophy and its aspirations in being a 'real' science (for example like physics), should be caught in this two-cultures tension. Snow's discussion of what it was like for a scientist like himself, who was also a novelist, to truck between groups, one that was for the most part uninterested in literature and the humanistic traditions and the other appallingly ignorant of basic science, paints a picture not unfamiliar to those who have watched theorists and institutionalists, orthodox and heterodox, and other categories among economists talk about the way they do economics.

There are many kinds of conversations going on within the profession, with very different conventions and interpretative structures. My suggestion is that amidst this diversity there is a pervasive and deep cultural divide. I shall employ an A/B categorization (which will be explained at the start of the next chapter) throughout this book to describe what I think of as the most important division within the profession. Of course, any such dualistic distinction oversimplifies the complexity of interlocking and overlapping positions but can have the virtue of sharply focusing on the tensions at work. In Chapter 2, after explaining the A and B modes of doing economics, I will have more to say about the claim that these approaches represent different capacities to do science, and then suggest something of the way economics, is theorized and taught by telling two stories commonly related by mainstream economists, which are deconstructed and retold to suggest the way assumption and pre-analytic vision color the project of doing economics.

Chapter 3 is devoted to the father of economics, Adam Smith. This is not because he was the first economist (he wasn't) but because *The Wealth of Nations* was the first book to describe something we can recognize as the economic world in which we live in a fashion that remains illuminating and accessible. Smith influenced millions who have never read him but who have absorbed something of what he said, or is reported to have said. Subsequent chapters take the story through (among others) Ricardo, Malthus, Mill, Marx, Marshall, Walras, Keynes, and Schumpeter. The last part of the book examines modern growth theory and then explores economic restructuring in our time, the experiences in combining market and state, especially with regard to globalization trends and its theorizations, labor market roles and the recomposition of classes that have resulted. Our project is one of revalancing these categories, which are at the center of the debates on the economic meaning of our time. This will be undertaken in the context of the rereading of the history of economic thought. This history reminds us of the wide canvas on which political economists once created pictures of social existence and discussed the relations that defined the way their world worked. As we shall see, a number of the profession's best and brightest have struggled to combine A and B mode approaches in their work. For their pains, they have typically been accused of eclecticism,[1] a charge that appears especially prominently in what are known as Whig histories (Samuelson 1988).

Whig history reads from the present back, looking for the origin of the accepted truths of the modern period. Whig historians are willing, as Herbert Butterfield writes, 'to praise revolutions provided they have been successful, to emphasize certain principles of progress in the past and to produce a story which is the ratification if not the glorification of the present' (Butterfield 1959: v). Thus Paul Samuelson, a confirmed Whig in his approach to the history of ideas in economics, remarks that 'within every classical economist there is to be discerned a modern economist trying to be born.' He builds models of classical economics that formulate their core ideas parsimoniously in terms of modern theory (Samuelson 1978: 1415). In response, those critical of such Whiggery call attention to the tendency in such an approach to imagine that one has discovered a root or an anticipation of modern phenomena 'when in reality he is in a world of different connotations altogether' (Butterfield 1959: 12).

An alternative to Whiggish history is the study of canon formation, which works at the level of the problematics rather than the solution to the problem. As Richard Rorty writes, it spends more of its time asking 'Why should anyone have made the question of – central to his thought?' or 'Why did anyone take the problem of – seriously?' rather than asking in what respect the great dead philosopher answered a question or solved a problem in a manner consistent with that of contemporaries. The study of canon formation, if one is to follow Rorty's suggestion, can be called *Geistesgeschichte*, or 'history-of-science-as-story-in-progress' (Rorty 1984: 57). If the German compound noun fails to fall trippingly off the tongue, the concept of political economy/economics as a story in progress has appeal.

Homo economicus

The struggle in contemporary economics over its core self-definition is long standing. In one version, economic thinking is a linear, modernist undertaking that looks to physics as the model of good science. In the other, evolutionary process, contingency, and social agency are privileged.[2] In the first, economics is seen as social *science*, an enterprise that seeks rigor by focusing attention on wealth seeking or the maximization of utility within a tight framework of determinism. Employing the construct 'economic man' allows for parsimonious models and a smaller subset of possible outcomes in models to produce and allow the testing of generalizations. As John Stuart Mill, to whom the construct *Homo economicus* is most indebted, declared in 1836 (Mill 1836), economic man (the term itself was not used by Mill[3] but popularized by John Neville Keynes somewhat later) is useful because in narrowing our view of 'man' abstracting, as Mill wrote, from 'every other human passion, or motive except . . . the desire for wealth,' economics avoids being hopelessly indeterminate, the fate of the weaker social sciences.[4]

Models that allocate scarce resources on the basis of narrow self-interest require agents to have a certain mind-set. The economics student is taught to see the social benefits of a kind of selfishness inconsistent with the values of caring and kindness that the religions of the world teach, which has long brought opprobrium upon the profession.[5] Economics is taught as an alternative socialization to such 'naive' viewpoints. Teaching students to think like economists is a very different enterprise to the moral philosophy that was once the profession's starting point, and different again to the sort of practical knowledge that the business world expects. It is a turn of mind that is often puzzling at best to outsiders.

Mainstream economics has been criticized in the wider society for not offering what it once did: guidance to those for whom decency, generosity of spirit, and an inclusive sense of community are valued. Economics claims to be about allocation of scarce resources, yet one may question why it insists on such a narrow sense of the allowable or optimal allocation process. As Myra Strober asks, 'Why does economics have so much to say about selfishness and competition and so little to say about individuals' aspirations for others' well-being or about cooperation? (Strober 1994: 146). Such excluding dualisms were not present in the Scottish political economy tradition before or after Adam Smith. In this remarkable group, which included David Hume, John Millar, and Adam Ferguson, as well as Smith, men who are considered the founders of economics and who also have claim to being the originators of sociology, the project was the philosophical study of people as socialized and social beings. Over the next century, the social sciences, and especially economics, developed the analytical devise of labeling some elements of the social system as given and assumed but not explained by the increasingly narrow concept of research into understanding the social world. As Aunt Diedre has put it, economists just have a lot of trouble endogenizing love (McCloskey 1997).

In mainstream economics in the twentieth century, the strict definitions drawn between exogenous and endogenous variables, between rationality and irrationality, knowledge and ignorance, and so on, are a departure from the tradition within which the father of economics worked (Dow 1987). They are a contested departure in that the rationality of isolated individuals it presumes and the narrowness of their vision and terms within which they maximize their own wellbeing can create social problems. Major figures in the field have written that those who behave in narrow economic man terms are 'rational fools' because egoistic payoffs consistently lead to suboptimal outcomes for all involved (Sen 1977). We are told that 'the substantial absence of others' utilities from one's own is a passable definition of a sociopath' (Aaron 1994: 15).

In recent years, feminist theory has raised questions about such narrowness 'not because economics is in general too objective, but because it is not objective enough' (Harding 1995; Nelson, J. A. 1995). By insisting on divisions that counterproductively narrow the vision of economists, A mode reductionism, it is asserted, does the profession a disservice.[6] Feminist economists[7] not only challenge the dominance of 'economic man' in the profession's thinking but, more basically, question the presumed neutrality of its governing constructs that support this dehumanized ideal: the mainstream's economics of scarcity, selfishness, and competition, and the very dualities they presume (scarcity/abundance, selfishness/altruism, and cooperation/competition). These feminists suggest that the mainstream's dualistic constructs reflect a politics and defend a preference set concerning the best way the world can be organized that is far from value neutral. For example, the

> more those among the 'haves' are told that the world is characterized by scarcity and that the path to well-being is through selfishness and competition, the less likely they are to behave in ways that foster altruism, cooperation, and more equal sharing of economic goods and services.
>
> (Moore 1994: 145)

A significant literature on other-regarding behavior and dictator games offers support for such views (Hoffman *et al.* 1996).[8] Experiments on the determinants of reciprocity show that the subject's degree of social distance is an important determinant of individual choice. The context of other-regarding behavior is important. People spending time in communities in which the benefits of mutual reciprocity are high come to value social generosity in ways those not so involved do not. The rat race and the dog-eat-dog ethos of those acting out extreme versions of economic man reinforce a gender gap in the economic sphere. Social context and the formation of norms influence 'individual' behavior and choice. Reputational concerns when decisions are made in the community have implications for labor relations and contracting more broadly. Spot exchange, the norm of mainstream economics textbooks, may be better thought of as the exception rather than the norm in exchange.

Economics-as-physics is under challenge from a number of quarters as the twentieth century comes to a close. The core requirement of A mode method is that each individual has stable and coherent preferences that the economist takes as given, and such isolated individuals act always to rationalize their preferences given available options and a set of probabilistic beliefs. Such a pure self-interest motivation has long been challenged by those who call attention to other motivations: fairness or revenge, for example, which turn out to be important in the work world as well as in other realms of human interaction. A growing body of experimental economics has offered evidence for the conclusion that it may be wrong to conceptualize some types of economic behavior in these traditional terms. Many mainstream economists deny significance for economic theory to such psychological tests. Matthew Rabin concludes a summary of literature on behavioral research in this area by commenting on 'the aggressive uncuriousity' shown by many economists unwilling to consider abandoning the hypotheses of rationality and self-interest that such research brings into question. In a larger sense of the way rationality is expressed, people seem to start out with a reference level concerning what is appropriate rather than from the sort of absolute characteristics of a situation that pure theory requires. People respond more to change than absolute level, fear loss more than they value gain of equal or even greater magnitude, and so on (Rabin 1998).

Amos Tversky and Daniel Kahneman (1991) find that people value modest losses as much or more as they do gains of twice the amount. Loss aversion seems to be a widespread human trait. People also value what they have far more than the monetary value an objective observer would impute to items. This goes not only for homes and neighborhoods but even for inexpensive and apparently trivial items. How can economists know such things? Experimental economics in recent years has been developing as a field of study by creating tests to shed light on such issues by putting people in simple choice situations. In one experiment, some students are each given a mug worth about $5. They, and another group of students who were not given mugs, were asked how much they would take for the mug, both choosing between a mug and money. It might be expected that the value of the mug in terms of an amount of money they thought equivalent would be similar for the two groups. Yet those given the mugs asked on average twice as much ($7) to sell their mug as those choosing whether to take money or a mug (on average they set the value of the mug at $3.50). The researcher's explanation is that those who had randomly been given the mugs saw them as part of their reference level of endowments and considered leaving without the mug to be a loss. Additional research shows this 'status quo bias' to be strong indeed (Kahneman *et al.* 1991).

Some organizational theorists offer similar criticism from a different starting point. Their argument, that decision making arrangements in which cooperation, relational contracting, and economies of scope in an information-intensive, knowledge-based economy are crucial to business success, requires a more sophisticated psychology than one-note economic man possesses. The critique extends to understanding the way economic thinking is done and new ideas are generated among the profession's innovators. It is partially a matter of whether A mode attempts to exclude considerations of subjectivities are not an important limitation in doing economics. I suggest that it is.

The impacts of institutions on economic outcomes encompass the ways situations are framed in the minds of participants. Institutions structure extrinsic motivations and can induce preference changes and the evolution of norms.

Institutions structure the tasks people face and influence their psychological functioning and the processes of cultural learning. The question is, how important is this to economics? How significant is it for economic questions that, for example, different preferences in child rearing and schooling have profound impacts on individual socialization and so preferences? Contemporary theory of the firm shows awareness of the importance of trust in relational contracting and of the impact of different normative commitments to the presence of information asymmetries. Awareness that one or both parties may have the capacity to structure the relationship and so affect the preferences of their exchange partners, and that preferences are endogenous with respect to economic institutions, means that economists must be more sensitive to the importance of institutional choice and not simply take institutions as given or unimportant to exchange outcomes. How people are socialized has major economic implications.

Samuel Bowles has made this distinction in terms of what he calls *Hobbes' fiction*, referring to Thomas Hobbes' state of nature starting point for social analysis which considers an initial state in which 'men,' in Hobbes' own words, are assumed to have 'sprung out of the earth, and suddenly (like mushrooms), come to full maturity, without any kind of agreement with each other' (Hobbes 1651; cited in Bowles 1998: 75). Such a fiction has for more than 300 years allowed social analysts, including of course A mode economists, to ignore the real-world origins of social arrangements and preferences. This simplifies model building, but at a cost. For if preferences are affected by institutional arrangements, political rules, social conventions, and so on, 'we can neither accurately predict nor coherently evaluate the likely consequences of new policies or institutions without taking account of preference endogeneity' (Bowles 1998: 75).

Public choice theory, in which social welfare functions are presumed to be a simple aggregation of individual preferences so easily presumed by mainstream economists for their tractability and solid micro-economic foundations, will not do in a political economy. In a political economy, the very mechanisms that aggregate interests do not simply sum, but reshape, interests by creating conversations and exposing participants to novel ideas, new perspectives and possibilities. Individuals taking part in such dialogic processes select differently from a multifacited set of interests and strategies based on the inputs of other actors. Mechanisms for collective decisions do not measure the sum of individual preferences and will depend on institutional rules for policy formation. Law and custom, norms and institutions shape preferences. The sort of 'natural' inequalities of a given society produce outcomes that emerge not from some presocial state but from a historically contingent social order (Immergut 1998).

The claim that preferences are endogenous and economics should model them as such, has had extensive implications for redefining the discipline. For if economic institutions not only structure tasks for individuals but also influence their values and psychological functioning and the way individuals acquire values and desires, then institutions do more than constrain and induce particular behavior choices: they also affect preferences *per se*. Thus economic institutions may induce specific types of behavior to become more prevalent in the society. Depending on the institutional context and the expectations and norms they encourage (these may be opportunistic or cooperative, more self-regarding or more other-regarding), society is re-formed in particular directions. Sharing the view that if preferences are in fact affected by the policies and institutional arrangements that mainstream economists in the past had tended to ignore, we cannot accurately predict or pre-scribe in this increasingly important area of institutional restructuring that has become so prominent with the fall of communism, crisis in the East Asian devel-opment states, and the creation of the European Union, to take three examples current at the time of writing.

Such investigations bring us back to the fears raised by political philosophers from Aristotle to Polanyi that, as Alvin Roth writes in the traditional language of economics, 'more closely approximating idealized complete contracting markets may exacerbate the underlying market failure (by undermining the reproduction of socially valuable norms such as trust or reciprocity) and result in a less efficient equilibrium allocation' (Roth 1995; cited in Bowles 1998: 104). The impact of the acceptance of economic man assumptions by the profession may be to make real men and women more like 'economic men' in reality.

Not only do we need a social side if economics is to be a social science, but if we are to understand how economists think about economics, we need to go beyond the formal models they produce. We can then consider the possibility, for example, that Austin Robinson may have more adequately captured the core of Keynes' eco-nomic 'model' building than contemporary Keynesians when he writes: 'I have long felt that Keynes' economic thinking was in reality, intuitive, impressionistic, and in a sense feminine rather than precise, ordered, and meticulous' (Robinson 1964: 90).[9] A person's place in historical time and in the life space dimensions of identity are not irrelevant to the economics that they do.

There are two issues here. The first is how a given thinker's pre-analytic vision affects their intellectual work. The second is the extent to which what are thought of as non-economic criteria are important to understanding the realm of the economy. A society that has no guiding ideology other than avarice may be prone to disintegrating tendencies of disturbing magnitude (Thurow 1996).[10] Yet 'most economists,' Daniel Hausman suggests, 'share a moral commitment to the *ideal* of perfect competition' and 'the theoretical world of equilibrium theory, rationality, morality, and the "facts" of economic choice become tightly interlinked' (Hausman 1992: 68). He sees the pervasive and deep commitment of contemporary econo-mists to equilibrium theory as coming from such a moral vision.

One of the most difficult aspects of an exclusively A mode focus is that in pre-suming laws on the same plane of generality as those of the physical sciences, free will is reduced to consumer choice, and moral considerations to narrowest self-interest. If we accept that social value judgements are a part of how decisions that effect economic outcomes are made, then they must themselves become part of the analysis of causal understandings. Further, if we believe that the more appropriate the value orientation of a society the greater will be its options and the possibilities of its members (Eichner 1985: 12, see also Hollis and Nell 1975: ch. 2) then there is no escaping what Hausman and McPherson (1993: 672) call the 'tough and tangled territory' of moral philosophy. Ethical matters cannot properly be avoided in most economic analysis (McPherson 1984), although economists do try. Almost every introduction to economics begins by making a sharp distinction, offered in its canonical form by John Neville Keynes, Maynard's father. This is the division of economics into positive and normative branches. A positive science, he wrote, 'may be defined as a body of systematized knowledge concerning what is; a normative or regulative science as a body of systematized knowledge relating to criteria of what ought to be.' He is worth quoting further, for whilst most texts (including his) after making this distinction do not refer to normative economics ever again, Keynes *père* is of the opinion that:

> The main point involved in controversies about economic method may be indicated in outline by briefly contrasting two broadly distinguished schools, one of which describes political economy as positive, abstract, and deductive, while the other describes it as ethical, realistic, and inductive.

Unlike many economists who claim at least in principle the total separation of the two, however, he goes on: 'It should be distinctly understood that this sharp contrast is not to be found in the actual writings of the best economists of either school' (Keynes 1890: 9–10).

To see why, consider Milton Friedman's famous 1953 essay on economic methodology with its Neville Keynes' distinction between a positive science ('a body of systematized knowledge concerning what is') and normative science ('a body of systematized knowledge discussing criteria of what ought to be'). Positive economics, according to Friedman, 'is to provide a system of generalizations that can be used to make correct predictions about the consequences of any change in circumstances. . . . [It] is to be judged by its predictive power for the class of phenomena which it is intended to explain.' To Friedman, 'Positive economics is in principle independent of any particular ethical position or normative judgments' (Friedman 1953a: 3). This essay by Friedman is probably the best known work in economic methodology of all times (Redman 1989: 3), and so it is not without great importance that Friedman's contrast of positive and normative insists on a sharp break between the two approaches. Friedman's intervention was influential in its advocacy of the capacity to make accurate predictions as the criterion for evaluating economics.

Often in mainstream discussion normative simply defines the opposite of the kind of passion-free objective research that serious economists do. It is used to contrast economists 'making value judgments' from economists doing 'scientific work,' pursuing the scientific method, and so enabling non-economists to make more informed judgments about current economic policy options (Klein 1988: 437). Of course, such a differentiation is not what the normative/positive distinction is meant to convey. An economist predicting the impact of a particular tariff, for example, is making a judgment call, albeit one perhaps based on tight reasoning and a model supported by econometrics results. Most economists, speaking in church, assert the validity, and indeed the centrality, of the distinction between normative and positive, but when claims are being made for findings and policy prescriptions, outsiders can perhaps be forgiven if the claim does not appear to be that the conclusion is positively proven by economic science.

The claim to being a science sometimes leads to the assertion that economics allows not getting one's feet wet in 'the swamps of moral philosophy.' The meaning of objectivity and the claim to doing value-free science is a perennial issue that continues to divide economists perhaps more than other social scientists (Dow 1985: esp. ch. 2). The use to which the power involved in what Hobbes called the capacity to 'give names and enforce definitions' is directed, has consequences for what is and is not considered legitimate economics. Those who consider their positions on such matters as legitimated by the consensus among their peers are always short with those who wish to reopen such discussions.

Mainstream economists have long complained of chatter that recycles grumbling about method and fails to offer effective alternatives (Hoover 1995). J.N. Keynes' 1886 book was met with 'a certain sense of relief that the final word seemed to have been said' on methodology (Skidelsky 1983: 45). Francis Edgeworth, the *Economic Journal*'s first editor, in reviewing *The Scope* wrote: 'For we cannot conceal a certain impatience at the continued reopening of a question on which authorities appear to be substantially . . . agreed.' And as Sherwin Rosen has more recently observed: 'Debates about methodology have opportunity costs. Most of us prefer to assess serious attempts to do economics, rather than to spend time arguing over which method should be used in those attempts' (Rosen 1997: 150). Mainstream economics has evolved virtually independently of explicit methodological analysis (Dow 1997: 73), and it is hardly our ambition to change this now. Rather our audience is those readers who wish to understand better what it is economists do and the relationship between this practice and understanding the social world of the economy in which we live. It is perhaps necessary, therefore, to reiterate that the deductivism of the a priorist approach, the logical empiricist testing of theories against facts, as well as the use of pure mathematics, are valued tools and have important uses. The issue is whether they are all there is to economics, that is whether economics as a discipline is defined by such methodology (or any methodology) rather than, as is the case in other fields, by the subject matter studied, and whether it should be open to the approaches grouped here as B mode economics or political economy.

The economics student, in the introductory chapter of most first-year textbooks, is told that the economist speaking as a professional is engaged in positive analysis. An economist offering opinions as to what should be, and advocating the 'best' course of action, bases advise to some extent on subjective valuation and so is engaged in a normative undertaking. Economists, the student is informed, always keep the two totally separate, or should do so; but it is often difficult for non-economists, when faced with normative conclusions from economists who support their views by a claim that they are applying economic science, to remember quite what the normative–positive distinction is meant to convey. Economics is the toolkit of positive economics, or so we are told. Students can use these analytics (once they learn them properly) as they like. Tools help do a job. What kind of job is not up to the tools. Paul Samuelson, at the end of his famous text, writes:

Like a gun, which can be used to defend a home or bully a harmless stranger, these tools have an efficiency whose final contribution to welfare must depend on how they are used and by whom. They also have a certain austere aesthetic grace.

(Samuelson 1967: 798)[11]

The 'austere aesthetic grace' is associated with a pure science which Samuelson, like many other economists, sets as the goal for a successful economics. On another occasion, Samuelson lauds the ergodic hypothesis. We theorists, he says, want to remove economics 'from the realm of genuine history' and move it into 'the realm of science' (Samuelson 1969: 184).[12] There is perhaps no better clarification of the A mode aspiration: it is escaping the complexities and contradictions of experience to a plane where pure logic reigns and deterministic models govern. It is on such a plain that it is possible to do positive economics.

The judgments of what it means to do good economics are not lost on the best and brightest who enter the profession. A survey of graduate students at America's top-ranked universities disclosed that the major factor in their desire to study economics was to do policy relevant work that would effect outcomes in the real world. What they found was a professional training obsessed with doing pure theory at the highest level of abstraction. Knowledge of the economy, they told interviewers, was unimportant for success in graduate school (68 per cent thought knowledge of the economy was unimportant; only 3.4 per cent believed it was very important). The interviews reflected student appreciation of the factors that make the profession so unappealing to many outsiders: 'We took a lot of derivatives, but we never really talked about how applicable these models were, how reasonable these assumptions were.' Another student noted that, 'To do the problems, little real-world knowledge of institutions is needed, and in many cases such knowledge would actually be a hindrance because the simplifying assumptions would be harder to accept' (Klamer and Colander 1990: 25 and 26). For most undergraduates, studying theory has much of the same quality, and whilst they are told that as they progress they will encounter more and more realistic models, this is rarely the case. Because of the abstract nature of the economic core, much of the policy advice given by the economics profession in practical matters is based on long-run tendencies in the models of economic systems, which may not be useful in the shorter-run adjustment period transitions that concern policy makers. Thus the narrowness of mainstream economics can have implications for society more broadly.

Economics and political economy

The great division for practicing economists is generally considered to be between theory and empirical economics. Of these two types of economics, Thomas Mayer writes, 'One, formalist theory, is abstract theory that is concerned with high-level generalization, and looks towards axiomization. The other, empirical science theory, focuses on explaining past observations and predicting future ones'

(Mayer 1993: 7). The usual divisi[on]
prefer to work out precise soluti[ons]
tractable and others who attempt t[o]
The latter is necessarily done in
'noise' in the real world. There
theory and get pure results that
or we can do empirical work th[at]
matter of 'truth versus precis[ion]
trade-off between simplicity, g[enerality]
and plausibility and recogni[zes]
(Hausman and McPherson 1
much prized.

For many economists, th[e]
and policy economics is th[e]
the formalists. The pecki[ng]
level of abstraction. This allows the[ory]
rather more clever than those dealing with practi[ce]
skills are more clearly judged than policy insight, good
builders of complex but non-empirical models get the status, whilst those w[ho]
with the messy realities of the world do not achieve the same recognition. We have
so many difficulties in need of wise solutions that reallocating prestige and other
emollients could increase the contribution of economists to making the world a
better place. The usual campaign for better balance is to raise the status of empirical economics and the value placed on contributions to problem solving in the real
world. This line of critique does not go far enough.

The policy irrelevance of much theory is not the only problem resulting from
overspecialization and pecking order reward structures. The model builders' mode
of operation cannot capture much that is of central importance to satisfying theory,
and a great deal of empirical work is suspect in that it tells a limited story about
how the world can work. The incompleteness of economics comes from a loss of
vision of social totality, a defect reinforced by the present-day division of academic
labor. This was not always the case in economics, or as the field was traditionally
called, political economy.

We may define political economy as the study of the mechanisms used or usable
by society to operate the social economy, understanding the social economy to be
comprised of the tools, institutions and human energies that produce goods and
services.[13] Social choices in production and distribution are constrained by governance structures and a cultural economy of attitudes, norms, and values embedded
in the historically specific institutions of a society. Oscar Lange defines political
economy more formally as 'the study of the social laws governing the production
and distribution of the material means of satisfying human needs' (Lange 1963: 1).
Political economy is a return to *oikos*, the Greek from which we derive ecumenical
(all in this together), economics (material providing), and ecology (interdependence of all the creation). The core differences between economics and political
economy from such a perspective are that economics presumes the isolated

individual as its key construct,
known resources, and allow[s]
mization as its determin[ing]
facing contingent choi[ces]
governance mechan[isms]
Political economy
ally held consta[nt]
in political-e
the basis o[f]
1981: 57
as the
wan

sees the core problematic as allocation of given and

s for a mechanical model of minimization and maxi-

nts. Political economy begins with the social individual

es and bounded rationality, and considers institutions and

sms that constrain and guide individual and group activity.

s an effort to study as endogenous variables the parameters usu-

it by economists – technology, property rights, the state. Changes

onomic organization assumed away by neoclassical economics are

theorizing sources of structural change in political economy (North

). It also has a normative side, understanding normative political economy

study of how societies can best change their institutions and why they would

t to make the rules that constrain individual choice different to how they are.

he driving idea behind normative political economy,' Ben Ward writes, 'is the belief that societies can change their economic institutions – not without premeditation and discussion, of course, but certainly in response to persuasive objections to the prevailing mechanisms and compelling mechanisms and compelling arguments for different ones' (Ward 1972: 180). The more interesting economists to most readers of the history of ideas are those who, from Adam Smith to John Maynard Keynes, offer such an avowedly normative perspective within a larger political economy framework, using tools of conventional analysis modified to meet their purposes. It is just such a project that, when successful in becoming sufficiently influential, becomes important to canon formation in the discipline.

2 Of dialogic debates and the uncertain embrace

Stressing the dialogic nature of the text of the economy implies that the economy too is characterized by disparate voices. In engaging with a text of this sort, economic discourse inevitably proliferates a range of theoretical approaches. But as even the heterogeneous interpretative resources of the discipline cannot exhaust the dialogic potential of the text of the economy, this process of proliferation is never complete. Just as the text of the economy has no determinate conclusion, so the process of reading it is open-ended.

(Brown 1994b: 379)

Not only will our successors have to be far less concerned with the general (leave alone the 'generic') than we have been, they will have to bring to the particular problems they will study particular histories and methods capable of dealing with the complexity of the particular . . . . Not for them the grand unifying theory of particle physics which seems to beckon physicists. Not for them, the pleasures of theorems and proof. Instead the uncertain embrace of history and sociology and biology.

(Hahn 1991:50)

I was at a gathering at which an irate scientist of international prominence told a story about how when the 'science' scientists where he teaches were thinking about undergraduate requirements, they decided to divide the sciences into two groups: an 'A' group in which replicable experimental knowledge formed the core (such as chemistry and physics) and a 'B' group of sciences in which history and detailed distinctions are central to what the science is about and in which experimentation is rare (for example geology and paleontology). The chairman of the Physics Department writing this up for the catalogue stressed how the B sciences 'were not yet' experimental sciences in the way the A sciences are. The man telling the story, thinking of himself as a scientist, not a second-class B team scientist, was outraged. The 'not yet' seemed singularly inappropriate to him as the distinguishing mark. Can we replay the era of the dinosaurs and then perform a test with and without a large meteor disrupting life as it existed? Can we try it with small and then medium sized disruptions? Can we raise the temperature of the planet on a controlled basis and see what happens to that Earth? Lower it on a second Earth and so on? How can these things be reduced to experiments, by humans? How exactly are the B sciences supposed to become like the A sciences? They, of course, cannot. They are about an alternative understanding because of their subject matter. One is not more mature than the other.

The twofold division of the sciences to which the professors agreed for their divisional offerings captures methodological differences that are widely evident. The simple dichotomous breakdown should not suggest that there are no differences among the fields grouped in the A and the B categories, but rather that for some purposes it may be helpful to simplify matters. This dualism suggests two modes of doing science. The broad and simplifying division highlights alternative conventions and employs distinct ways in which knowledge is to be judged, what counts as cause and effect for example, or in the importance of replicable experiments for drawing 'scientific' conclusions. Practitioners of science in the two categories are perceived as judging what counts as scientific knowledge in different ways.

The differentiation made between economics and political economy thus has its counterpart in the harder sciences. The former group attempts to build logically precise models at a high level of abstraction, the latter to understand and explain the world in its multifaceted complexity of historical time. They abstract differently from secondary details, and call attention to relationships that investigators see as relevant to the particular questions being raised. Those in the second group are the circles and the A mode thinkers are the squares of Arjo Klamer's terminology introduced earlier.[1] The distance between the two cultures in economics may not be as great as that which Snow finds between the humanists and the scientists. It may perhaps be closer to the one that our story of the A and B science division suggests exists among scientists themselves, or possibly be within what might to outsiders look like a coherent school, for example *evolutionary biologists*, where currently the Gould–Dawkins debate rages. The elegant mathematical perspective of population genetics led by Richard Dawkins is one in which genes of different kinds are presumed to swim around, and those that are most successful in getting copies into the next generation eventually squeeze out their competitors. There are obvious parallels to the physical world imagined from the seventeenth to the twentieth centuries by physicists who saw the world as consisting of invisible, independent particles, paralleling the philosophical metaphor of autonomous individuals. The parallel to A mode economics is equally evident. Stephen Jay Gould and members of the camp identified with his name do not deny the importance of changes in gene frequency, but see many more important forces at work in the living world with constant dynamic changes. In such a world, DNA is embedded in a web of interaction between cell and organism, organism and environment.[2] I suspect that there are A and B cultures in many fields and that academics as well as other people can to a remarkable extent be divided into circles and squares as Samuels suggests.

Whilst any dichotomy oversimplifies, and we could make meaningful subdivisions within both our A and B camps, it is useful to this undertaking to arrange economists into A social *science* economists and B *social* science economists. The A group takes physics as its model. Not modern physics, with its interest in chaos and complexity, but seventeenth-, eighteenth- and nineteenth-century physics, bolstered by a theorem-driven mathematical fundamentalism.[3] B science (which ironically is more like modern physics than is A type economic science) is historical, institutional, and comparative. Contingency and agency are important for B type economists. The hard-core A practitioners can be condescending to B economists, hoping they someday will learn to use deterministic mathematical models and test their theories by making predictions that they then verify statistically and so come to understand economic laws. B mode thinkers can think the As narrow and simple minded. They can also be critical of mathematical modeling and econometric testing, presuming that magicians' tricks are being used when they themselves lack comfortable familiarity with such discourse.

I would make three comments about the physics to which economics aspires. First, physics is not really like the A mode economics-as-physics caricature. Second, that 'science' science can be understood as itself a B mode exercise. Third, that the division, whilst useful, is a heroic exaggeration. Freeman Dyson, a Professor of Physics at the Institute for Advanced Study at Princeton, suggests that science is a subversive project, an alliance of free spirits against the dogma of reductionism. He tells the story of the great mathematician David Hilbert. Hilbert, after 30 years of high creative achievement in mathematics at its frontiers, walked into what Dyson describes as a blind alley:

> In his later years he espoused a program of formalization, which aimed to reduce the whole of mathematics to a collection of formal statements using a finite alphabet of symbols and a finite set of axioms and rules of inference. This was reductionism in the most literal sense, reducing mathematics to a set of marks written on paper, and deliberately ignoring the context of ideas and applications that give meaning to the marks. Since mathematics was reduced to a collection of marks on paper, the decision process should concern itself only with the marks and not with the fallible human intuitions out of which the marks were reduced. . . . Success was achieved only in highly restricted domains of mathematics, excluding all the deeper and more interesting concepts.
>
> (Dyson 1995: 32)[4]

There may be those who see this story as having relevance for economics, and so it is not without interest that in Hilbert's lifetime Kurt Godel 'proved' (the quotation marks are a measure of my own ignorance as to how one proves such a thing) that in any mathematical formulation it is impossible, as a formal proposition, to separate statements into true and false. The statement may well be right, even if I cannot follow the mathematician's 'strong' proof (known as Godel's Theorem) showing conclusively that reductionism doesn't work. I would suggest that many of the best economists share this view as well. Our discussion will hopefully establish that their idea of science is akin to that of the physicist Richard Feynman, who once put the matter, 'The scientist has a lot of experience with ignorance and doubt and uncertainty . . . we take it for granted that it is perfectly consistent to be unsure.' I myself do not claim to understand what goes on in contemporary physics, but if attempts to explain to the lay public are any indication, the sort of speculative theorizing being entertained (which cannot be tested and for which there is little if any real data) should lead economists of the hard A persuasion to look for another role model (Ferris 1995).

The usual grounds for the presumed superiority of A style economics is shaky. Economists as a rule do not follow the physicist's procedure in describing when a theory may be falsified. For the physicist, as Alan Coddington has pointed out, a theory may be falsified by experiment

> only if the physicist is committed to a rejection rule which says that, in the event of a conflict between observation and predictions, the blame will *not* be placed on the observer, the equipment, the data, the calculations, the theories on the basis of which the data were interpreted, the unspecified background knowledge which has guided the investigation or the concepts in terms of which the theory is expressed.
>
> (Coddington 1975: 592–3)

Brian Loasby goes further, suggesting that a list such as Coddington's is incomplete because 'It is impossible to test any proposition without assuming – usually unawares – the validity of a great many other propositions, each of which is forever open to challenge' (Loasby 1991: 5). Philosophers know this as the Duhem–Quine problem. Many economists tend to take such statements as sheer nonsense. How can anything be done on such a premise? The point is that the impossibility of 'doing it right' and getting unimpeachably correct answers goes with the territory and is the first thing economists (among others) should concede. The humility is both good for the soul and prompts an openness of mind conducive to good scholarship.

There is a necessary relativism to B economics. It depends on the particularities of given historical circumstance. The theories developed can appear ephemeral because of this historical contingency (Backhouse 1994: 3). If the Bs are judged by A standards, they are clearly poor economists. However, if one is concerned with how economies change and develop over time, how they deal with the problems that loom centrally in a particular period and place, the aspects of the approach that A economists deplore become virtues. B thinking is especially an economics for in-between times when the givens are crumbling or evolving. An A approach is better where matters are found in a steady state or are well represented by gradual extrapolation of past relations. If one is interested in the process of institution (re)formation and the breakdown and (re)making of the constraints under which individuals make choices, then B economics, the approach of traditional political economy, is a fertile approach.

I am sympathetic to the B side but this does not mean that I think the As are the 'bad guys.' The simple functional formulations of marginalist economics have proven powerful predictors in many respects. The impounding of dynamic considerations and holding constant of institutional norms has allowed a precision in model formulation and testing that is the envy of the social sciences. The parsimonious mathematical modeling of complex relationships and statistical testing have been responsible for innumerable important advances in our knowledge of the social world. The economist's way of thinking about the world has yielded powerful insights. Critics of orthodox theory can be accused of not appreciating the importance of a coherent theoretical structure and of 'underestimating the resiliency and absorptive capacity' of the framework (Nelson and Winter 1982: 48). The orthodox theorists, however, can be accused of claiming too much for their framework, overestimating its ability to deal adequately with a range of phenomena that, by their nature, are better analyzed in evolutionary terms. I think both assertions are valid. Choice of method is a matter of the task at hand and the way that problem 'looks' to various researchers, so the preferred method of approach is dependent in some measure on temperament as well as training.

The two traditions within political economy/economics, viewed from a different angle, are captured in Keynes' assessment comparing Edgeworth and Marshall: 'Edgeworth wished to establish *theorems* of intellectual and aesthetic interest, Marshall to establish *maxims* of practical and moral importance' (Skidelsky 1994: 412). The legacy of the Edgeworth approach is found in the 'austere aesthetic grace' of mainstream economic analysis of which Paul Samuelson speaks. And while Keynes has clearly selected to characterize Marshall by his B side (as we shall also do in Chapter 5), he was of course aware that Marshall's formulation of marginalism demonstrated quite a bit of austere aesthetic grace in its eloquent and precisely formulated partial analyses. It was Marshall's B side, however, that continued to inspire, among others, Keynes himself.

The two traditions

The A economists see established relationships as applicable in all times and places, once the noise of the messy real world is removed. The purer B mode economists see each conjuncture, a specific social structure at a point in history, as differentiated and its economy needing to be studied in terms of its unique reality, as a moment in an evolutionary continuum of non-reversible history. Dividing the complex history of economic thought in this way allows for a branching based on universal laws of economic behavior good for all times and situations, and an evolutionary view of economics in which the historical specificity of institutions matters a great deal and power is a principal consideration.

It is true that some of these disagreements are political. There are liberal[5] and conservative economists, Marxists and libertarians, and an overlapping between our A/B distinction and defenders of free markets as the best mechanism for allocating goods and services, on the one hand, and critics of capitalism (both reformers and revolutionaries), on the other. It is also clear that not all economists working within a neoclassical framework are politically conservative, and not all institutionalists politically progressive. Marxists can be A types (as advocates of central planning have been and as rational expectations Marxists are) and free market libertarians can be B economists (as the Austrian School is), and so can individuals who hold profoundly conservative political views such as, or so it shall be argued, Thomas Malthus and Joseph Schumpeter. Often such individuals have a foot in each camp.

A economics overlaps with positivism, which equates explanation with prediction. The goal of such science is to demonstrate that there are instances of well-established regularities in which the appearance of certain phenomena is associated with the presence of others. In Friedman's famous formulation, positivists are unconcerned with how the regularities are produced, only that they are. The debate is over what we mean by cause, and one economist's cause is another's exogenous variable. Some economists expect a scientific theory to describe structures and mechanisms that *causally* generate the observable phenomena, a description that enables the theorist to tell a convincing story of what they see. The positivists counter that theoretical explanations may not coincide with observed facts. Economic truths are correct in the same sense that pure geometry is, in the abstract. That is, they are true under certain suppositions that may or may not hold in particular real-world cases. Yet certainly such abstract models are capable of producing precise results that are 'true.'

In the influential Whig approach to the study of the history of economic thought, the past is valued only in terms of the beliefs of the mainstream in the present. Mark Blaug writes in the preface to his highly regarded text on the history of economic thought,

> My purpose is to teach contemporary economic theory. But contemporary theory wears the scars of yesterday's problems now resolved, yesterday's blunders now corrected, and cannot be fully understood except as a legacy handed down from the past. . . . [T]he focus is on the theoretical analysis, undiluted by entertaining historical digressions or biographical coloring.
>
> (Blaug 1985: ix)

Such an approach works backward from what is understood as true today to consideration of when and from whom these correct ideas emerged. The context of the times, and how issues were seen then, is of little importance since correct theory is always and everywhere true. This attitude encourages a certain perspective on the history of economic thought – for example that there is no point in the kind of project that we are involved in here. As J.B. Say remarked:

> What useful purpose can be served by the study of absurd opinions and doctrines that have long been exploded and deserve to be? It is mere useless pedantry to attempt to revive them. The more perfect a science the shorter becomes its history.

In Klamer's terms, Say is definitely a square.

The difference in approach is evident in the way economists, like Nobel Prize winner George Stigler, understand the history of thought. Stigler, reviewing a book on the idea of poverty (by Gertrude Himmelfarb), criticized the work, noting that 'Literature, as she surveys it lacks continuity, and the very nature of poverty seems to be different for each writer she considers' (Samuels 1992). This is an extra-ordinary statement. Why should all who write on poverty hold the same definition of the problem or not understand the nature of poverty differently? Stigler goes on 'there is almost no history in this book, in the sense of consecutive thought' and, he wrote, 'poverty is allowed to represent a constantly shifting set of unfortunate and deviant people' (ibid.). Robert Nisbet, a sociologist, responded to Stigler's review:

> Welcome to the world of ideas, Mr. Stigler, especially the ideas of philosophers and other opinion makers of an age. Discontinuity and differentiation are the very stuff of intellectual history . . . [and] until econometricians reduce human experience to some Benthamite calculus that I suspect is Mr. Stigler's dream, that is precisely what poverty will continue to represent.
>
> (ibid.: 50)

Stigler's comments are a measure of the distance the categories used in some economics have moved from social sciences, which take change as the norm and constancy as the exceptional case needing careful explanation. Stigler's criteria are of an A mode character; Himmelfarb's work and Nisbet's defense are in the B tradition.

Himmelfarb and Stigler also illustrate the diversity of positions on the political Right and Left, in their cases on the Right. Himmelfarb is a cultural conservative; Stigler is a libertarian, and also an economist who believes that if something exists there are efficiency reasons for its survival. Himmelfarb's enthusiasm for private charity as against government provision of welfare, and the relegitimation of morality as the basis of social policy, uses the language of virtue and vice (Himmelfarb 1995)[6]. Stigler, on the other hand, argues that government policies that have met the test of time are 'efficient,' indeed that all durable social institutions must be efficient: a very different conservative approach (Stigler 1992).

The issue of what kind of stories are to be told and what stylized facts they illustrate goes to the heart of economics as an intellectual practice. The definitions of 'poverty' or 'scarcity' or 'choice' are based on pre-analytic visions from which the social scientist proceeds. Joseph Schumpeter tells us that on the one occasion when he conversed with Leon Walras, the formulator of the general equilibrium framework, the holy of holies for A mode economics, Walras told him

> of course life is essentially passive and merely adapts itself to the natural and social influences which may be acting on it, so that the theory of a stationary process constitutes really the whole of theoretical economics and that as economic theorists we cannot say much about the factors that account for historical change, but we must simply register them.[7]

Walras' expression of A mode orthodoxy contrasts sharply with Schumpeter's own B mode view that 'The essential point to grasp is that in dealing with capitalism we are dealing with an evolutionary process. . . . [Capitalism] is by nature a form or method of economic change and not only never is but never can be stationary' (Schumpeter 1962: 82).

To A mode economists, the task, as Paul Samuelson suggests in a passage I have already cited, is to move from history to equilibrium modeling. To move from A mode economics to the B side, the tradition is, in Joan Robinson's pithy formulation to go 'from equilibrium to history.' The tension between the two approaches is inevitably at the core of the differences among economists stressed in this study. It helps to remember that even if we think in terms of movement from one equilibrium to another, we may privilege the occurrence of the equilibrium states or we may be more interested in paths, how changes take place in real time. The danger is in confusing comparisons of imagined equilibrium positions with movements through real time, of not keeping clear the distinction between logical time and historical time.[8]

The tension many of the best economists have felt between the attraction of pure theory *a là* Walras and the dynamism of evolutionary historical analysis of political economy is widely evident, as we shall also see. Joseph Schumpeter, who has just been quoted in his B mode understanding of the nature of the economy, regarded Walras' pure theory as perhaps the greatest contribution economists had made, saw the profession's highest calling as building such A mode theory at the level of high abstraction, even as he himself was drawn to the dialectics of capitalist evolution, seeing his own intellectual struggles as dialogue with Karl Marx, for whom he had the greatest respect. The annals of economic thought afford other such important examples, as we shall see. It is important to note, then, that I will frequently privilege aspects of a contributor's work such that, if taken as a summing-up of the total impact of an individual, would appear to be offering a false, or at best truncated, view of a particular economist. For example, Frank Knight, whose views on that archetype Robinson Crusoe will be discussed shortly, was as much a B type as an A type, something that will hardly be evident from my citation of his claims about realism in economic analysis. Knight's non-probabilistic concept of uncertainty and the battles it fought against formalism could be rehearsed to show his strong B mode reasoning.

Telling tales out of school

Economics does much of its teaching using parables and thought experiments. Economists tell stories to illustrate understandings of economics. Some of these parables are in the form of mathematical models, some use examples such as the lighthouse, emblematic of public goods, and stories of fictitious places and people, for example Robinson Crusoe allocating alone on his island, as prototype economic man. Often the stories are literally wrong, but are told anyway because they are such good illustrations of something that is believed to be true. Story telling is 'an attempt to give an account of an interrelated set of phenomena in which fact, theory, and values are mixed together in the telling' (Ward 1972: 180). For example, economists speak of the 'natural' rate of unemployment as the percentage out of work consistent with a stable rate of inflation, and suggest that efforts to reduce unemployment through macroeconomic policy below this rate will be unsuccessful. The story suggests that the best policy is non-intervention (the natural rate of unemployment is discussed in Chapter 8). As this is written, many economists accept such a story as more or less true in the same sense that at one time economists believed that income redistribution and job creation for the poor would only lead the lower classes to reproduce beyond the capacity of the land to provide food.

The power of such stories and the essentially arbitrary grounds on which many of them have been supported is easier to recognize after the passage of time when history has moved on, the stakes in the issues are no longer so high, and greater perspective is achieved. Most theorists who have made an impact on the thinking of their own time have been well aware of the great artificiality of their abstractions, that they are unreal, or, as Robert Lucas writes, that they are 'fictions,' and 'analogies' that are more or less useful depending on the questions they are used to answer (Lucas 1980: 697).

Alternative stories that are meant to approximate reality are important in distinguishing among the approaches of the various schools of thought and are more convincing in some contexts and eras than in others. In the last decades of the twentieth century, the economics of the (University of) Chicago School adopted what Melvin Reder calls the 'good approximation assumption' (Reder 1982: 12). This assumption is that 'in the absence of sufficient evidence to the contrary, one may treat observed prices and quantities as good approximations of their long-period competitive values,' and it seemed to speak to the *Zeitgeist* of the era. The burden of proof is on the 'Revisionists' (our Bs) to present convincing evidence that particularities of time and place are important.

The 'good approximation assumption' exercised profound influence within the profession, and the Chicago presumption that power is absent from the competitive system if properly structured (without government and trade union distortions) meant that market prices neutrally reflect demand and supply. This was the basis of the voluntarist society advocated by Ronald Reagan and others. Yet to ignore corporate power in the marketplace is also a political presumption. To maintain, for example, that '"You cannot buck the market", a slogan beloved of Margaret Thatcher, was another way of saying that "might is right", regardless of how right was distributed' (Sayer 1995: 104). This is a very different sort of story. What we consider 'good approximation' is hardly ever politically neutral.

In 1995, when Professor Lucas received word that he was the recipient of the Nobel Prize in Economics (the fifth University of Chicago economist so honored in six years), accounts rightly stressed that his contribution was to instill a more skeptical attitude toward the ability of government policy makers to do much to influence the economy effectively. At a news conference, he offered the view that 'The U.S. economy is in excellent shape. The Government is not trying to do things with economic policy that it isn't capable of doing' (Passell 1995: 1). Of course, other economists prefer the exact opposite story as their starting point, believing that models of perfect competition do not tell the stories they see as important (see for example Rogers 1989: 140); they perhaps also believe that for millions of Americans the US economy is not 'in excellent shape' and that a little sensible activism was indeed called for. Stylized facts are a matter of preferred stories. The stories economists tell convey a good deal about the economics they do.[9]

We are faced with such stories in economics all the time. Some are told in technical language, others are found in more popular discourse. The short-run and long-run cost curves are simple 'pictures' taught to generations of economics students to illustrate how firms make choices. They tell a story that has no place for either the entrepreneur or the dynamics of real-world competition driven by product design and process innovation. The cost curve fable is innocent of considerations of uncertainty and relies on a given distribution of wealth and resources. Issues of access to capital are reduced to the level of interest rates. The metaphors do the arguing in the same way that because the math is right, the argument that is supported by the mathematical syllogism is right. The flaw, when people believe they have found one, is rarely in the technical mathematics, but rather in the contestable assumptions built into definition of terms and so of relationships. To the extent that a technique obscures what these are, the economics in dispute becomes the absent center of the particular discourse.

The frequency of repetition establishes the presumptive legitimacy of a narrative. The conventional parables of economics are plausible within their assumptions and, when told in the absence of alternative stories, have a monopoly on the student's attention. Risk taking in the face of uncertainty, the reality businesses face daily, is not part of the story most students of neoclassical price theory learn. The stories we tell mutate over time, and even though most theorists are aware of the great artificiality of their assumptions, their models are the basis of policy advice. The economists' tools are socialization techniques. Teaching them involves acculturation. In the study of economics, they almost always reinforce A type myths told in the form of simple stories, allegories that are said to explain profound truths and are driven home through allegedly 'real-world' examples.

Consider two of the most widely used of these. The first is the example of the lighthouse. It is the paradigmatic case of a public good, used to explain the nature of government services provided when users cannot be excluded, and their enjoyment of a service comes at no additional cost once the item is available. The lighthouse story makes the case for the solidity of the terminological conventions of the field that freshman learn to identify, we hope correctly, on their short-answer tests (public good, non-exclusion principle, zero marginal cost, and so on). The second is the Robinson Crusoe story, which teaches how allocation takes place. Robinson Crusoe sets the stage for the methodological individualism that is at the core of type A analysis in economics. It is through such examples that new practitioners gain a sense of the ongoing thought process and grasp the essential language of the scientific community they are joining.

The lighthouse is the most familiar example used to explain a positive externality. Once the lighthouse is in place, all ships that pass can benefit from a lighthouse's protective warnings at zero marginal cost. They cannot be excluded from its benefits, which would be an incentive not to contribute to its construction and maintenance, or to be a free rider (those who don't pay but benefit anyway). Public provision of the service is the answer. The lesson of the story is that government should provide such public goods and that is why lighthouses have been a government service (since once they are in place, it is irrational for ship owners to pay for benefits voluntarily). Ronald Coase, rather than simply passing this story on to his students, took the unusual step of examining the history of the British lighthouse system. Coase found there was 'no correspondence whatever between the actual situation (a private sector existed for centuries) and what economists, starting with Mill, Sidgwick, Pigou, and on to Samuelson and others speculated about when either referring to this sector, or inventing models supposedly describing its characteristic features' (Brenner 1992b: 103). This led Coase to ask:

> How is it that these great men have, in their economic writings, been led to make statements about lighthouses which are misleading as to the facts, whose meaning, if thought about in a concrete fashion, is quite unclear, and which, to the extent that they imply a policy conclusion, are very likely wrong? The explanation is that these references by economists to lighthouses are not the result of their having made a study of lighthouses or having read a detailed study of some other economist. . . . The lighthouse is simply plucked out of the air to serve as illustration.
>
> (Coase 1974: 211)

Now one might think that the publication of his 1974 article would have had some effect. Ronald Coase is, after all, a well-respected economist, a Nobel Prize winner, and yet the lighthouse remains the standard example along with national defense of a public good. (There is, of course, an extensive literature on militarism that suggests that such expenditures harm most of us economically and serve to enhance the overseas interests of US-based investors rather than the protection of the territory of the United States, have a high opportunity cost for the domestic standard of living, and so are hardly a public good; but that is another story.) The lighthouse *pace* Coase should have been dropped, but it is such a satisfying story which proves what needs proving to students. Indeed, we shall encounter other such stories that economists know to be literally untrue, but because they are such good heuristic examples they continue to use them as if they were true.

Our other fable is equally worn. It is of the allegorical Robinson Crusoe, whom economists rehabilitate to illustrate allocation of scarce resources among competing ends, the core economic story. Most economists believe, as in the case of the lighthouse, that they have this story right. They do not. Numerous generations of young initiates have been exposed to the textbook tale of a Robinson Crusoe world (before Friday) in which an economic model is built to show allocation in its pure form before there is exchange, a story of individual choice which is then applied to the more complex contemporary society. Consider the following (typical) presentation by Frank Knight in his classic work, *Risk, Uncertainty and Profit*:

> We will suppose an individual choosing between the production and consumption of a large number of 'commodities,' in addition to the alternative of not producing any of them, but of putting his time, etc., to 'non-economic' uses. This is the situation of Crusoe on his island, of which many economists have made use . . .

In Crusoe's mind there would undoubtedly be built up something of the nature of a price system or value scale, if he seriously attempted to get the maximum of satisfaction out of the conditions of his environment. For an 'intelligent' use of his opportunities can be arrived at in no other way. He must ascertain the ratios in which different goods are to be obtained for subjectively equivalent sacrifices in 'effort,' and similarly form judgments of their relative subjective importance to him, and attempt to bring the two sets of ratios into coincidence.

(Knight 1921: 74)

Knight then goes on to offer eleven simplifying assumptions to make the economist's world accord as closely as possible with Crusoe's (as he imagines Crusoe's world). I shall not insist you consider all of these assumptions, the flavor can be conveyed well enough by a selection. Proposition #6 states: 'Every member of the society is to act as an individual only, in entire independence of all other persons. To complete his independence he must be free from social wants, prejudices, preferences, or repulsions, or any values which are not completely manifested in market dealings.' He goes on in this vein to define economic man, *Homo economicus*, independent, atomistic, innocent of cooperation or collusion with his fellows (Knight 1921:78). In all of this, Knight's view is that these simplifying assumptions are not far from the historical truth. 'Going back to medieval times or to the American frontier, we find relatively little joint activity, except for the division of labor between the sexes and in the family' (Knight 1921: 56–6). No feudal institutions for this knight, no barn raisings, just Robinsonade individualism and the (no doubt patriarchal) family.

In a moment we'll throw some water on his historical parade of economic men, but it is useful to cite the opening lines of this classic where its author makes an assertion that by now is familiar to us. It reminds us how essential the Crusoe behavior of economic man is to the claim economists make for the unique achievements of their science. As Knight puts it:

Economics, or more properly theoretical economics, is the only one of the social sciences which has aspired to the distinction of an exact science. To the extent that it is an exact science it must accept the limitations as well as share the dignity thereto pertaining, and it thus becomes like physics or mathematics in being necessarily somewhat abstract and unreal.

(Knight 1921: 3)

The economist's Robinson Crusoe is a rugged individualist, 'diligent, intelligent and above all frugal who masters nature through reason;' but of course the actual story of Robinson Crusoe as told by Daniel Defoe is one of 'conquest, slavery, robbery, murder and force' (Hymer 1971: 11).[10] This contrast between the economist's fictive parable and Defoe's written text carries over into the classroom and to blackboard economics in the way international trade is discussed, the way relations in labor markets are specified, in the discourse on the development of underdeveloped countries, and the treatment of gender (Grapard 1995). Indeed, the fictional recounting of Defoe's story tells us much about the basic story mainstream economics conveys. Yet, the model of the hunter and the fisherman who trade for mutual benefit (as equals) under conditions of Bentham and freedom in reciprocity is a striking departure from the way labor markets and trade relations were established historically. If we are to believe Defoe's story, the structure of subordination and inequality of reward 'has to be established and maintained by force, whether it be the structured violence of poverty, the symbolic violence of socialization, or the physical violence of war and pacification' (Hymer 1971: 12). Even the core use to which Defoe's hero is put, illustrating allocation in a scarcity setting (for to economists scarcity is always present and is what defines the rationale and core meaning of economic calculation), rings false when one actually reads the original text. Crusoe has access to the ample stores of his wrecked ship and to all he could use, the fruit of European science and productive know-how.[11] His needs, if Defoe's protagonist is to be believed, were entirely satisfied. 'But my time or labor was little worth, and so was as well employed one way as another. . . . The most covetous, griping miser in the world would have been cured of the vice of covetousness, if he had been in my case' (Defoe 1719: 71). When Crusoe says that he 'had nothing to covet; for I had all that I was now capable of enjoying' (ibid.) he confounds the unlimited wants presumption of mainstream economics.

Stephen Hymer suggests a contrasting and more persuasive reading in which Defoe's novel tells a Marxist tale:

> Robinson's greed went away because there were no people to organize and master. Marx's proposition was that surplus labor was the sole measure and source of capitalist wealth. Without someone else's labor to control, the capitalist value system vanished; no boundless thirst for surplus labor arose from the nature of production itself; the goals of efficiency, maximization, and accumulation faded into a wider system of values. . . . Later, when Robinson's island becomes populated, the passion to organize and accumulate returns. It is only when he has no labor but his own to control that labor is not scarce and he ceases to measure things in terms of labor time.
>
> (Hymer 1971: 19–20)

The neoclassical Robinsonades, of course, were not interested in such a story; nor are modern choice theorists who presume an individualism that precludes such outcomes. James Buchanan and Gordon Tullock, to take another example, employ the 'familiar Crusoe–Friday model' to explain their division of labor and political exchange for the common good without a hint of the superordination–suborbination which defines their relation as one of unequal power (Buchanan and Tullock 1962: 19).

For Marx to take the strong societal constrained-mode of production case of 'Individuals producing in society – hence socially determined individual production – is, of course, the point of departure. The individual and isolated hunter and fisherman, with whom Smith and Ricardo begin, belongs among the unimaginative conceits of the eighteenth century Robinsonades.'[12] We would, however, want to question Marx's reading of Smith in this context. Adam Smith is not a teller of the 'Robinson Crusoe as economic man' story. In Book I, Chapter I of *The Wealth of Nations*, Smith recounts the tale of the woolen coat that covers the day laborer; coarse and rough as it may appear, in his story it is a social product. 'The Shepherd, the sorter of the wool, the wool-comber or carder, the dyer, the scribbler, the spinner, the weaver, the fuller, the dresser, with many others, must all join their different arts in order to complete even this homely product.'[13] Adam Smith, as we'll see in the next chapter, is a far more complex thinker than is suggested by the passage from Marx or is considered by the young men with the Adam Smith ties who can be found running around Washington trying to undo government.

The misinterpretation of Crusoe's story continues to form an integral part in the education of the current generation of economists. The island parable is alive and well in the service of contemporary theories in which a single representative individual is assumed to make choices for the whole economy. The matter of the accuracy of the characterization to the original story and even more for the real world today remains germane.[14] The final irony of the tale is that whilst later economists might have an emasculate conception version of the origin of the coat, Daniel Defoe himself surely did not. His description of the woolen industry around Halifax in *A Tour Through the Whole Island of Great Britain* provides a graphic account of the domestic system extant in Yorkshire, of the dying houses and scouring shops and the people who worked together in the social process of production. Defoe cannot be accused of confusing fact and fiction and he was no believer in the fiction of isolated 'economic man.'[15]

Story telling needs to be taken seriously. It is the way core 'truths' are conveyed and whilst it seems the softer side of economics, it is present in the most formalistic models which are, after all, only another rhetorical vehicle to convey values and conclusions. Many of these stories seem convincing only because we do not bother to scrutinize them closely. To take history, real history, seriously is the undoing of economics, and the starting point of political economy. Many economists are loath to accept that their scientific method can be interrogated from such a vantage point, but as we look more closely at the history of economic ideas, this seems an inescapable conclusion. Like references to Robinson Crusoe and the lighthouse, discussion of the views attributed to Adam Smith or Karl Marx (whatever the school, the style of invoking authority is remarkably similar) contain an ideological overlay and claim to canonical veritas.

Whilst it is the fate of genius to be reduced to formulaic homily, (re)reading the masters plunges one quickly into controversy, for their complex insights more often refute than reinforce the simplistic inheritance of the mainstream. Explainers are also not innocent of the vision they bring to their readings, so that whilst the texts produced by the great minds may encourage better thinking on the part of us lesser mortals, such readings are filtered through highly differentiated systems of mainstream and heterodox interpretation. As we read *The Wealth of Nations*, *Capital*, *The General Theory*, and other classics, we are encouraged to rethink understandings of the contemporary world. We are both changed by, and change, the texts. (If modern literary criticism has taught us anything, it is the instability of the text, which is given meaning not only by the writer but, of necessity, by the reader.) The 'real' David Ricardo or Maynard Keynes are contested constructions.

There are high stakes involved in the contestation of claims to canonical authority for one's own positions. The reason Adam Smith and other canonical writers are open to multiple and conflicting readings is that the interpretation of these texts is a struggle over the construction of the discipline. The canon defines what a field is 'legitimately' about. Practitioners outside the mainstream needing to redirect the discussion can do worse than to reread important contributions and attempt to reorient their accepted meaning. Hence the task at hand. I argue for the usefulness of the B way of looking at the economy and wish to apply my understanding of such a methodology in interpreting our own time. I find it incumbent to reread the canonical literature of economics, to stress the importance of B mode economic thinking to our history, and to redress imbalance in the way the history of economic thought is conventionally presented. When the concluding chapters arrive at contemporary contributions, it shall be my assertion that 'rational' expectation models and 'real' business cycle theories, among other significant additions, are equally flights of fancy on the part of economists today. I can only suggest. With the perspective of time (and in the context of the needs and pre-analytic visions of future observers), contemporary economist metaphors will be reconsidered. One of the projects of this venture is to provide awarenesses adaptable to such an undertaking and so is integral to framing the alternative stylized story of where we are in economic history that is offered in the concluding chapters of the book. Between here and there a rereading of the history of economic thought is offered that highlights aspects of the mainline tradition in economics and positions them in relation to the economic mainstream.

3 Contestation and canonicity: the Adam Smith problem

[Didactick discourse] proposes to put before us the arguments on both sides of the question in their true light, giving each its proper degree of influence, and has it in view to persuade no farther than the arguments themselves appear convincing. The Rhetoricall again endeavours by all means to persuade us; and for this purpose it magnifies all the arguments on the one side and diminishes or conceals those that might be brought on the side contrary to that which it is designed that we should favour. Persuasion . . . endeavours to persuade us only so far as the strength of the arguments is convincing, instruction is the main end.

(Smith 1762–3; as quoted in Brown 1994a: 16)

There are many ironies to note in the historical outcomes of Adam Smith's discourse and the canonization of *WN* [*The Wealth of Nations*], as has been evidenced by the history of more than two centuries since *WN* was published. The argument of *WN* against the undue expansion of trade and manufactures has come to be interpreted as an argument in favour of such an expansion. The invective against merchants and manufacturers has been construed as an apologia for the new capitalist class that emerges in a later age. But one of the greatest ironies is that Adam Smith's discourse – indebted as it was to Stoic moral philosophy – has contributed centrally to the de-moralization of economic and political categories and to the construction of an economics canon in which moral debate has virtually no place.

(Brown 1994a: 2)

Professionals in any discipline tend to disparage those who put complex matters together simply – especially if they do so with clarity, insight, and grace. Very few such popularizers get anything but short shrift. This is true even of Adam Smith, the founding father of economics, although he is understood to have captured the broad sweep of economic history and to have explained some of the science's deepest truths with non-jargonated brilliance and vibrant prose. Adam Smith's virtues have led to an underestimation of his skill. Smith is thought to have been a theoretical lightweight, a reputation that many a fine theorist has argued is undeserved (Samuelson 1992). But such quibbling cannot challenge Smith's stature as founding father. 'Almost immediately after the appearance of Smith's work,' Maurice Allais writes with only moderate exaggeration, 'all previous or contemporary economic writings were forgotten' (Allais 1992: 31). In the popular mind Adam Smith has Parthenon status, and many schools of thought are anxious to claim him as their own. As D.P. O'Brien asserted in a bicentenary salute: 'the historical importance of Adam Smith as an economist is without any real parallel in the entire development of economics' (O'Brien 1976: 133).

None of this means that Smith was an original thinker in a Whiggish sense. There is general agreement that he was not. Jacob Viner offers the judgment that 'on every detail, taken by itself, Smith appears to have had predecessors in plenty. On few details was Smith as penetrating as the best of his predecessors' (Viner 1927: 118). Schumpeter concurs, declaring that Smith's magisterial work 'does not contain a single analytic idea, principle or method that was entirely new in 1776' (Schumpeter 1954: 184). It is a matter of taste whether such a Whig criterion is to be granted much importance. For example, it has been suggested that there is a canonical classical model that Smith, Ricardo, Malthus, Mill, and Marx can all be shown to share, a dynamic model of equilibrium growth and distribution that Paul Samuelson has formulated in modern terms in a mathematical model (Samuelson 1978). Professor Samuelson no doubt does modern economists a service in showing elements of commonality in these writers in this fashion. There may be those who would claim that reducing the complex insights and historically situated observations such economists offered to such a model can be said to capture the gist of their contribution to economics, but to those who understand these great political economists in B mode terms, such an assertion is travesty.

Adam Smith's fame rests in part on the enthusiasm of the reports of those who have read him and in great measure on his presumed message celebrating the magic of the marketplace, a popular (if unbalanced) reading (Stigler 1976).[1] It is necessary to flesh Smith out in more subtle hues before one can move on to a discussion of his conception of 'free' markets and the theory of the state. Our focus is to recast understanding of Smith so that he becomes a more complex figure in the history of economic thought, truly the progenitor of economics,[2] and not the sole property of *laissez-faire* economists as is often claimed.

It is the fate of canonical figures to be reduced to a one-sentence summary of 'what X thought' but like others who have made real difference, Adam Smith was hardly so narrow and shallow a thinker. His interests were incredibly broad – one has only to read some of his essays on philosophical subjects, for example, 'Of the Affinity between Music, Dancing, and Poetry,' or 'On the Affinity between certain English and Italian Verses,' to say nothing of 'The History of Ancient Physics' and 'The History of Ancient Logics and Metaphysics.' Whilst we confine ourselves for the most part to Smith's writings on political economy, it is not without interest that he was deeply steeped and well versed in the full range of intellectual developments not only of his own time but from the Greeks on.

In 1785 Smith wrote in a letter to the Duc de la Rochefoucauld of his ongoing intellectual projects, specifically

> he had two other great works upon the anvil, the one is a sort of Philosophical History of all the different branches of literature, of Philosophy, Poetry and

Eloquence; the other is a sort of theory and History of Law and Government. He wrote on rhetoric and the history of astronomy and of ancient Greece (some of the last found its way into the third book of *WN*).

(Wightman 1980)

In his age, such breadth was not unique, but in any age it is surely unusual. Moreover, importantly to the topic at hand, this breadth is surely not at the expense of a command of economics. Marshall is to the mark when he wrote of Smith that there 'was scarcely any economic truth now known of which he did not get some glimpse' (Marshall 1890: 757).

What is impressive is not simply the scope of his interests but the complexity of mind that could converse in the different discourses. One could imagine that Smith himself regarded his major works not as separate enterprises but as parts of a single whole, but if so, what this whole might have looked like to him is not possible to know, for, as he neared death, he ordered all his papers destroyed except for the few he judged ready for publication. As a result, sixteen volumes of manuscripts were consigned to the flames. As with many of the important figures we shall discuss, we work with only a very small part of his total concerns. His economics falls into both A and B mode categories, and some economists have perhaps for this reason seen 'two Adam Smiths' and suggested as a result that there is an 'Adam Smith problem,' matters to be discussed further in this chapter.

In our reading, whatever else he is, Smith is an institutionalist sympathetic to labor above other groups, who held to a Marxist-like theory of the state well before Marx, and was more of a protectionist, or as I would prefer to say, using yet another anachronistic term to characterize his thought, developmentalist, than most economists realize. His criticism of government was of the institution of his time run by a non-elected monarch and a small ruling class in which government was used to confer privilege on the favored few at the expense of the many. There is no reason to think he would have thought a modern democratic government could not take an active and progressive role in the economy. As is well known, he was suspicious of concentration of private power and saw the potential everywhere for collusion by sellers. Yet, as we shall see, he favored some interesting state policies in contemporary states in which far-sighted business interests ruled.

Writing midway between Adam Smith's time and our own, Beatrice Webb remarked:

> The Political Economy of Adam Smith was the scientific expression of the impassioned crusade of the 18th century against class tyranny and the oppressor of the Many by the Few. By what silent revolution of events, by what unselfconscious transformation of thought did it change itself into the 'Employers' Gospel' of the 19th century?
>
> (Rothschild 1992: 88)

We may ask concerning the years of state encouragement of capital's hyper-mobility, did all those young men running around the Reagan White House with

Adam Smith ties – telling each other, 'Just don't stand there, undo something!' – understand Adam Smith? Was he the prophet of deregulation and privatization they claimed? They, like Ms. Webb, picked the Adam Smith who suited their reading and their times. A century later, Ms. Webb's question is rarely asked. It should be.

It is more common today to read that: 'Adam Smith showed how the free market miraculously harnessed greed toward constructive ends' (Blinder 1987a: 27). He is not suggesting that greed is good, even if economists often invoke the founding father in a way consistent with such a view. Such an Adam Smith is an early Chicago economist, ready-made for an anti-Big Government and non-interventionist free marketeer climate (Stigler 1971). This is a one-sided reading that can be gleaned from Smith's writing, but it is not all Adam Smith taught.

The Adam Smith problem

Smith was a professor of moral philosophy and part of the Scottish Enlightenment, a school of thought based on natural theology.[3] As a philosopher, Smith was influenced by those ideas of natural law that pervaded the eighteenth-century intellectual environment. The use of the term 'natural' repeated throughout their discussion suggests that human beings can observe the nature of life and society, God's purposes, and the proper mode of behavior themselves (Meek *et al.* 1978). There are natural laws that can be grasped and are best followed to improve society.

The natural right Smith was most concerned with was each person's freedom to pursue their own interest, limited only by respect for the freedom of others. Rulers should not use their power to confer special privilege or to impose restrictions on initiative. Against the interventionist understandings, Smith offered the model of an atomistic marketplace where the invisible hand was free to do its miraculous work of turning self-interest into social good. These are the aspects of *WN* that mainstream economists stress, although it is also recognized that Smith railed against power being usurped by big business and their allies in government and used against the working people.

A second concept that Smith famously offered, the division of labor limited only by the extent of the market (specialization of labor functions to increase efficiency), led to the optimistic conclusion that as output increased, cost per unit would fall and living standards would go up. He also stressed the important role of savings as a way to increase 'the real quantity of industry,' and saw that if, as income rose, greater savings were channeled to increased production and further specialization, than the future was bright. Each nation could reach 'that full complement of riches which the nature of its soil and climate, and its situation with respect to other countries, allowed it to acquire.'

Smith faults mercantilism and state intervention in markets more generally with introducing bias into the natural order of things. Government subsidies induced trade and manufacturing over agriculture, manipulating growth and creating an 'unnatural and retrograde order.' He has something very specific in mind. There is a natural development in which stimulating trade or even private entrepreneurs choosing to invest their capital abroad has harmful consequence. Modern economists have, however, picked up on a different aspect of his thinking. Smith is responding to the idea that the legislator or statesman's task is to supervise in the interests of the public.[4] In his view, favoring a privileged sector at the expense of the rest of the economy would draw too many resources to it, other sectors would receive too little, and misallocation would lower overall efficiency. The gains for the privileged are not only unfair but amount to less than the losses accruing elsewhere. An impartial state should reduce disincentives by keeping taxes low, regulation minimal, and not allowing (certainly not supporting) monopoly franchises. The state was to maintain inter-individual justice, defense, and essential public works (Viner 1960). There was a natural order which, if left to function, would serve best.

Isaac Newton's influence on Smith and the broader intellectual world of emergent economics and political theory is not to be doubted.[5] There is an appreciation that random events could compose themselves into invisible processes of change. The intellectual impact of Newtonian laws of gravity suggested that the real (if invisible) structures of the world are subject to human understanding. Smith described Newton's mechanics as 'the greatest discovery ever made by man.' He was influenced by the development of science, though not by industrialism. Even though he wrote in the years when James Watt perfected a steam engine that freed manufacturers from dependence on water and animal power, there is remarkably little about real technology in his book. It may be noted that Smith failed to recognize the onset of the industrial revolution happening around him. The pin factory is the only example of industrial production described in *WN*, and it is a childhood memory of a small nailery on the outskirts of the then insignificant village of Kirkcaldy (Gray 1976: 154). Smith's examples are more likely to be the homely community and way of life of the butcher, the brewer, and the baker, from whom we expect our dinner.

Smith combined an appreciation of the productive potential of specialization with the natural liberty doctrine of his time. The inalienable rights to life, liberty, and the pursuit of property, in John Locke's original formulation (to be transposed in the US Declaration of Independence, written in the same year as the publication of *The Wealth of Nations*, as 'life, liberty and the pursuit of happiness'), put at the very center of his analysis the idea of natural liberty that was so important to the rising commercial classes. The linking of political freedom and economic freedom was both a continuation of moral philosophy and at the same time a departure from it. So much is familiar Adam Smith canon lore; but this is far from all Smith has to say on the good society and how it should function.

A small minority of economists have actually read *The Wealth of Nations*. Smith's other writings are hardly ever cited and, 'it is a fair inference that the set of economists who have also read closely *The Theory of Moral Sentiments* [*TMS*] and the *Lectures on Jurisprudence* is almost empty' (Field 1994: 684–5). Much of what Smith wrote was not economics as the subject is now construed. This by itself would not suffice to explain the situation, since economists do not hesitate to apply their science to issues of the family, crime, and other applications far from its traditional core. It is that when Adam Smith writes on other topics, the manner of approach is often not congenial to modern economics. Smith seems from the vantage point of modern economics to be schizophrenic. This has created what is called 'the Adam Smith problem,' which is usually put as, 'How do we reconcile the Adam Smith of *TMS* with the Adam Smith of *WN*?'

The answer of most economists is simply to ignore all other writings except *WN*. It is sometimes said that these earlier writings are 'less mature', whilst *WN* is Smith's 'final word.' The problem with such answers is that Smith revised *TMS* many times, both before *and* after completing *WN*. The sixth and extensively revised edition of *TMS* published a few weeks before his death had new sections concerned with theories of political justice in which he wrote of the 'corruption of our moral sentiments' which followed from the disposition 'almost to worship, the rich and powerful' (Rothschild 1992: 77–8). He situated his own ethical positions with Voltaire and Racine, not Gecko and Milken.

The answer given by ethicist Larry Rasmussen is a more fitting reconciliation:

[I]t is crucial to note that Adam Smith did not trust the morality of the market as a morality for society at large. He in fact did not even envision a capitalist *society*. He envisioned a capitalist *economy* within a society held together by noncapitalist moral sentiments.

(Rasmussen 1993: 41–2)

Even when we confine ourselves to only a consideration of *WN*, it is still true, as Nathan Rosenberg has written, that a

neglected theme running through virtually all of the *Wealth of Nations* is Smith's attempt to define, in very specific terms, the details of the institutional structure which will best harmonize the individual's pursuit of his selfish interests with the broader interests of society

(Rosenberg 1960: 559)

A number of scholars have noted that in *TMS* the social passions are equal to the selfish passions as motivating forces, whilst in *WN* the social passions are the source of cooperation without which the economy cannot operate. Is it the case that in *both* works social passions and interests are as important as self-interest? It came more easily to an eighteenth-century intellectual to suppose that society could function within an institutional framework of order and justice with moral grounding than it does to twentieth-century thinkers. The term moral philosophy is often misunderstood. In its eighteenth-century usage, philosophy meant the sciences and moral philosophy concerned the social sciences. Natural philosophy meant the physical sciences and mathematics. The standard course in moral philosophy included natural theology, ethics, jurisprudence, public finance, and economics. It is in this sense that Schumpeter can speak of *TMS* and *WN* as 'blocks cut from a larger systematic whole' (Schumpeter 1954: 141). Smith's successors, with a few significant exceptions (one thinks of John Stuart Mill above all), were unable to encapsulate in their thinking such a wider sense of moral philosophy. This was due in significant measure to Smith's contribution.

There is in Smith more of the Old Testament prophet than of the apologist for greed. Smith is emphatic: 'Justice . . . is the main pillar that upholds the whole edifice. If it is removed, the great, the immense fabric of human society . . . must in a moment crumble into atoms' (Smith 1759: II, ii, 3–4). Self-interest must have a stabilizing social context. This is clear from a close reading of *WN* and is amplified in the greater corpus of his writings. Whilst there is a simple, if not simplistic, Adam Smith message, the opening lines of *TMS* should give market experts pause for thought: 'How selfish soever man may be supposed,' Smith wrote, 'there are evidently some principles in his nature, which interest him in the fortune of others, and render their happiness necessary to him, though he derives nothing from it, except the pleasure of seeing it.' Natural law was about more than free markets. It concerned people as social beings, 'whose happiness is necessary to him.'

The realities of special pleading and the socially harmful outcomes of free markets that Smith recorded, as Viner has written, would provide ammunition for several socialist orations. Indeed, it is not only socialists who can find grist for their mill: 'every conceivable sort of doctrine can be found in that most catholic book, and an economist must have peculiar theories indeed who cannot quote from *The Wealth of Nations* to support his special purpose' (Viner 1927: 221). My special purpose is to note that for Smith labor is not just a commodity. He explores the social nature of work, the reproduction and control of labor power in class terms, the role of the state in determining wages, and the freedom of collective action or lack thereof for workers *vis-à-vis* employers, and places class power near the center of his analysis. He does not present land, labor, and capital as conceptually comparable categories. They are not factors of production outside of socially determined definitions and relations that are daily contested.

'With thy bloody and invisible hands'[6]

The expression 'invisible hand' appears only once in *WN*, yet the claim that it is central sets the tone for interpretation of Adam Smith's legacy to this day. The idea is presumed a riposte to the teachings of the Church, in which generosity and kindness to others and a sense of harmony and order in society were accepted as natural. Smith turns the moral world on its head by offering self-interest as the motor force for human improvement and societal wellbeing; but he does more than just that. He presents a model of capitalism that, whilst stressing the harmony brought about by free competition, does not omit the class nature of society, and the manner in which public power could promote inefficiency and private gain through illegitimate redistribution. Technically, he offers an understanding of price formation, value theory, the circulation of money, foreign trade, economic classes, the productive potential and the alienation implicit in the division of labor, and, of course, the nature and causes of the wealth of nations.

Singling out the invisible hand, as economists too often do, is a suspect enterprise. Emma Rothschild has gone so far as to suggest that Adam Smith did not particularly esteem the invisible hand and thought it 'an ironic but useful joke' (Rothschild 1994: 319).[7] Perhaps so, I do not know about this, but I do think that economists tend to get Smith's point about the invisible hand backward. As Jerry Evensky writes of the relation of ethics to early economic liberalism:

> Ethics is the *sine quae non* of the constructive competition envisioned by classical liberalism. Only in a community of ethical individuals can the invisible hand do its job properly, for it is ethics that keeps the hands of individuals from disabling, and thus distorting the actions of, the invisible hand. In the absence of such an ethical community, competition becomes destructive. In Smith's master metaphor, it is ethics that stands between a beneficent society and the Hobbesian abyss.
>
> (Evensky 1992: 61)

Patricia Werhane offers what I think is a correct judgment, that

> For Smith, the invisible hand is a result of economic interchanges, not the engine that drives these exchanges. Thus how the invisible hand 'regulates' the economy depends very much on the social framework in which market activities are conducted and the kinds of exchanges that contribute to it.
>
> (Werhane 1991: 12)

The invisible hand is created out of competition among individuals and can arbitrate the market only if there is a more or less fair balance among the competing actors. It controls self-interest only to the extent that there is a balance of interests in the market. It is not the market that assures this, but rather the balance among participants. 'Smith's thesis is that the invisible hand works because, and only when, people operate with restrained self-interest in cooperation with others under the precepts of justice' (ibid.: 14).

It is not really acceptable to assert, as many mainstream economists continue to do, that his version of the free market was about 'anything goes' and that the invisible hand would, through its mystical workings, preserve competition and provide optimal outcomes so long as government allowed it to do so. Smith's concern was to set up rules that allowed for individuals to act in their own interest, constrained by a moral order that was not lacking in understanding of the imperatives of social justice. Viner's summary judgment is on target:

> Adam Smith was not a doctrinaire advocate of laissez faire. He saw a wide and elastic range of activity for government, and he was prepared to extend it even farther if government, by improving its standards of competence, honesty, and public spirit, should itself be entitled to wider responsibilities. . . . He

did not believe that laissez faire was always good, or always bad. It depended on circumstances.

(Viner 1927: 112–13)

Smith commented positively on surprising interventionist state activities. For example, he approved of the elites of Venice and Amsterdam using the state to run public banks, seeing these 'mercantile projects' as 'extremely proper.' Sir Alexander Gray, after discussing such cases, writes, 'Now each of these exceptions opens a very wide door, especially so if they are interpreted in the light of modern times rather than of 1776' (Gray 1976: 165). Another level of understanding is to be gleaned from a contextual reading of Smith's use of the invisible hand in *WN*, which will appear momentarily. First, I will offer an alternative central understanding of Smith's sympathies by suggesting that rather than a defender of free markets in the modern Chicago School mode, Smith was an institutionalist and an advocate of working-class interests.

Adam Smith, labor economist

Smith's sympathy for the workers shines forth from the pages of *WN*. He describes their plight in graphic detail. Even in the celebrated writings on the dynamic benefits of the division of labor, he coupled these gains to an awareness of the harm done to the workers. He was hardly a solemnizer of commercial culture, which he saw as, to phrase it awkwardly, 'stupiding the people.' Making money lured young people away from education to the detriment of what they might be as they grew older. The cost to working people of the celebrated division of labor was severe:

> Where the division of Labour is brought to perfection, every man has only one simple operation to perform; to this his whole attention is confined, and few ideas pass in his mind but what have an immediate connection with it. . . . It is remarkable that in every commercial nation the low people are exceedingly stupid. . . . Another inconvenience attending commerce is that education is greatly neglected. . . . But, besides this want of education, there is another great loss which attends the putting of boys too soon to work. . . . When he is grown up he has no ideas with which he can amuse himself.
>
> (Smith 1776: 256–7)

He worried about the poor/working people (in his day the working people were the poor). In contrast to the allegedly Smithian doctrine that bans unions as 'restraints on trade,' Adam Smith favored trade unions. His sympathies were evident:

> Wherever there is great property, there is great inequality. For one very rich man, there must be at least five hundred poor, and the affluence of the few supposes the indigence of the many. The affluence of the rich excites the indignation of the poor, who are often driven by want and prompted by

envy to invade his possessions. It is only under the shelter of the civil magistrate that the owner of that valuable property . . . can sleep a single night in security.

(Smith 1776: 670)

Smith criticizes the non-productive classes that make claims on the productive ones, and also those among the productive, the merchants and manufacturers, who create the goods we require for our wellbeing. He worries that they profit overly by collusion and other unjust acts if they are not restrained. His mechanism for such restraint was understandably not the state, which in his time he saw as corrupt – the granter and enforcer of monopoly privilege – not the vehicle for promoting just dealings. Yet it is hardly true that he was ready to rely on markets outside of a supporting social context. He worried about class conflict that resulted from gross inequality. *WN* can be read as contributing to Marx's understanding of class struggle (Rosenberg 1960, 1979; Meek 1967). Inequalities of reward were not, in his mind, justified by differences in natural talent, as Locke or Madison for example, assumed. Smith wrote:

The difference of natural talents in different men is, in reality, much less than we are aware of; and the very different genius which appears to distinguish men of different professions, when grown up to maturity, is not upon many occasions so much the cause, as the effect of the division of Labour. The difference between the most dissimilar characters, between a philosopher and common street porter, for example, seems to arise not so much from nature, as from habit, custom, and education.

(Smith 1776: 15)

However small the innate differences among men and women of very different stations in life,

The man whose life is spent performing a few simple operations, of which the effects are, perhaps, always the same, or very nearly the same, . . . has no occasion to exert his understanding, or to exercise his invention in finding out expedients for difficulties which never occur. He naturally loses, therefore, the habit of such exertions and generally becomes as stupid and ignorant as it is possible for a human creature to become.

(ibid.: 734)

As later economists were to point out, separation of tasks does not need to mean a division of labor, which presumes specialization over long periods, perhaps for the working life of each individual.

The difference in compensation compounds the plight of workers. Whilst later economists attributed low wages to low productivity, Smith suggests it is the job that diminishes the worker, rather than the diminished worker who deserves only the limited value of his or her physical product, as the neoclassicals were to suggest.

Difference in class position figured prominently in the outcome of the wage bargain. He wrote:

> The masters, being fewer in number, can combine much more easily; and the law, besides, authorizes, or at least does not prohibit their combinations, while it prohibits those of workers. We have no acts of parliament against combining to lower the price of work; but many against the combining to raise it.
>
> (Smith 1776: 66)

The working men soon became desperate and must either starve or frighten their bosses into granting concessions, said Smith. But when they try to do so, the employer class can seek assistance from the civil magistrate, which usually results in the ruin of the workers and the jailing of their leaders. That masters collude to keep wages down and the state backs them up is not a conclusion often reached by popularizers of 'Adam Smith as market maven' thinking.

In the long-run, the workmen may be as necessary to the master as the master is to the workers, but 'the necessity is not so immediate.' The manufacturers in a dispute, he writes 'could generally live a year or two upon the stock which they have already acquired. Many workmen could not subsist a week, few could subsist a month, and scarce any a year without employment' (ibid.). Furthermore, the masters collude to keep down wages although this is rarely discussed in polite company, while if workers combine the magistrate is quickly upon them.

Adam Smith, unlike today's mainstream economists, understood the basics of class. He could appreciate the centrality of the division of labor for economic growth of nations, but could also see the impact on human beings who were subjected to the detailed division of task that made them stupid by boring them out of their skulls and sapping their strength through the forced repetitive motions of what was to become 'Modern Times.' Whilst employers favor piecework and other incentives to extract the utmost labor from workers, speed-ups do great harm to workers, Smith thought, even if in their need they 'voluntarily' agree to it. Piecework, he wrote, forces them 'to over-work themselves, and to ruin their health and constitution in a few years' (ibid.: 83). Smith reports that a carpenter in London, and in other places as well, is not supposed to last in his utmost vigor more than about eight years. He explains that 'Almost every class of artificers is subject to some peculiar infirmity occasioned by excessive application to their particular species of work' (ibid.). Writing here too with a very modern spirit, he suggests that masters working their employees to the breaking point would instead do better to ease up so that they could do better work and last. 'Where wages are high accordingly, we shall always find the workmen more active, diligent, and expeditious, than where they are low' (ibid.: 65). This explanation now goes by the name of efficiency wage theory.

Such long-run thinking embraced the importance of public funding of quality education and an inclusive stance towards the entitlements of citizenship. Like modern liberals, when he speaks of efficiency he has in mind both social efficiency and equity. In his great society, decent treatment of all members was the sign of civilized accumulation.

No society can surely be flourishing and happy, of which the far greater part the members are poor and miserable. It is but equity, besides, that the whole body of the people, should have such a share of the produce of their own Labour as to be themselves tolerably well fed, clothed and lodged.

(ibid.: 79)

Smith related the concepts of social efficiency and justice. The proper use of all members of the workforce count. Justice requires adequate compensation and the wealth of the nation demands the proper deployment and efficient use of labor. The opening lines of *WN* explain that the wealth of the nation is regulated 'first, by the skill, dexterity, and judgment with which its labour is generally applied; and, secondly, by the proportion between the number of those who are employed in useful labour, and that of those who are not so employed.' By such measure, the United States is well inside its production possibilities potential. We waste people most prodigiously. The cruel measure contemporary economists use – the unnatural unemployment rate – is premised on a rejection of this basic idea: that the proper use of potential people power is the measure of a society's greatness.

Not ready to write-off the hard core unemployed or to blame the poor, Smith believed that there was nothing natural about poverty in the midst of plenty. In his writings he connected questions of wealth creation with matters of fairness of social relations, a twinning that brought criticism from, among others, Malthus, who wrote in his 1798 *Essay* of Smith's 'error of mixing two distinct inquiries,' the one into the wealth of nations, the other into 'the happiness and comfort of the lowest orders of society' (Rothschild 1992: 85). (Our own contemporaries who invoke Smith as the patron saint of free markets are not troubled by such errors, for their Adam Smith shows little interest in the happiness and comfort of the lowest orders of society.) It needs be stressed that Smith certainly did not accept significant unemployment as natural, or a matter of moral blemish among the poor.

In the last chapter we saw how far Adam Smith is from accepting the isolated individual of the Robinson Crusoe neoclassical economics fable, which is still the starting point for mainstream economic analysis. Smith would not have us forget the hands of those who prepare our bread and our beer, and fashion the glass window that lets in the light and keeps out the rain. He details so many of the countless interdependencies of social existence that our debts are made clear and stand as admonishment to 'I don't owe anyone anything.'

Class conflict was overwhelmingly real in the lives of working people, and Adam Smith understood this quite well.[8] Smith, in describing how the master can call on the civil magistrate and the rigorous law to punish the leaders and drive the men back to work on his terms, acknowledged that it is the control of capital that gave them the advantage. The interests of master and worker 'are by no means the same. The workmen desire to get as much, the masters to give as little as possible' (Smith 1776: 66). He was aware, and put in context 'the most shocking and violent outrage' (ibid.: 67) to which workers could be driven partly because of having substantially less bargaining power. These were not matters of minor transition costs to a new equilibrium situation.

In a famous passage Smith notes that 'people of the same trade seldom meet together, even for merriment or diversion, but the conversation ends in a conspiracy against the public, or some contrivance to raise prices' (ibid.: 128). T.S. Ashton tells us more of such meetings in the period: 'Many an innocent-looking social or scientific group was, it seems likely, a business organization, the real purpose of which was to blunt the edge of competition and regulate output, prices, wages or the terms of credit, in some particular trade' (Ashton 1948: 128). Moreover, the isolated profit maximizer of the economist myth bears little relation to the social character of the life of the period in which masters and men were imbricated in overlapping networks of group identity. In the eighteenth century, the characteristic instrument of social purpose was not the individual but the club, and that concept extended from the cock-and-hen club of the tavern to the literary group of the coffee house, from the Hell Fire Club of the blasphemers to the Holy Club of the Wesleys. 'Every interest, tradition, or aspiration found expression in corporate form. The idea that, somehow or other men had become self-centered, avaricious, and antisocial is the strangest of all the legends by which the story of the industrial revolution has been obscured' (ibid.: 127). The pinmakers of Bristol and Gloucester had their own organizations, as did the silver plate makers of Sheffield and the file makers of Warrington. Isolated economic man was, and is, a figment of A mode economists' imagination, a story of primordial capitalist creationism without historic counterpart.

State 'policy'

Smith's sympathy for workers leads him to oppose state interference ('the policy of Europe,' the industrial policy of his era), which amounted to protection of privilege and grants by the crown to raise prices to consumers and to enrich the favorites. Monopoly is inefficient for reasons he made familiar to subsequent students of economics. Smith also approved the prevailing restriction of the maximum interest rate to 5 per cent, on the ground that if a higher rate were current,

> the greater part of the money which was to be lent, would be lent to prodigals and projectors, who alone would be willing to give this high interest. . . . A great part of the capital of the country would thus be kept out of the hands which were most likely to make a profitable and advantageous use of it, and thrown into those which were likely to waste and destroy it.
>
> (Smith 1776: 340)

To those who justify financial deregulation and the speculative excesses of the 1980s, the mergers and acquisitions, leveraged buyouts, debt pyramiding, use of junk bonds, and other such innovations on the grounds that the free market knows best and the invisible hand works it all out, such statements should at a minimum give pause for thought. Smith is hardly the prophet of the decade of greed, as those young men in red suspenders are wont to claim. As Viner remarks, Smith thought that 'the majority of investors could not be relied upon to invest their funds prudently and safely, and that government regulation was a good corrective for individual stupidity' (Viner 1927: 111).

Rather than advocating freedom of investors, Adam Smith saved some of his most critical comments for rootless transnational capital. He is worth quoting at length on the matter because it introduces us to the larger issues involved in the use to which he employs his most famous construction – the invisible hand. This term, which is the bedrock of mainstream understanding or, perhaps better, mis-understanding of markets comes in the context of Smith's advocacy of policies to create maximum employment for British workers. First the matter of footloose capital:

> 'The capital, however, that is acquired to any country by commerce and man-
> ufactures, is all a very precarious and uncertain possession, till some part of it
> has been secured and realized in the cultivation and improvement of its lands.
> A merchant, it has been said very properly, is not necessarily the citizen of any
> particular country. It is a great measure indifferent to him from what place he
> carries on his trade; and a very trifling disgust will make him remove his cap-
> ital, and together with it all the industry which it supports, from one country
> to another. No part of it can be said to belong to any particular country, till it
> has been spread as it were over the face of that country, either in buildings, or
> in the lasting improvement in lands.
>
> (Smith 1776: 395)

If we read Smith, the transnational corporations that take the proceeds of domes-tic accumulation, invest abroad and leave their former workers out in the cold, instead of spreading the capital over the face of our own country to the lasting improvement of the land of the working people who produced the wealth, are hardly to be praised for their callous disregard of working people. Smith might well have opposed the way a much more open economy and free capital move-ment has been forced on the world by America's international financial elites and their allies, at the expense of costly dislocations and an extended period of glob-ally high unemployment and slower aggregate growth, and dramatic increases in inequality as these internationalized capitalists have benefitted so exceedingly well.

To Smith there is a hierarchy among manufacturing, agriculture, and foreign trade that a nation would do well to respect. Smith's view was that a manufacturer's capital should reside in the country where it was created and be put to work there, where it would set in motion the greatest quantity of that nation's productive labor rather than going to where returns might be highest. Smith said:

> When the capital of any country is not sufficient for all three purposes, in pro-
> portion as a greater share of it is employed in agriculture, the greater will be
> the quantity of productive labour which it puts into motion within the coun-
> try; as well as likewise be the value which its employment adds to the annual
> produce of the land and labour of the society. After agriculture, the capital

employed in manufactures puts in motion the greatest quantity of productive labour, and adds the greatest value to the annual produce. That which is employed in the trade of exportation, has the least effect of any of the three.

(Smith 1776: 346–7)

The author of *WN*, far from advocating more international trade, thought that for the good of the nation its capital should be retained within its borders. Smith's free trade fans pass over all of this in embarrassed silence (Samuelson 1994). Smith thought that left on their own, individuals would (in pursuing their own advantage) invest at home rather than abroad; that is, self-interest would lead them to do the right thing. His reasons are not that important, although not without merit and insight. (He thinks 'every individual endeavors to employ his capital as near as home as he can. . . . In the home trade his capital is never long out of his sight. . . . He can know better the character and situation of the persons whom he trusts . . .' [Smith 1776: 223] and so on.) They are called to your attention because this line of argument is prelude to the following paragraph, which has within it the famous words concerning the ethereal digits. What is important to the argument is the context in which these words are found. The invisible hand is marshaled as part of Smith's stage theory. It is enlisted in supporting the argument that we should not allow investment capital to go abroad until the employment needs of the home economy are first met:

> But the annual revenue of every society is always precisely equal to the exchangeable value of the whole annual production of its industry, or rather is precisely the same thing with that exchangeable value. As every individual, therefore, endeavours as much as he can both to employ his capital in the support of domestic industry, and so direct that industry that its produce may be of the greatest value; every individual necessarily labours to render the annual revenue of the society as great as he can. He generally, indeed, neither intends to promote the public interest, nor knows how much he is promoting it. By preferring the support of domestic to that of foreign industry in such a manner as its produce may be of the greatest value, he intends only his own gain, and he is in this, as in many other cases, led by an invisible hand to promote an end which was no part of his intention.
>
> (Smith 1776 [Irwin edn.]: II, 22–3)

The paragraph goes on. The point to be highlighted is that it is about the support of domestic over foreign investments. The invisible hand leads the individual to carry through the natural order of things.[9]

Industry and trade

On the question of whether Smith's theory is correct in terms of the reality of English history, most economists endorse free trade as globally efficient, the best policy for a nation to follow. They also tend to use England as a case in point, attributing her high standard of living and global leadership to her presumed commitment to free trade. The story is read differently when we move from the fable to the historical text.

To tell the story of England's rise to world power without China, India, the West Indies, or to discuss its decline without consideration of the loss of empire is, if not quite Hamlet without the Prince of Denmark, still a rather shallow tale. Smith's take on British colonialism, as a matter of historical fact, would seem more wrong than right, hardly an account of the rise of British power (Lie 1993). Smith argues for free trade with the colonies and against restrictions, 'the invidious and malignant project of excluding as much as possible other nations from the colonial trade' (Smith 1776: 561). In doing so, England 'has subjected herself to an absolute and to a restrictive disadvantage in almost every other branch of trade' (ibid.). The fundamental argument, as in the case of the invisible hand, goes to his sectoral development theory:

> As the monopoly of the colonial trade has drawn from those other branches a part of the British capital which would otherwise have been employed in them, so it has forced into them many foreign capitals which would never have gone to them, had they not been expelled from the colony trade.
>
> (ibid.: 566)

He points out that trade may bring high return to the merchant, 'But the advantage of the country in which he resides, the quantity of productive labour constantly maintained there, the annual produce of the land and the labour must always be much less' (ibid.: 568).

Smith's argument is not just 'wrong' by modern trade theory standards, but it is also wrong when put against the historical record (with which trade theory is for the most part unconcerned). It was not by better meeting the needs of their communities that the butcher, the baker, and the candlestick maker brought about British prosperity. England's wealth was the result of its exports.[10] It should hardly have escaped Smith's notice that the prosperity of his own Glasgow was owed to trade in slaves and colonial products. The British navy was foundation for the nation's economic strength. What made England's shopkeepers such an unusual bunch is the local multiplier from the colonial trade and its spread effect in domestic markets that brought them prosperity beyond their peers elsewhere. A quarter century before *WN*, the Abbe Le Blanc, in his *Letters on the English and French Nations*, wrote:

> It must be owned that the natural productions of the country do not, at most, amount to a fourth part of her riches; the rest she owes to her colonies, and the industry of her inhabitants who, by the transportation and exchange of the riches of other countries continually augments their own.
>
> (Hobsbawm 1968: 25–6)

Economic historians will argue over the share of Britain's wealth accruing from her overseas adventures. Certainly, quantitative measures under alternative assumptions yield different figures. One thinks of Keynes' calculation that if the wealth Drake brought back from piracy for Queen Elizabeth had been invested at a modest interest rate, it would by his time have equaled the stock of British investment capital then extant. There should in any case be little argument that the triumph of the British economy had been achieved 'very largely because of the unswerving readiness of British governments to back their businessmen by ruthless and aggressive economic discrimination and open war against all possible rivals.' It was that triumph that made 'complete *laissez-faire* possible, indeed desirable' (Hobsbawm 1968: 23). To say that England gained advantage through mercantilist restrictions and armed interventions, colonialism and conquest, would be closer to the truth than to say she won world leadership through fair and open competition.

By the end of the Napoleonic Wars, Britain's position was 'unassailable.' As the only real industrial power, she could undersell other nations. The fewer restrictions on trade, the better she would do. Free trade was the best policy for Great Britain once she had achieved her supremacy, but not before – economists' abstract theories not withstanding. It may well be true that global welfare might have been greater if she had followed a free trade policy from the start, but British capital, like the Germans, Japanese, and Koreans subsequently, understood the benefits of mercantile stratagems. As Hobsbawm summarizes the British case, parliaments and governments

> Made war and peace for profit, colonies and markets and in order to stamp out commercial competitors. . . . British industry could grow up, by and large, in a protected home market until strong enough to demand free entry into other peoples' markets, that is to insist as a policy of self-interest on free trade.
>
> (Hobsbawm 1968: 32)

It is less useful to examine the matter from a free trade versus protection standpoint than to look at the economic interests arrayed on the two sides of the issue at different points in time. The struggle between commercial traders and manufacturing industrialists was carried out on the basis of political strength and not merely academic debate over the theory of optimal allocation. British producers won protection against Indian textile imports in 1700 when they needed it. By 1813 they were strong enough to deprive the East India Company of its monopoly on the Indian trade.

To the theorist, international trade is a positive sum game in which both parties benefit (or they would not freely exchange goods). To the economic historian, trade between the center and the periphery was not free but the result of colonialism, and the distribution of markets a matter of the comparative strength of naval power, not reciprocal demand in open markets. To the theorist, simultaneous economic expansion is more desirable than one nation attempting to monopolize industrial advancement. To the historian, it was the case that under pre-industrial conditions there was probably room for only one pioneer national industrializer, 'consequently also – at least for some time – for only one "workshop of the world"' (ibid.: 49). Again, it is primarily, though certainly not exclusively, the colonial trade and the dominance of an empire upon which the sun never sets, that gives Britain the lion's share of the economic surplus and the markets to feed the industrial revolution's potential.

Smith on mercantilism

One of our themes is that with the passage of time and shifts in perspective, the texts of the past take on new meaning as they are read with different eyes. In this section, let us consider how a revisionist reading of the East Asian experience and the powerful historical point made by industrial policy advocates, that 'During the past two centuries there have been few examples of countries other than microstates achieving an advanced industrial structure without selective industrial policies' (Wade 1994: 59), may reflect not simply on mainstream Adam Smith's reading of the limits of government, but on Smith's own treatment of the 'mercantilist' writers. That is, were the mercantilists right after all?

We have not talked of the economists who have come to be known as the mercantilists. (Neither they nor Smith recognize such a name.) The pejorative connotations of the term are shaped for us by Smith's criticisms, and to this day economists repeat the canards from the first chapter of Book 4 of *WN* about how they confused substance of wealth with the physical holdings of gold and silver. They advocated a positive balance of payments to pile up lucre, we are told.

Surprisingly contemporary understandings of the developmentalist state were published in major 'mercantilist' interventions in the year before *WN* appeared, 1775: Richard Cantillon's *Essay on the Nature of Commerce* and Josiah Tucker's *Elements of Commerce*. Steuart's *Principles of Political Oeconomy* had appeared about a decade before *WN*. It cannot be said Smith engaged the sophisticated arguments of these 'mercantilists' (the quotation marks are to denote that what we know as mercantilism today is not a fair representation of such works). Smith, and most contemporary economists writing on the subject, chose to attack only the less sophisticated and did not address the arguments of these economists.[11] As Michael Hudson writes:

> Modern scholars have demonstrated that Smith's accusations were only a caricature of the doctrines of economic statecraft developed by the third quarter of the eighteenth century. The fact is that mercantilists abhorred the hoarding attributed to them. They understood clearly that money was productive only when transformed into tangible capital. It was precisely for that reason, that hoarded funds were excluded from the mercantilist definition of the effective money supply. . . . A trade surplus was desired because it was a precondition for obtaining the money necessary to finance growth in investment and employment and also to hold down interest rates.
>
> (Hudson 1992: 47)

These economists understood the specie flow mechanism, but also knew that in the real world harmful inflation was unlikely unless an economy was truly at full employment. Below this point, more money provided definite benefits. Steuart dealt with the limitations of the 'self-adjusting mechanism' by showing its real-world limitations. Today, when economists celebrate David Hume's formulation, it is refreshing to remember Steuart's comment that Hume's theories

> are so pretty, and the theory they laid down for determining the rise and fall of prices so simple, and so extensive, that it is no wonder to see it adopted by almost everyone who has written after them . . . in this as in every other part of the science of political oeconomy, there is hardly such a thing as a general rule to be laid down.
>
> (ibid.)

There were A and B economists even then.

Steuart explained why in the real world, over the relevant short and medium run, an inflow of gold and silver stimulated growth and was not likely to be inflationary to any harmful extent. The long-run adjustment remained a theoretical possibility without immediate relevance. As we'll see over and again, the difference between the A type theorists' answers, correct in the abstract model, are often thought by B mode thinkers to be irrelevant and misleading as a guide to immediate policy issues. The difference is the frame: the pure science concern of 'economics as science' derives the rules that explain the pure theory, and the 'economics as instrumentality' provides a guide for observing events in real time.

These mercantilists thought that under changed conditions free trade may be the better policy choice. As to the special interests mercantilism was said to defend, we have Schumpeter's judgment, shared by other students of the original literature, that 'free-trade forces did not simply assemble outside the mercantilist citadel and storm it . . . but to a much greater extent formed up inside it' (Schumpeter 1954: 369–70). As in the case of Japan in the 1980s, when state technocrats advocated accepting more open trade, they did so for the same reason Smith's contemporaries among the mercantilists did: free trade had become a policy in the national interest under the new conditions of the period. To cite Schumpeter once again: 'If Smith and his followers had refined and developed the "mercantilist" propositions instead of throwing them away, a much truer and much richer theory of international economic relations could have been developed' (ibid.: 376).[12]

A conclusion and an addendum

The argument, to summarize, is that Adam Smith did not favor overseas investment, which he saw as taking needed capital from the home market. He was not an apologist for the rising capitalist class but its severe critic. He believed neither in free market allocation unfettered by moral consideration nor in *laissez-faire* distribution without the hand of the state to bring greater justice in allocation.

Adam Smith is the father of economics, of *both* two sides of its nature. B economists who stress social classes, their expenditure patterns, functional sources of income, the distinction between productive and the unproductive labor, power relations between the classes, value as measured by embodied or commanded labor time, profit as a residual, and the importance of institutions, of history, and evolutionary factors in economic outcomes, can point to Adam Smith as their patron saint. So too can the A economists, who start with the invisible hand optimally allocating resources in a free market, profit as renumeration to risk taking, and an atomistic view of society in which decisions are made by individuals who know what is best for them and need no interference from the state, except that it impartially enforce the rules.[13]

The canonical Adam Smith has been a convenient creature for mainstream economists, who claim him exclusively as their own. Their reading regards Adam Smith as an A-type economist, observing the natural workings of the system which follow laws that can be used to urge that intervention on moral, or any other, grounds in the market economy be prevented. Smith did not believe that real-world markets approximated perfect competition. Some authors have made much of Smith's utility and value paragraphs in Book I, Chapter 4, and in scattered digressions elsewhere, but Smith makes only passing reference to scarcity in his writing. It has been argued that it might have been possible during Smith's time to base a system of political economy entirely on marginal utility calculation (Kauder 1953), but Smith rejected such a path. Hutcheson had stressed scarcity and its usefulness as an economic construct. Smith, as Robertson and Taylor write, 'chose to alter decisively' such a focus 'in the direction of a one-sided almost exclusive emphasis on labour and cost of production' (Robertson and Taylor 1957: 181–2). In basic respects, Adam Smith was out of step with the modern economists who claim him as their oracle.

In this chapter Adam Smith's sympathies for the working class, his opposition to capital export, and to the abuse of wealth and power have been discussed. His endorsement of free markets was qualified in substantial ways and always rooted in an appreciation of the larger ethics of a good society. We will find that it is possible to build on some of his ideas and come to conclusions very different from the supporters of the status quo who invoke his name. If economics is to aspire to the status of a useful explanatory science, it would do well not only to hold to a more inclusive view of the insights it needs to draw from Adam Smith, but to embrace its origins, diverse levels of analysis, and realms of social understanding.

Much the same sort of discussion is necessary when, in the next chapter, the classical tradition he is considered to have founded is discussed. Our task there is to present the tensions in what is seen as a single school of thought, stressing less familiar themes that will be of subsequent importance. For all the differences among classical economists, there were commonalities that are clear in Smith's writing, and in the writers examined in the next chapters. For classical economics, the

> focus was on the ways in which capitalist production creates a social surplus in the context of the given social relations of production which governed the extraction and accumulation of the surplus by the capitalist class of their time, and on the effects upon the growth of the economy of the manner in

which the surplus was divided between capitalist accumulation and luxury consumption.

(Walsh and Graham 1980: 9)

The mainstream of the Classical tradition, if it passes through Ricardo and Malthus, draws on Smith the B economist. If one wants to bestow to Say and Senior the laurels of legitimate continuity, as the neoclassicals implicitly do, than Smith assumes the shape of an early Chicago economist. In the next chapter we examine the divergence of these paths.

4 The legacies of classical political economy

The completeness of the Ricardian victory is something of a curiosity and a mystery. It must have been due to a complex of suitabilities in the doctrine to the environment into which it was projected. That it reached conclusions quite different from what the ordinary uninstructed person would expect, added, I suppose to its intellectual prestige. That its teaching, translated into practice, was austere and often unpalatable, lent it virtue. That is was adapted to carry a vast and consistent logical superstructure, gave it beauty. That it could explain much social injustice and apparent cruelty as an inevitable incident in the scheme of progress, and the attempt to change such things as likely on the whole to do more harm than good, commended it to authority. That it afforded a measure of justification to the free activities of the individual capitalist, attracted to it the support of the dominant social forces behind authority.

(Keynes 1936: 33)

Classical political economy of the A type is, among other things, about laws – the law of diminishing returns, the law of population growth, the law of wages, the law of capital accumulation, the law of rent, and the law of markets and other laws. Such laws are in some tellings operational in the same impersonal way as physical laws. They are declared irrevocable and universal: true regardless of time, place, and existing institutions. As laws they are said to be neither good nor bad in the moral sense. They are then, in one interpretation, how things are; but in another, laws tell us the way things tend to be. Indeed, 'tendency' is widely used by classical political economists, often as a substitute for 'law.' The idea in such a usage is that the profit rate, for example, *tends* to fall (unless there is a more powerful offsetting tendency at work). At other times (often by the same people), 'tendency' is used to mean a presumed statistical relationship.[1]

The economists who stress the regularity and predictability of laws are A mode thinkers. Those who speak of tendency and who privilege contingent elements are B mode economists. Type A classical political economy is closely identified with David Ricardo and type B classical political economy with Thomas Malthus. The third economist of their rank who will be discussed in this chapter is John Stuart Mill. Mill, as much as any economist, is in both the A and B traditions. He is a superb technical economist to whom we owe many contributions of the first order, and yet he is also a philosopher, driven to ask questions in ways that undercut much type A thinking. He charts new ground for the Bs.

Malthus and Ricardo set the poles of the debate over the nature of classical economics (then political economy). For Ricardo the model is the physics one, for Malthus it is of a contingent *social* science. Robert Torrens, their contemporary, and an economist of stature, expressed the difference somewhat too strongly when he wrote: 'As presented by Mr. Ricardo, Political Economy possesses a regularity and simplicity beyond what exists in nature; as exhibited by Mr. Malthus, it is a chaos of original and unconnected elements' (Blaug 1985: 175). Today we would probably say that Malthus did not see chaos but complexity. He was skeptical of the A type tendency to oversimplify, to generalize at the level of parsimonious abstract modeling rather than to see limits imposed by the specificity of individual instances in their great unavoidable variations. Ricardo, as we shall see, was prone to passing judgments off as simple facts (a particularly compelling instance of the normative economics offered as positive economics problem).

Malthus and Ricardo

The friendship between Malthus and Ricardo is a wonderful story. The two men were close, respectful of each other, even in the way they discussed their differences through a dozen years of mutual criticism, as they sought answers (mostly in written conversation) to common questions. Their correspondence between 1811 and 1823 (the year Ricardo died) includes ninety-two known letters from Ricardo to Malthus and 75 by Malthus to Ricardo. Malthus' *Principles of Political Economy* (1820) is largely a response to Ricardo's *Principles of Political Economy and Taxation* (1817). Ricardo's extensive critical notes on Malthus' text are book length as well.

Ricardo built a tight analytic system of the sort A economists prize. His conclusions were drawn deductively from relatively few basic principles.[2] Like Smith, he saw 'The produce of the earth,' as he himself wrote in his major work *The Principles of Political Economy and Taxation*, as derived 'by the united application of labor, machinery, and capital' which he saw divided among 'three classes of the community; namely, the proprietors of the land, the owner of the stock or capital necessary for its cultivation, and the laborers by whose industry it is cultivated' (Ricardo 1817: 5). The question of the allocation among the three classes, in the form of rent, profit, and wages, is regulated by laws, and, wrote Ricardo in the Preface to his great text, 'To determine the laws which regulate this distribution, is the principal problem in Political Economy' (ibid.). Although the science had been much improved by the likes of Turgot, Smith, Say, and others, Ricardo thought 'they afforded very little satisfactory information respecting the natural course of rent, profit, and wages' (ibid.: 5).

To the historians of economic thought for whom economics is an A science, it is Ricardo who 'literally invented the technique of economics.'[3] Keynes fils captures the essence of why Ricardo continues to be the economist's economist, when he writes that Ricardo offers

the supreme intellectual achievement, unattainable by weaker spirits, of adopting a hypothetical world remote from experiences as though it were the world
of experience and then living in it consistently. With most of his successors
common sense cannot help breaking in – with injury to their logical
consistency.

(Blaug 1985: 192)

Keynes tempers enthusiasm for Ricardo with a desire for a policy relevant economics. He asks us 'to consider the assumptions required to validate' particular
Ricardian statements. The one Keynes has uppermost in mind is the usual classical one 'that there is always full employment.' This domination of abstract logic in
model building over meaningful assumptions drawn from the real world was, of
course, central to the classical economics Keynes opposed, and so it is not surprising that he wrote that 'the complete dominance of Ricardo's approach for a period
of 100 years has been a disaster to the progress of economics' (Keynes 1923: 33).
I should perhaps add that with the third edition of Ricardo's *Principles* (in its
Chapter 31), Ricardo finds that capitalist accumulation may cause the position of
the working class to deteriorate over time. He disassociated himself from the technological optimism prevalent in the opinion molding classes then, as now. But this
was a late admission, uncharacteristic, although it had influence on subsequent
rejection of *the* classical model.

'The first business . . . is to account for things as they are'

In his social views, Malthus is making value judgments explicitly in an area in
which most economists typically claim that in their role as economists they are
agnostic. Type A thinking suggests that the allocation of endowments reflects not
only chance (as per Malthus) but also intellect, effort, and sound application, and
that the economist *qua* economist could make no moral judgment in this area as to
the propriety of outcome. The economist's job, they think, is to report on the efficiency of resource allocation. Malthus has no trouble explicitly making judgements
that may appear to be absent in the work of other economists; positive analysis and
normative judgement are, however, unself-consciously mixed.

Most economists presume that Ricardo, as an 'economics-as-science' man, did
nothing of the kind, but they are mistaken. Schumpeter is certainly not the only
reader to have noticed the way Ricardo confused values and facts, piling up rhetorical arguments of questionable scientific validity, reflecting his clear personal bias.
Later A type economists learned from his technique, and follow Schumpeter's
cynical advice on the best way to proceed in such endeavors: 'boldly deny the obvious' (Schumpeter 1991: 205). From Malthus' perspective, the science mode
economist in looking for eternal laws is apt not to see, or even look at, what is actually going on in any particular instance and so to assume general causes that are
not applicable, or are of minor consequence. Ricardo thought such differences
could be reduced to Malthus' emphasis on the short run in which such 'details' are

important, and his own long-run emphasis in which laws can be shown to operate more smoothly. As we shall see when we come to the contemporary scene, this division is still evident and those taking Malthus' side continue to think the pure theorists are missing much of what is going on. Those siding with Ricardo see a great deal of *ad hoc* argument not grounded in theory. The Malthus types seem to come too close to sociology for the Ricardo side's comfort.

Schumpeter returns such criticism in spades aimed at Ricardo whom, he says, has 'no philosophy at all,' no sense of history, and 'not an inadequate sociology but none at all' (Schumpeter 1954: 471). He did not mean any of that as a compliment. Indeed, in describing Ricardo's method, Schumpeter gives an apt picture of the method of work of today's A mode economists. He writes of Ricardo that the latter's interest was in

> clear-cut result of direct, practical significance. In order to get this he cut his general system to pieces, bundled up large parts of it as possible, and put them in cold storage – so that as many things as possible should be frozen and 'given'. He then piled one simplifying assumption upon another until, having really settled everything by these assumptions, he was left with only a few aggregative variables between which, given these assumptions, he set up simple one-way relations so that, in the end, the desired result emerged almost as tautologies. . . . The habit of applying results of this character to the solution of practical problems we shall call the Ricardian Vice.
>
> (ibid.: 472–3)

These differences in method are what most importantly divide Ricardo and Malthus as A and B type economists. There is, however, also a contrast in their class orientations and their analyses of such substantive matters as to how markets work, the efficacy of government intervention, and the desirability of voluntarist understanding of economic developments. Interrogating their interplay in this paradigmatic case will, it is hoped, inform readers' judgments when contemporary examples are considered in later chapters.

Class politics and classical economics

It is from Ricardo, more than any other influence, that Marx took his economics. Among important items, Marx accepted Ricardo's version of the labor theory of value as a key starting point. Ricardo (even though he incorporated the role of time in explaining interest on capital) still conceived of machines as stored-up labor – their value reducible to embodied labor time, the result of 'the engineer, smith, and carpenter, who erected the building and machinery' (Ricardo 1817: 15). The value of the capital stock is determined by the sum of labor involved. Ricardo is rigorous in the manner in which he combines class analysis and a labor theory of value. He was thus quite naturally an economist Karl Marx held in high regard. Economists who found such views of class and value theory anathema were appalled by Ricardo. Stanley Jevons (whom we will encounter in Chapter 6 where we investigate the coming of neoclassical economics based on subjectivist under-standing of value), writes that Ricardo had 'shunted the car of economic science on the wrong track' (Jevons 1871: 72). Jevons surely appreciated Ricardo's mastery of comparative statics, but the great classical theorist's achievements in that line were as nothing compared to his placing class conflict and the labor theory of value at the core of his analysis.

The models Malthus and Ricardo built were constructed in a particular histor-ical context, that of the post-Napoleonic Wars years. Their economics was rooted in the class politics of that period. Napoleon had blockaded British ports, and domestic production of grains ('corn' was the general term in those days) in the British Isles had increased because of the war-induced high prices in that isolated market. The question after the war was whether the landed interests should be pro-tected against lower priced imports of corn. It was to answer this very practical question that Malthus and Ricardo developed their analytics. There is some irony here. Ricardo is thought of as the pure scientist thinking in terms of laws relevant across time: '[H]e nowhere displays insight into the fact that the constitution of his science was largely the result of his conception that the future of England depended, above all, on the manner in which the Corn Laws issue was resolved' (Rogin 1956: 3). When we examine contemporary issues it will be suggested that important current debates are about the nature of the present social and political arrangements in the same way. Since we are too close to them for this to be as clear as we should like, it is useful to get some practice, as it were, by examining these his-torically important debates as instances of this general phenomenon.

Malthus developed the basis of what is called differential or the Ricardian theory of rents,[4] the idea that an increase in demand for food brings into cultiva-tion less and less fertile land. This raises rents for all land, and those with the more productive lands enjoy greater income (since the higher rents are required to bring marginal land into cultivation). Whereas Ricardo criticizes the process (the landlords who do nothing get rich, food costs rise, profits fall, and growth slows), Malthus sees rent as just compensation to 'the powers attached to the soil' which are in the possession of the landlord per 'the great lottery of life.' Since production could not take place without natural resources, and since each class is equally enti-tled to compensation for the contribution of its factor inputs, this is a reasonable state of affairs. Indeed, for Malthus it is more than this. It is particularly useful because, whilst the landowner spends freely, hiring retainers and contributing to charitable works, the capitalist does not, withdrawing funds from the circular flow instead of creating employment with their surplus (a pre-Keynesian insight that we will return to, and an outlook that endears him to Keynes.)[5]

His views on population are well known, and Ricardo did not disagree with him on the matter of population growth causing high rents. The difference was that Malthus saw high rents as the result of economic growth and so an indicator of prosperity. Malthus also argued that landlords improve their property and, as noted earlier, believed that out of rents they conserve and create jobs for others. 'Rents,' wrote Malthus, 'are the reward of present valor and wisdom, as well as of past strength and abilities' (Malthus 1836: 216). (That would sound less preposterous to you, dear reader, despite the anachronistic use of language, if a landlord class still dominated our economic, political, and cultural life as they did in his time. Think about substituting finance in the sentence and it would seem unobjectionable, even obvious.)

The beneficence of existing property relations was a presumed given to Malthus, as was the folly of redistribution. He tended to see only the positive side of market allocation, writing in his *Principles* that, 'every exchange which takes place in a country, effects a distribution of its produce better adapted to the wants of society.' Rather than defining wealth as Smith did as the product of labor, Malthus wrote 'I should define wealth to be material objects, necessary, useful, or agreeable to man, which are voluntarily appropriated by individuals or nations' (ibid.: 33). No labor need be incorporated in an article for it to be considered wealth, he added. In turning his back on a labor theory of value, Malthus also moved away from a social understanding of production, as evinced in Smith's enumeration of the interdependence of each person on so many seen and unseen others, toward a subjective understanding of value as a characteristic of the commodity as perceived by the individual. Adding further to the asocial nature of his approach, he believed the initial distribution of assets held by each individual to be the result of a lottery. That 'one did not draw a prize' did not mean one 'suffers any hardship or injustice' (Malthus 1798: 143).

The Corn Laws and the victory of the free trade doctrine

Ricardo identified economic prosperity with capital accumulation and defended the interests of the rising capitalist class. He saw rents as threatening prosperity by raising labor costs and lowering profits, out of which new investment needed to be funded. Ricardo believed it is the profits of the farmers that regulate the profits of the other trades. He was wrong about this as a long-term matter, as he was in his pessimistic conclusion that the economic growth rate must eventually fall to zero and a stationary state reached, as rent on increasingly less productive land 'eats up' profits that must be paid out in wages to keep the working class alive. Malthus saw landlords as preservers of civilization and fosterers of economic stability. Ricardo believed that the interest of the landlord is always opposed to the interest of every other class in the community. Their class allegiances and economic analysis were internally consistent, and on this question Malthus and Ricardo took diametrically opposite positions. Ricardo may not have convinced Parliament to repeal the Corn Laws in his lifetime, but then Parliament was dominated by landowners. His reasoning and the model that he developed to present its analytics have impressed economists ever since. Eventually, free trade ideology did triumph as the industrial revolution changed the economic base of the nation and the class composition of the English elite.

British industrialists saw the political necessity of accepting agricultural imports if England was to convince other nations to reduce tariffs and protectionist measures against English manufactured goods. Then too, cheaper grains, as Ricardo had argued, lowered the cost of domestic labor and increased the profitability of English industry. The British Corn Law controversy was in many respects not unlike the contemporary debates in Japan concerning rice. Having built a powerful export machine selling its manufactured goods to the world, it was no longer politically possible, despite domestic protests, for Britain not to open agricultural markets to lower cost imports. Export success creates free trade advocates. For all the trappings of pure theory, justification of the benefits of free trade is for most participants in the debate a matter of self-interest. Economists are the major exception. They take great pride in their disinterestedness and believe in the power of their abstract theoretical model to apply to all times and in all situations.

The legacy

Ricardo's immortality rests on his having taken as exogenously given those elements that need to be explained, and in declaring fixed those quantities whose changes are most central to the process of economic development. It has taken economists well over a century after Ricardo to take seriously (at the level of theory) the reality that there is not a fixed amount of resources to be chosen from some waiting pile. There are underutilized resources and factors of production that are not perfectly mobile among uses (e.g. land in Portugal is not all good for growing grapes). The value of resources depends on their specificities and on the direction of development of the productive forces in a particular social formation. Growth is path dependent (as some contemporary economists we shall consider in Chapter 10 stress). Decisions today to move in one direction or another will produce different economies with different resource endowments over time. Nor is technology given. Returns are not constant (there are economies of scope and of scale, there is learning by doing). As with all economic theory, comparative static versions of comparative advantage rest on a number of unrealistic assumptions. The question is, are these patently false Ricardian assumptions close enough to give the model predictive power? Mainstream economics has traditionally claimed that they are. However, in a world in which people and capital are mobile internationally, and imbalances in international trade and payments a reality (they are not allowed in the pure theory), much happens that is not captured by the Ricardian theory, even with the modifications of later economists working in the traditional restricted frameworks (such as Hecksher, Ohlin, and Samuelson).

The economist's case (at least since Ricardo) is made by means of models from which most of the relevant considerations are eliminated by assumption. (Each country is assumed to enjoy full employment, there is no migration of labor, no international investment, perfect competition prevails, and there is perfect mobility of factors within each nation.) Foreign trade becomes the passive adjustment to factor endowment and relative prices in static allocation. This is the core of the theory of comparative advantage, attributed in the standard history of economic thought textbooks to Ricardo and taught as orthodoxy in international trade theory. However, the pure theory would seem to misrepresent Ricardo's more convincing argument.

Ricardo's interest in the repeal of the Corn Laws was motivated, as some readers noticed, not so much by a static 'gains from trade' argument but from a 'gains from growth' consideration underlying the effect of the repeal. By raising the rate of profit for the capitalist and reducing the rent of land (capitalists being presumed thrifty, landlords profligate), England's long-term growth prospects, Ricardo thought, would be greatly enhanced. The Ricardo of pure trade theory is a pale imitation of the real one. As Ronald Findlay argues, 'the very neatness and elegance of *the* Ricardian trade model has diverted attention from the more complex, rich and deep ideas.'[6] Ricardo's less orthodox contributions have been influential, but usually from the pens of those taking issue with pure Ricardian theory.

The dismal science

Malthus and Ricardo are both pessimistic on the prospects for the future. Ricardo's assumption of a static technology and Malthus' dire population forecast in the context of diminishing returns in agriculture set the tone for much of later classical political economy, which denies the prospect of progress through technological breakthrough or from organizational innovations. These assumptions, which underlay the expectation of a trajectory toward a stationary state, led Thomas Carlyle to dub economics 'the dismal science,' a sobriquet it has never really escaped, despite its innate modernist optimism.

Malthus' *Essay on Population* was a rebuke directed at the idealism of the Enlightenment. Things would *not* get better as human reason came to hold sway (as writers such as Condorcet and William Godwin argued). This was because, as Malthus in his most famous argument maintained, unchecked population growth would exceed agricultural capacity. In terms of historical fact, Malthus appears to have recanted. The data, he admitted, did not in fact support him. The theoretically logical 'tendency' was not a likely trajectory events would actually take. In a later edition of the *Essay*, Malthus concluded that diminishing returns in agriculture could be put off 'for some centuries to come' through improvements in agricultural machinery, better methods of land management, increased imports, and the decline in the price of manufactures due to improved machinery; but none of this entered the public consciousness once the terms of the initiating dramatic debate had been set. For a hundred years after Malthus' essay, English economists accepted his (canonical version) views as being valid natural law, 'an inexorable quasi-physical necessity' (Schumpeter 1954: 257); and posterity has the Malthus it prefers.

The canonical Malthus criticized Condorcet, who preached the desirability of government intervention to provide greater income equality and security through state provision of aid to the aged, widows, and orphans. Condorcet had also urged government intervention in financial markets to limit credit availability to the powerful capitalists and to rechannel it to working people. Malthus' second major target, William Godwin, countered the ever popular view that the poor were naturally lazy by pointing to the unjust social relations and institutionally enforced class inequalities. The criminality among the poor, Godwin wrote, was caused primarily by desperation, and if all people could have decent jobs, there would be fewer criminals. The historians of economic thought have given almost exclusive attention to the Malthusian thesis of arithmetic agricultural output gain versus a geometrically rising population. It should be noted that whilst the particular rationales for helping the poor, blaming them, and maintaining that 'science says nothing can be done to help them,' have all changed repeatedly over the history of the dismal science, there is also a basic similarity of rationales (Hirschman 1991). Economists are divided on the automaticity and optimality of free market outcomes, and because of their pre-analytic proclivities, the rationales and analytics often follows rather than being the unbiased conclusion to their disinterested scientific investigations. The language has changed somewhat but the contemporary debate over welfare and the work ethic would not be an unfamiliar one to Malthus and his contemporaries.

There can be no doubt that Godwin was working outside of what mainstream economists take for granted as the givens of their society. He had the habit of asking provocative questions such as: 'To whom does any article of property, suppose a loaf of bread, justly belong?' To him, as to Victor Hugo's Jean Valjean, the answer is to 'whom the possession of it will be most beneficial' (Hunt 1992: 89). The law, of course (as Inspector Javert reminds us), knows nothing of such logic. Malthus's understanding of matters would not be uncongenial to Monsieur Javert. It is that if the poor are fed, you simply get more poor. The problem was not, in Malthus' opinion, capitalist social and economic relations, or the fact that the law sided with the capitalists to keep the poor 'in their place.' Rather it is a matter of science, 'the inevitable laws of nature,' Malthus thought. 'No possible sacrifice of the rich, particularly in money, could for any time prevent the recurrence of distress among the lower members of society' (ibid.: 91). People whom Malthus' spiritual heirs call knee-jerk liberals, and whom Malthus called 'those benevolent, but much mistaken men,' just didn't understand the laws of economics. The Malthus side explanation typically understates the importance of the state, for the law plays its central role and must be enforced by the Javerts.

The only preventative check to which Parson Malthus accented was abstinence (he abhorred birth control as an abomination against God), but he thought that given lower-class lust, it would likely be inadequate. That left the horsemen of famine, war, pestilence, and death to do their work. If not natural catastrophe, then starvation would be the fate of the surplus population. The action of 'those benevolent, but much mistaken men' would only make matters worse. Malthus was certainly at one with the prejudices of the gentry and criticized the 'drinking, gaming and debauchery' of the poor. The decline of morality has ever been explanation enough for social decay: the poor have only themselves to blame. The want of frugality generally found among the poor, as Edward Banfield and others among our own contemporary academics were to say, had a short time horizon. That is why they are poor. Malthus said that even when they have the opportunity of saving they seldom exercise it.

The radical egalitarianism of a Godwin would result only in a shared poverty and a bestial existence for all. Malthus, like most conservatives, had a marvelous ability to presume that existing organization of production and social decision making would continue forever. The thought that productivity could be so increased, labor power employed so inclusively, society organized to allow a higher standard of living for the masses, were flights of imaginative thinking beyond his ken. His well-heeled readers could only agree: 'It would bring down the system if we limit child labor or the hours of women working in the mines. Any idiot knows that.' Indeed, many idiots did. They declared such measures were a threat to liberty, to human freedom. They proclaimed factories would all shut down and move overseas if child labor was restricted.

Despite such arguments, the mine and mill owners were challenged by the workers themselves through self-organization and militant struggle and by middle-class reformers who, in 1819, were able to pass legislation limiting the labor of children under 16 to twelve hours a day. After 1842, children under 10 were no longer legally allowed to work in the mines. Adult men's freedom of contract was not abridged. Women and children were not deemed free agents, and so legislation in 1947 allowed for a 55-hour week for young persons and women. Malthus' theory was an important bulwark holding back such reforms. The battle over defining the nature of poverty is a recurring theme in economics and policy debates, and whilst we cannot give sufficient attention to the subject, it is perhaps worth noting that just as Botero had fully developed the 'Malthusian' principle of population in a 1589 publication, and 200 years later Malthus 'really did little more than repeat it,' Malthus' critique of 'welfare,' that it would only encourage the poor to breed, was part of a supply side attached on the inefficiency and counterproductive nature of the welfare state of the Reagan Era. Between Botero and Malthus, as between Malthus and George Gilder (1981), a long list of other thinkers had recycled similar ideas.

If Malthus is such a reactionary, how is he labeled a B mode classical economist? The answer, and this bears emphasizing, is that one can be a conservative and either an A or a B economist or some mixture of both. Malthus is grouped with the B types for three important reasons. The first is that he envisioned social attitudes and behavior (his 'habits') as subject to change, and saw the economy shaped by the habits operating at a given time. One can appreciate his method of analysis even if one is not sympathetic to his stand on particular issues. Rostow, for example, celebrates Malthus for introducing 'a rather subtle notion of the dynamic interplay between material circumstances and social behavior' (Rostow 1990: 57). The second is that Malthus was one of the first economists to see beyond the automaticity of a return to full employment equilibrium and to take the theoretical problem of protracted depression seriously. Third, he strongly criticized deductivism and a priorism in social science. As we have seen, his criticism of Ricardo is much in this vein.

Ricardo rejected Malthus' categories, notably his measure of value, because they were oriented to what for Ricardo was the transitory issue of temporary unprofitability resulting from maladjustment of supply and demand. Keynes took Malthus' side and lamented how differently the history of thought and the tenor of policy in economic matters would have been if Malthus had won the debate. 'If only Malthus, instead of Ricardo, had been the parent stem from which nineteenth-century economics proceeded, what a much wiser and richer place the world would be today!' (Keynes 1923: 36). Schumpeter in turn criticized Keynes for carrying his judgments of Ricardo 'beyond all bounds of reason' (Schumpeter 1954: 623).

The A versus B nature of their differences needs to be appreciated. It is stated most effectively by George Stigler when he takes the position that 'the triumph of Ricardo over Malthus cannot be regretted by the modern economist: it is more important that good logic win over bad than good insight over poor.'[7] Indeed, Malthus's insight into the nature of England in the 1820s, a period much like England in the 1920s when Keynes formulated his ideas, is unacceptable to full employment equilibrium economists for much the same reason that 100 years later they were to declare Keynes' *General Theory* 'a special case' of the classical model.

Leo Rogin suggests that had Ricardo and Malthus recognized clearly that their theories were 'oriented to different economic problems, their thirteen year controversy might have been more fruitful both in their own time and for posterity' (Rogin 1956: 10). This is precisely the point, however. Economists are rarely ever able to see the significance of others' research agendas as being as valid as their own. To accept the alternative way of seeing as valid is, in general, to diminish the claim one is making for one's own approach. Each therefore has good reason to interpret through the lens of their own preoccupations. One can be sure that when Jevons wrote of 'that able, but wrong headed man, David Ricardo,' his criterion was not that of Keynes. The sort of thing Jevons had in mind was perhaps in reaction to Ricardo's thinking expressed in an 1820 letter to Malthus: 'You say demand and supply regulate value – this, I think is saying nothing.'

Where do we look for a value theory? At the level of profits, wages, and rents? Through the labor theory of value? At supply and demand? At the activities of people in relations of production with an emphasis on the formation and reproduction of social relations? Ricardo had an answer waiting for Jevons even if he delivered it directed at Malthus: 'The opinion that the price of commodities depends solely on the proportion of supply to demand, or demand to supply, has become almost an axiom in political economy, and has been the source of much error in the science' (Meek 1974). Marx, as we shall see in the next chapter, built on Ricardo's labor theory of value. In the subsequent chapter we shall turn to the neoclassical approach of Jevons and others.

First, however, a short comment is in order with regard to the relation of Malthus' thinking and the developments in the sciences, especially the development of Darwin's thinking. Charles Darwin, we are told by the historians of science, needed the social ideas of Malthus and other economists, for without them he could not have formulated the explanatory and theoretical mechanisms of natural selection. Just as Newton had influenced Adam Smith, there continued to be a reciprocal fertilization among intellectuals. As Appleby, Hunt and Jacob note, Darwin's wide familiarity with economics and social theory through the writings of Adam Smith and especially Thomas Malthus facilitated his development of an explanation of what he had seen on his voyage. They write:

As a liberal Whig with industrialists in his family, Darwin sympathized with the reforming impulse. His recent biographers describe his circle as a place where 'politics, science and literature were all of a piece'. . . . Reform suggested that the present was better than the past, that in effect the superior drove out the inferior. In addition, the idea that struggle was at the heart of the development of a species, the Malthusian vision of population survival of the strongest with containment of the weakest by plague and famine, set Darwin thinking.

(Appleby *et al.* 1994: 182)

As we shall see in Chapter 7, Darwinism[8] was seized upon by economic theorists and ideologues in the late nineteenth century, especially in the United States where, as Richard Hofstadter writes in his definitive study, it was seen

as a welcome addition, perhaps the most powerful of all, to the store of ideas to which solid and conservative men appealed when they wished to reconcile their fellows to some hardships of life and to prevail upon them not to support hasty and ill-considered reforms. Darwinism was one of the great informing insights in this long phase in the history of the conservative mind in America.

(Hofstadter 1944: 5)

The constant interplay expected as part of intellectual life among the sciences, humanities, and social sciences has been lost to a sad degree in our own time and it is sometimes difficult to remember how important such cross-fertilization has been in the history of ideas. In the present period, the struggle to renew such conversations is opposed on the grounds of greater gains from specialization. (We have said enough about Adam Smith's intellectual range to suggest that whilst he and other classical economists might speak of the gains from specialization, they also stressed the benefits of exchange in the betterment of the species.) The insights Darwin received from Smith and Malthus were fed back to the social sciences in late nineteenth-century Social Darwinism, and the resistance to it, which was formative to the founding of the American Economics Association by political economists who rejected the *laissez-faire* ideas Malthusianism had promulgated.

Gluts, Say's Law, and real-world markets

Whilst other economists dwell on the automatic working of the market system and either presume full employment as they would assume a can opener, or believe that markets work so fast to restore full capacity equilibrium that there can be no unemployment problem, Malthus was of a different mind. He wrote to his friend Ricardo:

I really think that the progress of society consists of irregular movements, and that to omit the consideration of causes which for eight or ten years will give a great *stimulus* to production and population, or a great *check* to them, is to omit the causes of the wealth and poverty of nations – the grand objective of all enquiries in Political Economy.

He also noted that eight to ten years, recurring not infrequently, represents a significant amount of time in a human life. 'They amount to a serious sum of happiness or misery, according as they are prosperous or adverse, and leave the country in a very different state at their termination' (Malthus 1836: 437).

Malthus, writing with the deep depression of 1819 firmly in mind, explained gluts and offered policies to mitigate them. He saw a periodic insufficiency of effectual demand – a good reason to talk up landlords who, being men of leisure, spend their income patronizing the arts, hiring servants, and generally recycling their incomes. Capitalists, however, receive too much, don't spend enough, and if there is no profitable way to invest, their savings create problems because they withhold income in the form of barren cash (capitalists hoard rather than invest it, fearing reduced or negative profits). They respond pro-cyclically to reduced effectual demand worsening the situation. Now there is some question of how much of this essentially Keynesian story Malthus understood, but there is little doubt that he was one of the first economists of note to challenge what came to be known as Say's Law.[9] Malthus' call for public works projects to employ the working classes in times of high unemployment included his retort to those who thought higher taxes to pay for jobs would diminish private incentive to investment.[10]

Ricardo's view on the impossibility of gluts is much like Adam Smith's. Smith had not worried about the problem because in his view 'What is annually saved is as regularly consumed as what is annually spent, and nearly in the same time too; but it is consumed by a different set of people.' There was no need to worry about the cumulative effect of purchasing power being withdrawn from the circular flow. This Keynesian fear of Malthus' just wasn't the way the world worked. For Ricardo

> No man produces but with a view to consume or sell, and he never sells but with an intention to purchase some other commodity. . . . By producing, then, he necessarily becomes either the consumer of his own goods, or the purchaser and consumer of some other person.
>
> (Ricardo 1817: 192–3)

There might be a glut of particular commodities but 'this cannot be the case with respect to all commodities.' Of course, Ricardo knew there were depressions, he too lived through them and wrote about their meaning, but like many other economists he saw them as the necessary period during which the economy adjusted to some abnormal changes in supply and demand. Once these disturbances had been worked through, the normal state of full employment was reestablished. There is no need for government intervention to attempt to repair the situation. Ricardo endorses Say's Law; Malthus does not.

Say's Law is the most prominent formulation of the idea that competitive markets quickly create full employment if allowed to function freely, that a given aggregate output creates a demand of the same magnitude. What buyers purchase provides income for suppliers as a group to become buyers. They then have the income to command what is produced. Say denies the possibility of an under full employment equilibrium. In Chapter 15 of *A Treatise on Political Economy*, Say himself put the matter this way:

> It is worth while to remark, that a product is no sooner created, that it, from that instant, affords a market for other products to the full extent of its own value. When the producer has put the finishing hand to his product, he is more anxious to sell it immediately, lest its value should diminish in his hands. Nor is he less anxious to dispose of the money he may get for it; for the value of the money is also perishable. But the only way of getting rid of money is in the purchase of some product or other. Thus, the mere circumstance of the creation of one product immediately opens a vent for other products.
>
> (Say 1821: 142)

Notice the use of 'immediately,' 'is no sooner created that it,' and 'from that instant.' Other economists were even more doctrinaire on the automaticity of the law. Yet these were years of serious economic crises. We are into 'tendency' and 'tendency' again: long-term tendencies of the system and short-term deviations. Say asserts that it is all very automatic: what is produced is immediately sold; what is received as income is spent. If one reads on beyond this widely quoted passage further down the same page, however, it turns out that all this is true only in principle, in a rational economy devoid of 'embargoes, oppressive duties . . . jobbing and speculation.' For those of us who live in such a less than perfect world, Say's Law is copybook fantasy. It is also textbook orthodoxy.

Please understand that it is surely not that Say denied there were economic crises or 'gluts' (as the terminology of the period described these occurrences of coexistence of unemployed resources and unsold goods). Writing of the post-Napoleonic depression, he asked:

> What is the cause of the general glut of all the markets of the world . . . ? What is the reason that in the interior of every state . . . there exists universally a difficulty of finding lucrative employment? And when the cause of this chronic disease is found, by what means is it to be remedied? On these questions depend the tranquility and happiness of nations.
>
> (quoted in Rogin 1956: 7)

Say recognizes the phenomenon of a 'general glut' sufficient to jeopardize 'the tranquility and happiness of nations', and maintained at the same time that – in principle – production creates its own demand.

In a mode of approaching real-world problems that should be familiar to any reader of contemporary economic theory, Say declares that in a rational economy things would work smoothly. If the world coincided with the model, the model would be a good description of the world. Well, yes it would. Such an approach may explain why economists can get so exasperated by the world's failure to conform, and why so much of their advise boils down to prescriptions that (if they worked) would make the world more like their models. The principle of a rational capitalist economy, of a mechanical social world, comes first and last. [11]

Classical economics after Ricardo and Malthus moves in a host of directions, only some of which can be detailed here. Before moving on, we may pause to note that little of pure Ricardian analysis remains in the mainstream of economics, and much by his critics does. Ricardo's legacy is rather his tightly reasoned analytic system of thought, which showed a methodological consistency that was not matched by his rivals. From a few simple assumptions (many of which were in his case historically not valid) there followed sweeping generalizations (Ekelund and Hebert 1990: ch. 7). Ricardo's immediate disciples exceeded him in dogmatic adherence to his theory, and where Ricardo in fact built his analysis, which was for him a matter of practical political import, on contingencies of time and place, what we have been left with are the formal trappings of the analysis (Rogin 1956: 4). Whilst Ricardo eventually yielded somewhat to Malthus' way of thinking, the real conversion was Jean-Baptiste Say himself who, in the fifth edition of his text (1826), openly disavowed the doctrine that there was no short-run limits to production. Indeed, he repudiated the Ricardian perspective and its 'obscure metaphysics' and 'vain subtleties.' Yet whilst Say may have admitted to Malthus that Say's Law was, ahem, 'subject to some restrictions,' none of this made the history books. [12]

Say, along with Nassau Senior and Frederic Bastiat, did much to move the classical economists away from the class theories of Adam Smith, Malthus, and Ricardo. They 'sanitized' classical political economy, in Kay Hunt's phrase, by rejecting the labor theory and class perspective. Another writer who paved the way for this redirection toward what will become neoclassical economics is Jeremy Bentham.

Bentham to Bastiat

It is useful to understand that Bentham's calculus of pain and pleasure, 'the two sovereign masters' he claimed nature decreed should govern mankind, dramatically recentered the attention of economists away from production and class relations to quantifying pleasures and pain subjectively. Self-defined utility became the measure of value. Today, Bentham has something of a theosophist caste, but his thesis is alive and at the core of contemporary writing on value theory. To Bentham, by utility

> is meant property in any object, whereby it tends to produce benefits, advantage, pleasure, good, or happiness (all this in the present case comes to the same thing), or (what comes again to the same thing) to prevent the happening of mischief, pain, evil, or unhappiness to the part whose interest is considered.
>
> (Bentham, cited in Hunt 1992: 158)

A great advantage of reducing human complexity to a single principle (that of maximizing pleasure, pain is merely the negative of pleasure), is that it can then be stated mathematically and, in theory, measured. Bentham enumerated the circumstances of pleasure – intensity, duration, certainty, and so on.[13]

Bentham grasped the difference between total utility and utility at the margin. He also believed in the diminishing marginal utility of money, which is an idea that in the hands of some of his followers had radical implications. For if money has diminishing marginal utility, total happiness can be increased by distributing from the rich (who get less satisfaction from holding so much) and giving it to the poor (who derive greater marginal utility from it than the incremental cost foregone by the rich). Bentham himself did not develop the iconoclastic implications of utilitarian thinking. Indeed, it has been argued that his development of utilitarianism (in contradistinction to natural law as the basis for economists to build a theory of the good society) was motivated by his impulse to disarm the growing radicalism of social thinking in his time.

Whilst classical liberals had used the doctrine of natural law and natural rights to fight the arbitrary power of the Church and the monarchy, radicals such as Tom Paine spoke of the natural rights of all men – which raised the specter of the tyranny of the majority in well-heeled circles, where it was thought they needed to be headed off. One way to do this was to reform the worst abuses of the system. Such a reformist course was inhibited by the natural rights doctrine which, as applied to property, suggested the right to property was absolute and inviolate. Utilitarianism proved more flexible. It offered a pragmatic basis for government intervention. Any reform that produced favorable consequences for the society as a whole could be validated. This legitimated reform to prevent revolt and revolution. Thus liberals, and John Stuart Mill is an outstanding example, were able to make the philosophical case for economic reform.

Bentham claimed that rights were not natural after all: they receive their legitimacy through the law. By passing new laws, government could legitimately create new rights and modify or displace old ones (so long as the laws served the public interest) (Clark 1991: 88). This became a powerful rationale in the hands of reformers.[14] Utilitarianism's justification by reason, the test for Mill's utilitarianism, is a 'let the chips fall where they may' readiness to dispense with traditions that should not be defended. There is a certain irreverence and intellectual openness to radical reform that would appeal to later English economists of the academic cultural elite, certainly to J.M. Keynes, although over time the explicit and unself-conscious moralism becomes muted and transformed into a liberal pragmatism.

Political allegiance tempted economists to strain the limits of their science in pursuit of influencing the politics, if not in the narrow, then in the broad meaning of the term. Apologists for the system like Nassau Senior discussed the relation of wages and profit in terms of 'the kindliness of a voluntary association' and would not entertain of even the possibility of class struggle. Those who could, Senior thought, were men 'whose reasoning faculties are either uncultivated, or perverted . . . ' (Hunt 1992: 184). Capitalists were entitled to profit because of the pain they endured to make it possible, i.e., 'To abstain from the enjoyment which is in our power, or to seek distant rather than immediate results, are among the most painful exertions of the human will' (ibid.: 182). Senior designed his theories to combat 'the threat of an arrogant laboring class, resorting to strikes, violence, and combinations, a threat to the foundations not merely of wealth but of existence itself' (ibid.: 182). One can almost hear the 'harrumph.'

Such views are not simply academic. Senior was a very influential member of the Poor Law Inquiry Commission, and the law that its report recommended enshrined principles popular to this day. They suggested that people should take whatever job is available, regardless of pay and working conditions, and that any person who couldn't or wouldn't work should be provided with only enough to be barely kept from starving, an amount well below the lowest wage commonly available. The stigma and the suffering of being on welfare should be calculated to discourage people from applying and to encourage them to take any job they could find, no matter how inadequate and oppressive. Hobsbawm's characterization of the poor law as 'an engine of degradation and oppression more than a means of material relief' is an accurate characterization of Senior's intent which, in turn, is consistent with his views of the way economic laws work. Senior did not see such views as political. He, and like-minded practitioners, both before and since, understand their work to be based on detached, objective, neutral, and scientific foundations, removed from class position. It was to help the poor and restore their moral fibre that reform was needed. Modern language versions of the theory are on offer from a large number of sources active in the current political debate on this very same subject.

The later classical economists were well aware that the intellectuals of the working-class movement were offering the masses an understanding of the world around them that led to a greater confidence that ordinary people could change the world. Mainstream economists such as the Frenchman Frederic Bastiat, whose influential work, *Economic Harmonies*, is written to refute the idea that class conflict is at all relevant to what economics is about, writes that 'the socialists conjure up a society out of their imagination and then conceive of a human heart to fit this society' (ibid.: 217). To Bastiat, however, it is more than a matter of warm heart–soft head: 'What makes the great division between the two schools is the difference in methods. Socialism, like astrology and alchemy, proceeds by way of imagination; political economy, like astronomy and chemistry, proceeds by way of observation' (ibid.: 216). The 'proof' Bastiat offered for his position, his ultimate justification for his own approach, was that his faith in *laissez-faire* was divine law. Sounding very much like the Christian Coalition so politically powerful in our own day (in message if not vocabulary), Bastiat testified: '[W]e, who are believers have the right to cry: *Laissez passer!* Let God's order and justice prevail. *I believe in God*' (ibid.: 217). The emphasis is in the original and suggests a powerful weapon is being marshaled against those who today would be called by the 'L' word. Then too they were considered godless socialists. Like later writers who also upheld faith in free markets and underlined that their conclusions were based on science (whilst those of the socialists were unscientific), Bastiat in *Economic Harmonies* attributes to the socialists the view that 'We [socialists] do indeed pretend to believe in God, but in reality we believe only in ourselves, since we want nothing to do with *laissez faire*, and each and every one of us offers his social plan as infinitely superior to that of Providence' (ibid.: 217). Today there are those who write off others in a similar manner. What is striking is the continuity of outlook and division on social policy.

The validity of his approach, Bastiat claimed, rested on two expressed grounds. We can skip over his appeal to divine endorsement (I find it hard to test such a claim) and move on to the assertion that, unlike his opponents, he proceeds by way of observation. This is the claim of the positivism of A type science against the constructed categories of the B types. These categories are not found in nature. They are built up not by aggregating data but rather by applying interpretative schemes, and so not only Bastiat, but many of our contemporary mainstream economists, would claim they are political, or perhaps non-economic, categories. The claim is the important one that the social categories of political economy are illegitimate and that individuals must be the unit of analysis. We shall return to this point, which is often twinned to another procedural convention, the reduction of all economic relations to relations of exchange between these individual actors.

Bastiat's dictum, that 'Exchange *is* political economy,' declares as 'not economics' all issues of distribution of wealth and the nature of social and political institutions into which women and men are born and which the B economists claim restrict and coerce the exchanges in which they take part. As Kay Hunt writes, 'Smith's few pages devoted to a description of the "invisible hand" had, with Bastiat, become the whole of political economy' (ibid.: 218). Bastiat need not look at all closely at the nature of property relations because private property was (he said) a natural law created by God. Indeed, property does not exist because there are laws, but 'laws exist because there is property.'[15] Contemporary discussion does not typically invoke God for this purpose, but property rights are still discussed within a framework that denies consideration to the origins of structured, or class, inequalities.

Much of the contemporary discussion of market efficiency makes the assumption that it really doesn't matter who owns property, since those with the greatest desire for it to be used in a particular manner would outbid others. Thus if the air and water could become property, those who want it to be clean could outbid the potential or actual polluters. The Law and Economics school takes such thinking into the legal system, suggesting that cases involving disputes between claimants can be settled on a marketized cost/benefit basis so that outcomes are efficient. Legislation is reviewed and in some cases to be judged permissible, based on the costs that enforcement imposes on public jurisdictions and private individuals. This contemporary line of thinking, in which market values come to dominate the political and social life of the nation, has a long history.

John Stuart Mill

John Stuart Mill is both the precursor of Marshallian economics and the last of the great classical writers. He does not defend the older order as Say, Senior, and Bastiat do. Along with Marx he is critical of capitalism, but unlike him sees its reform possibilities. Mill's *Principles of Political Economy*, first published in 1848, the year of revolutionary upheaval in Europe, was the dominant text in economics for close to half a century. (It was displaced only after 1890 by Alfred Marshall's *Principles*.) The younger Mill's writing today is more influential among philosophers and political scientists than among economists. This is partly because his thinking can seem eclectic and inconsistent. He states economic laws in an A mode, only to continue with extensions and exceptions to the rule.

The division within nineteenth-century mainstream economists between what we would call today in America liberals and conservatives, came into being over a profound disagreement on how to respond to the challenge of Marxists and other radicals. The threat to the status quo from the working-class movement was very real. The group that we call modern liberals was aware that *laissez-faire* policies were not winning converts among a wide segment of the population (whose views previously had not mattered because they were disorganized). Conservative defense of the unrestrained prerogatives of private property were blatantly antidemocratic, an increasingly losing stance. Given this conjuncture, modern liberals developed a new philosophy that could endorse social justice and government intervention to address blatant inequalities. The radical critique, and the threat of a left alliance of the productive classes, had the potential to overthrow the current order. Liberals acted to save the system by reforming it. The claims of labor had to be reckoned with, but through a moderating reform so that working people would have a stake in preserving the system, and not in rebelling and attempting to overthrow it.

Mill came around to an interventionist position, even in the realm of production. He was the first prominent economist to argue that the automaticity of the labor market was not sacrosanct. The wage fund theory employed by Senior and other classical economists presumed that the wages of labor were fixed in total by the size of the money set aside (the wage fund) and available for this purpose. This amount that was fixed at any one time was used to pay wages. More workers could be paid only by reducing the amount received by each. Nearly all the classical economists accepted the wage fund doctrine. In 1869 Mill repudiated it. In that year, in a book review, he argued that wages were determined by the struggle between workers and capitalists. There was no fixed amount of funds set aside exclusively for wage payments. Capitalists could increase their profits if they had the power, and workers could win gains through organized struggle. Such a recantation[16] allowed Mill to declare that trade unions could raise wages and to favor workers' organization.

As a brilliant A mode economist, Mill started from and improved upon Ricardo, and had general equilibrium down before Walras, but he was also influenced by the French philosopher Auguste Comte to create a complete science of society.[17] Mill made numerous and important contributions to technical–mechanical economics (he understood the movement and shift relations of demand and supply at a remarkably high level, introducing the concept of the reciprocal demand for products between nations into international trade theory, thus making the theory of comparative advantage far more sophisticated in its analytics). He also broadened the scope of political economy as a study of people, institutions, and customs, and moved it beyond just the formulation of laws governing production, exchange, and distribution.

Mill saw that in a barter economy Say's Law held, but that once money is used things were quite different. 'Now the effect of the employment of money,' he wrote, 'is that it enables this one act of interchange to be divided into two separate acts or operations; one of which may be performed now, and the other a year hence, or whenever it shall be most convenient' (Mill 1848: 70). Throughout Mill's writings there are points at which he recognizes that unemployment may result from the lack of effective demand. There are also some Keynes-like ideas about the impact of speculation and the business cycle, but these are not developed.

In what is perhaps Mill's greatest attempt at a Solomon-like solution to the contradiction between economics as science and economics as moral philosophy, he makes the distinction between pure and applied economics by deeming the laws of production of wealth as 'physical truths,' whereas those of distribution are partly human institution. Government can change distribution based on social justice concerns.[18] This expresses a profound projection of optimism concerning the productive potential to meet human need.[19] When we read further, on the next page, however, Mill tells us that 'Society can subject the distribution of wealth to whatever rules it thinks best; but what practical results will flow from the operation of these rules, must be discovered.' You can make whatever rules you want, but they may have consequences you won't like. He has taken back the blank check of volunteerist utopianism he appeared to have written a page earlier. The baby belongs to its true parent, the guardian of the status quo.

Mill as a reformer understands that almost all economics is political and that pure mode A thinking is limited to a fairly narrow range of phenomena. As he writes on the first page of the Preface to all editions of his *Principles*, 'Except on matters of mere detail, there are perhaps no practical questions, even among those which approach nearest the character of purely economical questions, which admit of being decided on economical premises alone.' In rejecting the emergent definition of political economy as exchange, Mill moves attention back to production and at the same time to the essentially arbitrary way wealth is distributed. Further, Mill does not think that all action is motivated by self-interest; we do have nobility and generosity as part of our character and, he is willing to say, some pleasures are 'better' than others. Mill freely makes interpersonal utility comparisons. In response to those who say the market knows best, Mill asserts 'better to be a Socrates dissatisfied than a fool satisfied.' Mill, whilst he claims to be a utilitarian, undermines the utilitarian understanding of motivation and markets. He is interested in the real world and how it works and how it can be made to work better.

In a similar vein of introducing realistic interpretations and relevant judgments, Mill showed that it was not only cost conditions but the pattern of demand that determined the barter terms of trade. He saw the relationship between England and its colonies in the following terms:

> Our West India colonies, for example, cannot be regarded as countries, with a productive capital of their own. All the capital employed is English capital,

almost all the industry is carried on for English uses. . . . The trade with the West Indies is therefore hardly to be considered as external trade, but more resembles the traffic between town and country, and is amenable to the principle of the home trade.

Further, Mill understood that 'The superiority of one country over another in a branch of production often arises only from having begun it sooner. There may be no inherent advantage . . . but only a present superiority of acquired skill and experience' (ibid.: 922). There is an important difference between the abstract theory of trade, which holds under the pure case, and the exchange in real time between nations. As these passages from canonical writers who have been discussed earlier suggest, the B side of economic analysis has always stressed the historical specificity of international relations and the shaping of the world system as a process of political economy. Mill, whose contributions to the pure theory of international trade are acknowledged, was not content to leave matters at such an abstract level.

Today, communication and transportation innovations bring the nature of international trade ever closer to intranational exchange. As financial markets have globalized, capital flows more freely, and it has become difficult to keep out undocumented workers. The first comer advantages described by Mill, and the transportability of physical capital, replicability of structures, and adaptability of foreign technologies, suggest that there may be little advantage remaining based on 'capital endowment.' In place of inherent advantage there is, as Mill suggests, only impermanent superiority, which can be based on acquired skills and experience. When development economists rediscover such truths, they are often chastised by their more A type colleagues for coming to conclusions that violate the findings of the established theory of comparative advantage. The founding fathers of the discipline had a different position. In real-world cases, the conclusions of pure theory may not, and frequently do not, hold. There is pure theory and there are real-world applications.

More radically still, he writes that private property is simply a convention, a matter of general expediency.[20] When it is not expedient, it is unjust. Private ownership for Mill cannot hide behind 'God's will.' Mill's search was for an economics that allowed a more egalitarian distribution of income and wealth than that provided by the market. Society had to find such an economics because, as Mill wrote in 1845 reviewing a book entitled *The Claims of Labour; an Essay on the Duties of the Employers and the Employed*, 'The claims of labor have become the question of the day.'

By common agreement, John Stuart Mill is the last of the great classical economists.[21] He is also a bridge to a later tradition of liberalism in economics. Mill believed there was a basis for making judgments concerning choices and therefore rational government intervention, but like many liberals he was inconsistent, seeming to take both sides on a great number of issues. He was for democracy but favored intelligent people getting multiple votes. He defended private property but advocated worker coops and flirted with decentralized socialism. He said government should do no more than prevent citizens from harming one another, yet also that government should provide birth control devices and tax inheritance to offset the concentration of wealth. As for the origin of current property arrangements, Mill accepts much of the socialist view, even if he ultimately rejects the Marxist solution.[22]

The complexities of Mill's positions, his statement of the general law in the A tradition only to follow it with contradictory specific cases and even alternative generalizations in a B mold, were partly a matter of Mill's character, but they also reflected the time in which he lived. Mill found it no contradiction to establish his economic analysis on a philosophical and moral base. Within decades, Alfred Marshall managed to convey to his students his own deeply moral feelings about the purpose of economics, even if in his writings he is generally more guarded than Mill. At the end of Victorian certainties there is so secular a culture that Marshall's ethics are subsidiary in ways Mill's did not need to be. By our own time, the confident moral judgments Mill made as a serious social philosopher have been removed from economics. Mill is read by philosophers today, not by economists.

One of the things that strikes this reader thinking about the classical economists is how fully some of them anchored their discussion of labor markets in considerations of household reproduction, from its biological dimensions to education and training, and embeddedness in community and structured by state policy. It is true that some classical economists, like most later economists, did not consider the relative autonomy of the sphere of social reproduction, but just saw the supply of labor as regulated solely by the wage mechanism. Much of what has captured the attention of readers then and since has been these wider discussions of the relationship between the sphere of production of goods and services and reproduction of labor power.

5   Marx and the long run

[W]hether that of the young Marx or of yesterday's Moscow slogan, forces us to confront: (1) every public issue of the modern world; (2) every great problem of social studies; (3) every moral trouble encountered by men [and women] of sensibility today. Moreover, when we try to observe and to think within the Marxist point of view, we are bound to see these issues, problems and troubles as inherently connected. We are forced to adopt an over-all view of the world, and of ourselves in relation to it.

(C. Wright Mills quoted in Foster 1990: 268)

In the crises of the world market, the contradictions and antagonisms of bourgeois production are strikingly revealed. Instead of investigating the nature of the conflicting elements which erupt in the catastrophe, the apologists content themselves with denying the catastrophe itself and insisting, in the face of their regular and periodic recurrence, that if production were carried on according to the textbooks, crisis would never occur. Thus the apologetics consists in the falsification of the simplest economic relations, and particularly in clinging to the concept of unity in the face of contradiction.

(Marx 1850–60: 500)

As Keynes writes in *The General Theory*, the 'classical economists was the name invented by Marx to include Ricardo, James Mill, and their *predecessors*, that is to say the founders of the theory that culminated in the Ricardian economics' (Keynes 1936: 3, fn. 1). These classical economists were the theorists of production and class relations. The economists of exchange, Jean-Baptiste Say, Nassau Senior, and Frederic Bastiat, Marx referred to as 'the vulgar economics.' Their vulgarity consists of a threefold departure: first, from the historical sense their predecessors had of capitalism as a system that comes into being, develops, and changes; second, by banishing class from their analytic framework; and third, by narrowing economics to issues of allocation. These are the very achievements for which mainstream economists today would praise them.

B mode economists celebrate aspects of the early classical tradition that Marx carries on and enhances. Ronald Meek suggests that what Marx added 'was a proper appreciation of the fact that problems of economic theory, even in such abstruse spheres as that of value, were not only problems of logic but also problems of history' (Meek 1973: 168). Joseph Schumpeter's judgment was that 'The so-called Economic Interpretation of History, is doubtless one of the greatest individual achievements of sociology to this day' (Schumpeter 1942). (The reference to sociology by Schumpeter was meant as a compliment.) These writers are in sympathy with Marx's criticism of the mainstream economists who, whilst they appeared to generalize over time and space, offered narrow abstractions – too narrow in the double sense of including too few connections and too short a period in real historical time. To Marx the mainstream focus on states of rest, whilst ignoring process and movement, is a serious methodological weakness.

In the light of our discussion in the last chapter of the differences between Ricardo and Malthus, it is not without interest to spend a few lines discussing Marx's views of the two men – both for the light this may shed on them and, as important in the present context, for what this may say about Marx himself. In *Theories of Surplus Value* he makes the following contrast:

> It is not a base action when Ricardo puts the proletariat on the same level as machinery or beasts of burden or commodities, because (from his point of view) their being purely machinery or beasts of burden is conducive to 'production' or because they really are mere commodities in bourgeois production. This is stoic, objective, scientific. In so far as it does involve *sinning* against his science, Ricardo is always a philanthropist, just as he was in *practice* too.
>
> (Marx 1850–60: 119)

Ricardo is contrasted to that 'shameless synchophant' Malthus, who also reduces the worker to a beast of burden for the sake of production. When these same objective demands of production call for curtailment of the landlord's rent or the Established Church's tithes, however, Malthus does not sacrifice these particular interests, but instead does all he can to sacrifice the demands of production to the particular interests of sections of the ruling classes. This is why Marx is so venomous in his criticism of Malthus: it is 'his *scientific* baseness, his sin against science, quite apart from his shameless and mechanical plagiarism' (Schumpeter 1942: 120). (Marx had read everything relevant to any topic in which he had an interest, and could be quite voluble as to who may have lifted what from whom).

There are two relevant points for us. First, for the purpose of scientific economics, Marx accepted that human labor was a factor of production (like land or capital). It was a different kind of factor of production – the human being could not be separated from the worker when engaged in the work relation, which involved exploitation and which was the origin of all surplus value. The second point is that Marx applauds Ricardo for his 'let the chips fall where they may' stance. If to foster historically progressive accumulation, capital gets devalued, or if Church tithes are swept aside – or workers treated like animals – this is part of the path of capitalism's progress. Malthus' sin is his double standard. The worker's interest is always sacrificed but never the landlord's or the Church's. He is a hypocrite, but his greater sin is not political bias but against science. In his praise of Ricardo's honesty, Marx writes:

> If the development of the productive power of labour halves the value of the *existing* fixed capital, what does it matter, says Ricardo. The productivity of human labour has doubled. Thus here is *scientific honesty*. Ricardo's conception is, on the whole, in the interests of the industrial bourgeoisie, only *because*, and *in so far as*, their interests coincide with that of production or the productive development of human labour. Where the bourgeoisie comes into conflict with this, he is just as *ruthless* toward it as he is at other times towards the proletariat and the aristocracy.

> (Marx 1850–60: 118)

The passage also conveys Marx's modernist core. The importance of material progress and development of the forces of production are always historically progressive. The case he makes for radical transformation, which we will come to subsequently, is that at a certain point in the development of capitalism, the social relations of production (capitalist class relations) come into conflict with the continued development of the forces of production, and that under these conditions the givens of the system, which have been historically progressive, no longer are so and the era of social revolution is at hand.

Class apologists such as Malthus were dishonest. Marx claimed that his own sympathies with the working class were, on the contrary, not in conflict with the scientific method. This is because in his reading of history's trajectory it is only the working class that holds the potential to form the universal class whose interests represent those of the entire human race (including capitalists, if we take seriously his view that oppressing others is alienating to the self). Capitalism, which he saw as a historically progressive, indeed revolutionary, mode of production, created both the conditions for human emancipation and self-actualization and also the social relations that fetter the future development of these forces to meet human need. Those in the A mode tradition have a very different understanding of what it means to be scientific, and judge Marx through the lens of their science and not his. One need not accept Marx's method to understand it.

The reputation of historically important intellectual figures can undergo dramatic revision over time. Economists and philosophers come into fashion and fall out of favor. This is true of no one else as much as of Karl Marx, though in the case of Marx, his standing has been derivative. Where radical movements claiming his mantle have been serious factors in contemporary history, he is a force to be reckoned with; but, as M.C. Howard has noted, mainstream economists have always constituted 'a thin market' for Marxist analysis. The bulk of Marxism was 'indigestible' (Howard 1995: 175) to mainstream thinking, and still is. Part of the difficulty is the politics and Marx's insistence that class struggle is the motor force of history and communism its ultimate end. Perhaps as important, however, is that Marx's methodological approach is so very different and requires an openness to dialectics, a mode of thought quite foreign, indeed antithetical, to the logic of mainstream economics and most other approaches in the social sciences. It is useful, therefore, to examine Marx's method in the context of explicating his economics. Indeed, one can hardly do the latter without undertaking the former. A further reason to look at what Marx said is that much of what is attributed to him, for example the labor theory of value (which he in fact took pretty much in whole cloth from Ricardo) and the distinction between use value and exchange value (which is found in Aristotle), are in fact part of an older tradition which he adopted and extended more than transformed.

Capital

To define properly and fully any one term Marx uses is to grasp all the other elements of the system of which that term is a part. His intellectual system is an integrated whole. It is this dialectical aspect of Marx's thinking that is both central and so difficult to understand and accept, especially for those raised in the economics-as-science tradition. 'Of course everything effects everything,' such a person might say. 'But you can't get anywhere unless you hold some things constant while you study specific relations in isolation.' 'Can't do,' says Marx. 'At least not the way you gentlemen do.' To Marx, each element of his system must be seen in relation to, indeed as inclusive of, every other. This is both absolutely essential and at the same time the hardest thing for those trained as positivists. The best way to see the difference is to take one of his concepts and see how it attaches. Marx does this by starting *Capital* with such a discussion of the commodity as a way of talking about the nature of capital. Consider one of the many 'definitions' Marx offers:

> [Capital] is not a thing but rather a definite social production relation, belonging to a definite historical formation of society, which is manifested in a thing and lends this thing a specific social character. Capital is not the sum of the material and produced means of production. Capital is rather the means of production transformed into capital, which in themselves are no more capital than gold or silver in itself is money. It is the means of production monopolized by a certain sector of society, confronting living labor-power as products and working conditions rendered independent of this very labor-power, which are personified through this antithesis in capital. It is not merely the products of laborers turned into independent powers, products as rulers and buyers of their producers, but rather also the social forces of their labor and socialized form of this labor, which confront the laborers as properties of their products.
> (Marx 1867: 194–5)

The reason why mainstream economists can concentrate their analysis on exchange value, the 'appearance' rather than the deeper reality of production, is that they take the existence of the commodity as a natural and hence non-problematic fact. But, said Marx, commodity production is not the only mode of production and even if it were the only mode of production we knew about, the question still arises prior to exchange of '*why* the product of labour takes the form of the commodity, why "human labour" appears as a value of "things."' For many readers this is about where their eyes begin to glaze over in a Hegel-induced stupor that overcomes their effort to 'get Marx.' Of course, others just nod along, 'yes, yes.' Which way you go is in part a matter of your willingness to think in terms of the connectedness of all aspects of his system of thought. Divisions are simply ways of presenting connections of totality.[1]

Consider the famous distinction between constant capital and variable capital. The former is, for Marx, the product of the latter. Capital is subsumed in this sense within the understanding of labor as the human power that creates value, that is, you can't understand capital separately from understanding labor (and vice versa). 'Capital' is the name of Marx's great work because it is the core for understanding the system. To Marx, capital is not a thing or group of things – plant and equipment or money capital – as it is for mainstream economists, although it is these also. Capital is a social relation of domination as well as the instruments of production, which are, after all, made by men and women under specific social conditions.

Workers are people who don't own capital and therefore have to sell their labor power to capitalists, who have a class monopoly on the ownership of, yes, capital. This view of things means that whilst the exchange of labor for wages is 'free,' it is also coerced. The worker may not have to work for any particular capitalist, but if (s)he doesn't work for someone there is no rent money. The social harmony of the mainstream theory of exchange omitting this misrepresents the essence, for Marx, of the system. 'Capital' includes an understanding of all this and more, much more.

Capital at a point in time is linked backward to primitive accumulation (to piracy, looting, conquest, and slavery), through expanded reproduction (the drive to innovate forced upon all competitors on pain of extinction as capitalists), to the creation of a single world market (the process he could foresee at a time when the working class itself was only beginning to emerge on the world stage). For Marx, 'Capital itself is the moving contradiction because forces of production can undermine settled social relations.' A full understanding for Marx includes a grasp of not only all that had produced the present moment and its near projections but also its eventual transition to socialism, which he saw, as we all know, as inevitable. Now, whether looking at the acorn anyone can really 'see' the oak tree if there is not already an oak tree in existence (and if there has never been an oak tree) is an important question. Marx had a supreme confidence that his science allowed him to make this prediction of socialism's inevitability.

Marx's method of investigation, which has come to be known as historical materialism, is not then the brittle thing some of his critics both within the mainstream and among post-Marxist critical theorists maintain. When Marx writes in gendered language of man making himself, he is concerned with the expression of identities by individuals whose activities are a definite form of expressing their lives, and it is in such a context that his comments on the nature of individuals depending on the material conditions determining their production may be seen (for example in Marx and Engels 1846: 7).

Whilst neoclassical economists expected that people would make whatever adaptation was necessary to accommodate the system's survival, Marx saw this contradiction as 'the material condition to blow this foundation sky high.' As a revolutionary, Marx tended to a historic optimism that was not borne out. In the *Communist Manifesto*, written on the very eve of the revolutions of 1848, Marx and Engels suggested that the Big R's time had come, that proletarian revolution had arrived and the death knell of capitalism was at hand.

Social knowledge and the long run

A very different trajectory is offered in his notebooks of 1857–8, known as the *Grundrisse*, which were only effectively published in the German original in 1953 and in English two decades after that. In the *Grundrisse*, Marx suggests that capitalism was nowhere near over, and that until the forces of production had advanced much further, capitalism would be with us. How much more advanced? Until it exhausted its capacities to exploit the enormous possibilities inherent in technology, which Marx envisioned as including automation (of a sort a century and a half later we are glimpsing). Despite its growing contradictions and crises, new technological breakthroughs would postpone the falling rate of profit until labor time itself had ceased to be the measure of value.

Moreover, the full analysis would not be of English capitalism but of the global system. Marx thought he could work all of this out in a step-by-step exposition in a reasonable length of time. In 1851 he wrote to a friend, 'I am so far advanced that by five weeks I will be through the whole economic shit.' In fact, he finished only the first volume of *Capital*, leaving others to work from his notes to bring out Volumes II and III and *Theories of Surplus Value*, Parts I and II of which form a sort of appendix to the work. Even these are a small part of the outline he had prepared for his project in political economy. On April 2, 1858, Marx wrote to Engels of his plan for a study of political economy: 'The whole shit is divided into six books: I. Capital; II Landed Property; III Wage Labor; IV State; V International Trade; VI World Market.' Marx left little guidance as to what would have composed the last three critical books.[2]

'Viewing the world devoid of the clear cut classificational boundaries that distinguish the common sense notion, Marx could not keep a definition of one factor from spilling over into everything else. For him,' as Bertell Ollman writes, 'any isolated definition is necessarily one-sided and probably misleading' (Ollman 1976: 25). The definition of categories also change over time as social reality changes. Marx himself said that 'Economic categories are only the theoretical expressions, the abstractions of the social relations of production. Thus these ideas, these categories, are as little eternal as the relations they express. They are historically given' (Marx 1846–7: 92–3).[3] When we enter a new historical period, those who would follow Marx need to reformulate economic categories to coincide with specific conditions under which the phenomena represented by the categories occur (see Lange 1963: 109). These categories would then need to be seen in their connectedness.

The seeming concrete categories through which mainstream economists present data and analyze the world are in fact more complicated. To deal with reality inclusive of a diversity of elements, they need to be deconstructed, to use the currently fashionable term. Marx's own categories, whilst they may seem vague in their elastic usage, are in his view more precise because they are abstractions based on the concrete historical elements and social relations of which they arc composed.[4] Ironically (or so it would seem at least to most non-Marxists), his claim is that his own abstract categories allow for a correct concrete use of terms.

Things are made more complex still because Marx distinguishes five levels of analysis (and he is not always clear on which he is operating in any particular analytical exercise). The first is the general abstract level 'which is more or less applicable to all forms of society.' The second level is of the categories 'which go to make up the inner organization of bourgeois society (landed property, circulation and credit, the three great classes and so on).' That is as far as he got for the most part. The design was also to consider 'the state in relation to itself' (where taxes and public finance would be analyzed), then international exchange (exports and imports, exchange rates), and finally 'the world market and crises' (which presumably would treat both globalization of the system and crisis theory not at the level of the nation-state as at level two but the comprehensive and emergent form at the level of the world system.

The last three categories are both more historically specific and attain fuller development with capitalism's maturity. He gives some indications of how he would treat the last three levels, each of which he considered worthy of a separate book. For example, with regard to the last level, he saw both crisis on a world scale and transformation occurring on that same broad stage. Soviet Marxism has obscured the scope of his vision (in this as in many other respects), and 'orthodox' Marxists who stick to the limited models in *Capital* preclude pursuing aspects of Marx's thinking most relevant to the third millennium AD. A great deal of the shape of capitalism's trajectory in our time can be gleaned from Marx.

'The industrial capitalist,' Marx wrote, 'always has the world-market before him, compares, and must constantly compare, his own cost-price with the market-prices at home, and throughout the world.' He saw the 'immanent necessity' for the capitalist mode of production 'to produce on an ever-enlarged scale.' It is the nature of the capitalist mode of production that it 'tends to extend the world-market continually' (Marx 1894: 333). It is remarkable that writing when he did he was ready to take on an analysis of the 'world market crisis' which as he said is 'the most complicated phenomenon of capitalist production' (Marx 1850–60: 501). He made clear the scope of the task he set for himself at this level of analysis:

> The world trade crisis must be regarded as the real concentration and forcible adjustment of all the contradictions of bourgeois economy. The individual factors which are condensed in these crises must therefore emerge and must be described in each sphere of the bourgeois economy and the further we advance in our examination of the latter, the more aspects of this conflict must be traced on the one hand, and on the other hand it must be shown that its more abstract forms are recurring and are contained in the more concrete forms.
>
> (ibid.)

Marx had a great deal to say about the emergence of the world market. He noted, for example, that if wages and prices are low in one country whilst interest on capital is high (he thought this would be the case in the underdeveloped parts of the world 'because the capitalist mode of production has not been developed generally'), whereas in another country wages and prices of land are high, whilst interest on capital is low, as it would later be called the core nations, 'then the capitalist employs more labour and land in the one country, and in the other relatively more capital' (Marx 1894: 852).

'Time's carcass'

The distinguished editors of *The New Palgrave* fault Marxist economics for not having a theory of relative prices and thus for not being able to solve the day-to-day problems that occur within a capitalist economy (Eatwell *et al.* 1990: xi). It is *not* that supply and demand analysis is irrelevant for Marx, but rather that price determination is a small part of what is going on. Moreover, 'demand' and 'supply' are dependent variables and need to be determined in a much different way than that of the mainstream analysis.[5]

Central to Marx's model is the distinction between labor and labor power. Surplus value is created by workers producing more than they receive. Compensation is determined by both the reproduction cost of labor power (the capacity to work) and the outcome of the historical struggle between capital and labor over income shares. The wage structure among workers and the level of wages as a whole does reflect to some extent differential costs of reproducing labor power at varying levels of skill. How much work an individual employee does – the contribution of labor to the production process – is negotiable and contested. Exploitation can be increased by prolonging the working day or intensifying work. It is not that Marx does not understand that technological change increases output;[6] that, after all, is the heart of the drive of the capitalist system in which all capitalists, on pain of being driven out of business and ceasing to be capitalists, must innovate or be left in the dust. Rather, his convention is to use the notion of socially necessary labor time. The new innovation raises the normal output per worker per unit of time.

Of course, when Marx develops his own reproduction schemas, very A mode in their conception, in which output is divided between the production of capital goods (his Department I) and consumer goods (Department II) in a two-sector growth model, he accepts fixed coefficients representing socially necessary labor time in production (not unlike what the neoclassicals do), but these proportional calculations are within the larger context as just developed. The schemas have been used by Marxists such as Otto Bauer and Henryk Grossman to develop mathematical models of the impact of changes in the organic composition of capital on the profit rate and to explicate the crisis tendencies Marx sees in the capitalist system. This framework is capable of sustaining very sophisticated treatment of contemporary growth theory. Indeed, among some economists, there is the inclination to use Marx's reproduction schemas to build a competitive comparative statics to contest with mainstream growth models, to start from the stability conditions as Marx did, but which he showed every indication of moving beyond in his formal modeling. In any case, this was only a small part of his more holistic analytical approach. A constant socially necessary labor time, which sets the standard in his comparative static model, for example, is put aside as changes in technology, the development of new products and processes become the driving force of capitalist development.

The labor process itself, Marx believed, is not a technical relation of fixed coefficients as it is in the neoclassical model (which will be considered in the next chapter). The actual surplus value generated in production is determined by the outcome of class struggle in the workplace, over not only compensation, but also the definition of job requirements, work norms, and rules. These are always a point of contention. There is no mathematical labor/capital output ratio that is invariant across job sites and institutional settings. Accumulation or economic growth is thus always the continuous extension and modification of class relations. The institutions of society always reflect class relations as well.[7]

The core of the economist's analysis, supply and demand, is premised on what Marx calls the fetishism of commodities. It is as if, as Colletti writes,

> the *real subject* indeed were not the man but labour-power itself, nothing being left to the man but to serve as a mere function or vehicle for the manifestation of the latter. The person does not appear. The product of labor does not bear the mark of the worker but is a thing.
>
> (Colletti 1977: 464)

As today's mainstream economists say, people as productive factors are human capital, analytically on a par with physical capital in the production function. Such an abstraction reduces men to things, from a Marx point of view. They are measured by the output they create per unit of work time, and, as Marx wrote, the pendulum of the clock becomes the god to those who control labor: 'Time is everything, man is nothing; he is at the most time's carcass.'[8] In place of consumer sovereignty, Marx believes individual desires are themselves the product of a particular social process and the individual's place within that process.

One of the impacts of the division of labor within the humanities and the social sciences has been for economists to background Marx's theory of alienation. Yet alienation is a central concept for Marx. The estrangement of the worker who does not experience himself or herself as an active agent is to experience oneself passively. Labor is alienated because the work has ceased to be part of the worker's nature. It does not fulfill the worker but denies their being. It creates a feeling of misery and does not allow the free development of the worker's mental and physical energies. It is because alienated work destroys individuality that Marx condemns capitalist social relations. The worker becomes object to the capitalist process, a part of the machinery of accumulation.[9]

Such views are not uncommon within the mainline tradition. Alfred Marshall, for example, believed 'Work, in its best sense, the healthy and energetic exercise of faculties, is the aim of life, is life itself' (Marshall 1873: 115). In his youth, Marshall had thought that the progress of society would eventually obliterate class distinctions, and in phrases reminiscent of Marx he wrote that 'no one is to do in the day so much manual work as will leave him little time or little aptitude for intelligent and artistic enjoyment in the evening.' For Marshall, as for Marx and Smith, 'a rise in the standard of life implies an increase in intelligence and energy and self-respect' (Coats 1990: 163). The simplifications of the thought of the mainline economists have meant that class is a subject reserved for Marx, and yet Marx, like the other figures we discuss, is part of a wider community of shared and overlapping concerns on a range of issues.

Capitalism in the very long run

Marx wrote so much and so diversely that there is room for many competing versions of Marxism and Marxist economics. The Marxist 'model' one finds in the textbooks of both friend and foe alike represents only the starting point of the vision he had conceived. Taking to heart Harry Magdoff's injunction that 'The aim of Marxists should not be to rehash how to read *Capital* but to concentrate on how to read capitalism' (Hillard and Misukiewicz 1988: 91), three related aspects of Marx's thinking claim our attention here. The first is the centrality of social knowledge as the dominant force of production in advanced capitalism. The second is his effort to anticipate the long-run trajectory of the system, which is one in which 'the tendency to create the world market is directly given in the concept of capital itself' (Marx 1894: 470). As he wrote in *Capital*, 'The specific task of bourgeois society is the establishment of the world market' (Marx 1867: 703). The third strand of Marx's work that merits our close attention is his theories of economic crises (note the double plural).

It is easy amidst Marx's calls for revolution and condemnations of the capitalist system 'drinking blood from the skulls of its victims,' the vivid descriptions culled from the factory inspectors' reports and so on, to forget that Marx celebrated capitalism's great achievements.[10] Capitalism's ceaseless striving for self-expansion is its historical mission. It 'strives toward the universal development of the forces of production' (Marx 1894: 540) by overcoming barriers that many of his followers assumed would bring down the system. Instead, capitalism has expanded to encompass more and more of the world, commodifying social relations and bringing 'the unconditional development of the social productivity of labor' (ibid.: 245). Capital strives to tear down every spatial barrier, to 'conquer the whole earth for its markets . . . to annihilate space with time, i.e. to reduce to a minimum the time spent in motion from one place to another' (Marx 1857: 539). 'Every limit appears as a barrier to be overcome' (ibid.: 408), and as it does it produces new needs and creates new use values. Capital drives beyond

> all traditional, confined, complacent, encrusted satisfactions of personal needs, and reproductions of old ways of life. It is destructive towards all of this and constantly revolutionizes it, tearing down all the barriers which hem in the development of the productive forces.
>
> (ibid.: 649–50)

Such is the transformative power of capital.

Marx saw the tension between capitalism's creativity: its revolutionary capacities as a mode of production as well as its destructive impacts on working-class humanity. This might go uncommented upon except for the fact that almost all Marxists of the contemporary period are unwilling to grant the historically progressive achievements of capitalism today. This is no small part of their inability to devise effective anti-capitalist strategies for the time in which they live. It is understanding the dialectics of capitalism's historical processes that is Marx's great achievement.

In the *Grundrisse*, but nowhere else to my knowledge, Marx extends an argument that has an almost contemporary ring. He writes that

> The principle of developed capital is precisely to make specific skills superfluous, and to make manual work, direct physical labor, generally superfluous both as skill and as muscular exertion; to transfer skill, rather, into dead forces of nature. The accumulation of knowledge and of skill, of the general productive forces of the social brain, is thus absorbed into capital, as opposed to labor, and hence appears as an attribute of capital.
>
> (ibid.: 693)

In our own time, this tendency has taken on a central importance. The products of generations of working people whose labor has built up the means of production created a social surplus which provides resources for the research and development that now become the major source of new productivity. The distinction between spending on R & D, which is counted as operating expense, and spending on a different category called investment, which is expenditure on new plant and equipment, is surely outmoded. The productive capacity of an organization is, as Marx said, not in direct physical labor but (in an information age surely) in 'the accumulation of knowledge and of skill, of the general productive forces of the social brain.'

Participants in discussions of the labor theory of value, who ponderously continue discussing what Marx 'really meant,' and whether he was correct to measure value in terms of labor time, would do well to think about why he, and other classical economists, chose a labor standard in their era, but also why value becomes so much more complicated a matter in our own time. It seems to me remarkable that Marx, writing when he did, could suggest the following:

> to the degree that large industry develops, the creation of real wealth comes to depend less on labour time and on the amount of labour employed than on the power of the agencies set in motion during labour time, whose 'powerful effectiveness' is itself in turn out of all proportion to the direct labour time spent on their production, but depends rather on the general state of science and on the progress of technology, or the application of the science to production.
>
> (ibid.: 704–5)

Two important implications of such a development seem evident. First, the extent to which this general productive force has been 'absorbed into capital, as opposed to labor, and hence appears as an attribute of capital,' leads not only to the devaluing of the traditional working class but also to those elements of the new working class, the knowledge workers and technicians, being identified with and identifying as part of capital, at least until, and to the extent to which, their work becomes routinized, rationalized, and proletarianized. In the interim, a division opens between capital identified labor (closely tied to the new social forces of production) and the older manual labor force, now devalued. The political consequences of this development are as important as the narrowly economic. Second, 'the general productive forces of the social brain' can only to a limited extent be appropriated as proprietary knowledge. The education, training, and organizational capacities of a social formation are also a crucial complex of productive capacity that represent what may be called 'a social externality.'[11] The private firm can be assisted or held back in global competition by the maturity of the social brain within the economic formation. The speed with which technological change takes place constantly devalues existing products and production techniques, as the definition of socially necessary labor time undergoes continuous transformation. The anarchy of production, which is the nature of capitalism, means than overinvestment can lead to system imbalance and crisis.

The few and tantalizing remarks Marx made foreseeing automation, and knowledge-based production more generally, like his comments on what form communism would take in a post-capitalist world, are only suggestive. In the 'Continuation of the Chapter on Capital,' Notebook VII of the *Grundrisse*, Marx writes that to the degree large industry develops

> the creation of real wealth comes to depend less on labor time and on the amount of labor employed than on the power of the agencies set in motion during labor time, whose 'powerful effectiveness' is itself in turn out of all proportion to the direct labor time spent on their production, but depends rather on the general state of science and the progress of technology, or the application of this science to production.
>
> (ibid.: 706)

The labor theory of value does not hold. Labor time no longer is the measure of value. It is at this stage that 'labor comes to relate more as watchman and regulator to the production process' and there is at last the prospect of 'the artistic, scientific, etc., development of the individuals in the time set free, and with the means created, for all of them.' Marx envisions the liberatory potential of human creativity. He expected that these truly revolutionary developments in technology would not be able to attain fruition under capitalism. Because the contradiction between the stage of development reached by the forces of production and the social relations of production under capitalism cannot allow their full development, working people (the term has new meaning as conditions are now very different and includes knowledge workers among others as dramatic class recomposition has occurred) will become revolutionaries.[12]

Such an analysis suggests that the crises that Marx expected to prompt the overthrow of capitalism come at a much higher stage of its development than he and Engels, optimistically (and incorrectly) in moments of revolutionary upsurge, would declare. But if we take the analysis of the *Grundrisse* as the relevant one, they have not been proven wrong.[13] The potential for human emancipation in which the full development of each is the need of all, may be present, but it does not spring into being on its own. The logic of the competitive system reinforces capitalist social relations despite the promise the greater power of science and social knowledge bring. Issues of the impact of knowledge- and information-based production on the trajectory of the system's development and on the consciousness of differently situated class fractions and geographically rooted communities of identity would need to be explored in any contemporary effort to do a Marx-type analysis.

How the contradiction of the greater productive potential of knowledge workers and the irrelevance of displaced workers and the growing surplus population on a world scale for whom there is little or no role in the knowledge economy is played out is the central question of our time, connected to the core issue of system stability and the character of the global political economy in the twenty-first century. Marx had insights helpful in these areas as well.

Crisis theory

The first major critique of Say's Law was not by Keynes but Marx, who asked: why would one buy immediately just because of having just sold a commodity? Money is both a medium of exchange and a store of value. Expectation of lower prices, or insecurity concerning future employment, may decrease spending by consumers. The lack of expectation of profit realization will retard investment in a dynamic capitalist economy subject to the anarchy of production (the lack of the perfect information presumed in the competitive model). Overproduction and crises are clearly not only a possibility but a regular feature of a system where money can be withdrawn from circulation. The separation of sale and purchase, a circumstance denied in the theories of Ricardo and Say, are a central reality of capitalism to Marx. The particular overproduction or undersupply of a single commodity, recognized as a temporary phenomenon by other economists, was seen as a potential trigger to crisis by Marx. The failure of planned savings to equal planned investment, which Keynes placed at the center of his theory, was anticipated by Marx who saw disproportionalities endemic to capitalism.

Marx struck a powerful blow at Say's Law when he constructed an analysis of capitalist production on the idea that its purpose is not the possession of other goods, but rather 'the appropriation of values, money, of abstract wealth.' Keynes, of course, was later to build a model in which the idea of ending up with more money than you start with is also at the heart of an accumulation process that can be interrupted with dire consequences. A real economy is in Keynes' phrase an 'entrepreneurial economy;' the one presumed by Say's Law is not. It is rather one that has the properties of a simpler barter or cooperative economy. The law does not hold in a capitalist economy once money is introduced, as John Stuart Mill noted (as we saw in the last chapter). It was such an understanding of the role of money that is found in Marx.

Marx's distinction between financial circulation and industrial circulation, and Keynes' distinction between the speculative and transaction demands for money, are essentially similar. The rate of profit emerges from industrial circulation; the rate of interest emerges in financial circulation. Both Marx and Keynes believed the rate of interest is the independent variable determining the normal rate of profit in long-period equilibrium, as opposed to the mainstream view going back to Adam Smith and Ricardo that the rate of interest is determined by the rate of profit (see Rogers 1989: ch. 7).

Credit and speculation play an important role in Marx's theorizings concerning crises. In expansion, capitalists spend more than they have, going into debt to expand production to meet expected demand. The banks lend them money. Marx sees the money supply as elastic and essentially endogenous, but as lending increases, interest rates rise faster than profits. The demand for money stays high because for some time speculation feeds on itself. As the real cycle turns down, as hopes are disappointed and costs of production rise, it becomes harder to pass them on in higher prices. Interest burden increases faster than profits. When speculators start to fear the future, prices fall. A realization crisis leaves producers and speculators with debts they cannot repay and holding collateral that is devalued. Bankruptcies lead to a chain reaction of failures.

Marx was quite expansive on the issues involved, but as we try and sort out the strands of his thinking in this area, it is well to bear in mind Schumpeter's view that Marx 'had no simple theory of business cycles. And none can be made to follow from his "laws" of the capitalist process' (Schumpeter 1965: 49). Marx nowhere presents a single coherent crisis theory. This should not be surprising, for Marx's science is not a deterministic one but a dialectical approach, with strong stress on the crucial nature of historically specific contingent factors.

At the same time, Marx did present a number of theories of crisis. It is therefore possible to argue that he believed in an underconsumptionist dynamic, a falling rate of profit explanation, that he held a disproportionality view of crisis, and that he maintained a profit squeeze analysis. He did hold to all of these and yet it would be wrong to say that any one of them was his theory of crisis, or that all of them can be summed to represent a total view of the business cycle. Each represents an important tendency immanent in capitalism. When one considers Marx's treatment of any particular economic crisis, causal explanations range from a lack of perfect information, which can lead to major bankruptcies (as in the ill-favored case of Gurney and Chapman, a firm that achieves a certain immortality thanks to Marx's attention to it in Volume III of *Capital*), to sectoral imbalance between investment and consumption which anticipates modern macroeconomic models.

When Marx and Engels talk of the crisis of 1850, they declare in the pages of the *Neue Reinische Zeitung* that the discovery of gold in California is 'a fact of even more importance than the February [1848] revolution.' They emphasize the importance of British investment in railways and the speculative fever of the prosperous years of 1843–5, mentioning merely the crisis of 1847 being not only a crisis of overproduction but also noting the unique circumstances of the cycle (the potato famine in Ireland and crop failures elsewhere in 1845 and 1846). From a reading of the numerous historically grounded discussions of this kind, it would seem that Marx and Engels were not the sort to tie up *the* causes of business cycles in a neat, one-size-fits-all package.[14]

In his more seemingly deterministic formulations, such as the falling rate of profit, Marx did not box himself in the inevitability department (remember tendency and 'tendency'). A falling rate of profit is not only a crisis tendency, a barrier to system reproduction, but can be a stimulus to innovation and, in that way, the source of further growth. ('Improvement, inventions, greater economy of means of production, etc., are introduced . . . when profits fall below its normal rate' [Marx 1850–60: 26; see Lebowitz 1976].) It was also the case that Marx explored quite extensively the sectoral composition of the economy of his time. He discussed cases of overproduction in cotton, linen, silk, and woolen fabrics, noting that 'it can be understood how overproduction in these few, but leading articles, calls forth a more or less general (relative) over-production on the whole market' (Marx 1850–60: 523). The equalization process between supply and demand in different industries may require a crisis and 'the crisis itself may be a form of equalization' (ibid.: 521). Energy, auto production, and computers play such a role today, so that an investigation of disproportionality, regional growth paths, and uneven development as the expansion trajectory of capitalism have not lost their usefulness to those interested in the growth and instabilities of capitalism in our own time. A strong case can be made that financial bubbles, excess liquidity, and speculative excesses are surely more recognizable phenomena within a Marx purview than the 'real' business cycles, 'rational' expectations, and 'efficient' capital market theorizings of contemporary economists.

Whilst Marx was a pioneer and important contributor to business cycle theory, he did not, as we have noted, try to build deterministic crisis models.[15] Some Marxists have endeavored to do so and have produced mono-causal models at the level of abstract capitalism. Yet as Paul Sweezy notes 'the crisis as a complex concrete phenomenon could not be fully analyzed on the levels of abstraction to which *Capital* is confined' (Sweezy 1956: 133–4). Since everything depends on everything, isolating one moment of the process is arbitrary, and what is more, crises are historically specific events that occur under specific conditions which must be studied in their concrete manifestations.

Thoughts about Marx's future

In any period in which mainstream economics sees its subject as the logic of choice and limits its core to allocation under given constraints, so that market coordination becomes the central focus of theory, Marx's project, the description of the historic processes of class domination and capital accumulation based on the alienation and exploitation of labor, is hardly likely to be part of its program. A Whig history of thought of such an economics is likely to see Marx as 'a minor post-Ricardian,' as Paul Samuelson said in the late 1950s, shortly before an upsurge in interest in Marx as part of the radicalization of a 1960s generation led him to include a respectful

chapter on Marx and radical leftist political economy in his textbook. In the 1990s, Marx is back to minor post-Ricardian status. As Anthony Brewer writes, he should not be accorded a significant position in the history of thought at all because he has 'little to offer, so mainstream neglect can be seen as a natural result of the normal winnowing process' (Brewer 1995: 113).[16] In relation to confidence in the system's stability, Marx can perhaps best be seen as a counter-cyclical indicator. Yet even in a period of capitalist hegemony, many of the issues of institutional embeddedness, property rights, principal–agent problems, path dependent equilibria, and contested exchange, many issues raised in Marx's thinking become digestible even if the uses to which he employed them remain unpalatable.

It is easy to see why Marx has excited and infuriated so many over the last century and three-quarters. His method of thought, always involving a grasp of the totality and the dialectical relationship of the parts, is not easy to grasp. Following his argument can be frustrating for those of conventional training who look for linear logic. Then too the scope of his project is dazzling. There is little about which he did not write. There are many areas of economic theory where he was there first, and often at a very sophisticated level, understanding developments that would not be visible to other economists for many years to come. (It is perhaps enough to remember, as George Lichtheim reminds us, that 'the German proletariat so confidently invoked by Marx scarcely existed' in 1848 when he and Engels wrote the Manifesto.)

It is an open question whether with the demise of the communist system Marx's writings will come to be read with fresh eyes. Much of what he had to say about capitalist development is of contemporary interest. Whether this is enough to overcome the dead hand of Soviet Marxism, and whether Marx's revolutionary message of the cost humanity pays for accepting class oppression and exploitation, and his vision of an alternative form of economic organization is simply utopian, have little to do with their intrinsic 'correctness,' if such a thing can be judged, but are a matter of how correct he proves to be in terms of the trajectory of capitalist development and the consciousness that emerges among a reconstituted working class in a knowledge-driven economy.

The reason Karl Marx, Adam Smith, and John Maynard Keynes make up the most popular top triumvirate in so many treatments of the history of economic thought is that they combine a breadth of vision, and each took up the necessary task, as Keynes wrote, of being 'unorthodox, troublesome, dangerous, disobedient to them that begat us,' and none more so than Karl Marx.

In what must be one of the most abrupt turns possible in any consideration of economic thought, the next chapter takes up the high water mark of the A type economic thinking, the neoclassical (counter)revolution. It comes in the wake of decades of decline in Ricardian economics and the crisis of classical economics which Mill's 'refutation' discussed in the last chapter did much to accentuate. The growth of workers' movements that took Marx's teachings to heart and the development of radical Ricardian thought encouraged many to look for an alternative to class analysis. The maturation of capitalism encouraged this trend, as allocation within a more or less fixed institutional setting came to hold greater interest for economic thinkers.

6   The neoclassical (counter) revolution

The change that has been made in the point of view of Economics by the present generation is due to the discovery that man himself is in a great measure a creature of circumstances and changes with them. The chief fault in English economists at the beginning of the century was not that they ignored history and statistics, but that they regarded man as so to speak a constant quantity, and gave themselves little trouble to study his variations. They therefore attributed to the forces of supply and demand a much more mechanical and regular action than they actually have. Their most vital fault was that they did not see how liable to change are the habits and institutions of industry.

(Alfred Marshall, Inaugural Lecture 1885)

[Suppose] it is possible for an egg to stay standing on its tip until it is disturbed. We should not attach great practical significance to this equilibrium of the egg until we are told some causal story of how it comes to be in that state. In exactly the same way, the proposition that, in certain circumstances, there is a set of prices which ensures equality between demand and supply in all markets tells us nothing of whether these prices will indeed be established by a market economy.

(Hahn 1984: 124)

Much of neoclassical economics was not new in 1870 when it is said to have appeared.[1] The concentration on allocation of resources – on exchange – that we find in neoclassical economics is strong in the *The Wealth of Nations*, but it is found there in a context in which historical, institutional, comparative dimensions dominate. Further, with Adam Smith, ethical sympathies are not overruled by efficiency arguments. Neoclassical reductionism takes the allocation decision under given conditions so as to allow for deterministic outcomes. It thus excludes much of the classical tradition which involves historically contingent outcomes and analysis. The narrowing of what it considered economics to be was of decisive importance for the direction economics has taken ever since and in (if you will excuse the expression) marginalizing the B mode culture.

For all the diversity among classical writers, the economic problem was growth (or accumulation). After 1870, economics came to be the study of allocating scarce resources among various and competing ends. The resources were taken as given, as were the ends to which they could be put. As Stanley Jevons wrote, the problem of economics is: 'Given a certain population, with various needs and powers of production, in possession of certain lands and other sources of material required, the mode of employing their labour which will maximize the utility of the produce' (Blaug 1985: 295).

This is the definition, or something quite close to it, that most economics students are taught today. It is quintessentially the A mode approach, wherein economic laws are considered to operate at all times and in all places. The 'needs and powers' of production become the subject of economics, reducing what might be a social science to maximizing and minimizing behavior within givens. The richer subject matter of earlier political economy discourse is deemed exogenous. Real historical events recede. The specifics of outcomes are less of interest than the regularities. In this lies the science of economics. The social world disappears. The marginalist revolution's central feature is captured in Stanley Jevons' assertion that his theory presumes to investigate the conditions of a mind, and bases upon this investigation the whole of economics.

To Leon Walras, 'The theory of exchange based on the proportionality of prices to intensities of the last want satisfied constitutes the very foundation of the whole edifice of economics' (quoted in Meek 1972). These and similar statements by Carl Menger, the third founder of neoclassical economics, celebrate the shift from the social to the individual, from the historic creation of values through institutional relations of dominance to subjective valuation, away from the politically tainted classical concerns with class and to, in Walras' phrase, 'Pure Theory.' Subjective does not mean lacking precision. The ability to calculate rates of change using calculus lent a new exactness to economic analysis and started the profession down the road to its obsession with mathematics as the language of its science. Jevons celebrates this development: 'I contend,' he writes, 'that all economic writing must be mathematical so far as they are scientific at all' (Hunt 1992: 311).

The powerful fourth developer of neoclassical economics, Alfred Marshall, is seldom treated in the same purview as the others. The reason is that despite the security of his claim, he is very much a man of both schools, perhaps at heart a B mode economist. The contrast is illuminating because like the Ricardo/Malthus conversations and the internal debates of John Stuart Mill, the division among the founders of neoclassical economics (and within Marshall himself and to some extent the others as well) tell us much about the deep A/B fissure that extends through the entire intellectual history of political economy/economics.

Thorstein Veblen, who coined the term neo-classical in 1900 to describe Marshall's approach, saw his work in terms of continuity with the classical economists. It was George Stigler who more than anyone else is responsible for extending it to include marginalism in general (Stigler 1941: 8). The term was popularized in the 1950s and was heavily used by Joan Robinson. Maurice Dobb suggested that counter-classical would be a better description for the mainstream orthodoxy, and Joseph Schumpeter (1954: 919) declared: 'there is no more sense in calling the Jevons–Menger–Walras theory neo-classic than there would be in calling the Einstein theory neo-Newtonian.'[2] The dispute is as much over interpretation of what properly constitutes 'classical' economics as the character and significance of 'neo-classical' economics. For an economist like Dobb, for whom the core of classical economics is its B mode tradition in which class analysis of production and repro-duction are central, could not but see the marginalism as counter-classical in its A mode methodology.

Not only Marxists, but market-celebrating Austrian economists could see much to be upset about in the new orthodoxy (Kirzner 1997). To take the guts out of the study of economic development by removing the entrepreneur, to replace gradu-alism for dynamic innovation as the governing mechanism of capitalism was for Schumpeter, and even more so for more Austrian-Austrian economists, an unwel-come departure. Menger asserted marginalist doctrine insistence that there is a correct economic analysis that discloses the one best way to proceed given any allo-cation problem. In purest A mode terms he writes:

> Only one road can be the most suitable. . . . In other words, if economic humans under given conditions want to assure the satisfaction of their needs as completely as possible, only one road prescribed exactly by the economic situation leads from the strictly determined starting point to the just as strictly determined goal of economy.

> (Meek 1972: 509)

With A mode neoclassical economics, the profession wrenched itself from concern with historically specific institutional grounding. Its value theory discusses market prices exclusive of considerations which were religious, ethical, or political. There was no philosophy of property rights, as there was in earlier political economy. Neoclassicals assumed them as given scientific categories (Dooley 1990). The study of economic agents maximizing behavior, optimizing exogenously given prefer-ences, the absence of information problems, and the focus on states of rest, movement from one equilibrium to another without concern for transition and adjustment, the avoidance of historical time, consideration of institutional speci-ficity and influence, the presumption of reversibility – all of this is foreign to political economy as a B mode undertaking.

The sharp break sets the terms of the contemporary dispute over method.[3] The economists who are looking for an economics-as-science capable of general explanations rigorously presented, find the neoclassical approach, and especially its general equilibrium formulation, fundamental. Mark Blaug claims that 'nearly all economics nowadays *is* Walrasian economics' (Blaug 1985: 585). In his light this is true. Most other approaches do not have this sort of parsimonious yet totalizing framework, and so are nowhere near as theoretically rigorous. The critics of A mode neoclassical dominance, especially in its general equilibrium form, see such 'strength' as false rigor.[4]

There is strong continuity from Bentham to the neoclassical revolution. As Leon Walras writes in the preface to his *Theory of Political Economy*, 'In this work I have attempted to treat economics as a calculus of pleasure and pain.' He notes that Bentham's ideas are 'the starting point of the theory given in this work' (Hunt

1992: 308). For Walras, relative prices guide all, and everything depends on every-thing else in an instantaneous self-adjusting way in a system of simultaneous equations with infinitely flexible wages and prices. The dependence is simultane-ous not dialectical. Value for Jevons depends entirely on utility. By value, he means price, or exchange value. Value thus arises in exchange. The goal of the individual, who for Jevons is a rational, calculating, asocial maximizer, is to consume up to the point of diminishing utility. Marginal productivity theory asserts that in equilibrium each productive agent receives a reward equal to the marginal productivity of the factor contributed (the quantity of inputs contributed by other agents held con-stant). Distribution is based not on class struggle but on marginal productivity.

Because in the neoclassical model inputs are paid according to their productiv-ity, each input is accorded the value of the output produced. The total product's value is fully accounted for; there is no surplus to be expropriated and there is no exploitation. It is easy to see why to Menger the labor theory of value is 'among the most egregious of the fundamental errors that have had the most far-reaching con-sequences in the previous development of our science' (ibid.: 320). Jevons too was at great pains to refute Ricardo's conclusions that the rate of profit varied inversely to the rate of wages. Such a doctrine was 'radically fallacious,' since both capital-ist and worker were compensated in proportion to their contribution. The capitalist is the friend of the worker, said Jevons, and the laborer should regard him as 'the trustee who holds his capital rather for the good of others than himself' (ibid.: 312).

It is clear why Marxists, Austrian school libertarians, and others for whom the constant struggle for profit is the motor force of capitalist development, reject the neoclassical approach. For conflict theorists, there is no conflict. For celebrants of capitalism's innate creative drive, there are no real innovative possibilities, no entrepreneurs introducing new ways of doing things. The neoclassical model leaves zero return to the organizer of production (although it does seem somewhat ingen-uous to think of the capitalists as acting more 'for the good of others,' as Jevons would have it, than for themselves). Neoclassical economics presumes it is a matter of indifference whether capital hires labor or labor hires capital. The compensation to each is the same either way. Some economists have spoken of Walras' capitalist as the 'Sisyphus entrepreneur,' for in equilibrium profits are zero. The entrepre-neur's job is to coordinate production taking techniques and prices as given. Any profits (above the normal rate of return to capital), from this theory's view, are instantly competed away. There is no reason why labor couldn't just as well orga-nize production – and equally no incentive to do so. As Walras explained, the entrepreneurs make their living not by being an entrepreneur, but as landowners, laborers, or capitalists earning returns in proportion to the contribution of the fac-tors of production they own.

It has been suggested that the acceptance of such models was a result of a political project of discrediting socialism and the economics of the working class that was having such a great impact at the end of the nineteenth century.[5] In the new theory it was certainly true that capitalists as individuals are unimportant, and capital itself is thought of, as John Bates Clark, an American who discovered the principles of neoclassical economics independently of the Europeans, put it, as 'an abstract quantum of productive wealth.'[6] Such abstruse treatment of the class struggle did nothing to calm the suspicions of critics. Clark himself can be understood as a conservative anti-socialist, defending property rights of capitalism as natural and fair to workers. Introducing his 1899 book, *The Distribution of Wealth*, Clark wrote: 'It is the purpose of this work to show that the distribution of the income of society is controlled by a natural law, and that this law, if it worked without friction, would give to every agent of production the amount of wealth which that agent creates' (Clark 1899: v). But whilst Clark is often invoked in support of a widespread belief that, as Joan Robinson suggests, 'the whole point of utility was to justify *laissez faire*' (Robinson 1962: 52), Clark was well aware of countervailing market powers and of the difference between theory as a guide to policy and real-world situations in which the existence of frictions were very much central to what was going on. Clark was also, like many of the neoclassical writers, a reformer.

Yet matters are more complicated. Jevons wrote movingly of the conditions of the working class.[7] Walras was a social reformer and no narrow mathematical plodder (indeed he was not a very good mathematician). His intellectual interests ranged from literature and art criticism to philosophy and history. He was a novelist and a journalist. As to their own views, the neoclassical theorists generally believed that they were involved in value-free science.[8] As Walras wrote, 'the pursuit of pure truth' is carried on with 'complete indifference to consequences, good or bad' (Hunt 1992: 345). Walras also thought of himself as a 'scientific socialist' and had always intended to write a treatise on social economics.

Most economists see marginal productivity theory as a positive analysis (as in positive rather than normative in the Neville Keynes usage), although many since John Bates Clark have suggested that marginal productivity provides a normative theory of distributional justice. To each according to the contribution of the factors they command. Markets produce outcomes that are both efficient and just. The extent to which its continued hegemony is a matter of its political implications is difficult to judge, but hardly a minor consideration. Its main attraction for theorists is that it has proven mathematically elegant and at the abstract theoretical level too powerful to be displaced. Neoclassical economics provides a robust A mode analytic framework.

Whatever the intent and the, in some ways, radical and socialist views of many of the leading neoclassical writers, there is surely evidence of a market driven acceptance of the theory at the end of the century. Thirty years earlier, Gosen (in 1854) had anticipated a great many of the results of the marginalist revolution, but the book was a failure. In 1889, when an enterprising Berlin publisher reissued it with a new date and short preface, it was a great success. It was in a context of criticism of socialism, in an era of mass industrialism, that this reformulated science of economics found its market, replacing labor-power, exploitation, surplus, and even capitalism from the very vocabulary of economists to this day (Screpanti and Zamagni 1993: 154).

Critics ask: is the initial distribution of wealth, income, and power just? If not, market outcomes are suspect. They point out there is no independent measure of marginal productivity and so the theory of wages involves an agreed upon circularity. They further ask: does the real world resemble the neoclassical model? Many lines of technical criticisms at the level of high theory have been offered (see Weintraub 1985), but for the last 100 years efforts to produce an alternative model of the economy have failed to garner anywhere near the support of as many economists as the neoclassical approach continues to enjoy.

For our purposes here, two areas of critique are important. These relate to labor markets and the state. On labor renumeration being equal to marginal productivity of labor, it is sufficient to express agreement with Lester Thurow's conclusion (contested by neoclassicals to be sure), that:

> There is practically no direct information on whether or not labor is paid its marginal product. Economists take it as an article of faith or else claim that it is the best null hypothesis, and economic theory is based on the assumption that labor is indeed paid its marginal product. Without this assumption, much of economic analysis falls apart. The theory of production certainly does. The convenience of the hypothesis for economists, however, does not make it correct.
>
> (Thurow 1970: 20–1)[9]

Empirical studies of wage inequality by occupation and industry in different national economies have found that trends differ in ways that are hard to reconcile with the theory, and they suggest that for discussion of policy issues the neoclassical model's generalizations may not be adequate, indeed may be misleading (e.g. Katz *et al.* 1995). It can be argued that the model was not meant to be applied in this way, and that economists should not draw policy conclusions from its abstract workings, although they do.

There is an absence of government from the neoclassical model, and the logic of the neoclassical mode of thinking leads economists to be suspicious of government intervention in the economy. To interfere in allocating resources that the free market, unaided, allocates efficiently seems unnecessary and unwise. In a perfectly competitive market, the kind assumed to exist, there is no market power, and because matters of technological change are excluded by the assumption that production functions are already known and there can be no economies to scale, outcomes are always efficient.[10] The inference in neoclassical economics is that government interference creates inefficiencies. Government is also coercive. It can redistribute to those it favors only at the expense of others. This would be against their will (or else there would be voluntary redistribution of this kind) and at the cost of an overall loss of efficiency.

Even if we accept all of the assumptions of the perfects – perfect competition, perfect foresight, perfect factor mobility, in fact the most perfect of all worlds of static allocation – the implication of fairness of outcome that is presumed because factors receive a return in exact relation to their contribution, does not follow. Distributional justice does not necessarily result. As Blaug writes:

It would be less misleading to say the very opposite: marginal productivity theory shows that market results are by no means 'fair' or 'equitable.' If a factor is relatively scarce, it will command a high price and there is no reason to think that a high efficiency-price for a productive agent will accord with our ethical notion of justice between persons.

(Blaug 1985: 427)

All of this is well-plowed-ground, but the controversies remain, and they are important to how the world is understood. Theory impacts policy and the consciousness of an age, although it may better be said that the dominant powers of the age shape consciousness, and lend support to the economic theories they find conducive.

Today, neoclassical economists move from such abstractions to advise developing nations to 'get the prices right,' to undo government regulations that interfere with 'free market' outcomes, and simply to open national markets to the advantages of free trade. Here it can be said that the recent performance of the East Asian developmentalist state regimes, nations such as Japan, Korea, and Taiwan, the three fastest growing economies in the world in the last forty years (measured by per capita GNP), have had intense government participation and direction of economic activity. As Sanjaya Lall summarizes their story:

> The lessons of the East Asian NICs [newly industrialized countries] are therefore rather different from those normally implied by the [neoclassical] development literature. They grew, not because they replaced imperfect interventions with efficient markets, but because they remedied imperfect markets by well-directed and selective interventions to promote entry into new sets of activities. The benefits of export orientation arose, not from the static benefits of resource allocation, but from the discipline and incentives they provided.
>
> (Lall 1995: 269)

A very different economics is necessary once these neoclassical assumptions regarding the nature of the state (essentially irrelevant to the growth process except as it interferes with the free market and produces inefficiencies) are discarded. For one thing, politics quickly enters and we are in the realm of normative political economics. Any significant event that involves labor and the state has a quick and easy neoclassical explanation. Labor unions raise wages above market clearing levels. The state can either reinforce the action of such special interests or insist on a free market outcome. The same events can usually be reinterpreted in a more ambiguous, but also more realistic, B mode formulation.

Consider another example, suggested by Ha-Joon Chang: the case of the coal miners strike in England in which the Thatcher government stated that their policies were simply a matter of common sense application of market principle. Britain could not afford to keep open inefficient mines and to pay the miners more than the value of the product they took out of the ground. As Chang writes:

[T]he British miners were told to accept 'world market' prices, which turned out to be determined by the 'political' decisions of the German government to subsidize their coal, of the French government to allow the export of their subsidized nuclear electricity, and of the Columbian government to allow child labour in the mines. . . .

(Chang 1995: 217)

we soon get a very different sort of story about this event which was such a milestone in British labor history. When we see the parameters 'given' by the market as politically constructed; and there is no shortage of such stories. Currently, watching China's market–Leninist leaders negotiate with Bill Gates and Rupert Murdoch, we see a powerful instance of market opening that turns out to be another version of developmentalist state industrial policy at work, in which *real politique* trumps models based on the 'good approximation assumption' of perfect competition.[11]

Because neoclassical economics takes everything else as given and only examines the relationship between a restricted number of 'endogenous variables,' much of what is going on is excluded by assumption. Neoclassical economics, starting with its founders, removed the political element from political economy, and, ironically perhaps, such an approach can be seen as serving political ends. Such shifts in emphasis undertaken consciously by the neoclassicals went along with the change in the name of the study itself, from political economy to economics. We owe this to Jevons, who thought that economics sounded more like physics and mathematics (Jevons 1879: 48). (Of course, it could sound like politics and ethics – even aesthetics. Contextualizing is in the mind of the beholder and some suffixes are promiscuous.)

To this point, neoclassical economics has been treated as a unity. There is, however, a significant division between those who develop a partial equilibrium framework and those who work with a general equilibrium analysis. The former hold everything else constant while they explore one particular relation, usually between two variables at a time. The latter work at a high level of abstraction. Such models allow everything to change at the same time, and outcomes are determined for the entire system simultaneously.

Menger and Jevons

It was Carl Menger who, as a young man, gave us the formulation of economics as the allocation of insufficient means – economics as scarcity and maximization; but this formulation always troubled Menger, who knew the world to be a more complex affair. He worked for fifty years revising his *Principles*. In the posthumously published second edition, he explained that economics had two 'elemental directions.' The economizing insufficient means were one and the 'technoeconomic, physical requirements of production/reproduction' the other. This second edition has yet to be published in English, and I do not read German, but from Karl Polanyi's account it would appear that Menger accepted two meanings of economics not totally divorced from our A/B understanding.[12] As Polanyi writes:

Menger himself thought that this theory [neoclassicalism] was not, in fact, capable of answering all the questions which were, more or less carelessly, put to it and explained by it. As a result, he never let his book be reprinted or translated because he wanted to find an even more general theory. Menger intermittently worked on this more general theory for about fifty years. After his death, it was published. In the second edition of the *Grundsatze* (1923), he retained his original theory – he retained, in fact, every word of the original book – but made a more general theory of the economy in order that he could make a place for history, and anthropology, and sociology.

(Polanyi 1971: 291)

Menger left a legacy that is at some variance to what we know as neoclassical economics. It is the Austrian School which has already been mentioned. Austrian economics stresses uncertainty in human affairs, subjectivity and distrust of the economics-as-science A mode approach. Friedrich Hayek, its leading light, was Keynes, major antagonist in the 1930s, but he also shared Keynes' critique of Walrasian general equilibrium theory (which will be discussed shortly). Hayek, unlike Keynes, however, stressed the centrality of local knowledge (Hayek 1945) and traced the importance of Menger to this line of theory he developed (Hayek 1973). What makes markets work is that each participant knows their own situation and acts on their individual understanding of their own interests in their particular circumstances. The sum of such action produces globally optimal outcomes. Social planners and interventionists from Plato to Voltaire, Marx, and Keynes were wrong to think that society could be organized rationally. The spontaneous social order uses knowledge optimally in ways no government can possibly hope to match (Hayek 1966). Unique individuals make very different choices based on a host of details that cannot be reduced to parsimonious mathematical modeling, and entrepreneurship is the engine of capitalist growth for Austrians.

Whilst Austrian economics remains a vital strain within the economics, the mainstream understanding of Menger, and the broad approach that has come to be known as neoclassical economics, is quite different. The domination of the concept of substitution at the margin gives pride of place to differential calculus, which is able to measure rates of change and demonstrate the principle of equalizing marginal values. The whole of neoclassical economics is nothing more than the spelling out of the equimarginal principle 'in ever wider contexts, coupled with the demonstration that perfect competition does under certain conditions produce equimarginal allocation of expenditures and resources' (Polanyi 1971: 297). Of course, this means that many interesting questions economists formerly asked are no longer considered. '[A]n unkind critic,' Blaug writes, 'might say that neoclassical economics indeed achieved greater generality, but only by asking easier questions' (ibid.: 299). A solution is found where the egg is on its end, in a state of rest, but there is no sense of how it would ever get up there.

Leon Walras

Leon Walras, who gives his name to Walrasian economics, a synonym for the general equilibrium approach, was the first economist who set out a theoretical structure in which all markets clear concurrently. Modern general equilibrium theory, which is descendent from Walras, is widely seen as the scientific counterpart or even proof of the 'invisible hand,' but as James Tobin writes:

> Where does the modern version of the theory leave the Invisible Hand? Two quite opposite responses are conceivable. On the one hand is the good news: the intuition of Adam Smith and many later writers can indeed be rigorously formulated and proved. The bad news is that the theorems depend on a host of conditions, many of dubious realism. Restrictions on preferences and technologies are stringent. . . . The theory does not describe a process in real time by which the economy reaches an equilibrium solution. . . . The modern version might be taken to refute, not to support, the applicability of invisible hand propositions to real world economics.
>
> (Tobin 1985: 106)

With general equilibrium theory, all the same issues therefore arise concerning the usefulness of a rigorous theoretical system; this, its critics suggest, makes it of little value, even in its most current versions and at what its exponents propose is the height of scientific rigor.[13] Examining Walras' contribution, we can readily see both sides of the question once more.

Since the forces of supply and demand in any one market will be dependent on prices prevailing in other markets, it is necessary that all prices are determined simultaneously in order to have a truly deterministic model. Walras arranges this in a system of simultaneous equations, that he abstracts from the possibility of market power: all markets are assumed perfectly competitive; all utility schedules are taken as given and exogenously determined. He has four sets of equations in the model. The first is the supply of productive services, which relate the quantity supplied to all prices in the system. The second is the demand for all commodities. The third is that the demand for each productive service is set equal to its supply so that the system is in equilibrium. Finally, the fourth set of equations assumes that the price of each consumer good is equal to its cost of production. These costs depend on technical coefficients of production that relate all inputs to outputs at constant cost.

The problem with all of this to most people who approach general equilibrium theory for the first time (and for other social scientists who do not accept the extreme methodological individualism of the approach) is the unreality of the assumptions. Aren't consumers influenced by what others are buying? Is perfect information available at zero cost, or at any cost? Are prices really always equal to the actual cost of production? Even if one accepts all of this, the question remains: what is the mechanism that makes it all happen? How is the *simultaneous* set of prices and quantities in each and every market reached at the same time? It must be simultaneous rather than sequential, because prices and quantities decided ear-lier would not be optimal in the light of new prices in other markets. There has to be recontracting until everyone is happy at the same time. How are these prices agreed upon? Walras' assumption of a *deus ex machina*, a crier or auctioneer, a dis-embodied voice somewhere over the oceans, calling out prices until the right ones are found to bring about equilibrium in the markets would be laughable if it were not the pride of the A mode economic analysis.

The assumptions of Walrasian models are not so much to simplify reality whilst retaining its essential elements but rather to preserve the working of the (unrealistic) model itself. As Rogers notes of the more sophisticated models in this tradition, 'additional factors [are] always introduced in such a way that they do not disturb any existing conclusions – for example, production is treated as a variety of exchange' (Rogers 1989: 191). The model can be made more complex but the same level of abstraction is always maintained. Efforts to return meaningful forms of choice and contingency, a real role for money and credit (these are essentially barter models and don't need money), fail because the complete specification needed requires that all decisions are coordinated and prereconciled at an instant of time in the first period when equilibrium is established. In the more sophisticated contemporary efforts in the Walrasian tradition, 'time' does unfold, but only in accordance with predeter-mined decisions and there is little relevance to historical time or room for real-world governance structures. Commodities and exchange must be structured so that the future is collapsed into present exchange decisions. The Arrow–Debreu model, to take the most famous of these, assumes the existence of all conceivable future markets. As critics have pointed out, a model in which all trades 'from creation to eternity' can be negotiated on the day of creation by prereconciling all choices lacks a certain desirable level of realism. If each market is settled one by one, the prices in one auction become input information for subsequent auctions, and, with recon-tracting, it can all work out. Ironically, this process resembles nothing so much as iterative central planning, only here, instead of a Soviet planning board, we have an imaginary auctioneer and a process of 'groping' (Walras' word) toward a set of prices in each market which simultaneously clears them all.

This brings us to Frank Hahn's egg standing on its end. It would seem an uphill grope to this simultaneous optimal outcome. Walras, having proved that there exists a set of market clearing prices, has his model make no attempt to discuss real-istic mechanisms. The egg can stand. Assume the economy starts from a position of equilibrium that is disturbed; the model brings it back to equilibrium. Prices increase and decrease. Quantities buyers bid for change. There is a reallocation of resources and a new competitive equilibrium. The egg is back on its end.[14] Some economists today accept all of this as the price of hard science.

The break after 1870 meant that what had been the mainline tradition in polit-ical economy was displaced by the neoclassical mainstream. There are many economists who did not, and do not, accept models that produce full employment by assumption and competitive outcomes by the fiat of perfect information, ease of entry and exit, which abstract from power in the economy, and uncertainty with regard to the future. Further, the near disappearance of moral and ethical considerations from the job description has not gone down easily. It is in fact increasingly difficult to use the descriptor 'neoclassical' in a generally acceptable and so unproblematic way. If we accept Frank Knight's view that neoclassical economics rests on the premise that actors have complete information and that information is free, then neoclassical economics is probably no longer really accepted by most practitioners; yet its presumptions are often implicit, and a neoclassical world is the background assumed for many rhetorical purposes.

Perhaps one of the sharpest divisions within the field is between those who continue to think Walrasian general equilibrium theory to be the highest achievement of modern economics and those who consider it a cul-de-sac, as Lord Kaldor has expressed it, which far from assisting economic science 'has inhibited progress and has created a brake on the development of an integrated system of knowledge' (Kaldor 1984: 8). The idea that the allocation of a specified amount of resources under known technological possibilities to produce a set of given ends, which is the legacy of Walras, Jevons and Menger, is best considered a counter-revolution when counterpoised to the dynamic investigations into the nature and causes of the wealth of nations in a context of a process of the constant evolution of societies, which is at the core of the classical economics of Smith, Ricardo, Malthus, Marx, and Mill. Efforts to incorporate intertemporal equilibria into a Walrasian framework to make such 'growth' models 'dynamic' seem a promising next step to some, but to others make the whole theory 'more absurd,' since nothing can happen in the future using such models that is not foreseen in Period 1. As Kaldor would have it, economics is still dully static: 'From period 2 on, life must be very boring!' (ibid.: 7).[15]

Many other economists, however, continue to prefer parsimonious deductive models at a high level of abstraction and generality, the formalist mode of A style economics-as-science economics. To understand reality and the especial complexity of human nature using such models is an inadequate starting point for others. The debate is once again between circles and squares (Hirschman 1984). There is a great deal of resistance to dependence on such versions of price theory as a framework for all of economics. Information problems, increasing returns from social knowledge, and other real-world problems intrude into, indeed are central to the concerns of, the last of the founders of neoclassical economics, Alfred Marshall, to whom we now turn attention.

Alfred Marshall

Alfred Marshall, the great Cambridge economist, is more responsible than any other individual for the establishment of academic economic science in the English speaking world. Through his own influential teaching (half the chairs in political economy in England came to be filled with his students), Marshall created modern Anglo-American economics. For over twenty years Marshall taught material that was later to appear in his great principles text in 1890. (Had he published earlier he might have eclipsed the claim of Jevons and the others with regard to founding neoclassical economics.) Interested in plain communication, and given to illustration of economic principles with real-life examples, he exuded the same kind of common sense one finds in Adam Smith. His lifelong efforts to pursue a moral agenda using the tools of his craft make him the exemplary mainline economist. Marshall started his academic career studying metaphysics and ethics. Told by a friend, as many with such interests are, that he 'really had to understand economics,' he read Mill and got very excited. His career changed directions.

Today, whilst students are taught Alfred Marshall's image of supply and demand as two blades of the scissor (which cannot cut without the coming together of the separate cutting edges), they are rarely helped to see that in this analysis Marshall reconciled the older classical cost of production theory with the subjective utility understanding of the determination of value. Like Paul Samuelson's Keynesian–Neoclassical Synthesis over half a century later, Marshall codified a new orthodoxy, offered a textbook version of the theoretical core that was to provide a coherence for the profession.

Marshall's contributions to A science are legion. His stress on scarcity and choice was a brilliant formulation of optimizing rules and formalization as the basis of the definition of the field of study (symbolized by his success in pushing metaphysics out of economics with the establishment of the Cambridge Economics Tripos in 1903 after Sidgwick's death deprived Cambridge of a powerful defender of philosophy as a necessary part of the training of an economist). Marshall, wishing to professionalize the disciple and, fearing the influence of people like Sidney Webb and Austin Chamberlain, presented a formalization that removed the subjectivist judgement that earlier economists at Cambridge had felt part of political economy's legacy from moral philosophy. Yet matters of values were more complicated for Marshall as we shall see. Scientific judgments were to be made contextually and to serve moral ends in ways that could not comfortably admit any final separation.

His method of partial analysis, the concepts of elasticity of demand and consumer surplus, the distinction between the short-run market period and the long period, and how equilibrium was determined differently in each, Marshall's presentation of maximization by the firm as essentially the same as utility maximization by the household, all reenforced mechanical balance as the way the laws of economics were understood. The symmetry – for example of the firm maximizing revenue, producing a fixed output at minimal cost by substituting factors at the margin, just in the way that households maximize utility by substituting work for leisure, or leisure for work, giving up one as the cost of getting more of the other in a way that depended on relative price and utility – was beauty to behold. Marshall deduced the negative demand curve from a given and constant utility of money for the period of the analysis. By summing individual demands at different prices, Marshall produced the total demand curve for the commodity. For Marshall, time is the chief difficulty in economic analysis. This insight led to some of the most brilliant innovations in the neoclassical framework. He used comparative statics to impound (as temporarily constant) the magnitude of variables that would be transformed by dynamic change over time. He thus attempted to mimic the general equilibrium problems of dynamic change with a sophisticated precision possible using comparative statics. By breaking up complex questions into their parts and analyzing each separately, Marshall provided great insight into the dynamics of the system as a whole.

Most of what students do in intermediate price theory courses comes from Marshall. What these students hardly ever get is a sense of the feel he had about the way attitudinal factors, the relevant institutions, and societal dynamics affect any real-world application. As Marshall wrote in one of his extended exercises in self-clarification:

> The rate of interest depends on the labour which can be got in exchange for a given amount of the produce of past labour. This depends on (I) the amount of wealth already accumulated, (ii) the number and efficiency of the people, (iii) the scope that the arts of production offer for the use of machinery and other forms of capital, and (iv) the relative importance of the future enjoyments as it appears on the one hand to spendthrifts and others who borrow wealth for the purposes of immediate enjoyment, and on the other their creditors.
>
> (Rostow 1990: 165)

He goes on to include so many variables as he thought relevant to the determination of interest rates, variables difficult and some impossible to measure. He is soon into what Rostow, in this context, describes as his extended method, a 'wide-ranging descriptive, institutional mode of exposition' (ibid.: 166; see also Shove 1942).

Marshall's outstanding achievement is widely understood to be his success in A mode economics, in giving economics a 'range, precision, and predictive reliability [that] would compare with that of the natural sciences' (Maloney 1985: 24); but he taught his students more than this apparatus. Indeed, for Marshall there remained a lifelong conflict between the development of the science of economics along these lines and the moral uses to which that understanding was to be put. The apparatus could get us only part of the way toward solving the economic problems of mankind. The great irony in considering the canonical Alfred Marshall is his own ambivalence toward the approach his *Principles* takes to the study of static microeconomics theory. Time and time again the reader is told that the conclusions of static analysis are unreliable, that microeconomics fails to come to grips with the vital issues of economic policy, and that the central problem of economics is not the allocation of given resources but rather how the resources became what they are (see Blaug 1985: 420 and Screpanti and Zamagni 1993: 180). The man who did more than any other economist to set out modern microeconomics, found the method unreliable and criticized its inability to deal with the vital issues of policy that had drawn him to study economics. It is, Marshall wrote,

> especially needful to remember that economic problems are imperfectly presented when they are treated as problems of static equilibrium, and not of organic growth. For though the static treatment alone can give us definiteness

and precision of thought, and is therefore a necessary introduction to a more philosophic treatment of society as an organism; it is yet only an introduction.

(Blaug 1985: 161)

Moreover, as some economists have been unable to help noticing, his *Principles*, besides being a great work in modern economics, is 'an impressive book of "sociology" of nineteenth-century English capitalism, and is permeated with a sense of history' (Screpanti and Zamagni 1993: 248). The gap between Marshall and his mainstream followers is in large measure a result of their not sharing his cultural and philosophical interests. Almost afraid of the power to mislead and coerce ascent through displays of technical sophistication, and rejecting the claim that economics had reached the state of 'Science,' Marshall attempted to qualify the claims of his own apparatus. The study of pure theory, he feared, would lead economists away from the urgent tasks of the day. As John Vaizey writes:

> His pupils were not to sit on their bottoms theorizing; he found mathematics dizzily exciting and, like chess, put it behind him. The poor were always with him and their poverty cried out for relief. His powerful mind was perfectly capable of drawing up abstract schemes, but his emphasis was put continuously on the hard recalcitrant stuff of reality.
>
> (Vaizey 1977: 11)

Marshall offered many grounds for misgivings as to the effect on economics of the extensive use of mathematics. Not least of these was the harm done by the mathematical model building the followers of Walras celebrate. The mathematical approach required rigorous abstraction and this took precedence over the concrete of the situation which Marshall thought more important. Marshall believed, in Viner's formulation, that 'economics must become more complicated and more biological in character, whereas economics tended toward excessive simplification and sought its prototype rather in mechanics than in biology' (Viner 1941: 123). Whilst some economists prefer mathematical presentation for this very reason, believing that because economics is so complicated it is best made clear by using the precise language of mathematics, Marshall took the reverse position. Mathematics cannot catch the important nuances that make up economic reality.[16]

What set him apart from so many of today's neoclassically steeped economists is both this clear sense of the limited capabilities of mathematics as a tool to build economic understanding and the need always to translate any conclusions he derived using mathematics into clear English. It is the verbal version that is the economics, not the mathematical one. As he wrote in a frequently cited letter to A.L. Bowley in 1906,

> [I] had a growing feeling in the later years of my work at the subject that a good mathematical theorem dealing with economic hypotheses was very unlikely to be good economics; and I went more and more on the rules – (1) Use mathematics as a shorthand language, rather than as an engine of

enquiry. (2) Keep to them till you have done. (3) Translate into English. (4) Then illustrate by examples that are important in real life. (5) Burn the mathematics. (6) If you can't succeed in 4, burn 3. This last I did often.[17]

Marshall and the working class

In 1919, in his Preface to *Industry and Trade*, Marshall described how when as a young man while reading Mill, given his own interest in the causes of inequality which he believed 'were not wholly beyond human control,' he developed what he called 'a tendency to socialism.' Mill's *Fortnightly Review* article of 1879 was a strong influence, we are told:

> But the writings of the socialists generally repelled me, almost as much as they attracted me; because they seemed far out of touch with realities; and, partly for that reason, I decided to say little on the matter, until I had thought much longer.[18]

Marshall seems to have thought about such matters over much of his lifetime. Writing to John Bates Clark in 1900, Marshall offers the view that the marginal productivity principle, though correct and important, 'covers only a very small part of the real difficulty of the wages problem.' Marshall, like Mill, was drawn to the situation of working people. When he was younger, he and his wife would sometimes spend their summer vacations visiting factories and wandering around working-class areas talking to the men and their bosses. As Marshall grew older, 'he became increasingly preoccupied with ethical ideals, historical development, and problems of economic and social policy' (Coats 1990: 157–8). On his deathbed, Marshall told Keynes how he first came to study economics as a sort of religious work for the sake of mankind. What he was not able to do was reconcile his radical reformist instincts with the constraints upon any man of the Establishment to channel these proclivities carefully within accepted boundaries. The tension led him to contorted moralisms.

Political economy to Marshall was the study of human welfare and not merely the study of material wealth. Further, ethical forces must be taken into account, Marshall said, because they directly and significantly affect individual and social behavior. Marshall's treatment of human nature as endogenous was a rejection of Bentham's reliance on current revealed preferences as an unambiguous guide. Like many other economists, Marshall saw the benefits of type A science as a system of measurements and careful calculation, but he also moved beyond such a limited view to embrace non-measurable aspects as well. He was drawn to do so by a moral commitment that was dissatisfied by the capacities of the very science he did so much to develop. His ethical imperatives were hardly a normative afterthought to his work. As Levitt has written, 'Marshall's constant sermonizing page after page was integral and substantive to his work, that indeed in a strange and fundamental way *was* his work' (Levitt 1976: 44).

Marshall's ethics were of the enlightened middle class, those of an elite technocrat, if so ungenteel a term is permitted for one whose task is to prompt the moral evolution of society. His Victorian desire for earnestness is seen in his effort to assimilate capital and labor to a consensus. He wanted to prevent the ruling-class weakness for simply making money from growing to the point where the moral distaste of the middle classes would find unity with radical working-class elements to demand revolutionary change. Marshall feared militant socialists. Whilst they painted pretty pictures, they both overstated the economic evils of the age and called for change that could not be brought about within their time frame for political action (and surely not the rules of the game Marshall felt constrained to accept). He had no choice then but to criticize that mixture of 'ardour and haste' that he felt remains characteristic of socialist critics. Human progress, Marshall thought, was very slow and proceeded by minute marginal steps. As the credo for his *Principles* stated: 'Natura non facit saltum' – 'Nature makes no leaps.' Economists would be wise to emulate nature in their own habits. 'The only good work,' Marshall wrote in 1901 to Professor Richard T. Ely (the American institutionalist whom we shall encounter in the next chapter), 'is slow work.'

Such a personal temperament, Marshall's fear of change, made him a very peculiar, though hardly unique type of socialist. His sympathies were with the Mill of *On Liberty* rather than of the *Essays on Socialism*. In his dealings with trade unionists, he favored the class collaborators and wanted the radicals who, as he saw it, stood in the way of progress, beaten at all costs. He opposed 'ill-considered measures of reformly Utopian schemes' (nationalization and municipalization), fearing the heavy hand of the bureaucrats. His own inclination was toward 'Economic Chivalry,' by which he meant an assimilation within business life of a moral consensus that would include schemes for mild income distribution, improved working-class housing and health care, which would raise productivity. Social contentment would provide stability. It was not merely morally right but, he thought, good for business. Whilst he believed the socialists to be utopian, in his own good society 'No one should have an occupation which tends to make him anything less than a gentleman' (Skidelsky 1983: 47). It was his fervent hope, as Robert Skidelsky writes, that 'with the growth of earnestness, society could increasingly rely on voluntary sacrifices from capitalists and workers to sustain economic progress' (ibid. 46–7). No utopian he.

At another level, Marshall was too keen an observer not to be concerned with the issue of national competitiveness. Rostow finds 'in the sequence of Marshall's work – stretching over a half century – a gathering awareness that Britain's critical economic problem was how to meet the challenge posed by the rise to industrial maturity of the United States and Germany (Rostow 1990: 187). This question, whilst of serious importance, was difficult to conceptualize. His basic comparative static framework was perhaps forced on him by his definition of self in the context in which he lived and worked. Even supplemented by his awareness of the evolutionary nature of real economies and the importance of historical and institutional embeddedness, he was simply not bold enough to make the jumps in consciousness necessary.

Perhaps it is just a matter of his cautiousness and the constraints of his intense professionalism that does not allow him to speculate beyond these self-imposed boundaries. He was hesitant in giving policy advice for, as he wrote,

> We have reached very few practical conclusions; because it is generally necessary to look at the whole of the economic, to say nothing of the moral and other aspects of a practical problem before attempting to deal with it at all.
>
> (ibid.: 168)

Marshall, whilst he tried to be scrupulous in such matters, was tortured because he understood that a positive economics was not really possible and yet the basis of moral judgements (to say nothing of the complex interactions in any real-world instance) made the giving of advice a most weighty matter. Marshall was honest enough to see the implications of giving primacy to his moral conviction. Taken seriously, as part of an economist's framework, making such matters endogenous to the analysis would undercut the claim to scientific precision to which his technical work aspired. Like other economists we have encountered and some we are yet to consider, Marshall's belief that a value-free science was not possible led him to tiptoe around the issues of class and power.[19] He wrote, for example:

> When a workman is in fear of hunger, his need of money is very great; and, if at starting, he gets the worst of the bargaining, and is employed at low wages, it remains great, and he may go on selling his labor at a low rate. This is all the more probable because, while the advantage in bargaining is likely to be pretty well distributed between the two sides of a market for commodities, it is more often on the side of the buyers than on that of the sellers in a market for labour.
>
> (Marshall 1890: 335–6)

Once such considerations are introduced, many of the basic tools of neoclassical thinking are blunted. Maurice Dobb draws our attention to the implications of Marshall's introduction of uneven bargaining power, viz. that an aggregate supply curve independent of the aggregate demand curve for labor is untenable. The later Cambridge economists, steeped in Marshallian concerns and endowed with his economic assumptions and technique, critiqued the independence of supply and demand for labor more widely (as in Piero Sraffa's and Joan Robinson's work). These arguments flow from Marshall's insight into the nature of the wage bargain. A change in the price of labor changes distribution, and, through its effect on the marginal utility of income, changes the supply and demand curves for labor. There is no longer a determinative equilibrium.

The same sort of qualifications should be made in accepting the use of cost curves. Marshall's theory of the representative firm can be seen as a substantial departure from the other neoclassicals. Using biological imagery, he contemplates the birth and maturity of economic enterprises. These are not, to his thinking, interchangeable units. The representative firm is not meant to represent all firms in an industry. The passive price taker of the contemporary textbook is an anemic descendant of the Marshallian firm. For Marshall, firms make real choices even as they are coerced by laws of competition. The possibility, and indeed prevalence, of internal and external economies moves the focus away from smooth and predictable cost curves towards a consideration of the advantages accruing to better management.

Marshall also recognized that the more successful firms can enjoy advantages that lead to monopoly power and oligopolistic industrial structures. Indeed, as Marshall wrote, great corporate giants were being created that had advantages over smaller competitors. His answer was an evolutionary theory, the lifecycle of corporations, which led him to expect that like young trees in the forest, newcomers could eventually grow, though initially they stood in the shade of older and larger rivals who would, in time, die off and the new ones would force their way upward. As a firm ages, he wrote, 'it is likely to have lost so much of its elasticity and progressive force, that the advantages are no longer exclusively on its side' (Hunt 1992: 370). Industries were different in their technique, labor relations, and geography of suppliers and markets. They need to be studied concretely. Marshall did not believe in either timeless models or industry-wide truths. He was at heart an evolutionary economist and can be read as such.

It is this theme that runs through much of our consideration of the history of economic thought. The broader interests of the seminal figures are rarely reflected in the narrow-gaged work of the mainstream, which incorporates their innovations into the profession's self-definition. The focus on technique to the exclusion of broad vision is evident in any comparison of Marshall's or Mill's approach to the writing of a principles text, with most modern versions geared to the explication of graphical analytics and deterministic mathematical models.

'Economics has too little to do with ideas'

In the first sentence of the *Principles*, Marshall tells us that: 'Economic conditions are constantly changing, and each generation looks at its own problems in its own way.' Further, Marshall thought, people just did not have given tastes over their lifetimes, nor was human nature constant either within or across generations. Understanding such changes and developing frameworks that take evolution in real time to account, were tasks for economists. How different from Jevons' version of marginalism in which interpersonal comparisons are not allowed, every mind being 'inscrutable to every other mind' and therefore 'no common denominator of feeling seems possible' and no point of analytical entry for the social scientist (Hunt 1992: 312).

Unlike in that other neoclassical tradition discussed in the first part of this chapter, which is the basis of so much of today's economics-as-science thinking, Marshall was quite comfortable with the possibility that equilibrium, once disturbed, might not be restored. He was interested in whether the egg could get up on its end. Under realistic assumptions, conventional microeconomic equilibrium analysis does not operate, according to Marshall.[20] It is for these reasons that Marshall is important to the B culture in economics. Indeed, his internal battle is a significant instance in the history of economic thought in which an economist who contributed much to laying down tools for textbook A mode analysis struggled to surmount its limitations and methodological presumptions.

One is struck over and over as one reads Marshall at his appreciation of the dynamic evolutionary nature of economics.[21] In the qualifications to the theory's static confines, we see an evolutionary economist desiring to take on real-world complexity and impatient with the bloodless constructs of economics and its 'economic men.' Writing in the *Economic Journal*, memorializing the master, Keynes quotes Marshall as saying, 'If I had to live my life over again I should have devoted it to psychology.[22] Economics has too little to do with ideas. If I said much about them I should not be read by businessmen.' This unease, the tension between wanting to be read and to have influence in the world, and wanting to tell things as they are, which leads to phrasing issues carefully, nuancing pronouncements discretely, is a tension felt by many economists.

For Marshall, professionalism required a distancing from the real world so that it could be reengaged with powerful tools. The point of struggling through mastery of the tools was not to worship the 'austere aesthetics' of a narrow and rigorous economic science but to get about the business of making the world a better place. Sir Dennis Robertson, reflecting on his upbringing as a Cambridge economist, writes:

> We thought we knew pretty well what sort of things we wanted to know about and were glad to take the counsel given by Marshall himself nearly at the beginning of the *Principles*: 'the less we concern ourselves with scholastic enquiries as to whether a certain consideration comes within the scope of economics the better.'
>
> (Deane 1989: 143)

This is why Marshall can make neoclassical economists uncomfortable and why many of those who sought both to follow Marshall and to do A type economics, slight the heart of his B side teachings.

The most important legacy of what is known as the neoclassical revolution is the sea change shift from value and distribution in class terms and the broader social and political understanding of the economy to a view of society, or at least the economy, as a natural mechanism in which independent, freely acting agents interact to produce the best possible allocation of resources. All larger categories are reducible, determined by the preferences and actions of individual actors. Efficient outcomes are achieved naturally and stable equilibrium states are the norm. The Keynesian revolution was to challenge as a myth the idea that prices and quantities automatically adjusted in some optimal fashion and that enlightened self-interest always operates in the public interest. Yet fifty years after the Keynesian revolution, the tenets of neoclassical economics once again are dominant. It will take us a number of chapters to tell this story, but first we detour to consider versions of B mode heterodoxy that, after becoming influential at the start of the twentieth century, are finding new converts in various modernized versions at the century's end.

7 Heterodoxy and holism

In scientific thinking logically disparate elements, which are often impossible to separate from one another, tend to mix; and as the main viewpoint changes constantly. Instead of trying to establish sharp borders between disciplines and approaches, we must realize that everything flows together.

(Schumpeter 1991: 87)

After having been nonexistent for a large part of the twentieth century, there is now perhaps a chance for a meaningful interaction between economists and sociologists. Maybe it will even become possible again – as in the days of Adam Smith, John Stuart Mill, and Karl Marx – to get an analysis of central social problems that is informed by both economics and sociology. In a sense, then, things would simply be returning to normal, since the radical separation between economics and sociology is relatively recent.

(ibid.: 5)

The fracturing of political economy in the last part of the nineteenth century into neoclassical economics and the emerging disciplines of sociology, political science, anthropology, and geography, represented both an increased distancing of the field from the other more 'social' social sciences and a marginalization of its ethical dimension in favor of a search for more scientific groundings. The evolving nature of social phenomena continued to be studied, and there were economists who retained as their central interest historical processes and the relationship between political power and economic development. The first of such groups to be considered is the German Historical School which, whilst not really a major influence in the same sense as others discussed, is part of a debate that took place in the last decades of the nineteenth century, the *Methodenstreit*, which is of interest. In this debate, the historical school is the B side in combat with what was to be the triumphant A mode neoclassical economics.

Institutionalism, an American creation, is another of the heterodox alternatives to the neoclassical mainstream. As a movement in the decades both before and after the start of the twentieth century, it was the dominant school of thought in economics departments in the US. Institutionalism considered the economy in evolution and asked how its defining features came to be and how they came to change. It is the quintessential B mode school of thought and offers an interesting comparison to what Oliver Williamson has named New Institutional Economics of recent decades. This seeks to extend the neoclassical framework to encompass an explanation of institution formation and development and to what has been called historical and comparative analysis (Greif 1998), which identifies relevant institutions and sets of self-enforcing expectations and social structures relevant to a political economy understanding of particular episodes under consideration. Because of its historical and comparative approach, respect for historical specificity, and examining of the limits of rationality, cognition, and knowledge and incentives for and obstacles to institutional innovations, such an approach being developed by contemporary economists seems to capture much of the earlier institutionalist project, but it remains to be seen how such tendencies develop. What is clear is that at the end of the twentieth century, as at its start, there is broad ferment within the social sciences that is indebted to the early institutionalism, which will be discussed in this chapter.

Initially, what we know as the old institutionalist school was characterized by a positive regard for the potential of state action in the economic realm. One of its founders, John R. Commons, was in touch with Maynard Keynes. Commons believed that wise government action could correct the defects found in an unregulated, or rather poorly regulated, capitalism. Wise institutional reform based on a broad understanding of how individuals' incentives were shaped, and could be better shaped, were the core of his economics. The viewpoint is strikingly similar to that of J.M. Keynes, and it is therefore not altogether surprising that Keynes could write to Commons respectfully in 1927, 'there seems to me to be no other economist with whose general way of thinking I feel myself in such general accord' (Skidelsky 1994: 229).[1] This tribute is a reflection on Commons' intense interest in how markets work in practice and how incentives could be improved upon for the public good through government regulation. We shall also discuss Richard T. Ely in some measure because of his role in founding the American Economics Association, the umbrella formation under which the profession meets in the United States and through which it publishes its leading journals, and comment on the radical origins of this now most conventional organization. This chapter also considers the most famous of the institutionalists, Thorstein Veblen, as well as Joseph Schumpeter, whose career and interests combine a particular awareness of culture and institutions with a secure acceptance within the mainstream, and whose influential opinions come up repeatedly in commentary in our travel through the history of economic thought.

The *Methodenstreit*

The victory of neoclassical economics, especially in England, was in historical terms quick and lasting. Whilst the victory of neoclassical economics should not be confused with a victory of pro-market policies, Walras, Wicksteed, and Wicksell among its important figures were, as we saw, radicals or socialists, Marshall was motivated by a concern for the poor (and incidentally praised the German Historical School's method in an appendix to the *Principles*), and Menger accepted a role, if limited, for the state. Yet on the continent, where late developer nations ceded a significant role to the state (most especially in Germany), marginalism and general equilibrium theorizing seemed too restrictive to those who saw statist leadership as essential to national wellbeing. Hegel's privileging of the mystical state spirit, and Bismarck's very practical use of bureaucratic reformism in his revolution from the top, were part of a nationalist tradition of great suppleness, capable of encompassing capitalist nation builders and junker militarists. Germany, and Prussia before unification, as a late industrializer was more comfortable with mercantilist regulation and bureaucratic control. Public administration was a science to be cultivated and the masses encouraged in a servile nationalism. Whilst in England free trade doctrines reigned supreme and abstract models of capitalism as a universally homogeneous ahistoric reality were congenial (with Great Britain ruling the waves and the sun never setting on its empire), in Germany the governing class took the role of building state power quite seriously.

In the academy, the German experience produced the Historical School, which may be dated from the publication in the 1840s of Frederick List's defense of the protection of infant industries as a strategy of state-led development. He had been influenced by Alexander Hamilton's 'Report on Manufactures,' which had urged temporary protection of the domestic market from superior British manufactured goods as a way of stimulating industry in the newly independent United States. List presented a petition for a customs union to the Federal Assembly on behalf of an association of merchants and manufacturers he had organized. The idea was to create a large, unified, internal market in Germany, where thirty-eight customs boundaries crippled trade. Whilst List ended up in prison for eight months and was deported for this radical act and related activities, in 1834 the *Zollverein* was established and the influence of his thinking widely appreciated.[2]

What is known as the older historical school, which reigned in mid-century, saw its historical approach as supplementing classical political economy's laws and theories. The five volume textbook *Economic Science*, written by the most prominent of the older historical school figures, William Roscher, had taken him forty years to complete. Roscher was a child of German romanticism and idealism. He was a conservative for whom sociological considerations were uppermost. His was a political economy in close collaboration with the other 'sciences of national life, above all those of law, politics and culture' (Stark 1994: 5). The flavor of the way he saw the study of economics is captured in the focus on public administration and the science of finance, both in service to the state and bound up in a historic approach to the organic essence of the national economy. He writes:

> If, by the public economy of a nation, we understand economic legislation and the government guidance or direction of the economy of private persons, the science of public economy becomes, so far as its form is concerned, a branch

of political science, while as its matter, its subject is almost coincidental with that of political economy.

(Marx 1968: 123)[3]

The applied administration of the public household idea of economics continues with Gustav Schmoller, who founded the Association of Social Policy and was leader of the younger historical school which wanted to supersede the English approach to economics root and branch. Schmoller holds that the essence of the economic process is lost once there is a fragmentation and a consideration of separate elements in isolation. The essence of Schmoller's approach to economics, Yuichi Shionoya tells us, 'was the recognition that institutions are not only physical and technical but also ethical and psychological, thus enabling the individual agent to behave on plural motivations' (Shionoya 1991: 199–200). In 1897 Schmoller wrote, rather over optimistically as things turned out, that:

> Contemporary economics has arrived at a historical and ethical perception of state and society, in contrast to rationalism and materialism. From a mere theory of market and exchange, a kind of business economics which at one time threatened to become a class-weapon of the propertied, it has once again become a great moral and political science, which along side the production of goods investigates their distribution, institutions, which once more places man at the centre of the science instead of the world of goods and capital.
>
> (Hennis 1987: 39)

The school loses importance in the eyes of most historians of economic thought after 1915, the year of Schmoller's death, although as a matter of historical record some of its members aligned themselves with Nazism, and social market thinkers in the years after the war were also influential. The economic thought literature concentrates on the defeat of the historical school in what has come to be known as the Battle of the Methods *(Methodenstreit)* in the closing decades of the nineteenth century. Schmoller opposed Carl Menger's attempt to make economics more exact, abstract, and deductive. To Schmoller, Menger's models were empty formulations. He criticized the Robinsonades of the 1880s for their ahistoricism. To Menger, the Historical School with its 'so-called "ethical orientation" of political economy' is simply 'a confusion in thought' and 'devoid of any deeper meaning.' The *Methodenstreit* was characterized by insults and polarization, out of which the neoclassicals carried the day and came to dominate the profession.

Menger's achievement was to give pride of theoretical place to autonomous, atomistic, economic man (and by extension the individual unit patriarchal household) and to the business firm (also presumed to be run by an owner who held single-minded authority over its employees). The proper unit of analysis is these 'individual economies,' as he called them. One could not scientifically aggregate to such confused categories as classes or even nations. The reason there can be no such collective interests is a simple matter: only individuals have interests. The national economy, thought Menger, is not really an economy itself in the strict meaning of the word; it is merely an organized complex of individual economies. Today, economists who take the position that there is no such thing, strictly speaking, as national competitiveness or macroeconomics, but only microeconomic analysis built on individual economic units, follow in this tradition. Collective categories not built from atomistic or individualistic microfoundations are illegitimate according to both. Indeed, Menger is seen by some as the true founder of the tradition of methodological individualism (Bostaph 1978).

The Historical School is not without important influence in Europe, however, where both state policy and local historical specificity in analysis are part of accepted economic science (Frey and Eichenberger 1993), and in America through the influence of those who studied in Germany and came back to take part in founding American institutionalism. The American institutionalists were able to move beyond the enumeration without theory and data collection as almost an end in itself. Veblen was very critical of the school, expressing the view that no economics was farther from being an evolutionary science than the Historical School (Veblen 1919: 217).

Even though Schmoller's name rarely appears in the American institutionalist literature, he was an influence on writers like Joseph Schumpeter and Karl Polanyi. The latter, an anthropologist who has had major influence on many institutionalist-inclined economists, took from Schmoller

> the historical analysis of the centrality of the state in organizing and developing what was allegedly a natural phenomenon – the growth of markets. Schmoller argued that national markets were foreign to natural progress, but had been historically foisted onto emerging national territories as critical phases in nation-state building for purposes of both internal unification and external war-making.
>
> (Somers 1990: 155)

The reason such a seemingly secondary insight is important is that in denying that markets were 'natural,' Polanyi is led to examine how they are instituted and the forms of resistance to the market mentality. He shows that it has been necessary to limit the functioning of free markets to preserve the capitalist system from being undone by the disruptions to the social order that it unleashes. Markets function best in a socially constrained setting in which rules are imposed on it and enforced in socially acceptable ways. It is this claim that limitation on markets is essential to a better functioning economic system that is at the heart of the institutionalist project. Polanyi's contention was that the success of market development was dependent on political regulation in order to preserve the existing social coherence of the society in which markets were embedded, but also because states were far more effective in pushing trade and capturing fields of enterprise than the unhampered activity of individual economic actors could have been. Polanyi's argument, that the greater the significance of markets, the greater the role of the state (ibid.), is worth considering in an era of neoliberal restructuring.

As the battle with the landowning class was behind them, and a rising working class looked to the state to regulate the power of the employer class, the powerful interests that controlled the state became less enamored with legislative interventions which they thought they no longer needed to impose market relations, and which should not be used by others to limit the power of the market. In defense of the freedom to accumulate, a new version of natural law appeared attractive. It was embodied in the neoclassical approach to economic science. Policy was to be discussed within narrow limits circumscribed by the new division of labor, which took the outlines of the existing distribution of resources in society for granted. Conservatives in the German Historical School interpreted matters differently and looked to the government to produce a more internationally competitive economy and to project German state power. To some extent we may suspect that the clash originated not in the debate over scientific method but with the pre-analytic vision of participants that led them to a socially holistic approach. German economic science in the nineteenth century retained a strong ethical component and never questioned the interdependence of state and economy (Melton 1991: 147). The legacy of the Historical School is still evident in the different manner in which most continental economists do economics to this day.

In the academy, Max Weber, a generation younger than Schmoller and Menger, proposed ending the split through a synthesis of theory and history to reconstruct economics. In pursuit of this goal, Weber started upon a major project – a giant handbook of economics – and invited theoretical economists, historical economists, and practitioners of the emerging discipline of sociology to contribute. He hoped they would each see that the work of the others was necessary to the success of their own efforts. Weber, a professor of political economy and sociology at Fribourg, considered himself to be an intellectual descendant of Schmoller, but he also tried to hold the social sciences together. His most famous work, *The Protestant Ethic and the Rise of Capitalism*, is still a classic, although read more by others in the social sciences than by economists.

Weber advocated socio-economics as a broad tent undertaking combining economics, history, and sociology. Such breadth would allow economics to be combined with the historical approach and so enable economists to absorb a keener appreciation of the ways ideas and material conditions interrelate. Richard Swedberg, a person very attentive of the need for the renewal of such a project, paraphrases Weber's message this way:

> [H]istorians mainly look at details and economists at what is general; but there is also a need for an intermediate perspective – sociology – which puts these two into contact with each other. This, however, did not mean that Weber wanted sociology to replace theoretical economics or history. On the contrary, all three are essential to a full analysis, and 'socioeconomics' was to be constituted through a dialogue between them.
>
> (Swedberg 1991: 34)

Something along the lines of such a socio-economics was attempted in America, where it went by the name of institutionalism.

Institutionalism

This influence of the German Historical School, and even the American version of *Methodenstreit*, took place in the 1880s between that particularly American application of the competitive model, in which markets provide for the survival of the fittest, that we call Social Darwinism. Its influence on the profession was substantial and led Richard T. Ely, a student of German Historical economics, to come back to the United States and to challenge *laissez-faire*-oriented deterministic social science. Indeed, his purpose in founding the American Economic Association (AEA) was to fight the influence of 'the Sumner, Newcomb crowd.' (William Graham Sumner was the leading Social Darwinist and Simon Newcomb a follower of Jevons.) Among the strong influences on institutionalism was the Christian social gospel movement of the period. Both Ely and Commons were participants in, and strongly influenced by, the Christian socialism of their time and very much of the milieu among whose other public faces were Henry George, Eugene Debs, Lester Ward, and Josiah Strong (Gonce 1996 and Cort 1988).

Ely, whose 1893 *Outline of Economics* was the American textbook most widely used by economics professors for forty years, believed in a progressive activism in which economists did their part to make the world a better place. He wanted to purge the profession of the idea that natural laws beyond human manipulation governed social existence. Since Newcomb advocated the benevolence of the invisible hand and thought that economics, through greater use of mathematics, could become a positive science free of the contamination of moral judgment, the cast seemed to have the lines of the *Methodenstreit* down fairly well – as translated into the American idiom. It is a sign of the trajectory the American mainstream has taken that on the occasion of the hundredth anniversary of the Association that he founded, Ely was denounced, personally calumniated as an opportunist. Celebrants were urged to toast Simon Newcomb as their true spiritual progenitor (Barber 1987).

It is important as an antidote to such 1980s-style thinking to see why Ely's political economy is hardly mentioned in such attacks. The founders of the AEA, and not only Ely, 'maintained that there is a close relationship between ethics and economics, considered economic truth relative rather than absolute, championed the inductive method, and criticized the assumptions of the laissez-faire credo with respect to self-interest and competition' (Fine 1956: 200). Ely wrote that the emergent political economy he wished the AEA to represent 'does not acknowledge laissez-faire as an excuse for doing nothing while people starve, nor allow the all-efficiency of competition as a plea for grinding the poor' (Hofstadter 1944: 146). It is easy to see why some *au courant* economists of the Decade of Greed wished to deny such paternity. There is an old-fashioned morality here that hardly accords with contemporary conventions. The most important aspect of the thinkers who founded the American Economic Association, which sets them at odds with the *Zeitgeist* of the Reagan Era and its legacy, is their attitude toward government. As Ely made clear, what the Association was committed to was advocacy of a positive, fostering role of the state which, he said, should be construed as not paternalism, but fraternalism. Henry Carter Adams, another of the founding fathers, wrote, it is not 'the best government which governs least, but which governs the most wisely' (Adams 1891: 43)[4]. The normative political economy of these founders of the American Economic Association, from my perspective, holds up quite well a century later.

This chapter cannot be the occasion to join in this particular possible canon revision contestation, although we may share William Baumol's observation that these earlier economists 'were able to offer a great deal by way of innovation and insight dependent on no well-defined methodological approach. Their procedure was free swinging reliance on an amalgam of intuition, observation, erudition and sheer opinionatedness' (Baumol 1985). Over the hundred years since the Association's founding, while the profession has grown more systematic in its methods, and not simply in the use of mathematics, Baumol suggests that whether we see this as an unqualified improvement remains a matter of opinion.

Baumol's characterization of these economists' 'free swinging reliance on an amalgam of intuition, observation, erudition and sheer opinionatedness' surely is apt for characterizing the person whose work we consider next, who, like Ely, was a founder of the institutionalist tradition and a man widely considered to have been 'the most significant, original, and profound social theorist in American history,' and 'the most creative mind American social thought has produced' (Lerner 1948: 2). He is Thorstein Veblen, a giant that not one economist in a thousand has read.

Thorstein Veblen

Thorstein Veblen grew up on the Wisconsin frontier. His father was a master carpenter and builder whom the son later described as having the finest mind he had ever known. He sent his children (girls and boys) to college. Veblen went to the small Minnesota college, Carlton, where his economics teacher was John Bates Clark. It is not quite true that Veblen was 'an early Chicago economist' (even if he did edit the *Journal of Political Economy* while he was on the economics faculty at the University of Chicago); his books like *The Theory of Business Enterprise*, which described the 1880s and 1890s as the 'sleaziest decades of American civilization,' were hardly a celebration of the magic of the marketplace. For Veblen, production is always a social process. 'This natural rights theory of property makes the creative effort of an isolated, self-sufficing individual the basis of ownership vested in him,' Veblen writes of the neoclassical position.

> In so doing it overlooks the fact that there is no isolated, self-sufficing individual . . . .Production takes place only in society – only through the co-operation of an industrial community. This industrial community may be large or small . . . but it always comprises a group large enough to contain and transmit the traditions, tools, technical knowledge, and usages without which there can be no industrial organization.
>
> (Veblen 1964: 33–4)

Veblen was more than an institutionalist; he was a political radical. For Veblen, freedom in the economic system of his time means freedom for capital. Capital controlled the government, he thought. The socialization process and the indoctrination working people receive is part of what keeps the system going. Government selects its administrators and policy makers from the ranks of lawyers and bankers, 'practical men' whose conceptions and convictions 'are such as will necessarily emerge from continued and successful experience in the conduct of business of that character.' To such people, says Veblen, 'the logic of ownership becomes second nature.' What American society of his time witnessed, he thought, was the reduction of human society to business society, the complexity of human emotion to monetary and market relations. Not only is the social harmony presumption of neoclassical economics far from the mark, but Veblen understood labor relations in terms of class conflict.

Economics to Veblen was not simply a matter of the logical and the rational. He rejected the idea that we can have a useful economic science that banishes 'wasteful, disserviceable or futile acts.' He saw too many of them all around him. As to the neoclassicals economics of 'a friendly rivalry in the service of mankind at large, with an eye to the greatest happiness of the greatest number' (Hunt 1992: 396), he also saw appropriations that took place at the expense of weaker participants and/or the community at large (Hodgson 1992b).

Veblen is sensitive to an aspect of the nature of capitalism that has become increasingly important in our own time among transaction theorists and the new institutional economists who, though in a different manner than Veblen, also talk about the importance of legal rights, contract, understandings, and mutuality of expectations for the functioning of markets. Without the fabric of relating that institutions provide, and the expectations that a culture leads one to have of others, markets would break down. The economy shapes people's habits for good and ill. It produces deformed human beings such as the lawyer, 'exclusively occupied with the details of predatory fraud, either in achieving it or in checkmating chicane.' The lawyers who succeed, says Veblen, are those with 'a large endowment of that barbarian astuteness which has always commanded men's respect and fear.' Veblen reserves his admiration for the engineer and the skilled craftsperson who do their job well out of the instinct of workmanship. It is easy to see why economists are uncomfortable and insist that Veblen is not really an economist, a sociologist maybe, but not one of us.

It is no more possible to summarize his thinking and the areas of our understanding to which his contributions are important than it has been with the other economists we have discussed, though one can list sharp dichotomies between Veblen's thinking and that of the mainstream. Veblen's celebration of the engineer, the craftsman whose pride in workmanship drove him to make the best products he could, in contrast to the businessman who only wanted to make a profit and would sell any shoddy thing to do so, is not a judgment mainstream economics accepts. The dualities of Veblenesque economic categories are at the theoretical core of his thinking: workmanship contrasts to salesmanship, technological proficiency to pecuniary management, the engineer to the price system. He had some hopes for the technically trained workers who would see how a better system could be built to replace the profit grubbing and destructive one he saw operating around him, but he was not a Marxist: he thought the workers could be bought off.

What Veblen left was appreciation that economics needed an adequate psychology and a greater respect for the centrality of institutions and culture in economics. His message, above all, was that economics needed to be an evolutionary science. Numerous Veblenesque signatures appear in the history of the profession's engagement with its own nature. For example, when one reads in Kenneth Boulding's presidential address to the American Economic Association, forty years after Veblen's death, the following, one thinks of Veblen:

> One of the most peculiar illusions of economists is a doctrine that might be called the Immaculate Conception of the Indifference Curve, that is, that tastes are simply given, and that we cannot inquire into the process by which they are formed.
>
> (Boulding 1969: 1–2)

It is not surprising that Boulding credits the idea to Veblen that 'we cannot afford to neglect the processes by which cultures are created and by which preferences are learned' (ibid.: 2); and we suspect that Boulding was proud of his trope, 'the Immaculate Conception of the Indifference Curve,' which brings to mind Veblen's mocking description of neoclassical economic man.[5]

Because of Veblen's biting ability to turn a phrase and his facility to cut to the quick of the issue, his very phrases – 'the leisure class' or 'conspicuous consumption' – have become part of our vocabulary. It should not be thought that other astute contemporaries did not understand the nature of advertising and its ability to shift demand curves. Alfred Marshall, whose exposition of demand and supply in the marketplace continues to set the standard treatment observers, even as he impounded such concerns in *ceteris paribus* assumptions necessary to produce rigorous A mode comparative static results, suggested on other occasions, as in the following passage from *Trade and Industry*, that he certainly was not oblivious to the importance of such matters of interpersonal utility and the power of salesmanship:

> Changes in fashion are not now products of a wayward fancy, which is its own reward. They are, in large part at all events, deliberately planned several months before they obtain vogue. They are planned with a view to successful effect; for if they fail in that, they reap only a short-lived commercial success. But those who control them have always a general interest in causing anyone, who wishes not to be out of fashion, to discard the costumes of last season
>
> (Marshall 1919: 809)

A useful institutionalism speaks to the central economic issues of its time (as Veblen did) and does so in a way that is interesting, recognizable, and accessible to its audience. This is unlikely to be in six volumes of minutely recorded idiosyncratic efforts striving for completeness. It is therefore not Roscher or Schmoller but

Veblen whose living genius still dazzles new readers, but by its nature there can be no 'Veblenism.' In 1925, four years before he died, Thorstein Veblen was offered the presidency of the American Economic Association. He refused it. Having been kicked around from school to school, unable to find a steady university job for most of his life, he asked 'They didn't offer it when I needed it, why should I take it now?'

Few economists have written about the nature of our civilization with such facility. The writer who comes closest, although as a stylist he is in a different mold, is not an economist but the anthropologist Karl Polanyi, whom we have cited in a number of places. The division of the social sciences makes his work less than familiar to economists than Veblen's. The institutionalist tradition continues in America, of course, and its major tenets remain important for a profession that continues to ignore them. Ray Marshall, drawing on the writing of Wendell Gordon, suggests that institutionalists, despite their differences, agree with the view that 'the economy is an ongoing process, causing them to be skeptical of orthodox economics' assumption that there was a large body of positive economics unrelated to time, place, and circumstances.' Institutionalists stress 'the importance of the interactions between institutions, technology, and values.' They criticize orthodoxy for 'being too deductive, static, and abstract' (Marshall 1993: 302, drawing on Gordon 1980).

John R. Commons, institutions, and the New Institutionalism

John R. Commons is the final institutionalist singled out for discussion before moving on. His study of collective action and what today would be called governance made the important distinction between three types of transaction costs, which it is interesting to compare to later more restricted understandings of contemporary transaction cost theorists (Ramstad 1996). The bargaining transactions of buying and selling that concerned economists needed to be understood in the context of the managerial transactions, those concerned with the command relation of employer and employee and other superior–subordinate situations, and a third category which contemporary transaction cost theorists are yet to valiance properly, rationing transactions, the sharing out of costs and benefits in organization of a society. The last is important because growth is always (re)distributional, and the legal system and broader institutional context, what has been called the cultural economy (Tabb 1995: 293–4), plays a major role in structuring the incidence of costs and rewards. Transactions, for Commons, involve psychology, jurisprudence, ethics, and politics, as well as economics more narrowly (Commons 1924: 5). They are a conceptual tool of B mode analysis. Later transaction theorists were to narrow the usage so that it would fit determinative A mode analysis. The New Institutionalism is not concerned with the sociopolitical institutions of the larger society or the cultural structures that constrain and guide choices and are themselves shaped by the economy. We will return to these issues in Chapter 10.

Commons thought that the biological metaphor was inappropriate in its Darwinian implication of natural selection. Such a usage, he thought, rather than being a departure from the mainstream was simply a variant of natural law theory (since people could only adapt to conditions and not change them). Social evolution allowed for artificial selection. Humans could meet challenges, he thought, by modifying their environment. Evolutionary economics is the study of the process of change, institutional creation. We are influenced by habit and tradition, constrained by past and present, but we also make choices, and make up new collective possibilities through collective action, above all though government.

Commons declared that 'the highest individualism' comes from an enabling governance structure, writing:

> If governmental control serves to stimulate the self-reliant energies of the people, if it opens up new avenues for private enterprise, if it equalizes and widens the opportunity for employment, if it prevents injustice, oppression, and monopoly, if it stimulates a noble ambition, inspires hopefulness, and vouchsafes rewards where they are earned, then government is not socialistic but rather is supplementing the highest individualism.
>
> (Commons, as cited in Fine 1956: 210)

These American institutionalists, as the passage just cited attests, maintained a middle course between the radical socialism of their day and its economic orthodoxy. Very soon, however, the American Economic Association (having grown to be an inclusive professional organization) moved away from its founding declarations and assertive sympathies. If, in 1887, the AEA could publish Adam's most significant contribution, 'Reflections of the State to Industrial Action,' the 1888 convention abandoned the statement of founding principles and declared that the association would 'take no partisan attitudes,' or 'commit its members to any position on practical economic questions.' Such institutionalization, as any good institutionalist should know, was inevitable. There can be no binding orthodoxy for a broad scholarly organization open to all members of a profession, but the reforming and crusading moment, and its wider impact on American politics, should not be missed. Professor Barber's account of Ely and the early days of the American Economic Association (cited earlier in this chapter) should not be allowed to stand unchallenged. We may ask, no matter how appropriate to the state of economics and political caste of economic policy in the 1980s, if there is more that is worth remembering concerning what should and should not have been celebrated on the centennial of the Association's founding.

Economics students are more apt these days to learn about a New Institutionalism than to be aware of the older institutionalist tradition. For 'old' institutionalists like Commons, all transactions are 'instituted' phenomena, they are structured arising from chosen practices, strategies, customs, and so forth. To Ronald Coase or Oliver Williamson, the most important figures in the transaction cost approach of the new institutionalism, costs, including transaction costs, are natural and given within the technological interfaces of production and organization, and neoclassical principles can be extended to explain the economics of the firm and its governance. In general, the new institutionalists focus on the ways individuals create institutions and emphasize formal techniques, whilst the old institutionalists describe how institutions mold individuals and employ non-formal techniques. Government and power are important to the latter, whilst individualistic normative criteria are the focus of the former.[6] The difference between the two conforms quite nicely with our A/B distinction.

New institutionalists explain the emergence of institutions as the intended or unintended consequence of rational individual behavior. The analysis presumes individuals as given and prior to the creation of institutions. Such methodological individualism preserves the neoclassical understanding of the individual with autonomously determined preferences. In this regard, the crucial point made by institutionalism (meaning 'old' institutionalism) is that institutions are long lived, typically outlasting individuals who are born into institutional settings. This temporal priority suggests that individuals are socialized within specific institutional settings and so institutions are logically privileged over a general historical model of the individual agent (Hodgson 1998). Individuals, in turn, modify the operation of inherited institutions but within a context of relative institutional invariance over long periods, which also constrain individual behavior. It is not so much that we have to make a choice of one method to the exclusion of the other, but that we need to remember that men and women make their own history to be sure, but not in any way they choose. They are constrained (but not determined) by the situations they inherit.

Healing the breach?

McCloskey and others have called attention to the cost to economics of its isolation from the other social sciences, suggesting that there is much to be learned from conversations not only within the discipline but across its borders (McCloskey 1985). This is not a new concern. In the early years of the twentieth century when the separation of the social sciences was still new, Albion Small, a founder of American sociology, expressed the view that 'sterility must be the fate of every celibate social science' and worried about the deliberate and 'abstinent programs of non-intercourse' proposed by the economists (Small 1972: vi). Economics represented a narrowing down, a devolution from the richness of political economy before the division of the social sciences in the late nineteenth century. There are a number of people who are now redefining the boundaries, with the most explicit dialogues taking place between economists and sociologists, although some economists think the conversation should be much broader. (George Akerlof, for example, has called for the development of a psycho-socio-anthropo-economics.) At the start of the 1990s, Richard Swedberg suggested that 'the opportunity now exists to break with old habits and to redraw the boundaries between economics and sociology' (Swedberg 1990: 3). It is possible he was right, but it will not be an easy undertaking.

Progress in such an enterprise faces the same A/B division we have encountered so often in discussing the history of economic thought. In addition, there is the matter of disciplinary partisanship. and even chauvinism. James Coleman, for example, thinks economics will one day become part of sociology. Gary Becker, whose approach is the economic-sociology (with the hyphen), believes it will be the other way around – sociology will be part of economics. Within sociology, Mark Granovetter, an economic sociology man (without the hyphen and a staunch Becker foe), is closer to the political economy of Veblen than to the sociological tradition of Talcott Parsons, whose elaborate abstractions, systems, and subsystems of coordination and pattern maintenance are called structural-functionalism or normative functionalism, and is very A mode. Parsons is perhaps the most influential sociologist of the last half century and a lightning rod of A/B debate in sociology. Robert Solow's brief on Gary Becker's work is that it 'oscillates between the obvious and the false' (ibid.: 276). His judgment is not untypical of economists' reactions to Becker's economic-sociology:

> I just find that when I read him, my response usually falls into one of two categories. Either I feel that I do not need all this apparatus to reach these obvious conclusions. Or I say to myself, 'How could anyone believe this to be true?'
>
> (ibid.: 135)

Kenneth Arrow (like Solow and Becker a Nobel laureate in economics) finds Parsons' theoretical work 'tautological,' 'preposterous,' 'very empty and grandiose' (ibid.).[7]

This does not mean that even traditionalist sociologists accept Gary Becker's efforts to enlighten their discipline through applied neoclassical economics. Neil Smelser, who investigates economic sociology from the sociology side, says of Becker's unrealistic assumptions (for example that there is complete knowledge in the 'market' for spouses, and of the judgment criteria of economic benefits derived from spouse selection), 'Now, this is patently ridiculous, if you will excuse my language' (ibid.: 208). One might also point to other examples that originate in an extreme atomistic modeling that have raised hackles, such as explanations that discrimination against African Americans is a matter of taste (some people prefer opera to rock, pizza to burgers, white people to black people), or that the white who discriminates against a qualified black hurts themself and so pays for indulging their taste. Competition will solve the problem in any case, since in the marketplace competition will drive out discriminating employers, in this view.[8] Reconciliation will clearly not be easy, in large measure because of intra-disciplinary A versus B complications. Analysts look for causal explanations within different realms. The methodological individualism of A mode theorizing is essentially similar across the disciplinary lines, and B side theorists can have more in common with colleagues in other departments than with A mode colleagues in their own.

From its beginnings, neoclassical economics has had substantial influence within sociology. Pareto's circulation of elites (it was he who, deriving the idea from Mosca, gave the name elite to the ruling few) followed his formalization of the

Walrasian general equilibrium model (he had succeeded Walras in the chair at Lausanne). His aim at mapping the sources of non-rational behavior, to create a general theory of sociology, reflected a belief in the possibility of going beyond economic man in a science of society while still basing the work on methodological individualism. Pareto's distinction is that economics studies rational action and sociology studies irrational action. After his significant contributions to economics he turned to sociology because, he said, it was more of a challenge. Indeed, Pareto is an interesting case in terms of conventional economics understanding of him, which is limited to 'Pareto optimality,' a term understood by all economists and frequently taught to freshmen. It is the criterion that a redistributional act is unambiguously acceptable if it makes even one person better off without making anyone else worse off. Economists like to limit redistribution to cases that are Pareto optimal, which is to say, to very, very few cases.[9]

Of course, economists do not actually read Pareto, and it is a good thing, for this is another one of those Robinson Crusoe stories. Pareto's own work demonstrates the importance of power in the economy. His intention was to provide a general equilibrium model of the total socio-politico-economic decision making or policy process in terms of a complex psychology and politics of choice. As Warren Samuels tells us, Pareto's work demonstrates

> the presumptive and narrow character of the new welfare economics which pretends to speak in terms of the Pareto rule; he demonstrates how the actual economic world is, as a matter of fact, almost exactly opposite to the picture conveyed by the rule and the microeconomics supporting it.
>
> (Samuels 1974: xi)

Within sociology, there has since its early days also been a strong scientistic strand that urges the field to stick to positivist analysis and stay away from normative pronouncements. At the first meeting of the German Sociological Association, Ferdinand Toinnes argued for the positive (as against normative) non-partisan nature of sociology of the A mode character, asserting: 'We wish therefore as sociologists to concern ourselves only with what is, not with what, from whatever the viewpoint, or whatever grounds, should be' (Frisby 1969: xxiv). Comptian sociology shares the modernist aspirations of economics in its search for invariant laws. In this tradition, Talcott Parsons (although his writing has not appealed to many economists) was quite reverential toward the queen of the social sciences and tried in his own work to build a science along precise taxonomical lines.[10]

More recent efforts to heal the breach by James Coleman have been received with interest by some economists. Coleman's formal models assume people start out with exogenously determined interests and endowments but expand the framework of rational action to include norms, social capital, and other group-dependent elements. Whilst his work has been applauded by these economists (Frank 1992), major figures in sociology have been critical of what is seen as 'individualism askew' (Tilly 1991). If economics and sociology are coming together, and there is some evidence that they are (Baron and Hannan 1994), it is with regard to economists' growing interest in incentives, information, and strategic action, which brings them closer to non-market explanations based on cooperation, custom, and bounded rationality. This is a return to concerns close to the heart of the founders of sociology.

In the first section of *Economy and Society*, Weber defines sociology as a science that attempts the interpretative understanding of social action. He notes that 'Action is social insofar, by virtue of the subjective meaning attached to it by the acting individual (or individuals), it takes account of the behavior of others . . . .' It is just this *social* nature of choice that is denied by neoclassical economics; to the extent that we deny the usefulness of the economic man assumption, we are starting with sociology and not with economics, or, more accurately perhaps, we are returning to political economy before 1870. This perspective was marginalized within economics but carried forward by Weber, and is implicit in the social terrain of sociology. It is an effort to capture the holism of social experience, which economic science would fragment into the discourses of the post-*Methodenstreit* division of the social sciences.

Weber's first chapter of *Economy and Society* makes clear that social relations based on calculated attempts to achieve desired ends is only *one* type of social relation. Others are based on sentiment, long-established custom, and belief in the intrinsic value of acting in certain ways. An appreciation of moral philosophy needs to be part of any economic sociology. The reductionism of given institutions and limited incentive structures that made economics a science in the eighteenth-century physics sense, is what is at stake in the defense of economic-sociology as against economic sociology. In 1994 Neil Smelser and Richard Swedberg published what may prove to be a landmark volume: *The Handbook of Economic Sociology*. In a very real sense it is the modern incarnation of Weber's design for such a defining compendium of essays by leading practitioners of both economic-sociology, and economic sociology along with other important scholars who may not be easily classified in either camp. Economists may be less inclined to consider such a volume (due to the broadness of its coverage and the presence of so many non-economists).[11]

Schumpeter

Joseph Schumpeter saw the Battle of Method as a disaster for economics. In 1926 he published an essay, 'Gustav von Schmoller and the Problems of Today', in which he lauded Schmoller's research program as a prototype for social economics or economic sociology, suggesting it might be the solution to the *Methodenstreit* (Schumpeter 1954: 20). This is what Weber had proposed two decades earlier. Schumpeter (like Weber) tried to go beyond the *Methodenstreit* and develop a positive synthesis of historical economics and analytical economics (Swedberg 1991: 83 and Shionoya 1991). He offered the injunction that economics (or rather as he chose to say *Sozialoekonomik*, social economics) should consist of four fundamental fields – theory, economic history, statistics, and economic sociology.[12] All are crucial to scientific economic analysis in Schumpeter's view. This was a logical conclusion given Schumpeter's background and interests.

When Schumpeter completed his university education, he applied for permission to lecture in three areas: economics, statistics, and sociology. (He could also have taught law or political science.) In his appointment as the only professor of economics at Graz, he lectured on all aspects of economics as well as social science more broadly. Before coming to Harvard he was a banker and Minister of Finance in his native Austria. In training, experience, and breadth of interest he was an anomaly in the American economics profession. Schumpeter, a good mathematician, was critical of the uses to which economists put mathematics, and though appreciative of what he considered the proper place of mathematics and statistics in economics, came to see the approach as beginning to monopolize and so diminish the field.[13]

He saw the indispensable need for there to be a sociological core of economics. He also believed strongly in the need for history. How the system performs at any one point in time cannot meaningfully be considered aside from the question of how it performs over time (Coe and Wilbur 1985: 5). Needless to say, the institutional investigations he had in mind are not those of the neoclassical model. He argues against the view that because a perfectly competitive economy is statically efficient, it is therefore superior to monopoly. Market power gives capitalists the ability to take risks and provides the excess profits that allow the new to be tried. Schumpeter wrote 'The introduction of new methods of production and new commodities is hardly conceivable with perfect – and perfectly prompt – competition from the start. And this means that the bulk of what we call economic progress is incompatible with it' (Schumpeter 1942: 105). Economic progress requires being able to capture economic rents from successful innovations.

Success of the enterprise in Schumpeter's mind was not a matter of equating marginal cost and marginal revenue but actively seeking changes in technology and organization. It can certainly be argued that it is still the case today that 'non-recognition of this is the most important single reason for what appears unsatisfactory to us in economic theory' (Schumpeter 1961: 61). Schumpeter thought perfect competition not only impossible but inferior, and certainly 'has no title to being set up as a model of ideal efficiency' (Schumpeter 1942: 106). The Schumpeterian world is dominated by large firms who know how they exercise influence over the market. Capitalism is a dynamic system and no model of steady growth comes near understanding its essence. What happens over time is not more of the same on some improved basis but revolutionary changes in production processes and product mix. The fundamental impulse that sets the capitalist engine in motion and keeps it churning comes from new commodities, ways of producing and selling them, from new markets and modes of transportation, and forms of organization that capitalist entrepreneurs create. It is this dynamism that 'incessantly revolutionizes the economic structure *from within*, incessantly destroying the old, incessantly creating the new one. This process of Creative Destruction is the essential fact about capitalism' (ibid.: 83).

The essential point to grasp, Schumpeter thought, is that in dealing with capitalism we are dealing with an evolutionary process.[14] Indeed, he thought it strange that anyone can fail to see so obvious a fact which, moreover, was long ago emphasized by Karl Marx.[15] 'Yet the fragmentary analysis which yields the bulk of our propositions about the functioning of modern capitalism persistently neglects it' (Fellner 1981: 82). Schumpeter discusses the similarities and differences between himself and Marx extensively, but what he left out, for the most part without much comment, was the construction of class that was so central to Marx and absent from his own way of thinking.

To a Marxist it is the case, as Michael Kalecki writes, that whilst many economists assume 'at least in their abstract theories, a state of business democracy where anybody endowed with entrepreneurial ability can obtain capital for starting a business venture,' this picture of the activities of the 'pure' entrepreneur, Kalecki critically comments, 'is to put it mildly, unrealistic. The most important prerequisite for becoming an entrepreneur is the *ownership* of capital' (Kalecki 1952: 94–5). For Schumpeter such details of how the entrepreneur gets access to necessary funds is quite secondary. The centrality of the entrepreneur in organizational and technological innovation is the dynamic heart of capitalism. The 'perennial gale of creative destruction' represents a threat to the most established entrepreneur. The drive to be rich and famous spurs all on to the next great breakthroughs, whether they be Teenage Mutant Ninja Turtles or interactive video.

Schumpeter was well aware that this pattern of growth imposed what economists are inclined to call 'short-run costs' on society. A dynamic society creates unemployment, bankruptcies, and farm foreclosures. He thought that eventually, on the one side, the victims would grow unwilling to pay these costs and, on the other, the corporate structure would systematize the entrepreneurial function. He also worried about the family and feared that if the rich did not have children they would be less inclined to accumulate and build dynasties. Other aspects of Schumpeterian thought have also become popular, such as his ideas concerning the 'tax state', for example; although the contrast between Schumpeter's own formulation and its popular political formulations is substantial.[16]

Whilst Schumpeter had contempt for Marshall's notion of the representative firm, he shared the latter's lifecycle view of companies, like trees in the forest competing for light, the most successful growing to great heights but eventually succumbing to age and dying. Believing that innovation and entrepreneurial vigor came from the new firm, he saw the process of the incessant rise and decay of firms and industries as central to the nature of capitalist development. Schumpeter used Simon Kuznets' findings from *Secular Movements in Production and Prices* (1930) that the key trends in prices and in production were systematically associated with the lifecycle of a given technological or other type of innovation, new discovery of natural resource, the opening up of a new territory. The phasing of rapid then decelerating growth is the impersonal formulation of Schumpeter's theory of the entrepreneurial-led cycle. Empirically, both Kuznets' twenty-year cycle and Schumpeter's bunching of innovations as the driving force of capitalist development have been questioned (and the fit is surely not precise), yet for certain periods the episodes of cyclical growth do seem to be explained in these ways. Historical specificity and not some *ex cathedra* explanation is suggested.

He considered the subject matter of economics as essentially a unique process in historical time. His view was that 'Nobody can hope to understand the economic phenomena of any, including the present epoch, who has not an adequate command of historical *facts* and adequate amount of historical *sense*.' He believed that the historical report could not be purely economic but must inevitably reflect 'institutional facts.' Understanding how 'economic and non-economic facts are related to one another and how the various social sciences *should* be related to one another' was part of the task of being an economist. It was the lack of historical sense more than any other shortcoming that led to fundamental errors committed in economic analysis (Schumpeter 1954: 12–13).

After his theorizing on the role of the entrepreneur, Schumpeter is perhaps best known for what Paul Samuelson has called his 'predilection of capitalism's psychosomatic demise as a result of self-induced will not to resist dying' (Samuelson 1981: 5). That a democratic society would inevitably produce a majoritarian coalition that would use the state to socialize the means of production so as to avoid the social costs of the uneven nature of capitalist development, was hardly a new idea. It was not only Marx but a long line of eminently conservative establishment figures who have, over the centuries, held similar views. Schumpeter believed that this process, once initiated, would mean the demise of capitalism.[17] It was this gradual disintegration, born both of its success and its reproductive failure, that augured a socialist future. The parallel to the Marx of the *Grundrisse* is striking.

For Schumpeter what made such socialization possible was not simply self-interest but the fact that the social function of the entrepreneur was being undermined as 'economic progress tends to become depersonalized and automatized and bureau and committee work tends to displace individual action' (Schumpeter 1942: 133). Schumpeter saw the bourgeoisie as sociologically as well as economically dependent on the entrepreneur, and 'as a class lives and dies with him.' The large bureaucratic corporation, as Schumpeter portrayed it, was not all that different to an efficient Soviet industrial combine. Schumpeter, of course, did not advocate socialism, and the socialism he saw emerging had important differences from Marx's version (which he skillfully drew himself in *Capitalism, Socialism and Democracy*, where he diagnoses observable tendencies and states how they would work themselves out according to their historic logic). Schumpeter says he does not 'prophesy or predict' socialism (ibid.: 422), but what he said does not amount to prediction because factors external to the chosen range of observation may intervene, and also because there are counter-tendencies that offer resistance to the main tendencies working themselves out completely or leading them to 'eventually "stick" at some half-way house' (ibid.). Ironically, Marx's socialism based on the potential emancipatory potential of shared social knowledge in which the working class was freed from alienation and exploitation is antithetical both to Soviet Marxism and Schumpeter's statist socialism. Schumpeter's discussion of the trajectory of capitalist development does not involve class politics or agency, and in this sense is both deterministic and idealist. Schumpeter argues that capitalism

> creates a critical frame of mind which, after having destroyed the moral authority of so many other institutions, in the end turns against its own; the

> bourgeois find to his amazement that the rationalist attitude does not stop at
> the credentials of kings and popes but goes on to attack private property and
> the whole scheme of bourgeois values.
>
> (ibid.: 143)

Marx's conclusions in his longer run democratic transition version are not, however, so different, although class consciousness and agency are involved. For Marx
it takes more than rationalist attitudes to produce epochal change.

Finally, in this respect Schumpeter is closer to his great status competitor, John
Maynard Keynes, than to Marx. Schumpeter thought that the corporate bureaucracy could function just as well under the loose guidance of government officials
as a multitude of absentee owner stockholders. So long as the state left basic business decisions to the executives (but served on boards of directors for review and
oversight), efficiency losses would be minimal. Expert supervision rather than political meddling for patronage or electoral gain was envisioned. What Schumpeter
calls socialism bears a striking resemblance to state-regulated corporate capitalism
(Samuels 1985). What he was announcing was the expectation of the demise of
laissez-faire, perhaps capitalism's most dynamic, but also socially costly, phase of
development. Schumpeter's socialism was very bourgeois. If structurally it resembles Hilferding's organized capitalism more than Marx's socialism, it was because
he assumes continued hierarchy and restricted democracy rather than the coming
to power of a new dominant class and the creation of an essentially different
mode of production. There is a smooth societal transition aspect to Schumpeter's
historical scenario which contrasts with both the creative destruction that motivates
capitalism's economic development and the class struggle Marx envisions. In my
view (discussed in the concluding chapter), after the period of disassembling the
post-war nation-based regime of accumulation has sufficiently freed the forces of
capitalism on the global plane (and the costs of this freedom become widely appreciated), there will be movement towards a reregulation on both the levels of the
nation-state and on an international scale. When this happens, much of what
Schumpeter had to say about the tendency toward socialization will have greater
salience than in the period of neoliberal ascendancy.

'Most of the creations of the intellect or fancy pass away for good after a time
that varies between an after-dinner hour and a generation,' Schumpeter wrote
(1942: 3). The creations of his own intellect have not faded. Perhaps the reason the
same can be said for so few economists (and thinkers in general) is that in rooting
themselves ahistorically in their immediate moment, when that Warhol ephemeral
fifteen minutes passes, so too does interest in what they have had to say.
Schumpeter's influence has hardly been a constant, consistent presence. At the
time of his death he was the most frequently cited of economists. Unlike Marx and
Keynes, he was not a progenitor of a school of practitioners who see themselves
carrying on his work, though there is some evidence that this may be changing, and
he is now the topic of retrospective appreciation. Herbert Giersch, in a 1983 cen-
tenary celebration of Schumpeter's birth which coincided with a revival of
Schumpeterian economics, called ours 'the age of Schumpeter' (Giersch 1984) and

(as we shall see in Chapter 10) there is a large 'Schumpeterian' literature in the area of growth theory.

Conclusions

The question that remains in the minds of many mainstream economists, those who grant the brilliance of insights of these and other B economists is: Is there a systematic alternative to neoclassical economics? The argument we make is that, of its nature, the answer must be no. The method used needs to be appropriate to the questions asked, and, to a significant degree, different questions are being asked by mainstream and mainline economists. The legacy has been a division in which evolutionary theory was 'squeezed out' of economics. As the twenty-first century approached, some rethinking was underway. A number of economists came to the conclusion expressed by Richard Nelson that 'many economists put too high a value on formal argument, and underestimate the worth of carefully constructed theoretical discourse that seems to capture the gist of what actually is going on but is not expressly formal' (Nelson 1994: 110). This greater interest in substantivist discourse (our B mode economics), whether it goes by the label of evolutionary theorizing or institutionalism, suggests that the range of economic possibilities have not been adequately captured by the formalist determinism of A style thinking. The contrast between the two methods and the advantages of embracing the B side of the menu have gotten more respectful hearing, and evolutionary and institutionalist thinkers have been able effectively to compare and contrast their own approach to the neoclassical methodology.[18]

Complexity grows as we approach the contemporary literature because there are so many active voices in the conversation(s). Disagreement is usually handled by separating out discussions. There is a tendency to prefer to talk to those who basically agree with our ideas and are working to advance a common understanding. This reduces the need to go back to first principles too often, so that development of a line of thinking is slowed. Separating into interest groups allows for more manageable conversations, although much is lost when comparisons across borders are discouraged. As we turn in the next chapters to more recent developments in economics, disputed issues seem to take on greater complexity and ever more controversy. The literatures become larger and their rate of increase substantial. Equally affected are the immediacy and weight of the implications for policy, with real impacts on the distribution of income, wealth, and power. The difference is evident in the next chapter's consideration of John Maynard Keynes. Dead for half a century and acknowledged as the greatest economist of the twentieth century, Keynes' meaning remains contested. In two crucial areas especially his insights do not command a secure influence. These are the role of speculation and expectations in a money economy and the dangers of uncontrolled internationalized markets. Continued controversy over 'what Keynes really meant' and means today is highly contentious.

8   Keynes and the world turned upside down

One and a half generations of ostensible political and economic peace in Western Europe from 1870 seems in retrospect to have been marvelously apt as a setting and illustration of the subjective, marginalist theory of value. The most essential and powerful difference between this world and the world of the 1930s was the loss of tranquility itself. Problems of 'the price of a cup of tea' as Professor Joan Robinson put it, no longer counted much against the failure of the incentive to invest, which failure itself was due to the sudden oppression of business minds by the world's incalculable uncertainties. There was no longer equilibrium in fact, and there would no longer be equilibrium in theory.

(Shackle 1967: 289–90)

How, then, can it be that the total cost of production for the world's business as a whole can be unequal to the total sales-proceeds? Upon what does the inequality depend? I think that I know the answer.

(Keynes 1930a: 141)

John Maynard Keynes was a product of the Cambridge moral science tradition, in which Cambridge economics developed 'side by side with Cambridge moral philosophy' (Skidelsky 1983: 10). Keynes, following the same path as Marshall, moved from mathematics to economics via ethics. It was a different ethics than Marshall's Victorian moralism, a different mathematics as well,[1] and it was surely to lead to a different economics. Yet the influences of Marshall were strong, as would be the case at Cambridge, even if it had not been Alfred Marshall who had worked on the young Keynes, finally succeeding in interesting him in pursuing a career in economic studies. Keynes, whose father, John Neville Keynes, we met briefly in Chapter 1, was not only an economist but a prominent figure at the university. The son was born in the right place at the right time to become a world famous economist and he was to become not simply a man of establishments, but part of the elite of each establishment of which he was a member. 'There was scarcely a time in his life,' Skidelsky writes, 'when he did not look down at the rest of England, and much of the world, from a great height' (ibid.: 1).

Early in 1881, Marshall commented on a review by the young Keynes (of Edgeworth's *Mathematical Psychics*) that he showed signs of genius, and a promise of great things to come. 'But,' he added, 'it will be interesting, in particular, to see how far he succeeds in preventing his mathematics from running away with him, and carrying him out of sight of the actual facts of the economy' (ibid.: 60). Marshall need not have worried. Keynes used mathematics in the sense of looking at the numbers, as he said, 'messing around with the figures, and seeing what they must mean' (ibid.: 223). This was an intuitive flash sort of procedure and not the use of mathematics to work out the logic, as it had been for Marshall.[2]

Keynes was an undeniable genius in just about anybody's book. This is not the same as saying that his ideas were fully original or that he single handedly made that revolution; a rather large literature exists on the question of who was first with what.[3] The Polish economist Michael Kalecki has claim to priority, and perhaps to a better version of the theory. Others were working along the same lines.[4] The Swedes Gunnar Myrdal and Erik Lindahl, basing themselves on Wicksell, can be said to have been there first too. Myrdal, in a 1931 review of *A Treatise on Money*, spoke of the 'attractive Anglo-Saxon kind of unnecessary originality,' which comes from not reading outside of their native language.[5] Among Keynes' associates, Dennis Robertson saw the possibility of divergence between savings and investment (Robertson 1949).[6] In addition there was Richard Kahn, whom Schumpeter suggests was not short of meriting co-authorship of the *General Theory of Employment, Interest and Money* (hereafter simply the *GT*), an opinion shared by other knowledgeable contemporaries.[7] Some would go back at least to Marshall himself, who emphasized the sluggishness of nominal wage adjustment and multiplier effects. There is no end of debate on the question of proper paternity of the Keynesian Revolution (McCollum 1986).

It is unclear whether all those practical men of affairs, even in America, did not understand the basics of Keynesian economics pre-Keynes. Politicians knew that increasing spending in periods of high unemployment would create jobs and stimulate the economy. Before the *GT* and Keynes' advice, the President's Conference on Unemployment, chaired by the Secretary of Commerce at the time, a man named Herbert Hoover, proposed setting aside 10 per cent of the nominal level of public works as a reserve to be used when recessions struck. The explanation was that by spending money in construction, incomes generated would be spent and there would be further economic stimulus. It was not yet called 'the multiplier,' but the idea was clear. The committee spoke in terms of 'multiplying effects' producing more employment. Between 1929 and 1930 new construction in the public sector rose 20 per cent. The much maligned Hoover as president attempted to increase spending and keep wages high, but all those years of studying economics convinced policy makers that deficits were evil. It was here that those practical businessmen, fearing for their own interests, declared on the very best available advice of economists that government spending would crowd out private investment, even though it was evident that there was precious little private investment going on. It was not that political leaders or even most economists did not support public works to relieve unemployment, they did.[8] In England, Keynes wrote perhaps only a touch misleadingly, 'I know of no British economist of reputation who supports the proposition that schemes of National Development are incapable of curing unemployment.'[9] They might know this but they also believed that deficits were to be avoided in season and out. The rising deficit had to be a worry, because without a balanced budget there was the expectation of loss of business confidence. Loss of business confidence was to be avoided at almost any cost.

Keynes' life interests and pre-analytic vision are important in understanding his work and to appreciate that there was not, as some have maintained, a disjuncture between his early interests in mathematics, philosophy, and probability and his later economics (Skidelsky 1991). As some want to see a young Marx of the *Manuscripts* concerned with alienation and an older Marx of *Capital* writing scientifically about capital, and in the same manner as there is an 'Adam Smith problem,' the continuity of Keynes' work is also both questioned and equally evident.[10]

The key in all of these cases is bearing in mind the difference between the two cultures in economics. Keynes' way of thinking is framed by B mode norms. The mainstream culture with its deterministic models is one in which markets out of joint are set right with dispatch by automatic equilibrating mechanisms. This is exactly the supposition that Keynes strove to escape, and yet the dominance of A mode thinkers has provided the ether of ideas through which Keynes is interpreted. His approach to economics as an engaged practice, for example, was to be transmuted into a particular kind of A mode science in the postwar period. The argument will be detailed through much of the next chapter, but it is useful to state it here more briefly. Keynesianism was to be defined as an instrumental policy orientation in which the stability of the macroeconomy was to be achieved through what can be thought of as a large plumbing system (Phillips 1950).[11] It is represented in the textbooks as a circular flow in which one sector, households, provides another sector, firms, with factors of production, and receives in a reverse flow wages, salaries, rents, profits, and interest. The firms use the factors to produce goods which are paid for by the households. In this familiar picture story, the hydraulics engineers (the economists) watch to see that the money flows through the pipes unimpeded.

Diagrams show leakages from the circular flow in the form of taxes paid, imports, and savings, and inflows back to the circular flow from government spending, exports, and investment. The job of the hydraulics engineer, the Keynesian economic adviser, is to estimate the flows and recommend government action that will harmonize the flows. Instrumentally the easiest and presumably most effective channels for this are increasing and decreasing taxes and government spending. By raising or lowering these sluice gates, the right amount of effective demand would circulate through the system. This, in brief, was the Keynesian economics of the postwar period. The idea that an economy did not automatically find the right level of output and required statist engineering to help it do so was, of course, a startling one for orthodox economists of the period.

Today it is hard to remember that Keynes' impact was revolutionary in a manner that would never have been accepted were it not for the profound loss of confidence in *laissez-faire*, a product not primarily of any clash of ideas but of the very real collapse of world capitalism. Hobsbawm captures the mood of the period when he writes that Keynes formulated what was to be the most intellectually and politically influential way of saying that capitalist society could only survive if capitalist states controlled, managed and even planned much of the general shape of their economies, if necessary turning themselves into mixed public/private economies.

(Hobsbawm 1987: 334).

Pre-1914 capitalism was dead, and for the forty years after the early 1930s the intellectual supporters of pure market economics were an isolated minority. These lessons had been learned, writes Hobsbawm, 'because the alternative in the period of the Great Slump of the 1930s was not a market-induced recovery, but collapse' (ibid.). Most economists do not believe such a story these days. Rational expectations and efficient capital market stories, government failure and regulatory excess are widely understood to be the culprits, and business cycles, as we shall see, have become 'real' in ways Keynes might well have thought quite preposterous.

In this and subsequent chapters, retelling the history of economic thought becomes more difficult. Assertions about the meaning of Smith or Malthus still stir emotion among economists, but tempers rise even more quickly, and debate rises to a sharper pitch, when we consider Keynes and living economists. Because so much of contemporary debate still responds to Keynes' assertions (either directly or more frequently through contested interpretations of his meaning), the issue of his legacy remains passionately contested. Since the economists we now consider have written so much (and in the case of the living ones can be expected to write still more), we cannot easily speak of 'the history of thought' in our times but can only conjecture as to meanings and interpretative debates that may have lasting significance.

We start with Keynes' views on probability, which are especially important to his theories of expectations (and, more broadly, how he theorizes about economics). These are at strong variance with the rational expectations and other manifestations of a New Classical Economics which has become so intellectually influential (and are taken up in the next chapter). Keynes' views are very much in the B cultural tradition, and their rejection in recent years has much to do with both their interpretation through A mode filters and the inadequacies of the A mode version of Keynesianism that was to triumph, especially in America, in the postwar period (Kregal 1976).

Avoiding the position of Buridan's ass[12]

Keynes believed that one intuits possible outcomes and can have only a 'degree of belief' in the conclusions one draws. We have what we may think are good reasons for preferring one conclusion to another, but this probability is a matter of logic as opposed to mathematics. People incorporate the widest variety of facts in developing expectations,[13] but when it comes to predicting the future, knowledge of what will happen is simply not possible. Statistical forecasting models, Keynes thought, were based on 'mathematical charlatanry.'[14] Ordinary language is the most appropriate language for probability. The symbolic formulations in economics are restrictive: they force limiting conditions and closed categories. People's understandings are matters of habit, instinct, and desires (much along the lines American institutionalists suggested). Thus, Keynes did not think the future knowable or that investors' views concerning what was likely to happen were totally, or perhaps even mainly, rational.

Such views on probability, with their implications for the way humans forecast, play a large role in his thinking about instability and are core to Keynes' model (though not to contemporary Keynesian thinking). There is a continuity of approach from his *Treatise on Probability* through the *GT* that draws on Keynes' Cambridge roots.[15] This attitude toward uncertainty led him, like Marshall, and unlike many modern economists, to be suspicious of the neat mathematical models that solved the world's problems. The more sophisticated the mathematics, the greater the grounds for suspicion. Given developments over the last half century or so in the mainstream, it is perhaps useful to quote him at length on the rhetorical power of mathematics as language in argumentation:

> It is a great fault of symbolic pseudo-mathematical methods of formalizing a system of economic analysis . . . that they expressly assume strict independence between the factors involved and lose all their cogency and authority if this hypothesis is disallowed; whereas, in ordinary discourse, where we are not blindly manipulating but know all the time what we are doing and what the words mean, we can keep 'at the back of our heads' the necessary reserves and qualifications and the adjustments which we still have to make later on, in a way which we cannot keep complicated partial differentials 'at the back' of several pages of algebra which assume that they all vanish. Too large a proportion of recent 'mathematical' economics are mere concoctions, as imprecise as the initial assumptions they rest upon, which allow the author to lose sight of the complexities and interdependencies of the real world in a maze of pretentious and unhelpful symbols.
>
> (Keynes 1936: 186)

It could also have been written yesterday, and immediately attracted the amen of those dissatisfied graduate students at our more prestigious universities interviewed for *The Making of an Economist*, who found their professors more concerned with teaching technique and sophisticated mathematics than conveying much sense of real-world economies.[16] It is equally relevant to considering the policy prescriptions of those economists who, forecasting from these uncertain models, urge actions that will pay off 'in the long run' despite their obvious and severe cost in the short run.

With regard to the particular passage, another word is required. The assumption concerning the power of economists' prediction, which led Keynes to be skeptical of simplistic long-run planning, should not be taken as indicating that Keynes did not think about the long run as well as the short term. He did so in a different mode of thought than that which he here criticizes (as we shall see). The problem is really in the A mode confidence of economists who claim the world follows mechanical laws. The trust economists place in their abstract modeling reveals a misplaced faith. Writing in a far less confident time, Keynes declared

> Our power of prediction is so slight, it is seldom wise to sacrifice a present evil for a doubtful advantage in the future. Burke ever held, and held rightly, that it can seldom be right to sacrifice the well-being of a nation for a generation, to plunge whole communities into distress, or to destroy a beneficent institution for the sake of a supposed millennium in the comparative remote future. We can never know enough to make the chance worth taking, and the fact that cataclysms in the past have sometimes inaugurated lasting benefits is no argument for cataclysms in general. . . . It is the paramount duty of governments and of politicians to secure the well-being of the community under the case in the present . . . .[I]t is not sufficient that the state of affairs which we seek to promote should be better than the state of affairs which preceded it; it must be sufficiently better to make us for the evils of the transition.
>
> (Skidelsky 1986: 1565–6)

Readers in depression-torn Britain were not unlikely to accord such a pronouncement nodding approval. To encounter such a passage at the end of the twentieth century, as historic transition from the postwar Keynesian governance system was well underway, is to experience a sense of cognitive dissonance in two regards. First, Keynes' views on probability, herd behavior, (ir)rational frenzies, and crashes are viewed as thoroughly outmoded by the contemporary mainstream. Current fashion interprets learning behavior and rationality differently, so as to explain them within a neoclassical context of efficient market theory, often in terms suggesting asset volatility, and is based on extreme sensitivity to new information or noise trading models in which fierce self-amplifying reactions of speculators produce such outcomes. Second, a historic transition is taking place in which citizens are being told that weakening safety net protections put in place as part of a Keynesian response to the Great Depression will increase economic efficiency under contemporary conditions and increase growth. Such a newer economics is urging pain now for gain later. Keynes' words just quoted may be read as stern rebuke to the expectations of this newer economics.

Keynes warned that the problem with political formulations of the future is that the promise of gain later is rarely ever kept to those who are asked to sacrifice now for this uncertain future. More typically, the claim that sacrifices must be made today for the good of tomorrow are constructed in a politicized process to benefit those who profit today – and tomorrow – from the policies everyone is told are in the general interest. Transition costs can be substantial in terms of lost jobs and income and regressive distribution of wealth. In the case of the United States average family wages in real terms were actually lower in the mid-1990s than in 1968 (Folbre 1995: Table 2.5). The richest ten per cent of American families garnered 85 per cent of the wealth generated by the record rise in the stock market (Wolff, 1996). Matters are little different in the UK.

Keynes did not agree with the trickle down premise that if the rich could make money all would be well for the rest of the population, and he might appreciate the irony of the policies that have replaced his being so successfully sold to the majority on a basis comparable to that which politicians in the 1920s attempted in selling austerity for the masses to fund income distribution to the rich. Keynes was convinced that in seeking their own private ends, the financial speculators and the rentier class who dominated the England of his time did great harm to society.[17] The reason was not only that finance removes money from the productive sphere, but also that greed is not stabilizing in an uncertain world, but destabilizing. It discourages long-term investment.[18] This brings us to two central questions: What forms expectations? To what extent is speculation in financial markets (especially a substantially internationalized capital market) stabilizing and/or destabilizing?

Expectations and the state

We are guided, Keynes thought, 'to a considerable degree by the facts about which we feel somewhat confident, even though they may be less decisively relevant to the issue than other facts about which our knowledge is vague and scanty' (Keynes 1936: 148). It is the case of the drunk looking for his house key under the street lamp not because he thinks that is where he dropped it but because the light is better there. The knowledge one really wants is not obtainable, and what one has is likely to be 'ephemeral and non-significant' yet can be expected to have 'an altogether excessive, and even absurd, influence on the market.'[19]

If their confidence is weak, investors will hold back, withdrawing money from circulation, not spending on new equipment or building factories; their doubts intensify pessimism and feed a potentially cumulative process. The reason the classical self-adjusting market model is wrong in many policy matters, even when it may be true 'in theory,' as Keynes famously writes, is that

> this *long run* is a misleading guide to current affairs. *In the long run* we are all dead. 'Economists set themselves too easy, too useless a task if in the tempestuous season they can only tell us that when the storm is long past the ocean will be flat again.'
>
> (Skidelsky 1994: 156)

We can hear in such a statement echoes of the longer debate, for example Malthus addressing Ricardo on the measure of cycles in the 'serious sum of the cost of happiness or misery, according as they are prosperous or adverse, and leave the country in a very different state at their termination.'

Whilst Keynes' analytical framework is generally said to be only a short-term one, there is an important sense in which the present moment is contextualized in terms of an extended time frame that allows Keynes another avenue of critique of neoclassical thinking.

The whole object of the accumulation of wealth is to produce results, or potential results, at a comparatively distant, and sometimes at an *infinitely* distant date. Thus the fact that our knowledge of the future is fluctuating, vague and uncertain, renders Wealth a peculiarly unsuitable subject for the methods of classical economic theory. . . . About these matters there is no scientific basis on which to form any calculable probability whatever. We simply do not know.

(Keynes 1937: 213)

Many, perhaps most, contemporary economists would disagree, believing that such calculation is indeed possible and that assignment of risk to uncertain outcome can be carried out with a substantial degree of confidence.

Keynes, like Marx, saw freedom as taking control of the blind forces of economic life that threatened destructive consequences, and subjecting them to conscious direction. For Marx, freedom required ending class rule by capitalists and the conscious direction of economic forces by working-class actors. Keynes' view was that the world was being ruined by stupidity, not wickedness, and that competent management by an intellectual elite could set things right. Witnessing the Soviet Union in practice, he was impressed by the lack of capacity of the 'workers' state' to administer the economy. In terms of British politics, he was surely skeptical of the capacity of the Labour Party. He saw its very nature as a class instrument as a handicap to proper administration.

At the same time, it is important to remember what he affirmed as well as what he reproached:

I criticize doctrinaire State Socialism, not because it seeks to engage men's altruistic impulses in the service of Society, or because it takes away from man's natural liberty to make a million, or because it has the courage for bold experiments. All these things I applaud.

(Keynes 1926b: 316)

Keynes' criticism of the Stalinist version of communism was, as he put it, because it was 'little better than a dusty survival of a plan to meet the problems of fifty years ago, based on a misunderstanding of what some one said a hundred years ago' (Keynes 1926b). Keynes thought the Soviets had it wrong when they wanted to control and centrally direct the means of production:

It is not the ownership of the instruments of production that it is important for the State to assume. If the State is able to determine the aggregate amount of resources devoted to augmenting the instruments and the basic rate of reward to those who own them, it will have accomplished all that is necessary.

(Keynes 1936: 378)

He thought this could be done gradually and without a break in the general traditions of society.

It is this aspect of Keynes' mode of thinking, that solutions need 'to fit,' not simply to solve abstract problems but be appropriate to the particular conditions of the times, that places him so clearly in the B tradition. It offers a warning to 'Keynesians' who would apply Maynard Keynes' solutions in all contexts as 'applied theory.' His authority, and the reason he is so very much in the mainline of the economic greats, is that he unashamedly holds to a commanding pre-analytic vision, and an evolving social philosophy, while consistently developing new analytics rooted in the rationality of the need of his time. There are general understandings that offer guidance to what is possible and desirable, but there is awareness of limits to idealism. We must be both principled and wise. Men can make their own history, as Marx (who Keynes claimed not to understand) maintained, but not in any way they choose.

Keynes did not make pronouncements for all time, only for immediate conditions and circumstance. He thought that economic evolution would be a matter of cooperation between private initiative and the public exchequer, and that the 'true socialism of the future will emerge . . . from an endless variety of experiments directed towards discovering the respective appropriate spheres of the individual and the social' (Skidelsky 1993: 185). Keynes did not think this would be at all easy, but he had faith that intelligence would overcome stupidity and wickedness. He had perhaps more of Marshall's Victorian morality than he himself would admit. He, like Marshall, saw himself as an intellectual administrator. His kind, the Platonic Guardians, claimed the technical capacity to help make the transition 'from economic anarchy to a regime which deliberately aims at controlling and directing economic forces in the interests of social justice and social stability.' He knew this task presented enormous difficulties both political and technical, but he had immense confidence that his New Liberalism's 'true destiny' was to seek their solution (Keynes 1926a: 335).

There is both challenge to capitalist practice and support for its reinvigoration in this credo. Keynes wanted not to destroy the system, as some of his critics claimed, but to take from capitalists' privileges that they considered integral to the definition of capitalism but which he did not. Keynes, writing of the metaphysical principles upon which *laissez-faire* had been founded, wrote: 'There is no clear evidence from experience that the investment policy which is socially advantageous coincides with that which is most profitable' (Keynes 1936: 157). There is no doubt he saw the essential characteristic of capitalism, the 'dependence upon an intense appeal to the money-making and money-loving instincts of individuals as the main motive force of the economic machine,' but he did think a time would come when such ignoble motivations could be superseded. It is especially important to underline that Keynes did not celebrate the speculators whom he saw often making money at the expense of costly dislocations for the larger society. Keynes' view was that the speculators seeking individual advancement also cause unemployment, and that the cure to the economic problem of unbridled markets cannot be through individual actions but via deliberate social control (Keynes 1926b: 318).

Markets and the business cycle

What started Keynes on the road to the Keynesian Revolution was not some theoretical inconsistency, but the lack of real recovery from the 1920–2 depression.
Nothing like this collapse of prices, output, and employment had been seen in
England since the Napoleonic Wars, and when the position stabilized in 1923 it
was on the basis of 10 per cent unemployment (which was to last for the rest of the
decade). Then came the depression of 1929–32. Over the whole inter-war period,
lasting almost twenty years, Britain never experienced anything like full employment. Hitherto, large-scale unemployment had been seen as a problem of the
business cycle. It now seemed that it might be endemic, and 'It turned out that economics had very little to say about all this' (Skidelsky 1993: 130).

Until Keynes, almost all economists held to Say's Law, which Keynes summa-
rized as 'supply creates its own demand.' That is, by producing a certain quantity
of goods and services and paying the cost of their production, the purchasing
power was created to buy back the sum of what was produced. Of course, they
understood shoemakers didn't buy back the shoes they themselves made; rather in
the aggregate all consumers together received enough income to purchase the
products that came to market. There could be temporary gluts (due to especially
bountiful harvests or overproduction of a unpopular article), but by lowering prices
the market would clear. In this world of Say's Law there is famously no involuntary
unemployment, since by accepting lower wages, workers can always find a job.
There could also never be too much saved or too little invested, since the interest
rate would rise or fall to equate the demand for investment funds and the supply of
savings. This perfect market world, which textbook economics today again suggests
we more or less live in (or would except for government, unions, and other interference which needs to be removed or at least minimized), is the world Keynes did
not live in, as he said in a powerfully argued manner. He explained how the real
world could, and did, depart from this economists' paradise. The Great Depression
made the pretensions of the orthodox seem ludicrous indeed. Their theories were
obviously inadequate.[20]

The *GT*, as is surely well known, is a critique of the presumption that the economy automatically and in accordance with its nature corrects any tendency toward
under- or over-production. The classical law of markets, Keynes thought, is wrong.
To the extent that marginalism presumes this self-correcting mechanism, and is
based on this assumption to its core, it is wrong. Keynes' famous statement that 'in
the long run we are all dead' speaks to the mainstream predilection that, when con-
fronted with evidence that markets don't clear, maintains that 'in the long run' they
will. Given time, equilibrium conditions will prevail and the economy will eventually move into a new equilibrium, if conditions of the old equilibrium are
disturbed. In the real world (and not the blackboard world of such a pure theory),
the economy does *not* move automatically to a satisfactory new equilibrium, nor
was it in an equilibrium to start with. The ability to think in terms of such models
obscures the pure theorist's vision and his or her interest in the specifics of the trajectory of the real economy. The theorist puts down temporary maladjustments to

rigidities and market imperfections, but these 'rigidities' and 'market imperfections' are the defining characteristic of markets as they exist.

Keynes challenged the idea that all unemployment had to be voluntary and that cutting wages would solve the unemployment problem. The key difference between Keynes' model and mainstream thinking is that as opposed to assumptions that the total quantities of exchangeable items are fixed and everyone has perfect knowledge of prices (allowing all traders to attain optimum satisfaction consistent with their income constraints), and in which trading, because of perfect information and simultaneous exchange, is riskless and costless, in which all expectations are realized, and money need play no role except as a medium of exchange, the *GT* 'presents a model of a *production* economy, using *money*, moving through *time*, subject to *uncertainty* and the possibility of *error*,' as Victoria Chick (1981: 59) reminds us.

The theorist in the Walrasian tradition implicitly wants the real world to be reconstructed to approximate more closely the model in which markets will adjust unless state sanctioned monopoly and command structures are allowed to distort the natural order. Orthodox economists in the 1930s taught (as they do again today) that the central problem of economic analysis is the allocation of scarce means among different uses. Keynes challenged this view, too, and did so at just the right time. Joan Robinson observes

> in 1932 it was clearly impossible to deny that millions of workers were unemployed or that, in the U.S. real national income had fallen by 50 percent in three years. But these phenomena were attributed to 'frictions' that held up the working of market forces; to the shortsighted folly of trade unions in preventing wages from falling faster, or to a scarcity of gold that was constricting the monetary system.
>
> (Robinson 1976)

Before Keynes, the stress on equilibrium conditions had led to an emphasis on 'the static state where there is no changing future to influence the present.' This, said Keynes, 'had the result of breaking the theoretical link between today and tomorrow,' resulting in a large element of unreality in mainstream economic thinking. Keynes set about to answer what it was that determined the future if the future is understood to be uncertain. By the end of the twentieth century, confidence in economic agents' capacity rationally to command their future based on individual maximization has been re-established, and, as in pre-Keynesian models, workers are assumed to be in a position to set real wages and be responsible for determining the level of employment.

Equilibrium can mean market clearing by prices, as it does in the Walrasian model and also in new classical economics (to be discussed in the next chapter), but the term was used by Keynes to refer to a position of rest. For Keynes, therefore, there can be an equilibrium outcome with involuntary unemployment as well as equilibrium with full employment. The issue, and this separates him from most neoclassical economists today as well as before he wrote, is whether a general excess supply can exist for significant periods and whether such a state can be called an equilibrium. Whilst his answer to both questions is yes, theirs is no. In the new classical models to be discussed, the economy will instantaneously adjust to shocks so that no actual discrepancy between supply and demand will occur. Shocks are absorbed by markets and won't even be observed. In a Walrasian world there is perfect flexibility of prices, and money does not matter since real equilibrium is independent of nominal prices.

Unemployment vs. full employment equilibrium

Keynes pointed out that labor market bargaining takes place in terms of money wages. He saw workers as concerned with relative wages compared to reference groups (note the parallel to the findings of recent experimental economics discussed in the first chapter) and their actions affecting the distribution of the aggregate real wage between labor groups and not its average amount per unit of employment, which he saw depending on the level of aggregate demand. He thought there was no way labor as a whole could reduce its real wages. This is not a matter of rigid money wages or money illusion. Employment is dependent on conditions in the market for goods and services, on the level of aggregate demand. The demand for labor is a derived demand (Asimakopulas 1991: ch. 3). The rigid wage assumption explanation for unemployment (held by many Keynesians today) is the classical explanation that Keynes criticized. The efforts to make Keynes' economics part of a new orthodoxy by synthesizing the neoclassical and 'Keynesian' approaches are therefore highly suspect (Rogers 1989: ch. 4).

Workers *as a group* accepting lower wages in hopes of reversing this process could not succeed. Lower wages for a few workers might create employment for them, but generalized lower wages meant lower demand for goods and services and so less employment in the aggregate.

> [I]t is a delusion to suppose that they [employers] can restore equilibrium by reducing their total costs, whether it be by restricting their output or cutting rates of renumeration; for the reduction of their outgoing may, by reducing the purchasing power of the earners who are also their customers, diminish their sales-proceeds by a nearly equal amount.
>
> (Keynes 1930a: 141)

In the context of a relatively closed economy this is certainly the case. What seems most dated in the approach is not the underlying mode of thinking about cycles but the nation-state level of the analysis of macroeconomics.

Keynes feared that the greater openness of the postwar economy offered corporate capital and the speculators the chance to invest outside their home country to an extent not seen since before the First World War. As transnational capital calculated its marketing options globally, the sort of national expansion Keynes saw as the route out of underconsumptionism became less viable. Tax cuts leaked out of the domestic circular flow and growing imports created balance of payments problems, a leakage addressed by austerity measures that canceled the initial stimulus. All of this lay decades ahead, although clearly the outlines of the problem were evident to Keynes and much of his thinking about a proper regime for the global economy after the war was addressed to such considerations.

Keynes was no Keynesian

The structure of Keynes' argument in the *GT* at first seems to be very mainstream in its short-run time frame and its holding all elements of the social structure constant. Indeed, it was criticized by orthodox growth theorists on the grounds that he neglected stock concepts and stock-flow relations which were better treated in neoclassical models. In attempting to construct a model in such a short-run manner, however, Keynes introduced a different type of dynamic consideration in his use of the psychology of expectations.

The difference between Keynes and the economists of the immediate postwar decades was, as Hyman Minsky has written, that 'The models of the neoclassical synthesis are essentially timeless, whereas Keynes in the *GT* was always conscious of time, process, and the transitory nature of particular situations' (Minsky 1975: ix). Keynes' economy has particular institutional characteristics, not stylized stocks and flows. Keynes did, however, compromise with received method. He used a comparative static treatment as an approximation to his understanding of the dynamics of market operation in time. He treated demand side elements within a new framework and the supply side conventionally, and so in a manner inconsistent with his overall theoretical ambitions. This created problems. It also allowed model builders of conflicting orientations to be 'Keynesians.' It also meant that to be Keynesian need have nothing to do with John Maynard Keynes' basic ideas. As N. Gregory Mankiw has answered, 'If new Keynesian economics is not a true representation of Keynes' views, then so much the worse for Keynes' (as quoted in Davidson 1996: 47).

The rational expectations theory, the most important framework for responding to Keynes' approach as this is written, has been answered by Keynesians such as Alan Blinder, who first admits to Keynes' alleged faults. Blinder, debating Robert Lucas, quotes from the *GT* about how 'a large proportion of our positive activities depend on spontaneous optimism rather than on mathematical expectations.' Keynes, Blinder implies, has an attitude problem what with all his talk of 'animal spirits,' which leave 'a big loose end' in the *GT*.[21] Business investment is supposedly driven by the state of long-term expectations, but these 'are not pinned down by one theory.' Some defense. Given Keynes' views we can hardly have a tight theory, can we? It would hardly seem a consistent reading of Keynes to suggest either that he was unaware that he had left outcomes indeterminate – this is central in terms of his theory – or that he *wanted* to tie up this indeterminacy since it is an important element of his framework.[22]

One of the most striking features of Keynes' analysis in the *GT* is the central place he gives to the volatility of expectations and the instability of any marginal efficiency of capital schedule based on these expectations and the prime role he gives investment behavior. In his definition of the marginal efficiency of capital (as that rate of discount that would make the present value of the series of annuities given by the return expected from the capital-asset during its life just equal to its supply price), he underlines the role of expectations. It is the expected yield that counts in decision making in the face of uncertainty. The original cost of a capital asset is irrelevant and only its expected rate of return counts. This is why low interest rates may not help stimulate new investment in the face of an exceedingly bleak outlook. As he explains his thinking in Chapter 11 of the *GT*, 'The most important confusion concerning the meaning and significance of the marginal efficiency of capital has ensued on the failure to see that it depends on the *prospective* yield of capital, and not merely on its current yield' (Keynes 1936: 141).

Here is the key difference between Mr Keynes and the classics and the neoclassic analysts of perfect markets. In such models the marginal productivity of capital is equal to the real cost of capital in equilibrium. Keynes' model is characterized by the absence of such a perfect capital market and so the consequent divergence between the marginal product of capital and the real cost of capital. Uncertainty over the future can lead to rates of interest that result in a rate of investment inadequate to provide full employment. Investors hold money due to precautionary and speculative motives. In these aspects Keynes' theory involves monetary and financial aspects that are not found in the formal models of the Keynesian system. The importance of market psychology is for the most part dropped.

Subjective determinants and motivations of two sorts are key. The first is the state of confidence, 'a matter to which practical men always pay the closest and most anxious attention,' which leads to a herd mentality that intensifies the amplitude of fluctuations. Second is the matter of risk propensity, the 'animal spirits of capitalists.'[23] Keynes also gives substantial attention to the matter of liquidity. Investors who of necessity are speculators face uncertainty, and their natural fears lead them to prefer some degree of liquidity, which increases with growing uncertainty. The best brains on Wall Street are devoted to the game of staying ahead as the market rides up and bailing out just before the downturn. Of course, all do not succeed and there is no such thing as liquidity for the entire investment community. Further, Keynes' stress on uncertainty and the wide swings in long-run expectations that he considers natural in an unrestricted market economy led him not to expect easy adjustment or stable equilibrium. Add to this the longevity of existing capital stocks concretely embodied in specific capacities and resources, and the tendency for wages to rise before full employment is reached, and we have adjustment problems that unaided markets do not handle well. Constructing an optimal growth path was 'a political rather than an economic problem.'

In a period of historically high and volatile interest rates in the 1980s, very different from those conditions Keynes is describing, Keynes' thinking seems outmoded. It is not at all clear that Keynes, were he writing at the end of the twentieth century, would not think in quite different terms about interest rates. During his lifetime, up to 1936 when he finished the *GT*, interest rates had averaged 4 per cent a year and had varied at the extremes in either direction by only 1 per cent. He explained their stability and was concerned with the impact of their lows.

Had he been writing a half century later, the wide swings would no doubt have captured a central place among his concerns.

The central role of money

There is a tendency, after decades of 'Keynesian versus Monetarist' debate, among non-specialists to assume that Keynes didn't care about money and that progress has been made by monetarists establishing that 'money matters.' A large literature on Keynes' extensive writings on money, however, makes clear to anyone with an interest in what Keynes himself was about, that 'Keynes was pre-eminently a monetary theorist' (Davidson 1989: 2).[24] (Indeed, every major publication in the Keynes *corpus* contains the word 'money' or 'monetary' in its title.) Harrod is not alone in characterizing Keynes' monetary analysis as 'a study in depth of a magisterial quality not matched in the previous century' (Harrod 1969: 152, as cited in Davidson 1989: 3). The point is central. It is the contrast between essentially barter economy models, where money is non-existent or neutral and simply a veil, and a monetary economy, in which asset valuation is the key factor and entrepreneurial attitude toward risk and borrowing are determinant, that distinguishes Keynes and is integral to fundamental psychological aspects of his model, the attitude toward liquidity and subjective expectations as to the return from capital assets as presently valued. Keynes' project in the *GT* was to construct a monetary theory of production. Yet 'Keynesians' neglected money, leading to the ironic spectacle that it was this non-monetary Keynesianism that Milton Friedman and the monetarists responded with the assertion that 'money matters.'

What Keynes had come to reject in his monetary economics was the very version of the quantity theory of money that has once again become popular within the profession. Keynes believed the quantity of money could affect either velocity or real income or both, and that under some circumstances the money supply could be endogenous. Unlike much contemporary monetary theory, which is a useless appendage in a Walrasian world, Keynes' could be used to operate an entrepreneurial economy. The non-neutrality of money can be seen as the starting point for the Keynesian Revolution, for it provides the basis for understanding the devastating impact asset deflation can have in a world of flexible prices (Davidson 1993 and Minsky 1986).[25] Those who say that Keynes ignored money do not have to address his core belief that money is not neutral or compare his (as opposed to later Keynesians') theoretical system to that of the monetarists. After all, it was Keynes who said of those who assume neutral money that they are like Euclidean Geometers in a non-Euclidian world (Keynes 1936: 16). Those who seek Walrasian macrofoundations for their theory are following in the footsteps of such Euclideans, and Keynes' critique has much to teach us that goes beyond the liquidity trap, which is about all that is left in mainstream texts of Keynes' thinking on money.

Money matters for Keynes, indeed matters far more than for monetarists for whom money is merely a veil; but it is in terms of the distinction he makes between enterprise and speculation that money markets count. Keynes, both in the *Treatise* and in his 1937 and 1938 papers on finance, lays out the mechanisms by which investment (independent of savings) is provided through a banking system ready to meet increased demand for credit. In Keynes' story an increase in demand for credit is met prior to an increase in saving.[26] The point his interlocutors missed then and reject today is the meaning that the production and purchase of capital goods, because they involve the assumption of debt and are themselves based on long-term expectations, has for the determination of the interest rate. The characteristics of money impart a particular character to a modern economy in which finance plays so central a role, and suggest an important reason why the whole of the economy is not simply the sum of its individual isolated elements and why the interests of speculators can be destabilizing.

Based on the experience of the 1920s and 1930s, Keynes suggested that capitalism's tendency toward stagnation, which was created by a preference for holding cash balances at low interest rates, reinforced the case for an activist fiscal policy focusing on aggregate demand. For if it is true that autonomous growth has slowed down, and low interest rates are not sufficient stimulus to bring forth new investment at a sufficient level to produce full employment, only the state is capable of stimulating a satisfactory growth rate in a mature capitalist economy. Keynes thought that not only did the cure to deflation lie outside the operation of individuals; it may even be to the interest of individuals, Keynes thought, to aggravate the disease. What was rational for an individual employer or investor might not, indeed under the conditions he was describing and that millions were living through, be in society's best interests. With regard to savings and investment, Keynes believed

> that some co-ordinated act of intelligent judgment is required as to the scale on which it is desirable that the community as a whole should save, the scale on which these savings should go abroad in the form of foreign investments, and whether the present organization of the investment market distributes savings along the most nationally productive channels.
>
> (Keynes 1936: 318–19)

It is ironic then that for decades (especially in the United States and most extremely in the 1960s and 1970s) Keynes' views were contrasted with those of monetarists as if Keynes had nothing to say himself about money or, like many Keynesians, denied its importance. To Keynes, money mattered;[27] but money did not mean monetary theory in the contemporary usage of the term. Keynes' interests were primarily financial. 'In the Britain of his time,' as Marcello de Cecco writes, 'it would have been impossible not to be. So clear a hegemony of finance over every other form of economic activity has never existed anywhere else' (de Cecco 1977: 19). Perhaps not, but the contemporary United States, indeed the current world system, is dominated by finance as at no other time in history, with consequences economists today have only begun to explore. Keynes has much to teach us in our present situation, for at a basic level the situation has important similarities.

As I write, most economists accept the Efficient Markets Hypothesis (the idea that prices reflect available information about individual companies and the economy as a whole and so market prices are 'correct' and markets allocate efficiently). Modern theorists of finance express confidence that markets understand risk, are able to separate out its component parts, and minimize loss from the unexpected while taking advantage of opportunities inherent in a dynamic, changing economy. Such theories are at striking variance with those expressed by Keynes in the 1930s. Modern theorists of finance offer the judgment that their financial theories can tell us how to manage our affairs so that the uncertainties of human existence do not defeat us. The perfection of capital markets is contemplated as the triumph of economic law (Bernstein 1992).

We cannot know what Keynes would think of this were he writing today. The experience of the prolonged Great Depression produced a less confident outlook on these matters, and it is possible that the hubris of present-day financial theory may be challenged in some similarly unpleasant fashion. Fisher Black suggested in his 1986 Presidential Address to the American Finance Association, after considering the scientific status of the profession's work, 'In the end, a theory is accepted not because it is confirmed by conventional empirical tests, but because researchers persuade one another that the theory is correct and relevant.'[28] The empirical proof supporting contemporary macroeconomic thinking is in fact exceedingly thin (Summers 1991 and Learner 1983). New generations may reread Keynes and come to the conclusion that his story makes more sense to their own historical period's experience.

Reflecting on reactions to Keynes, and macroeconomics more generally, what is most impressive is its responsiveness to the *Zeitgeist* of the era rather than the convincing proof offered for new departures. The discussion of Keynesian fiscal policy from the 1950s well into the 1970s (and to this day in many texts) is a hydraulic version in which when recession threatens, government is urged to lower taxes and increase their spending to pump money into the circular flow (and to do the reverse in a period of inflation) (Coddington 1976). Keynesianism is thought to have failed when an economy, plagued with slow growth and rising prices, is unable to fine-tune a solution due to the contradictory elements required. Given the trade-off between inflation and unemployment, governments are helpless to lower both at the same time.

Disillusionment with fiscal policy in general increased as theories in the 1970s and 1980s suggested there wasn't even a trade-off: any effort to lower unemployment must fail as soon as people knew what the government was doing and acted rationally in ways that undermine the rationale for its action. Indeed, macro models in the 1990s show lower interest rates, tax cuts, and higher government spending initially having the effect of increasing economic growth but also creating inflation and producing bigger budget deficits that push up long-term interest rates. In the long term, the opposite measures, cutting government spending and balancing budgets in the context of more flexible labor markets, produces more growth. This was seen as turning Keynes 'upside down.' Budget cuts, the new orthodoxy suggested, can be expansionary, a budget stimulus contractionary. Keynes is made the fall guy, given the blame for policies he did not endorse. The ironies are thick here. As Michel Beaud and Gilles Dostaler have written:

Paradoxically, by the time political leaders were adopting the objective of full employment, and with or without reference to Keynes, it had already been several years since Keynes had begun to worry about the difficulties which would emerge with the approach of full employment.

(Beaud and Dostaler 1995: 53)

The international economy

In a broader global perspective, Keynes believed, market forces were at least as much to blame as violence-prone nationalisms for the world's difficulties. His fears of the power of international product and financial markets to destabilize a nation's economy and move the cure to such developments beyond the capacities of national governments have not proven unfounded (Crotty 1983). The loss of local autonomy by the nation-state and the costs of the sacrifices demanded by internationalist capital had been a persistent theme in his writing.[29] Aware that foreign investment was not necessarily good for the nation (as opposed to the investor), he urged a balanced national growth strategy. Like most Englishmen, he wrote, he had been brought up to respect free trade not only as an economic doctrine 'but almost as a part of the moral law. I regarded ordinary departures from it as being at the same time an imbecility and an outrage' (Keynes 1936: 372). Yet he had changed his mind on this most basic teaching. He did so perhaps because he saw some variant of what has come to be known as managed trade as necessary to overcome what he thought to be the outstanding faults of the economic society in which he lived, and in which we live as well, 'its failure to provide for full employment and its arbitrary and inequitable distribution of wealth and income' (ibid.).

In the Bretton Woods negotiations, without holding many cards, Keynes,[30] on behalf of his country, tried to convince the Americans that it was preferable and feasible to set up a system of international balances that would not penalize the weaker economies in the adjustment process. His proposal would tax countries running payments surpluses to encourage them to import more and so stimulate employment in the debtor nations. The failure of the world (and most especially the United States) to heed Keynes now haunts the global economy, where international capital markets dominate the waking hours and sometimes the sleepless nights of treasury officials and central bankers.

The mainstream does not appear unduly concerned. Indeed, in the long run, it is suggested, capital flows will prove not destabilizing but will produce full employment and convergence in standards of living (we will discuss the current debates in subsequent chapters). Keynes would have much to say writing today when daily speculative international fund movements exceed the combined foreign exchange reserves of the G7 governments. Consider that in 1971, when the fixed exchange rate (Bretton Woods) system broke down, 90 per cent of foreign exchange transactions financed trade and long-term investment. The remaining 10 per cent were speculative. Twenty years later the relation was reversed. Speculation drove global currency markets accounting for well over 90 per cent of their volume. Market volatility was a source of immense speculative profits but also proved profoundly costly to millions of working people who, while the theorists ignored them, had become unwilling participants in these markets through the impacts such markets have on employment and compensation levels. The alleged overriding benefits of free capital mobility presumed by contemporary mainstream theory leads to both an underestimation of such costs and a belief that little can be done to restrict capital markets that is not counterproductive. The power of theory is its power to coerce assent to the proposition that there are no alternatives. Keynes' great contribution was to challenge orthodoxy on the truth of such basic assertions.

A Keynes-based Keynesian economics that avoids consideration of the internationalization of speculative finance and the spatial reorganization of production, would seem unthinkable. Such openness has profound costs that, whilst they are dismissed as 'transitional' and 'unavoidable,' must be borne by the society. The easy presumption that it will all be better in the end (even though the costs are enormous in the 'transition') was rejected by Keynes. In the long run we are all dead. Keynes' message – that citizens need to interrogate the logic of free markets when they are in the service of the fraction of capital that benefits from globalization – would be understood to be relevant to our own period.

In the mid-1990s, writing in a spirit reminiscent of Keynes on the importance of developing stabilizing mechanisms, John Eatwell suggests:

> Attempting to maintain stability in international currency markets under the current deregulated regime is like trying to cross an uneven field carrying a large volume of water in a shallow pan. It would be much easier if the pan contained a number of baffles to prevent all the water from slopping in unison from side to side. Financial baffles are needed to slow down the rush of short-term capital from one currency to another.
>
> The technical problems involved in creating suitable baffles in the international financial markets are typically overrated.
>
> (Eatwell 1996: 16)

This is not the place to explore what such mechanisms might look like and the procedures for their development, or even the question of whether Eatwell is correct in claiming that the difficulty of creating such mechanisms is overrated. The point is rather that the normal science of economics in the late twentieth century for the most part rejects consideration of these issues that were so central to Keynes' thinking about the operation of the world economy.

The financial system, now as then in England, is one in which the bond market holds the rest of the economy to ransom. Capital markets prevent economic expansion, cowing decision makers who fear its retribution. As Keynes saw it, replacing the landowning aristocracy, which once extracted extortionist rents, and imparting a deflationary bias to the system was precedence for England doing the same to the rentier class. In his 1923 *Tract on Monetary Reform*, Keynes writes that deflation is far more damaging than inflation all things considered (though neither is desirable), because it is worse 'in an impoverished world, to provoke unemployment than to disappoint the *rentier*.' A Keynes today in America would not have much of a chance to be appointed to the board of the Federal Reserve System. In his own time he did continuous battle with the holders of the same objectionable positions – then known as the Treasury view.[31] Keynes was fascinated that a circuit could exist between savings and financial assets in a vicious cycle of perverse rationality and exclude the real economy. The financial sphere could grow fat while much of the rest of the British economy could suffer, reduced to working at half-steam. 'This understanding,' in de Cecci's opinion, 'is perhaps the greatest of Keynes' achievements. . . . Once the rentier class and the financial system had reached a certain critical size, the same interaction . . . which had made Britain great plunged it into a permanent slump' (Keynes 1931: 21).

From Robinson Crusoe to our grandchildren

Concluding our discussion of Keynes, it is useful to comment on the three levels at which his thinking on money is of contemporary importance. The first is the role of his understanding of money as more than a 'veil,' which helps us grasp what is wrong with the neoclassical world of our old friend Robinson Crusoe. The second is the impact of the growth of the financial sector to an extent that speculation becomes the tail that wags the economy. The third, of which we will not comment extensively, is his Marx-like appreciation of the difference between exchange value and use value.[32]

The world of Robinson Crusoe, or the existence of hunters and gatherers, is one of barter. Things are exchanged and must be consumed before they perish. Production, exchange, consumption – the steady state circular flow – is interrupted with the introduction of money. With an uncertain future, withholding purchasing power in hope of finding a better way to expend it tomorrow makes sense. Money in the presence of uncertainty changes things profoundly.[33] Money debt, in the form that allows current use of funds in exchange for the promise to repay at a future date, creates default risk, interest loss or gain risk if the price level changes and the interest at which the debt is to be paid is fixed. It creates foreign exchange risk if the loan is in a foreign currency. These basics of modern finance are all implicit in the introduction of money. Finance is about risk. When banks and their customers are optimistic, they are willing to increase indebtedness. Their actions expand the money supply. Pessimism has the contrary effect. Money is thus an endogenous variable with consequences that are important for the usual way economists look at money and monetary policy.[34]

Keynes' willingness to put the speculators' footloose capital under social control rattled the Establishment of his time. It would take an equally deep crisis for such suggestions to have such an impact again. Depending on circumstance, the appeal of such a step as a necessary one may seem more obvious. The existence of huge speculative activities cannot, despite the hubris of the moment, be forever divorced from real production and the valuation of assets, for they are in the last instance based on expectations of realizable profit. There is nothing simple about such relationships.[35] Keynes' view was that a function of money is a store of value and not just about purchasing power, but trust and mistrust in the future leads to the conception of interest as a reward for parting with liquidity. This is a different and more useful emphasis than the neoclassical view of interest in periods of significant uncertainty. Contracts, most prominently debt contracts, are based on expectations concerning the price level. Prices, for Keynes, do more than allocate resources in a static sense (as they do in the mainstream model where changes in prices lead to a new set of preferences). Absolute levels of prices validate profits or fail to validate profit expectations.

Keynes' preference for leaving business decisions in private hands stems from his skepticism that bureaucracy can deal with risk and uncertainty in as productive a fashion. This does not mean that he was unaware of the corrupting influences of monetary valuation on human relations and self-development; however, the time for a better value system was not yet. In his 1930 essay, 'Economic Possibilities for Our Grandchildren,' he suggested that at least for another hundred years 'we must pretend to ourselves and to every one that fair is foul and foul is fair; for foul is useful and fair is not' (Keynes 1930b: 372). This was a state of affairs to be tolerated and not celebrated. At the same time he was clear in his own mind as to what economic necessity meant. All manifestations of avarice were not desirable or, in his moral universe, allowable.

In the case of Keynes, as in each of the canonical economists discussed in this book, there is more to what they had to say than the received versions suggest. Adding fuller dimension to their economics typically has meant illuminating their B side, how they see matters in historical time and the importance of uncertainty in their thinking. Keynes held an 'organic' view of society, and as he famously wrote to Roy Harrod (July 4, 1938), 'economics is essentially a moral science and not a natural science. That is to say, it employs introspection and judgments of values.' B mode analysis is never divorced from normative values and has a very much 'in this world' moral purposefulness. In the case of Keynes, and more specifically his thinking on unemployment, international openness, and money, this is particularly evident (Skidelsky 1993: xxiv). As in the case of other B economists in the great tradition, Keynes has a moral vision of the way the economic organization of society can be reorganized and individual and social energies redirected. The response to Keynes by the mainstream has been an effort to avoid these radical insights.

In the absence of counter factual history it cannot be known what place in the history of economic thought Keynes would hold had the Great Depression not occurred. As lived memory of the depression fades, so too has the prestige of Keynesianism in the mainstream. The very micro/macro distinction that for a half century has organized theory, and now the boundaries between such major subfields as labor economics and international trade, are increasingly blurred.

In the next chapter a skeptical review of the last fifty years or so in the mainstream proposes that the theoretical departures that have received most of the attention may have limited value. In Chapter 10 the suggestion is made that versions of growth theory have asked more significant questions and have given more interesting answers by reframing those issues that have been discussed only obliquely in macroeconomics. It is possible that the trajectory of important schools of thinking within the profession are leading to a return to the issues that were once the terrain of political economy. In this process, Keynes is being reread inclusively of aspects of his thought that were banished by the now collapsing, postwar, Keynesian–neoclassical synthesis.

9 The last half-century in the mainstream

The left Keynesians understood that '. . . the Keynesian revolution would lose its force and usefulness if it were assimilated to the old concept of *science*: if it were frozen into a closed, determinate theoretical system which purported to model the main economic relationships in a formal and determinate way. Understanding that danger, Robinson, Kaldor and a few others proposed an open-ended analysis of the determinants of economic activity, one which saw economic activity always in its social and political context, alert for the uncertainties and continuous historical changes to be expected from that environment.

(Balogh 1982: 5)

When formalization first took the profession by storm it could boldly promise an emancipation from the 'dark ages' of literary economics. But after roughly a half-century of increasing formalization its premises are starting to sound hollow. Instead of vague verbalizing about real problems we have precise modeling of artificial ones. In place of dubious assumptions hidden behind eloquent prose we have equally dubious assumptions hidden behind dazzling mathematics. The ideological debates that used to rage in the open in verbal confrontations have not been decisively ended but simply buried underneath *technical* paraphernalia. Instead of Keynes vs. Hayek on the causes of unemployment we have Keynesians vs. New Classical interpretations of Rational Expectation Models. Economists disagree as much as they used to; it is just more difficult to see exactly why and how they disagree.

(Caldwell 1990: 275–6)

The mood of the historical moment exercises powerful influence over the subjectivities of economic actors and theorists. In *The Economic Consequences of the Peace*, Keynes attributes the prosperity of the nineteenth century to the 'organization and psychology of society.' The Great War shattered that delicate social machinery of wealth creation and the optimism that underlay its psychology. At the other extreme, perhaps, the hydraulic Keynesianism of the post-Second World War era was imbricated in the optimism of that period, especially in America, and created a heady growth psychology as the pendulum swung once more. The sustained prosperity of the long post-Second World War expansion renewed faith in the neoclassical verities and the dream of a formal determinate and mechanical economics. With the decline of (by then) no longer so great Britain, the United States dominated the era. Among its scientists there was a resurgence of confidence that technology could dominate nature. Social engineers saw prospects of understanding and manipulating societal developments to produce desired outcomes. Among the economists a new balance was also evident. Keynesian macropolicy, it was promised, could produce full employment equilibrium. Free markets could be counted upon within this context to allocate resources efficiently. There was also a renewed confidence in Walrasian general equilibrium thinking which placed free markets back at the center of professional analysis after the Keynes–Great Depression hiatus. The lengthy depression was blamed on government blundering and ignorance of monetary relationships.[1] Depressions came to be seem as a phenomenon of the past.

The Cambridge (England) tradition never accepted this narrowing but sought instead a more solid theoretical basis for opposition to the American Neoclassical Synthesis. In a slim, mathematically and densely reasoned Ricardian approach to production and distribution, Piero Sraffa recast the Cantabridgians' foundational idea that distribution is a matter of politicized struggle. Particularly galling to the mainstream was the revolutionary conclusion Cantabridgians drew from the Sraffa model that profit cannot be explained by the contribution of some factor of production called 'capital' but remains a surplus whose magnitude depends on social and technical relationships.[2] To determine the value of capital it is necessary to know the rate of interest; but to determine the rate of interest it is necessary to know the value of capital! The core belief of neoclassical thinking was based on a tautology. This Cambridge attack on the presumption of an exogenous value of capital in neoclassical production functions and in (Wicksellian) general equilibrium models, focused attention on the conditions under which heterogeneous capital goods could be aggregated into some homogeneous entity 'capital' in a one-commodity world. In such a very abstract blackboard model the theory can be made to function, but in a slightly more realistic world (in one in which there is more than one commodity) it doesn't work; not at the level of high theory and the rigor economists expect of such models (Rogers 1989). The premises of neoclassical distribution theory, as one of its defenders, Charles Ferguson, famously acknowledged at the time of the controversy, must be based on 'faith' and not premised on solid theoretical grounds (Ferguson 1969).

Paul Samuelson, summing up the controversy, granted that there often turns out to be no unambiguous way of characterizing different processes as 'more capital intensive' except in an *ex post* tautological sense, and that if the Cambridge (England) economists have 'caused headaches for those nostalgic for the old time parables of neoclassical writing,' that's just how it is. 'We must,' he concluded, 'respect, and appraise, the facts of life' (Samuelson 1966: 583). The implications of the outcome might have been considered significant for a number of reasons. For example, Vaizey writes of the consequences of Cantabridgian economics: 'There is no longer any intellectual reason to suppose that the price system allocated resources any better than any other system; in any particular case it was a matter of fact and judgment (Vaizey 1977: 14). It is not, however, always intellectual argument and logical force that carry the day. The Cambridge (England) people were able intellectually to cut the theoretical grounds from under the neoclassicals in this 1960s debate on the theory of capital. Yet the Cambridge Controversy (Cambridge, England versus Cambridge, Massachusetts) simply petered out as neoclassicals, after losing on points, simply ignored their critics.[3] It was clear from the language in which the debate was carried on that participants simply preferred different stories or 'parables' to explain capital and interest in a real market economy (Harris 1980; see also Harris 1975 and Samuelson 1962).

In England, the Cantabridgian analysis continued to recognize the system as being principally in disequilibrium, and because the key figures in the English economics profession had studied with Keynes and were well versed in *The General Theory* and his method of thought, they hardly accepted the 'modernized, expurgated version,' as Sidney Weintraub called it. Joan Robinson described American Keynesianism as 'a dash of Keynes in the Walras soup.' The subversive idea that is part of the legacy of Marshall, Keynes, Kahn, Sraffa, and Robinson remains the road not taken by economics as the influential center of gravity within the profession crossed the Atlantic in the postwar years.

This American economics became the mainstream economics of the world. The mild recessions in these years and the growth in real living standards under a welfare–warfare driven economic policy fed the belief that the economics profession's brilliant advice had been responsible for postwar prosperity. Keynesianism was reduced to the hydraulic view of the economy (pumping purchasing power into the economy to keep profits and employment rising). What is interesting about this mechanistic Keynesianism is that it is very A mode in its presumptions. Indeed, much of the left-liberal theory of the period paid obeisance to economics-as-science. In India, for example, the first and the most important of the nations to receive its independence in the decolonial aftermath of the Second World War, the idea of planning that was so central to the non-aligned philosophy of Third World development of the time, depended most directly on an appreciation of the scientific socialism of Soviet central planning, which viewed the economy in terms of exact relations among physical quantities and their precise technical coefficients, and also on the work of men of such unquestioned brilliance as P.C. Mahalanobis, the Cambridge trained physicist turned economist to whom a rational economy could be managed with the precision of a physics experiment. It was indeed this chimera that social relations could be reduced to exact laws of science that was to undo both the Keynesian and the planning variant of liberalism and scientific socialism in the face of social conflicts arising from developments in the forces and relations of production as the postwar period unfolded.

Most importantly for our purposes here, whilst 'Keynes' appeared to have been vindicated in the initial successes of hydraulic Keynesianism, and the problems of stabilization and growth appeared to be susceptible to fine tuning, mainstream economists found a way to reenthrone the automatic growth assumptions of neoclassical economics whose overthrow had presumably been at the center of the Keynesian Revolution. In part, the basis of its defeat was already present in the very foundation of American Keynesianism with its central A mode presumptions.

The apparatus of what was called the Keynesian–Neoclassical Synthesis, produced in Samuelson's fabled text (from which directly and indirectly American students learned economics in the postwar period), stressed an automaticity of markets – so long as government took care to do the plumbing, keeping leakages and injections from and into the circular flow in balance. Within such a mechanistic framework, Walter Heller and other New Frontier economists claimed the capacity to fine tune the economy, to make the business cycle obsolete, and to create permanent prosperity. So long as streams into the circular flow matched those passing out, economic stability was maintained. The 'pipes' with their leakages and injections were pictured in a circular flow diagram and expressed algebraically. The government, through operation of tax policy and regulating the level of spending, could be counted on to restore equilibrium to the system. This exposition gave hydraulic Keynesianism a presumption of precision Keynes would have found problematic. Just as 'Keynesian' hubris reached its peak (at the end of the Great Society years), the downturn from the expansionary phase of the long postwar cycle struck, taking the Keynesians – we speak here of the kind Joan Robinson was fond of calling nasty names – by surprise. In applying what was taken to be Keynes' message of aggregate demand stimulation, the Keynesians continued to advocate pumping money into the economy under conditions in which it seemed increasingly inappropriate. The resulting serious inflation (accompanied by severe unemployment) would be blamed on Keynes.[4]

Keynes' invocation of psychology and interdependence of the social sciences effectively created a new (new to the mainstream) understanding which, after Samuelson's synthesis, was quickly segregated into the box 'macroeconomics,' so that existing economics could continue pretty much unchanged as microeconomics. This division Peter Temin has observed,

> corresponds to the split in the nascent social sciences of the late nineteenth century between the thinkers who emphasized the interdependence of human affairs and the people who denied the importance of history or the other social sciences for the study of economic phenomena.
>
> (Temin 1982: 73)

In a similar vein, Alan Coddington in discussing the implications of hydraulic Keynesianism, a term he introduced to the literature, found the implications of its 'reductionism' quite limiting. Reducing market phenomena to stylized, individual choice 'of a particularly stereotyped and artificial kind' that was pursued for its mathematical tractability, meant that unlike Keynes, Keynesians did not consider 'the elusive and wayward manner in which actors make up their minds' (Coddington 1976: 1259).

Samuelson's contention that all properly economic problems reduced to the issue of constrained maximization was the signature statement of the postwar quest for more effective formulation of the optimal properties of a competitive equilibrium and brought the Walrasian approach to the core of economic theorizing. Samuelson achieved this at both the level of high theory with his 1947

Foundations of Economic Analysis and then for millions of introductory economics students in his principles text, the first edition of which appeared in 1948.

Kerry Pearce and Kevin Hoover suggest that the success of Samuelson's text over the others produced in the 1930s and 1940s was that he did not attempt a faithful reproduction of Keynes' ideas. Noting Joan Robinson's famous labeling of this hydraulic model as 'bastard Keynesianism,' they suggest that in the case of Samuelson it may be closer to the mark to absolve Keynes of paternity altogether (Pearce and Hoover 1995). They suggest he is rather the Joseph of the story and that in some sense Samuelson's macroeconomic model is the product of a virgin birth. In this telling, it is Samuelson rather than Keynes who serves as the god of the new economics. Other parentage can be recognized in the offspring's features. The particulars of the model that was soon to be widely familiar to undergraduates from national income accounting, the multiplier, and so on as a guide to government action, were those elements that had been stressed by Abba Lerner and not by Keynes himself. Functional finance, the use of fiscal policy as the balance wheel, and much of the rest of the 'key element in the textbook policy revolution, deserves to be called Lernerian rather than Keynesian' (Colander 1984: 1573).

The four decades or more of argument between monetarists and Keynesians (which still commands center stage in many principles textbooks), a skirmishing over whether 'money mattered,' the relative effectiveness of fiscal versus monetary policy, the revived importance of quantity theory thinking, and other episodes, were not, as was noted in our chapter on Keynes, faithful to his views. Indeed, monetarism's challenge to Keynes was about not money but pre-analytic vision conflict. Monetarists were committed to efficient markets which they saw as inherently stable and in need of no government intervention. Producing a stable money supply that grew predictably at the rate needed by secular expansion was not only its monetary policy but its entire agenda. Milton Friedman's libertarian politics were at the center of his, and monetarism's, agenda. As Franco Modigliani among others made crystal clear in his 1976 Presidential Address to the American Economic Association, the debate reduced to a struggle between believers in activist government macroeconomic policy and advocates of non-intervention (Modigliani 1977). The latter group claims that basically markets work (left to their own devices). The former group suggests that markets work, but not in a timely fashion, and government policy can speed adjustment and cut the cost of restoring the economy to healthy growth. Each side has a different theory of state and market, which as much as matters of technical economics are at the heart of the division among macroeconomists.[5]

In the downturn of the postwar long wave, the redistributive aspects of liberalism (in the phrase's American usage) appeared too burdensome and outright counterproductive in their incentive impacts. A new political understanding formed around lower taxes and privatization. This consensus followed and was a response to the slow economic growth starting at the end of the 1970s. Liberal Keynesianism was blamed for the creeping stagnation. Monetarism, and then supply side economics, rational expectations theories, new classical economics, and new Keynesianism, emerged on the cutting edge of theory within the academy and reflected political developments in the wider society.

The world of IS and LM

For most of the postwar period the debate has been framed in an IS–LM context. The IS–LM model, as all students of academic economics are supposed to know, shows the economy as a balancing of forces, predictable relations between income generation and spending, interest rates and investment and the connecting conditions of harmony between the real and the money sectors of the economy. These came together in this core heuristics of the postwar period, a four quadrant diagram demonstrating the interdependent establishment of system equilibrium after any exogenous shock to the self-regulating economy. Generations of economics students were taught to work through the steps. From a B perspective, they do not really learn much about the economy from doing so. It is all very neat and deterministic. There is a sense of precise causation being captured in the approach the students were taught, but as Joan Robinson suggested, 'It is impossible to understand the economic system in which we are living if we try to interpret it as a rational scheme. It has to be understood as an awkward phase in a continuing process of historical development' (Robinson 1967: 3).

If it is the evolutionary development of capitalism that primarily needs to be understood then it is, as Robinson was fond of saying, history and not equilibrium that needs to be at the core of economics. She was not alone as a defender of the political economy culture of economics. The excesses of synthesis theorists who had created hydraulic Keynesianism to fit their vision of how the economy functions produced mechanical regularity at substantial cost to the revolution Keynes and others had produced in the 1930s. Within the framework of the IS–LM model, if the assumption of downward, rigid, money wages is replaced by an assumption of perfectly competitive wages and prices, then markets clear, and we are back in a classical world.[6] John Hicks, who developed the IS–LM analysis, went on to regret his contribution. After observing its elaboration in the neoclassical synthesis, Hicks wrote, 'I could see that it was nonsense. It does deliberate violence to the *order* in which the real world (in *any* real world) events occur' (Hicks 1977: v–vi).[7] Keynesians who accept the synthesis model have little choice but to stress rigidities in an otherwise neoclassical world, if anything at all is to remain of their Keynesianism. They therefore spend a great deal of creative energies explaining why wages stay above market clearing levels (which does not happen within the traditional neoclassical model of markets, which is still the norm in the dismal science). Their opponents spend equal amounts of time and brilliance arguing that they are wrong and that their creative explanations are inconsistent with basic economic theory.

The textbooks say Keynesians favor fiscal policy to monetary policy because they believe the IS curve is more stable than the LM curve. In the textbook tale, monetarists believe the demand for money is more stable and so the LM curve, which connects points of equilibrium in money markets at different levels of economic activity, is more stable. Keynesians point to the variability in the velocity of money. Some following Keynes stress the destabilizing impact of the speculative demand for money and the non-responsiveness to interest rates, but basically the ones who follow Keynes stress the greater importance of the IS side because changes in the interest rate would not be enough to do the job. The causes, as they see it, of the instability in expectations need to be addressed on the demand side with active fiscal policy (see the discussion in Hillier 1991: 77).

The main point here is that this model, as the rest of the synthesis, is essentially timeless whereas 'Keynes in *The General Theory* was always conscious of time, process, and the transitory nature of particular situations' (Minsky 1975: ix). To Keynes himself (staying with the synthesis terminology), instability is caused by volatile shifts in the IS curve, which result from swings in expectations. Because the IS–LM framework is so elegant, and allows for the use of comparative, static, graphical presentation in which the alternative assumptions about the slope of curves allow a clear if unrealistic clarification of the difference between blackboard monetarism and blackboard Keynesianism – the model endures. Whilst the framework was rarely used at the graduate level or in the journals, it was retained for decades, retailed to college students by the millions for whom the first course in economics is the only course they will ever take.

From the neoclassical side of the synthesis, macroeconomists imbibed from the Arrow–Debreu formulation of the Walrasian model well-behaved preference and production functions that allowed contracts to cover all contingencies at a point in time and to eliminate market uncertainty (Begg 1982). Keynes' sequential economy in which everything is not known at one point of time and all cannot possibly be simultaneously and mutually agreed upon (so that the real world can get into no end of troubles) is pushed from the consciousness of the economic theorist (see Buiter 1980). Economists moved from Keynes' diachronic analysis of how an economy acquires its determining features and how these vary over time to a Walrasian synchronic analysis abstracted from reality and existing in universalist splendor, suspended beyond any particular time or place by its transhistorical mode of theorizing. Samuelson's ergodic grail is attained.

Other forms of Keynesian thinking had a comeback in the 1980s as persistently high levels of unemployment made it harder to accept that these millions of workers had suddenly caught some disease that led them to reject work, giving each a psychological preference for leisure, or were afflicted with misperceptions of the price level (lasting year after year).[8] The Keynesians offered explanations, but these were deemed to be *ad hoc*, plausible perhaps, but not grounded in micro-economic axioms. Whilst the Keynesians might capture what appeared to be part of the actual ongoing practice, their stories were inconsistent with Walrasian assumptions. Given a choice between retaining the unrealistic premises of Walrasian general equilibrium and a more realistic view of the world, there was no contest: the model's purity came first. Thus, for example, the thought that workers with valued skills and tacit knowledge of the particulars of the workplace who were already employed by a firm (the insiders) might command high wages, while outsiders who offered unsuccessfully to work for less, remained unemployed without driving wages down, seemed an *ad hoc*, and so unacceptable, explanation. That it might not be worth it for employers to break implicit contracts by forcing down wages in periods in which they had, temporarily perhaps, greater bargaining strength, was, well, 'ad hoc' (Sargent and Wallace 1976: 169). That labor was not simply another factor of production but came attached to real human beings who were not as malleable as the putty neoclassical economics assumed all factors of production essentially to be, was declared 'amateur sociology,' even though it continues to gain ground by accretion in mainstream modeling (certainly by the late 1980s).[9]

In the 1970s the view became prevalent in neoclassical circles that if only labor were fully informed about the true situation, workers in periods of unemployment would promptly accept a lower wage rather than continue a fruitless search for employment at the going rate. Unemployment is transitory, in this view, largely frictional. Keynes' unemployment equilibrium 'is just a disequilibrium that lasts a long time' (Tobin 1975). The modern neoclassicals deny the theoretical possibility of an under–full employment equilibrium. Unemployment, in the pure neoclassical model, represents errors in judgment or is caused by exogenous shocks to which the system will adjust (Phelps 1970: 56). Workers who believe higher wages can be found and so wait, continue to search longer than they should, and show up in the unemployment statistics. They do not act like good little factors of production, taking the first job that offers the lower pay to which they are entitled. The idea is that at each moment there are jobs at some wage and that anyone who will work can find employment. Unemployed workers are either irrational, have made a mistake, or voluntarily 'prefer leisure.'

Such economists speak of the leisure–employment tradeoff which, by assumption, makes all unemployment voluntary. This model allows workers to have higher utilities from not working than they would with jobs. It explains unemployment as a matter of choice by maximizing individuals (Blinder 1987b: 131–2). Under such assumptions, markets clear at full employment. Such reasoning presumes a decision at a margin removed from the real choices most workers face. Traditional Keynesians such as James Tobin offer the view that the unemployed would be 'well pleased to accept renumerative work based on current real salaries not superior in reality, to marginal labor productivity,' and that whilst market economies do have automatic stabilizing mechanisms to (re)adjust aggregate demand and potential supply, these are often slow and unreliable and so government activity can reduce fluctuations (Tobin 1992b: 3–4). Even this mild claim, once widely accepted as conventional wisdom, was challenged by new classical economists. They extend the neoclassical synthesis drive to make Keynesian economics the special case to its logical conclusion – that the Keynesian model is illegitimate.

After decades of skirmishing within the mainstream there came to be an increasing willingness to meet in the middle. In the new neoclassical approaches to fiscal policy there are mobility costs, incomplete information, and of course distorting taxes within the familiar equilibrium approach.[10] Despite powerful guild restrictions against admitting sociological insight, some economists have been willing to suggest that because workers care not only about real absolute wages, but also about their compensation relative to workers in other firms and industries, they may resist wage cuts by their employers, whilst at the same time they would be willing to accept a social contract that limits their wages (that even cuts their real wages) as part of a package that affects others proportionately. This has been the experience over protracted periods of European social democracies with corporatist wage bargaining. In practice it meant greater wage dispersion and the creation of a more privileged sector with jobs and a significantly large group without work (although with state benefits).

The Phillips Curve

It is not necessary to retell each of the episodes in this long running debate over interpretations of unemployment. One topic that managed to hold a central place in the profession's thinking about macroeconomics over decades is the Phillips Curve, which began its career in a 1958 article[11] in which A.W. Phillips proposed, based on evidence for the UK over a long historical trajectory, an inverse relationship between unemployment and wage inflation. Phillips Curve thinking encouraged economists to accept the view that there was a tradeoff between more unemployment as the cost of less inflation and more jobs but a higher price level. The idea of a societal menu choice involving such a reversible tradeoff was influentially endorsed by Samuelson and Solow in a paper delivered at the 1959 meetings of the American Economic Association (Samuelson and Solow 1960). This paper has come to be seen as the crucial Keynesian intervention of the period, linking the reputation of American Keynesianism to the validity of the relationship's stability (Leeson 1997). The paper was met with some skepticism, even at the time, and the original work by Phillips on which it was based was also subjected to reanalysis of the data and scathing criticism (Routh 1959; see also Reynolds 1950). Most influentially, in terms of the defeat of the (non-expectations augmented) Phillips Curve–Keynesianism, even before evidence showed that this relationship did not hold for the 1970s and 1980s, Milton Friedman and Edmund Phelps were arguing that whilst there might be a *temporary* tradeoff between unemployment and inflation, there was no permanent tradeoff. This, they said, is because it is real wages (money wages adjusted for inflation) that matter. Once expectation of future price increases (due to policies aimed at reducing unemployment) were established, people would not be 'fooled' and would make decisions based on these expectations.

There was no way macroeconomic policy could get unemployment below a certain point (designated as the 'natural rate of unemployment'). Activist macro policy was impotent or even counterproductive. Friedman argued that this 'natural' rate of unemployment existed for an economy based on the structural characteristics of the labor and commodity markets (Friedman 1968: 8). There is thus an optimal level of long-term unemployment (Phelps 1967: 134). It is only unexpected price increases that will matter because they will lead to wrong forecasts. In the short run there appears to be a tradeoff, but in the long run, as adjustment takes place, the

Phillips Curve becomes vertical at the natural rate of unemployment. Once it is realized that mistakes have been made, workers and employers adjust, and real wages (and demand for employees and work) fall back to their 'natural' rate.

Economists have been using *natural* in a variety of uses for centuries. Adam Smith employed the 'natural price' as part of his natural law philosophy, for example, but the extent to which 'free' trade or 'free' markets, 'moral' hazard and 'rational' expectations form such a large and significant part of the working vocabulary of economists generally goes unremarked, although some economists sensitive to the implicit claim being made try to avoid the use of the term *natural* with its implication that the rate is god-given, or use quotation marks around the word. There is a rhetorical impact in such usages. Thomas Sargent, for example, a pioneer in the rational expectations approach, which is discussed shortly, talked about natural and unnatural rate theories of macroeconomics (Sargent 1976). Economists wishing for less rhetorically loaded terminology use NAIRU – the 'non-accelerating inflation rate of unemployment' – a more neutral, if awkward, formulation.

Yet as economists sought to track the NAIRU and use it in forecasts for policy purposes, they found it a slippery construct. When unemployment was close to 6.5 per cent, it was said the NAIRU was 6.5 per cent. When the actual unemployment rate fell to 6 per cent without inflationary pressure, it was said the NAIRU was 6 per cent. When actual unemployment fell well below 5 per cent and then 4.5 per cent in the United States, home of the NAIRU threat, and there was still no sign of inflation, some economists were willing to say that after a quarter of a century and more during which real wages increases had lagged the price level, and productivity growth was quite substantial, it was time to dump the theory. One review of the state of the art models concluded that precise knowledge of what the NAIRU actually is at any point in time in the United States 'is not very important' from the standpoint of inflation forecasting, since deviations of actual unemployment from presumed NAIRU are similar whether NAIRU is presumed to be 4.5 per cent , 5.5 per cent, or 6.5 per cent. It seems the reason it is so hard to pin down NAIRU is that it doesn't correlate closely with coming inflation and so is hard to determine and what it is, or is presumed to be, doesn't matter very much in practical terms (Staiger et al. 1997).

It is likely that future generations interpreting the NAIRU episode in intellectual history will see it as integral to the neoliberal policy agenda that swept the world in these years, and suggest that free market economics used versions of the NAIRU as support to drive up unemployment rates, weaken labor, and make economies 'more flexible.' Economists enamored with the NAIRU warned policy makers of the dangers of inflation if the unemployment rate were to fall below its 'natural rate.' Inflation, they said, would accelerate and there could be no reduction in unemployment in the long run. In 1997, when the unemployment rate in the United States fell to its (then) lowest rate in a quarter of a century and there was no sign of inflation, economists began presenting calculations showing that even if the unemployment rate was kept a full percentage point below its estimated equilibrium (NAIRU) rate, it would take eight years for the inflation rate to double from

3 to 6 per cent, and in that period the lower unemployment rate would allow the federal budget to balance and the Easter Bunny to be elected president if she ran on a dump-NAIRU platform. In any event, the NAIRU was not the 'cliff' it had been portrayed as (fall off and it is a disaster) but perhaps a gradual beach. You don't drown when you pass this limit; you can merely turn around without experiencing harm. Thus experimenting with the lower limits of unemployment made sense. The key point was that 'gradually falling unemployment has never resulted in a rapid slide toward inflationary catastrophe. The process is, at worst, extremely gradual – and reversible' (Galbraith 1997: 66–7). The sudden increases in inflation had come from exogenous shocks such as oil price jumps, crop failures, and wars. Inflation had not been wage led in the US over the years in which the 'natural' rate of unemployment had dominated policy debate.

In Europe, where high levels of unemployment persisted through the 1980s and 1990s, versions of the NAIRU were used to argue that the social wage was too high and that competitiveness required lower wages. Governments, it was widely argued, had inadvertently raised the NAIRU by expanding the Welfare State too much, producing inefficient labor markets. The logic of the position seemed unassailable. Stephen Nickell, however, found that this broad brush 'generous benefits = rigid labor markets = high unemployment' oversimplified to the point of being wrong. High unemployment is associated with some labor market features, but other labor market rigidities do not appear to have serious implications for average levels of unemployment (even though they were widely presumed to). These include strict employment protection and general legislation of labor market standards, even generous levels of unemployment benefits (as long as these are accompanied by pressure on the unemployed to take jobs, duration limits, and resources to increase their ability and willingness to take jobs). High levels of union strength are not a problem in this regard, so long as they are accompanied by coordination of wage bargaining. Based on his research comparing Europe and North America, Nickell concludes that 'there is no evidence in our data that high labor standards overall had any impact on unemployment whatever' (Nickell 1997: 72). Along these lines Edward Leamer has written,

> Having been taught that unemployment is caused by inflexible wages, I imagined that a measure of the gap between actual wages and predicted wages from some 'equilibrium' model would explain the level of unemployment. I could not find a model that would work.
>
> (Learner 1996: 313)

Other researchers using a different approach find that whilst employment in the United States adjusts more quickly than does employment in (the then West) Germany, hours worked adjust at about the same speed, since the Germans simply spread the cost of downturns more broadly (Blank 1994: 165). Reporting on National Bureau of Economic Research-sponsored research on the social protection–flexibility tradeoff, Rebecca Blank explains: 'there is little evidence that labor market flexibility is substantially affected by the presence of these social protection programs, nor is there strong evidence that the speed of labor market adjustment can be increased by limiting these programs (ibid.).

One might think that awareness of such findings and of the extent of the personal pain and larger social costs of persistent unemployment would lead not to a consideration of NAIRU as a given and constant unalterable element in the system, but to discussion of how this non-'natural' rate could be reduced. Yet despite the questionable basis of any scientific status useful to forecasting in a real-world policy context, for those believing in minimalist government intervention, acceptance of the 'natural' rate of unemployment served as a suitable replacement for the iron law of wages that was discredited in the last third of the nineteenth century to support a new policy pessimism.[12] The augmented Phillips Curve served to foil efforts to restore full employment through institutional reforms, and encouraged the development of the new classical economics, which is virtually Say's Law with the addition of random shocks or disturbances to explain economic fluctuations. In the absence of these exogenous shocks, continuous market clearing would take place. This classical model becomes a special case of the new classical model when random errors are zero and expectations are the best forecasts that can possibly be made. This brings us to the central question of the nature of expectations once again.

Rational expectations

The importance of perfect information in the older models asserting the allocative efficiency of markets finds its contemporary counterpart in the rational expectation theorists' suggestion that economic actors make predictions of the future based on all available information and are able to form the most accurate expectations of the future that can be formed. Everything that can be predicted is predicted. Mistakes are caused by random errors that cannot be forecast correctly, and if markets are not perfect, the implication is that economists cannot predict any better than anyone else. (Admittedly, many people have long felt this to be true which gives the theory instant wide credibility.) Government cannot know more than anyone else and models cannot guide policy to make the future better than it will be without government intervention.

This conclusion is a generalization that may be incorrect under other assumptions. For example, it is quite possible that 'everyone' knows the future looks bad and so reduces consumption and investment. Because everyone shares this belief, it is not only self-fulfilling but may turn out still worse than 'everyone' thought it would. If the government steps in and takes substantial action, by cutting taxes, by increasing employment through public works programs, or whatever, things look up because actual spending is greater than formerly expected, and expectations improve. The monetarist and new classical presumption is that public spending will increase public debt, which drives up interest rates, 'crowding out' private investment and cutting off the expansion. Keynesians, however, say that public spending does not crowd out private investment that was slack because of pessimistic expectations now reversed. Within normal bounds, state spending does not drive up interest rates. So long as significant excess capacity exists, stimulation should produce growth. This is the Keynes case. Is it the relevant one?

In the current period, official fears have revolved around inflationary expectations. If the government spends more and runs a deficit, or is expected to do so, markets react. Interest rates rise, cutting off investment. Wage demands increase in anticipation of these pressures, and so on. Expectations, the heart of Keynes' model, are turned against the possibilities of successful Keynesian policy. Whilst the Keynesians continue to do battle on the limited grounds of the presumption that sticky wages validate the Keynesian special case, more conservative economists and elected officials, especially in the United States and Great Britain, but elsewhere as well, work to remove the stickiness of wages by cutting unemployment benefits and other safety net programs, reducing the power of trade unions, and take other actions to make labor markets more efficient. In conceding the heart of Keynes' approach for the tactical, and pyrrhic, victory of fine tuning, the very project of activist government was compromised. Most Keynesians also accepted the need for a neoclassical micro grounding for macro analysis. As Robert Solow has pointed out, the demand for microfoundations is a demand that macroeconomics be built on Walrasian foundations (Solow 1986: 191). Andrew Kirman suggests the Walrasian model has so little to say about aggregative behavior that abeyance to this emperor 'who has no clothes' in this context makes little sense (Kirman 1989: 138). Of course, as always, other economists stand ready to defend the need for microfoundations along Walrasian lines as strongly. The critics of the microfoundation approach fault it for denying the possibility of, and the need for, a different kind of analysis when one considers the economy as a whole. To Keynes and economists in the B mode tradition, the economy is more than the sum of its parts. It is not that if each individual is allowed to maximize for themselves the sum effect will be the greatest good for the greatest number. This is precisely what Keynes denied.

There has been an interesting sea change in mainstream theory over the last quarter century or so, from an analysis of market determination of resource allocation, to choice theoretic analysis with particularly restrictive behavioral assumptions, embodying a further narrowing of the understanding of human nature, as the core of economics. This is a logical extension of the effort to reduce all economics to the result of individual choice and to limit the kind of choices so-called rational actors make (Sargent 1979: ch. 16). Reversing Keynes, this orientation maintains that any apparent disequilibrium, when looked at properly, will be seen to reflect the best possible outcome for all participants, given the constraints they face. What Keynes saw as a problem, the new classicals see as an optimal outcome. The strength of the new classical economics is in its suggestion that whilst poverty and business cycles exist, they are part of dynamic equilibria. Its insistence on microfoundations for macroeconomics logically leads to the end of a separate macroeconomics. The division, accepted since Samuelson's Keynesian synthesis, is ended, and economics is once again the study of markets, of the allocation of scarce resources among various and competing ends. This is, from the earlier Keynesian point of view, an instance of fallacy of composition. The sum of individuals acting rationally may not lead to the best outcome (as in the case when recession threatens and individuals rationally choose to save more and so, in the aggregate, reduce demand for goods and services, worsening the situation for all). Such possibilities are dismissed in the new classical economics.

The idea of 'rational expectations' theorists, that future values can be proxied based on rational expectations because economic agents forecast correctly based on available information and because errors are random and remain small, would have seemed ludicrous to Keynes. That economic policy is impotent, that systematic policy changes can do nothing to increase output and employment (because the public takes actions that offset the changes), would have made no sense to him and he surely would have denounced these new theories as he did their counterparts while he lived. The strong form of rational expectations assumes people actually know the structure of the model that truly describes the world and use it to form expectations.[13] The focus on conscious choice as the determinant of global outcomes has extended the power economists attribute to narrowly conceived rational action, on the one hand, and the power of the individuals (divorced from any wider socializing context) to make optimal choices, on the other. Versions of perfect information and best possible information have been revived to strengthen individual capacities at the level of theory.

Such thinking has not gone uncontested. A variety of behavioral models associated with influential thinkers such as Herbert Simon, James March, Richard Nelson, and Stanley Winter, among others, have offered rival views of richer psychological intricacy and organizational complexity. An important literature has grown up on the periphery of the profession which stands in stark challenge to the efforts to maintain parsimoniously motivated economic man, as was noted in Chapter 1. Especially with regard to the theory of the firm, major challenges to traditional neoclassical thinking have begun to make an impact within the profession (as will be discussed more fully in the second half of the next chapter); but in general economists continue to prefer parsimonious and deterministic to realistic and contingent explanations. A mode thinking dominates.

Business cycles, now and then

Where, before, business cycles were seen to be endogenous, caused in Keynes' way of thinking by cycles of over optimism and then protracted pessimism that are worked out with costly consequences in real historical time, economists came to see business cycles as caused by exogenous shocks to the system which are corrected by the natural tendency of a self-equilibrating economic system. By the end of the 1980s, 'Real business cycle theory thus pushed the Walrasian model farther than it has been pushed before' (Mankiw 1989: 81). Among such theorists there was a resurgence of pre-Keynesian thinking on the business cycle, a blotting out of the Keynesian Revolution. Many macroeconomists were back to a world in which business cycles are caused by exogenous shocks and fluctuations in employment are fully voluntary. Individuals are seen as just reallocating leisure over time. This was part of the research program of giving macroeconomics solid micro analytic foundations.

A host of neoclassical schools, most importantly rational expectations theory, claim the mantle of the A science systematizer against the B style, which is to stress consistency with the world over consistency with the theoretical abstraction.[14] The significance of the rational expectations hypothesis was, as David Begg has written, that 'it appeared to offer a clear-cut answer,' that it 'seemed to remove the ambiguity' (Begg 1982: 132–3). For Keynes, ambiguity had been inherent in expectations, as our earlier discussion of the distinction between risk and uncertainty hopefully made clear. Rational expectations avoids Keynes' question, which is how the diversity of economic agents with conflicting valuations and different expectations interact: bulls and bears, creditors and debtors. Tobin suggests 'To assume away this diversity is to default the responsibilities of the profession to maintain seriousness and relevance' (Tobin 1992a: 127). Other critics of 'rational' expectations thinking have been equally scathing in their reaction to this effort to undo the Keynesian Revolution by assumption.[15]

Words are used to communicate and to convince. They can be weapons to make partisan, ideological, and theoretically contested points. Like so many of the recent developments in economics that describe 'real' business cycles, 'natural' rates of unemployment, and so on, through the rhetorically charged use of familiar words, 'rational' conjoined with 'expectations' has come in for such criticism. Fritz Machlup wrote in the last article published before his death:

> I am using the term rational expectations under protest, since rational and correct are quite different things. Economists who had read Max Weber – and at one time every educated economist was supposed to have done so – have agreed that rationality meant consistency with one's preconceptions and prejudgments, right or wrong. . . . John Muth may be charged with an infraction of terminological discipline when he misused the term 'rational' to denote 'correct' expectations (or expectations in conformance with those of some economic theorists of the neoclassical school).
>
> (Machlup 1983, as quoted in Redman 1992: 35)

The line of demarcation of approach is clear. Robert Gordon has characterized rational expectations as a theory that 'proceeds with impeccable logic from unrealistic assumptions to conclusions that contradict the historical record.'[16] To Robert Lucas, on the other hand, 'progress in economic thinking means getting better and better abstract analogue models, not better verbal observations about the world' (Lucas and Sargent 1989: 696). The rational expectations theorists pursue and, in the minds of some, succeed in what has been called 'the mission impossible of voluntaristic individualism,' the production of robust and tractable models of continuous market clearing (Hillard 1992: 65). It was the rigor and precision of their mathematical style of arguing from a methodological individualism that impressed colleagues, even those who were not ready to buy the model.

The new classical economics paradigm accounts for business cycles and emphasizes external shocks and misspecifications in an otherwise perfectly competitive equilibrium economy. Random outside events, most notably changes in technology that affect productivity, are theorized to produce cycles. The purpose of the models is to show that fluctuations in economic activity are consistent with competitive general equilibrium. The implication of real business cycle thinking is that the existence of cycles is no reason for activist government. Cycles happen. The real business cycle theorists take the rational expectations hypothesis and explain cycles as caused by external unpredictable shocks to the system. Looking back on the Great Depression close to a half century later, a leading rational expectation theorist sees that it was obviously caused by a whole bunch of people making a lot of individual mistakes. Robert Lucas explains:

> If you look back at the 1929 to 1933 episode, there were a lot of decisions made that, after the fact, people wished they had not made; there were a lot of jobs people quit that they wish they had hung on to; there were job offers that people turned down because they thought the wage offer was crappy. Then three months later they wished they had grabbed. Accountants who lost their accounting jobs passed over a cabdriver job, and now they're sitting on the street while their pal's driving a cab. So they wish they'd taken the cab-driver job. People are making this kind of mistake all the time. Anybody can look back over the '30s and think of decisions which would have made millions – purchasing particular stocks, all kinds of things. I don't see what's *hard* about this question of people making mistakes in the business cycle. From the individual point of view, it's obvious.
>
> (Klamer 1984a: 41)

Indeed, from an individual point of view perhaps it is, but if social science is about more than the choices of individuals in isolation from larger social forces, it is both trivial and in the larger sense wrong to say that if all of these folks had decided to take the cab driver job or whatever, there wouldn't have been a depression.[17]

A prominent assumption of these models is that workers plan their labor supply over a fairly long period, some years in fact. Unemployment results because wages are always equal to the marginal productivity of labor, and so when external disturbances cause wages to fall, the labor force works less. When productivity rises again, workers will work more. The logic is impeccable, given the assumptions about behavior. Exogenous shocks produce an inter-temporal substitution of leisure, but is this line of reasoning plausible? The idea that people choose not to work because, given current wage rates and expectations concerning the future, it is advantageous to enjoy leisure now and earn income at some future date (and so choose to be unemployed voluntarily), is difficult to swallow. Robert Solow writes:

> If it were true, for instance, you would expect sales of goods complementary with leisure – like golf clubs, beachwear, skis and Caribbean cruises – to be higher in recession when there is a lot of measured unemployment than in

prosperous periods when the unemployment rate falls. There is no sign that anything so amusing is true.

(Solow 1990: 29)

The assumptions required to make such models work are not unlike the manipulations required in Ptolemaic astronomy. For example, consider the presumption of risk-sharing contracts, which help resolve the otherwise unexplainable problem of the cyclical behavior of labor's share of income. (In such models, entrepreneurs provide optimal risk-sharing contracts and workers obtain insurance against job and income losses due to cyclical fluctuations.) Even if one accepts for the sake of argument the real business cycle theorists' assumptions, there is no evidence for the large economy-wide disturbances of the sort they presume, nor is there other evidence in formal econometric testing of competing models to support such model presumptions as 'recessions are induced by rashes of bureaucratic intervention in the market process' (Stadler 1994: 1771).

Older understandings of business cycle theory were messier but I think more useful. Consider Wesley Clair Mitchell, the institutionalist founder of the National Bureau of Economic Research. As he saw it, 'A theory of business cycles must . . . be a descriptive analysis of the cumulative changes by which one set of business conditions transforms itself into another set' (Mitchell 1913: ix). The key phrase is 'transforms itself.' Cycles are seen as endogenous, natural occurrences in which prosperity sets the stage for crisis, depression, and then in turn for revival and new prosperity. 'Business history repeats itself, but always with a difference,' Mitchell writes. He thought

A thoroughly adequate theory of business cycles, applicable to all cycles is consequently unattainable. . . . Every business cycle, strictly speaking, is a unique series of events and has a unique explanation, because it is the outgrowth of a preceding series of events, likewise unique.

(ibid.: ix and x)

Schumpeter offers a similar view. He notes that:

the assumption that business behavior is ideally rational and prompt, and also that in principle it is the same for all firms, works tolerably well only within the precincts of tried experience and familiar motives. It breaks down as soon as we leave those precincts and allow the business community under study to be faced by – not simply new situations, which also occur as soon as external factors unexpectedly intrude but by – new possibilities of business action which are as yet untried and about which the most complete command of routine teaches nothing.

(Schumpeter 1939: 98)

This is what is intolerable to A science. For Mitchell, 'probabilities take the place of certainties' and 'moods' have 'a large share in shaping business decisions' (ibid.: 5). Similarly, for Schumpeter the future is always about 'new possibilities as yet untried.' The indeterminacy that accompanies a patterning of endogenous cycles does not fit the rational self-equilibrating model. Hence the science generates ideas such as rational expectations and real business cycles. It should be recognizable as Robinson Crusoe economics – a single representative individual makes choices for the whole economy.[18]

In making this distinction between the kinds of business cycle theorizing Mitchell (and Keynes) preferred, it is worth noting that this is part of another important episode in the development of economics, which cannot be adequately dealt with here. It is the often acrimonious debate between partisans of the National Bureau of Economic Research approach, represented by Mitchell, and those of Arthur Burns' 1946 business cycle study, which was reviewed in a highly critical fashion by Tjalling Koopmans, director of the Cowles Foundation. This debate was in large measure about whether econometrics, which integrated theory, mathematics, and statistics in a way then new to the profession, was a major breakthrough and vastly superior institutional approach endorsed by Mitchell, and the business cycle theorizing of Keynes, which was in real historical and institutionally contingent space. Advocates of the latter approach criticized econometrics for simplifying reality by ignoring uncertainty and real irreversible time. The modeling approach advocated and practiced by Koopmans (and by Jan Tinbergen and Ragnar Frisch) was part of a 'probablistic revolution' replacing Keynes' approach by reducing uncertainty to risk. These models in turn were the basis of work by Lawrence Klein (who had worked with Samuelson mathematically formalizing economic theory) and others, which produced large macro–micro models explaining the operation of the economy in Keynesian terms and used in forecasting and policy work starting in the 1950s.[19] Ironically, the critique Robert Lucas was to make of these models had in some respects a very J.M. Keynes flavor.

The New Keynesians

More generally, the disagreements among contemporary theorists concern what distinction if any needs to be made between the presumption that agents use available information efficiently and how specific assumptions about the available set of information are made. Within the rational expectations literature, attention focuses on costs of information, learning models, expectations formation, and forecast errors. Finding a good testable model has proven difficult. At the level of theory, the model can be said to be logically constructed, but many, perhaps most, economists still find it improbable as a description of the real world. New Keynesian economists have used information and contract theory to pour the vintage wine of institutional labor economics into presentable new containers and to model social behavior in individualistic terms (see e.g. Baker and Holstrom 1995). These New Keynesians have proposed alternative models in which markets do not clear and in which sticky prices are strongly justified, in the sense that convincing imperfections are identified and mechanisms specified that produce equilibria in which there are suboptimal levels of employment and output (Blinder 1994). Because sticky prices can be both privately efficient and socially inefficient, business cycles, according to New Keynesians, result in suboptimal adjustment of prices in response to demand shocks and so call for policy measures. Even small changes in such things as menu costs are believed to cause large welfare losses, and such an economy 'does not recommend passive monetary policy' (Mankiw 1985: 537). Such models with non-neutral money, structured coordination problems, and sticky wages have been presented using sophisticated mathematics, building and testing models empirically, which are found more convincing by New Keynesians than their adversaries (Mankiw and Romer 1991a).

New Keynesians are not the Keynesians of the monetarist–Keynesian debates, but rather precede from the terrain chosen by the New Classicals: both the need for rigorous microanalytic foundations for macroeconomic analysis and the suspicion of active government policy. They do, however, argue that unfettered markets can produce inefficient equilibria, and their models often show that government intervention can lead to improved resource allocation. They do not argue for traditional demand side Keynesianism, but offer supply side rationales for government actions. The New Keynesians believe that real market imperfections are crucial for understanding economic fluctuations, and that changes in nominal values (money wages and the money supply, for example) influence real variables such as employment and output. The New Keynesians argue that the many 'small' imperfections in the relevant markets add up to large impacts.

New Keynesian studies show extensive stickiness at the micro level and model how these substantial and complex frictions impede the market adjustment process presumed in the New Classical models. Real rigidities exist in real economies. Some prices get out of line and the nature of different markets produces important consequences for price adjustment. Models demonstrating self-fulfilling prophesies and chaotic dynamics provide alternative stories to characterize the complex world. They therefore should be part of a rigorous microeconomics, say the New Keynesians. Notions of fairness, far from being mushy constructs of interest only to the warm fuzzies of the profession, have predictive power when considered in the context of explicit contracts and other aspects of long-term relational agreements. Such models of employee–employer cooperative bargaining prove to have explanatory power to predict wage behavior and employment over the business cycle. Temporary shocks are demonstrated to have permanent effects in hysteresis models. Credit imperfections based on asymmetric information between lenders and borrowers and credit rationing mechanisms are found to explain financial market behavior. These real imperfections suggest roles for government and a need to question the New Classical Economics' story of markets (Mankiw and Romer 1991b).

Whilst modern economists rarely speak in terms of their pre-analytic visions, or acknowledge the extent to which their intellectual pedigree informs their positive economics, such matters are hardly far below the surface. The tension between agency and structure can be seen across the spectrum of theorists and policy makers. For this reason it is difficult to discuss contemporary theory. The sheer size of the literature and the impossibility of knowing which economists and what of their economics will be considered of importance in the longer perspective makes valancing contemporary discussions difficult.[20]

Political implications of modern theory

Modern theorists with their efficiency wage and shirking theories claim to break new ground by offering microanalytic foundations for equilibrium unemployment. The big improvement is that these theories are consistent with the reality that unemployment is not temporary in the frictional meaning of the neoclassicals. In a neoclassical system, the existence of competition guarantees that no one undertakes erroneous (read wasteful or inefficient) activities so that resources must always be optimally allocated. The idea of efficiency wages (firms do not pay the lowest possible wage that anyone would accept to do a job, but pay a higher amount than this market clearing level so that workers have an incentive to do their best) is put together with the shirking model insight that wages are above equilibrium level (so that workers will not risk shirking since to be fired means the likelihood of an inferior wage in alternative employment) and a quitting model (quits are minimized by higher wage payment and so turnover costs such as training new workers are saved).

In a more conservative political climate, efficiency logic more influentially asserts that unemployment benefits increase the real wage firms must pay in order to induce a given level of effort, turnover, and shirking. Government benefits to workers are 'a subsidy to leisure' and so raise this efficiency wage. The availability of benefits diminishes employed workers' concern over possibly losing their jobs and so they reduce equilibrium employment. These explanations account for above equilibrium wage payments. There will be other potential workers who would like employment at these wages but are not hired. The firm is presumed to have the number it needs, and the availability of those willing to work for lower compensation does not lead to hiring, as in the neoclassical model. To do so would lower morale and the productivity of already employed workers. Thus there is equilibrium and unemployment.

The effects of real interest rates on labor demand is another explanatory theme. Edmund Phelps, for example, places higher interest rates, which bring about rising unemployment, at the heart of the exercise (Woodford 1994: 1804). In a moment I will quote Phelps on the causal relations he assumes to be central to explaining the present era's 'structural slumps,' but first it should be pointed out that whilst there may be an association between higher interest rates and higher unemployment, it need not be a causal relationship as Phelps presumes. Indeed, Michael Woodford argues in an effective critique that both are cyclically sensitive. When the economy goes into recession, the public debt rises and unemployment goes up. Deficits caused by revenue shortfalls or unexpected inflation lead to higher interest rates. The reduced form correlations Phelps offers can be explained by many alternative theoretical frameworks and do not offer proof of his position. Phelps's is one story on offer among others. Is it convincing?

Believing that government spending that increases consumption is a bad thing, primarily because unemployment and real interest rates are thereby increased, Phelps offers a theoretically coherent and influential explanation of how government spending in the 1980s was the cause of the deep slumps of that decade, and argues that the worst thing governments can do is stimulate consumption and investment (since this will produce unemployment). The channel through which the most damage appears to be done, as noted, is through high interest rates causing unemployment, because workers get so much income from their asset portfolio that they choose more leisure when interest rates rise and *this* generates the problem levels of unemployment. His hope is that once real interest rates fall back to the neighborhood of 3 per cent, around which they seemed to center for so many decades, workers will not have such 'plump cushions, their own and their relatives', provided by the various incomes from wealth as exist today' (Phelps 1994: 373).[21]

Realities of asset distribution and especially the statistics on unearned working-class income hardly support such an edifice for modern equilibrium theorizing. Indeed, his model is built on stylized facts that do not stand up to scrutiny.[22] Most working-class families had zero or negative net financial assets. In 1989 the richest 1 per cent of Americans had 14 per cent of total income but owned over half of all net financial assets (including government bonds). In total, the bottom 95 per cent of the population lost income to the top 5 per cent over the decade. Most families lived from paycheck to paycheck, but the 'modern' theory of employment developed in this decade stressed the ability of workers to stay unemployed longer because of their non-labor income from mostly non-existent financial portfolios. It is true that income from capital assets rose (from 10.7 per cent of all income in 1959 to 19.7 per cent in 1989) but at the latter date the bottom 90 per cent received only 10 per cent of their income from capital (dividends and interest). Very little of this went to persons outside of the managerial–technical–professional strata, and hardly enough to offer the workers the 'plump cushion' central to the Phelps story.[23]

As to the increased government spending presumed as fact by not only Phelps but many others, federal spending did grow by 39 per cent between 1980 and 1995; but the ability to finance that collective obligation, the Gross National Product, rose by more: 43 per cent (both adjusted for inflation). The burden increased for the average taxpayer even as tax cuts reduced it for the top 10 per cent and especially the top 1 per cent of the income distribution. The structural deficit created by the Reagan Era tax changes stimulated the much commented upon increase in the national debt to national income ratio. The fiscal crisis of the state was a political construction. The response to slower growth was increasing inequality sponsored through a politics of misrepresentation. There is a great deal of evidence of rising inequality and redistribution to the top and very little to suggest that the incentive effects of redistribution to the workers or the unemployed created the problem, rather than the 'plump cusions' of government transfers and higher interest and dividend income for workers.[24]

The retrogression of modern theory

Whilst such a brief account can hardly do justice to contemporary debates, and it would surely be premature to characterize the world of contemporary mainstream theory as that of Senior, Say, and Bastiat revisited, I believe there are important parallels in the reaction to the Keynesian Revolution to the century earlier rejection of the classical mainline tradition. Such a view on my part accounts for a certain unhappiness expressed in the manner in which the trajectory of 'modern' theory with its 'rational' expectations, 'real' business cycles, and 'leisure seeking workers' with their 'plump cushions' has been recounted. These are not the only theoretical perspectives on offer but they are the most energetically promoted and seem to speak to the (dis)temper of the times. For economists, their success comes in their microanalytic foundations, parsimonious assumptions about human nature, and faithfulness to an extreme methodological individualism. The new Keynesian opposition has internalized these values. The A science core demands of the mainstream have constricted the vision of those with oppositional proclivities among many of the best and brightest of our economic theorists.[25]

Rational expectations are invoked in a way that returns the centrality of harmony to the way the economy is presumed to work, a stability that Keynes had taken away. If, as John Muth's work suggested, private actors dynamically optimize their individual positions by adjusting to the available information, they will always be on an optimal adjustment path. As Robert Lucas saw it, they adjusted immediately and rationally to new information, including what they expected government to do. The brilliance of rational expectations is that it is a more convincing substitute for the assumption of perfect foresight that is much harder to maintain, and serves the same function. The uses to which the natural rate of unemployment have been put are ideologically reminiscent of the classical economists' natural wage and wage fund doctrine. Current business cycle thinking speaks of fluctuations as caused by shocks to an essentially stable system. Government mistakes, faulty information, and external events have their impact on a system that is believed to be basically self-correcting. The new classical proofs are either simple assertions of how the world works that are easily contested or, as their critics maintain, are based on models of such unrealism as to be irrelevant for policy purposes. The anti-government economics of the new *laissez-faire* theorists, as William Buiter has argued, 'has no sound foundation as a generally valid proposition, either in economic theory or in careful empirical observation' (Buiter 1980: 45). Yet it is tremendously popular, and that popularity is what needs explaining.

Stepping back to look at the view of macroeconomic policy that has prevailed at the end of the 1990s, the consensus that emerged was that activist fiscal or monetary policy to stimulate output and reduce unemployment beyond their sustainable level (understood as the natural rate of output) and reducing unemployment beyond its sustainable level would simply lead to inflation. The policy would act only to increase the price level but not to lower unemployment or higher output persistently. Activist fiscal policy was abandoned and then activist monetary policy, as the lags involved in their implementation came to be understood as variable and long. Timing uncertainties were as likely to result in pro-cyclical as anti-cyclical impacts and so be counterproductive, even if they worked as the earlier theorists had assumed. The general acceptance that there was no long-run, and likely not even much of a short-run tradeoff between inflation and unemployment, convinced mainstream theorists that attempts to exploit such a presumed tradeoff would have no real benefit. The greater role attributed to rational expectations and the consensus that inflation, even at low levels, resulted in slower real growth, drove additional nails into the coffin of activism in the minds of most of the mainstream. The best that policy makers could do was target inflation and provide a stable environment for private economic actors.

A broader B mode contextualizing of contemporary normative economics suggests other possible frameworks that consider the power of the bond markets and of capital strikes to prevent expansionary policies from working and their ability to enforce a low wage, slower growth path on national governments, and stagnant wages on workers. In the next chapter we start with the pure theory of growth that was popular in the 1950s and 1960s, and which is the basis of the more complex modeling by endogenous growth theorists and others coming out of the neoclassical tradition, producing an important literature in the 1980s and 1990s. We will also consider approaches grounded in B mode understandings of processes of the accumulation process, and the importance of the forces that have come to be known as globalization.

10 Theorizing economic growth

In the world of simple theory, firms everywhere are assumed to operate with the full knowledge of all possible technologies. Given the right (market determined) prices for inputs and outputs, they pick the one that is appropriate to their national endowments. All firms in an industry facing the same prices, chose the same technologies; otherwise they are allocatively inefficient. The international technology market is assumed to work efficiently, and all firms are taken to have full knowledge of the technologies available so that they can buy the right one 'off the shelf'. All firms can, moreover, immediately use imported technologies with the same degree of efficiency (and at best-practice levels). There is no theoretical reason to expect the persistence of technological inefficiency. If such inefficiency exists, it is, *ex hypothesi*, due to managerial slack or incompetence, and to government interventions that allow inefficient firms to continue in production.

This approach gives rise to simple policy prescriptions.

(Lall 1995: 259)

There is no question that, in taking on board this complexity, one often ends up with a theory in which precise predictions are impossible or highly dependent on particular contingencies, as is the case if the theory implies multiple or rapidly shifting equilibria, or if under the theory the system is likely to be far away from any equilibrium, except under very special circumstances. Thus an evolutionary theory not only may be more complex than an equilibrium theory. It may be less decisive in its predictions and expectations. To such a complaint, the advocate of an evolutionary theory might reply that the apparent power of the simpler theory in fact is an illusion.

(Nelson, R. R. 1995: 85)

We have seen that the framing of research questions about economics and the economy create overlapping conversations that, like the blind men of the fable, employ diverse procedures to look at the elephant. The viewpoints of different economists can be grouped into schools of thought, and the parts of social reality appear different from these many angles. Even when seemingly comparable questions are being considered, for example about trends in productivity growth, A and B mode economists see different factors at work. Likewise, debates within a national context produce a different picture from an internationally comparative one, from the perspective of pure theory.

In this chapter we start with formal models of growth, explore how their failure to speak to postwar complexities led to the empirical researching of determinants of growth, discuss extensions of the neoclassical approach, and then move beyond these perspectives in various directions. Neoclassical theory, econometric explanations of productivity, new growth theory, international trade and especially strategic trade approaches, social knowledge and organization-based theories of economic development, and models of the postwar regulatory regime are considered. These approaches are part of a resurgence of interest in the question that inspired the early political economists: the nature and causes of the wealth and welfare of nations.

There have been a number of such challenges by models in which production takes place in real time and geographical space. Many of the 'hot topics' in economics at the end of the twentieth century represent striking departures from existing mainstream theorizing; 'Pervasive increasing returns and imperfect competition; multiple equilibria everywhere; an often decisive role for history, accident, and perhaps sheer self-fulfilling prophecy: these are the kind of ideas that are now becoming popular,' writes Paul Krugman (1991: 9).

In the last chapter we discussed the increasingly limited vision of macroeconomics that accompanied the policy ineffectiveness proposition and the anti-Big Government political climate, in which widespread skepticism of interventionist made macroeconomics a less interesting field within economics because there was little that economic policy could do except get out of the way of the market. Macroeconomics reduces to microeconomics, and as a field it comes to be demoted from the preeminence it held in the days of activist macropolicy making. Indeed, both macro- and microeconomic theory have become more abstract and, since they rely on the automaticity of markets, have similar things to say about the way the world is presumed to operate. Yet internationalization and the global–local reorganizations of production and the economics of technology, the possibility of replication of goods and services at minimal cost for consumption in distant markets, the reorganization of corporate governance structures, and a host of new thinking about transaction costs are having an impact. New models are abandoning neoclassical simplifications and looking with increased curiosity into the black box of technology and the production process.

It is possible that a next phase economics will be created from such inquiries. The new macro, if it is thought of in such terms, would be a return to the classic concern with the nature and causes of the wealth of nations, in which increasing returns from social knowledge and institutional re-formation are central. A new micro that takes entrepreneurship, innovation, and factor specificity as central to explaining allocation of resources and generation of corporate profitability may produce a next stage microeconomics that contrasts sharply with the 'allocation of given resources among known competing ends' (Robbins 1932).[1] In contrast to the disjuncture between micro and macro of the years of the Keynesian–neoclassical synthesis, which was produced by the need to weld Keynesian macroeconomics to a neoclassical microeconomics, a next generation synthesis would allow for easier movement from the small to the large and indeed for greater trucking and barter across more open borders to neighboring social sciences.

In the next chapter more attention is to be paid to the possibility of such a reconstitution. In this chapter we discuss some of the major interventions in the area of growth theory, broadly construed, that have piqued professional imagination in the period since the decay of the mainstream Keynesian–neoclassical synthesis. This is a vast, sprawling, overlapping, and often oddly intersecting set of discourses that is yet to be codified. They continue to develop too rapidly to expect easy closure. In my view, they point economics forward in an exciting direction: back to the classic concerns of the early political economists.

In 'our armchair omniscience'

In 1965, in one of the authoritative review studies jointly published by the American Economic Association and the Royal Economic Society, Frank Hahn and R.C.O. Mathews surveyed the field of growth theory. They found the variety of models to be great and noted that 'with ingenuity can evidently be almost infinitely enlarged.' The purity of the Walrasian framework, far from being a virtue, enabled proliferation of stories that were so abstract as hardly to connect with any picture of a recognizable economy. It is one thing to use abstractions in order to understand basic rules and regularities of the economic system, but growth theory had become something else. Scathingly they wrote:

> As far as pure theory is concerned the 'measurement of capital' is no problem at all because we never have to face it if we do not choose to. With our armchair omniscience we can take account of each machine separately. Moreover the measurement business has nothing whatsoever to do with the question of whether imputation theory is or is not valid. In an equilibrium of the whole system, provided there is perfect competition, no learning by doing and no uncertainty, the neo-classical imputation results hold. This should now be beyond dispute. It is also of little comfort to the empirically inclined.
>
> (Hahn and Matthews 1965: 110)

After going on a bit about the way stylized facts – if they are defined narrowly enough – can be used to produce 'fascinating models' (the assumptions they refer to specifically are that there is no government and no international trade), Hahn and Mathews suggest that the undertaking was essentially a frivolous occupation. Such damning criticism would perhaps not have influenced economists enamored with neoclassical growth theory but for the fact that, within a few years, by the end of the 1960s (and showing up as a statistical trend break in 1973), growth in the advanced capitalist nations plummeted. GDP, which had been increasing at close to 6 per cent over the 1950–73 period, fell to below 2 per cent thereafter and stayed at a low rate for more than two decades. These developments led to a focus on empirical growth models.

Measuring the determinants of growth

Since the pioneering publications by Solow and Swan (both in 1956), neoclassical theorists have been building growth models under a variety of assumptions concerning the extent of factor mobility for open and closed economies. There have been debates concerning core predictions of the model, most prominently what explains growth and whether there is a tendency for poor economies to grow faster than rich ones. The literature suggests there has been convergence among countries within striking distance of the leaders; that relative backwardness, if not too extreme, allows room for catch-up through imitation. In terms of the leading neoclassical models, however, the presumption that capital accumulation will explain observed growth does not seem to hold up (exogenous growth as measured by the 'Solow residual' is uncomfortably large compared to what the early versions of the model predicted). Edward Denison's pioneering empirical measurement of the determinants of productivity growth described this residual as 'the measure of our ignorance.' Since Denison's 1979 book, economists have made progress in reducing the size of the unexplained variance. Yet the stylized neoclassically construed factors of production, labor, and capital inputs explain about half of historical growth in the industrialized nations (see Solow 1956 and Swan 1956).[2]

As there has been considerable occasion to remark, the postwar Keynesian economics represented a dramatic redirection of the economics that had broken in upon the mainstream under conditions of world depression. The 'Harrod–Domar' model is in fact another instance of such reconstitution. Harrod's original model had explained overheating chronic unemployment and the general dynamics of cyclical fluctuation as an extension of Keynes' economics (Harrod 1948). Evsey Domar, who worked in a tradition going back to Marx, was concerned with underconsumption and the link between employment and capital accumulation, criticizing and extending Keynes' frame to include increased productive capacity produced by investment as a source of future problems from overcapacity. He was critical of abstract growth models. His work was multi-disciplinary and drew on ideas from all the social sciences (Domar 1957). Textbook 'Harrod–Domar' models are part of the restructuring of the economics identified with Keynes and other like-minded economists of the 1930s and 1940s.

It is not clear that the synthesis Keynesian innovations of the 1950s were an improvement on the earlier direction. The assumptions of constant returns to scale and full employment in steady state models in which all countries have access to identical production techniques produced a neoclassical world that was not mirrored in the data.[3] The real innovation has been the increasing appreciation of the importance of social knowledge as the cause of growth. Formal education is the easiest aspect to measure, but organizational competence, and even such vague and all-encompassing constructs as 'social capability,' have captured attention. The role of knowledge (as a form of capital in some models hoping to save the neoclassical version by expanding it in unorthodox directions), increasing returns and spillovers, externalities, public goods aspects, and social returns are prominent in newer growth theories that see scope for government policy to bring about welfare enhancement as aspects of B style realism and interpretative power to the earlier, more parsimonious abstractions.

The economic historian David Landes, after laboring for two decades to produce, in 1998, *The Wealth and Poverty of Nations*, a majestic economic history of the world, concluded that culture, the values and attitudes that guide members of society, is the key to economic development of nations. Variants of this idea were heard with increased frequency in the 1980s and 1990s. A related notion, social knowledge as the major source of economic growth, has also become popular, with the inference that there are increasing returns from ideas developed in one place and copied elsewhere at low marginal cost. Knowledge can be a non-rival form of property. In a world of increasing returns, competition can be a positive sum game, producing faster economic growth from rapid learning in multiple relationships – from suppliers, customers, and workers. Rather than proprietary secrets as the route to higher profitability, in a world of fast obsolescing, knowledge-based products, getting more knowledge earlier through wider networking can pay high returns (Kanter 1995: Pt 2). Improvements in understanding and best practice technique can be spread by 'contagion' as it were (Baumol 1994).

The idea that productivity depends in some dependable mathematical way along Harrod–Domar (Domar 1947 and Harrod 1948) lines on some homogeneous input investment in physical capital has lost favor. We are brought back to Marshall's judgment that 'Capital consists in a great part of knowledge and organization; and of this part is private property and other part is not. Knowledge is our most powerful engine of production. . . . Organization aids knowledge; it has many forms.' Among these it may be noted that Marshall listed the State 'providing security for all and help for many' (Marshall 1890: 138–9).[4] Marshall's preference for biological concepts over mechanical analogies has found respectful hearing.[5] For example, Nelson and Wright look at the postwar period in longer historical perspective and discuss the rise and decline of American leadership in terms of actual technology development in historical time. They trace the rise of mass production in the US in the nineteenth century, considering the impact of America's uniquely favorable access to natural resources, the world's largest internal market, the high investment in R & D and in scientific education and training. Nelson and Wright suggest that the skills of mass production were hands-on capabilities, more like a private than a public good, but that in the post-Second World War period, key technological capacities are more like public goods. It is 'the internationalization of trade, business, and generic technology and the growing commonality of the economic environments of firms in different nations that have made it so' (Nelson and Wright 1992: 1961).

Productivity growth in world perspective

Whilst there has been a tendency for researchers to concentrate on developments in their own countries, over time it became clear that similar forces may have been impacting across boundaries. It is not only the United States but the other advanced capitalist economies that exhibit slower growth. The OECD economies grew at an average rate of 4.2 per cent between 1962 and 1979 but only 2.4 per cent from 1979 to 1992, according to the World Bank. How is it that with all of this technological sharing that is possible, specialization, and gains from trade, there was such a slowdown? Economists have expended a great deal of creative energies attempting to explain the troubling decrease in the rate of productivity growth that struck the world economy at the end of the 1960s.

William Baumol, Sue Anne Batey Blackman, and Edward Wolff have sorted out the various issues of the productivity debate and offered an influential reading of what is known of the facts involved. In doing so, they take a longer view, assembling data from 1870 that show a remarkably stable productivity growth of around 2 per cent between 1870 and 1929. After that, productivity growth drops to 1 per cent during the Great Depression and leaps to 4 per cent in the 1940s. Growth is rapid until the 1970s, when it falls to slightly below the long-term trend (of 2 per cent) (Baumol *et al.*1989). Their conclusion is that the United States had simply returned to its long-run growth path and, as other nations have recovered from the Second World War, the United States was about where it should be. The productivity slowdown was widespread and it has been suggested that this too represents a return to trend. Whilst the slower growth following post-Second World War rebuilding explains some of the changes, more is involved.

Angus Maddison looked at labor quantity and quality, capital and a set of proxies for capacity utilization, foreign trade effects, economies of scale, energy cost impacts, and government regulation across the industrialized nations. His is a neoclassical model with variables for exogenous shifts that statistically correlate with events. His regression equations significantly 'explain' GDP growth and slowdown by period (Maddison 1987: 679, Table 20). In a 1987 review article, Maddison looks for proximate causes and does not examine institutions, sociopolitical conflicts, ideology, or policy impacts, and criticizes those who do who use 'loose descriptions, untestable assertions, and literary modes of persuasion' (ibid.: 677). However, he himself has some conflicting feeling, for in a later essay Maddison takes a more generous position, suggesting that consideration of institutions, ideologies, socioeconomic pressure groups, historical accidents, and other 'ultimate' causality, whilst virtually impossible to quantify, are valid concerns and so 'there will always be legitimate scope for disagreement on what is important' (Maddison 1994: 32).

Glyn, Hughes, Lipietz, and Singh ask the same questions, adopting a historical approach that looks at macroeconomic structures to explain the relation between wage changes, productivity, profitability, capital, investment, and consumption. They examine the organization of work, techniques of production, rules of coordination, and the international order. They are concerned with the institutions of the postwar accommodation and its stability conditions. Their approach is that of profit squeeze theorists. Their regressions show that rising input costs, tighter labor markets, and increased competition led to the decline in productivity (Glyn *et al.* 1991).

The correspondence between Maddison's work and that of the Glyn, Hughes, Lipietz, and Singh team can be judged in terms of their variables. Maddison's precise findings and abstract causal categories can be read in conjunction with the latter's more eclectic stories reviewing some of the same statistical evidence, telling their tale in dynamic system terms rather than comparative statics. The first is an A project; the second is a B undertaking. For me, the A findings may be accurate (in factor input terms) but tell little about the way the economy works, how choices are made, what makes a difference in terms of how private and public decision makers act in the real world. In a Maddison-style analysis, economies function in mechanistic fashion, varying input combinations produce outcomes, but there is little sense of human agency, of real people making difficult choices in the face of an uncertain future. The laws of economic science are, however, shown to function fully and to explain what transpires. The Glyn *et al.* study looks at political coalitions, institutional accommodations, and the choice social actors have made, which contribute to the outcomes in economic indicators observed. The choice of approach, which has major significance for how we see the social world, is a matter of Klamer's circles versus squares. There is no mutually agreeable standard of comparison as to which is the 'better' way to envision the economic order.

Much of the framing in this 1980s discussion was reduced to the issue of how the productivity slowdown caused economic stagnation. This debate grew more complicated as it came to be agreed that the economic slowdown, with its troubling sustained high unemployment could not neatly be explained by a productivity slowdown (Bean 1994: 588). Moreover, the usual neoclassical suspects were found innocent in influential studies. These familiar all-purpose villains – trade unions, social insurance (such as too generous unemployment benefits), high taxes, the other sins of Big Government and so on – interfere with the operation of the 'free' market. High taxes were exonerated because they were rising in Japan and non-EC Europe. Union strength was everywhere declining (in the test case, 'the Thatcher government has clearly emasculated the unions without any noticeable beneficial effect on wages and employment' [ibid.: 591]). Generous unemployment benefits do increase unemployment duration, but statistically the effect is quite small. The impact of the minimum wage in European social democracies – a familiar suspect – 'is effectively zero.' Whilst there is some impact on youth unemployment specifically, 'its overall effect is marginal.' Thus the ever popular 'blame the Welfare State' view is not supported. Charles Bean, summarizing the evidence, suggests

> The bottom line of this is that no single factor stands out as the cause of the rise in European unemployment, although it seems difficult to believe the terms-of-trade shocks of the seventies and the counter-inflationary policies and high interest rates of the eighties do not have some part to play in the story.
>
> (ibid.: 596)

We have discussed similar findings in the last chapter. The frame of such debates shifted somewhat by the late 1990s as Japan and German growth rates slowed and American performance improved. In terms of methodology, looking at comparative studies we see a different kind of tension – between findings in trade theory and labor economics.

Comparative advantage and international trade

The principle of comparative advantage is broadly that economic actors engage in an activity that they are relatively better at performing, and exchange with others whose advantage lies elsewhere. Both benefit from the gains from trade. Anyone questioning the general validity of this view has (until fairly recently) been denounced for incompetence and marginalized within the profession.[6] Yet the pure theory of international trade, like much pure A mode theory in economics, is not realistic in its assumptions and is being used for purposes other than those for which the model was designed. Wolfgang Stolper himself, writing fifty-five years after the Stolper–Samuelson theorem was proposed, notes the lack of realism of its assumptions – that not only labor but final products and technology to make them were the same domestically and abroad and the amount of inputs are all assumed to remain constant. As a Schumpeterian, he felt the need to point out that real economies are evolutionary and that new types of goods are produced as a result of technological changes, and so in reality the structures of economies change continuously. The kinds of labor needed shifts as well, and individuals are not easily shifted. Alterations affected by trade on the structure of an economy must be considered. 'This becomes crucial,' Stolper wrote (1997: 6), 'in an evolutionary context.'

The basic Heckscher–Ohlin–Storper–Samuelson trade model, which assumes identical production functions in the same industry in all countries, presumes that low labor cost from an abundance of unskilled labor translates into a comparative advantage in that factor, just as capital abundance suggests specialization in capital-intensive products for trade. Because it is about proving conclusively the advantages of trade, the theory must keep to simple assumptions that are tractable. It is taken for granted that if the simple model is correct then more complex ones will be too. In the short run, the comparative advantage of nations is presumed given. The theory states that labor and capital are perfectly mobile within countries but immobile between them. As firms combine factors they respond to changes in cost and expected returns that are presumed to be known. The working of the market produces full employment. Under such conditions, each participant within a country, and the countries themselves benefit from specialization and exchange (Leamer 1984).[7] This case for free trade is the strongest economists make for any policy advocated on a presumed basis of positive economics. Beyond the two commodity–two country matrix, however, all sorts of judgments quickly and of necessity intrude, and the generalized findings are not theoretically secure. Indeed, in a world in which capital is mobile between the two countries, a world something like the one we live in, such a pure trade model would produce very different results. Assuming no taxes or transportation costs, the nation with the absolute advantage in unit labor costs for the production of both commodities will attract enough capital to produce both locally and export both to the other nation. In such a simple two commodity–two country model, in which we allow for capital mobility and available sufficiently trained or trainable workers in a Lewis Model of surplus labor (Lewis 1954), production and employment in the second nation fall toward zero.

If unemployed labor is not readily rehired for other tasks, and large segments of the higher wage country's industrial workforce, the less skilled and older workers especially, permanently lose out, it is possible, in theory, as economists since J.S. Mill have said, to compensate losers out of the gains from trade. As a matter of practical politics, such assistance has never been successful. The case can also be made, as it was by Adam Smith and of course many other economists since, that rapid shifts that suddenly displace workers should be slowed to assist the adjustment process and reduce the pain that new trade patterns can bring. In a world in which floating exchange rates can make a nation's industries uncompetitive for periods long enough to destroy the industry (before exchange rate movements are reversed), protecting the industry on a temporary basis may also be called for, although as a matter of practical policy doing so efficiently and effectively is unlikely to be easy. There are thus two levels of debate surrounding trade. The first is at the level of believable general theory and the second concerns adaption of the best short-run policy matters. In the case of extremely high domestic unemployment, a convinced free trader, as Keynes, for example, was at the start of the depression, can conclude that tariff protection is the best available practical policy (Eichengreen 1984 and Radice 1988).

Because so much actual trade is intra-industry, between advanced economies, and less likely to be natural endowment based, economists have been moving away from the Heckscher–Ohlin assumption of identical production functions. Gary Burtless has offered the paired formulation that 'Although trade economists are confident of the implications of the Heckscher–Ohlin model (given its assumptions), they are not very confident that its assumptions are true' (Burtless 1995: 804). Dynamics is, of course, beyond the approach that assumes that the long run is simply the sum of short runs. The point is a most important one and can be put more strongly. Indeed, it often has been. Warren Samuels suggests that the proposition that free trade results in a Pareto-optimal solution is 'non-operational, non-testable, and non-refutable' (Samuels 1980: 139). It is a matter of logic perhaps and true at the abstract level; but even there the presumption that all parties benefit requires restrictive assumptions that do not hold in real-world cases. The two key elements built into the model by assumption, that the total volume of employment in both trading countries is no smaller after trade than before and that there are constant costs of production, are not really acceptable bases for policy making. Yet until Japanese success and the rise of the other East Asian developmentalist states it was, however, accepted as an article of unquestioned faith (Fishlow *et al.* 1994).[8]

Diminishing returns to transferable factors, or increasing returns from economies of scale – say from limited availability of high quality soil for vineyards in Portugal, or increasing returns in manufacturing textiles in England – could produce a situation in which Portugal could end up a poorer country after trade than before. If there are learning-by-doing effects in England's textile industry, and if vineyards do not absorb unemployed former textile workers in Portugal, we have a different story indeed. From what we know about increasing returns in industry, a country with an initial lead may increase the distance from its lagging competitors. The technology may be freely available (although that too may be doubtful) and still not be adopted because of market scale differences. Which outcomes prevail are hardly matters of different mathematical skill levels of analysts, but rather the assumptions each finds believable. The central point is that the classical and neoclassical conception that the opportunity to trade necessarily benefits a country by reallocating resources in such a way that each unit of labor will directly or indirectly make a greater contribution to the national output than it did before, is false – or rather, it is true only under highly restrictive and unrealistic assumptions (Kaldor 1984: 62).

When capital is internationally mobile and where subcontracting and commodity web organization by transnational corporations dominate real-world trade in manufactures, we find different kinds of links between trade and relative wages, ones that fall outside the Heckscher–Ohlin framework. Skill bias in technological change and monopoly power at one strategic point in the commodity chain allows for appropriating greater value added to such transnational corporations (Feenstra and Hanson 1996). The politics of trade increasingly claims attention as the costs of reaching long-run equilibrium mount. In this regard, a perspective offered by David Ricardo and Jacob Viner, the so-called specific factors approach, looks at which sectors of the economy gain and which lose from changed trade patterns. It suggests that political division on trade is between sectors rather than exclusively owners of factors of production, with workers in some industries lining up together for or against freer trade as exporters or importers.

The pattern of trade characterizing the contemporary era is heavily intra-industry, and takes place between (and within) transnational corporations among countries that are relatively similar. Moreover, trade has been increasingly replaced by Foreign Direct Investment for sale in these markets, so that even the rise of intra-industry trade may be transitional, displaced by location of production facilities to meet local demand. James Markusen concludes from an examination of the trends to the mid-1990s that 'Although far from decisive . . . evidence may indicate that a process of multinationals displacing trade has begun' (Markusen 1995: 181). Sales of US-based transnationals abroad exceeds exports from the United States by these same companies. Strategic product differentiation in imperfectly competitive markets (independent of comparative advantage traditionally understood) is central to contemporary trade among the industrialized economies, which account for 80 per cent or so of total international trade.

Because these economies work at a level of pure trade theory that does not make such qualifications and is methodologically disinclined to see transitional costs as a major part of the analysis, or part of the analysis at all, mainstream economic theory concludes that globalization will reduce inequality both between and within states as resources are more efficiently allocated across borders. Many trade theorists slight the important losses to unskilled and semi-skilled labor in the richer countries like the United States when their economies become more open. The extent to which factors of production are specific to factor uses in the short run, and perhaps over a longer relevant horizon and so not easily redeployed, means that both capital and labor in trade-impacted industries may suffer substantially

(Mussa 1974 and Neary 1978). It is also the case that greater openness, which puts US-based low wage workers in competition with a larger, global, labor pool, pro- duces labor market. This means that import surges, given the increased elasticity of demand for labor in a more open economy, increase the costs to workers affected (Rodrik 1997). A growing number of studies confirm that rising inequalities in the US are related to skill premiums in just such a manner (Richardson 1995). This employment effect of a more elastic demand curve for labor is consistent with the increased instability of earnings in the United States (Gottschalk and Moffit 1994). Mainstream economists have begun to develop full employment trade models that predict the sort of 'race to the bottom' competition that hurts low wage workers if the upgrading of skills demanded in Third World exports from movements of capital and technology is sufficient. Less skilled workers in both the more developed and the less developed countries may suffer from an increase in trade (Feenstra and Hanson 1996).

The possibility that some nations might benefit from policies that consciously and purposefully violate free trade has been strongly and successfully denied by economists for hundreds of years. Yet the success over decades of some East Asian countries, most prominently Japan and South Korea, puts pure trade theorists on the defensive in the 1980s as rationales for strategic trade and industrial policy were proposed at the level of high theory (Brander 1986). Such imperfect competition models featured such elements as investment in excess capacity to deter competi- tion, large R & D expenditures, strong learning by doing and first comer advantages, knowledge spillovers, and high risks of producing and marketing – all aspects stressed in the discussion of the Japanese model and later considerations of an East Asian model of state-led development.

The dramatic consequences of applying new trade theory to real world situa- tions was a disturbing prospect for many mainstream economists. By and large, therefore, there was a re-embrace of conventional simplifying assumptions even though these were so evidently at odds with the norms of East Asian development state cases. For example, Avinash Dixit (1984) demonstrated that the greater number of domestic firms, and so the closer the market was to perfect competition, the less export subsidies are advisable. Well yes, but of course in development states the typical case is state-sponsored oligopolistic structures, *chaebols* and *keiret- sus* that maximize collective gain under state guidance and limited market entry. Calum Carmichael constructs a model in which the domestic firm chooses its price, knowing that the subsidy depends upon its price, and uses information in deciding what price to set (Carmichael 1987). Such a model is useful for under- standing inefficiencies in European state champion strategies but is not relevant to the East Asian cases. Douglas Irwin, after reviewing the literature filled with assumptions in models not designed to consider the East Asian cases, concludes that 'plausible but slight modifications' (Irwin 1996: 215) make such strategic trade models unconvincing. The case for free trade is thus, in his view, confirmed. Similarly, Robert Baldwin answers the question, 'Are economists' traditional trade policy views still valid?' in the affirmative (Baldwin 1992).

This is a rapidly evolving literature that can certainly not be adequately dealt with here. We may note that there appears to be a robust relationship between openness and total factor productivity growth (Edwards 1998), but that in East Asia total factor productivity growth has not been an important contributor to growth, which seems to be a matter of extensive utilization of factor inputs (Collins and Bosworth 1996). It is a matter of the assumptions about collusion, government ability to enforce cartel-like arrangements, and the specifics of the way subsidies for product development and marketing are designed and implemented by state planners and their ability to produce results that enhance their firms' competitive position that is at issue. Using more subsidized capital, however, has the tendency to lower profit rates and cause capital to invest elsewhere. Continued exploitation of labor breeds resistance and political unrest. The trade models do not really capture these elements. They are, however, captured by institutionalist models and political economy approaches, which focus on rent seeking and changing power relations as industries mature and state agencies become corrupted (Ades and Di Tella 1997). It is not so much at the level of pure trade theory but in the shifting power relations and ability to extract rents, capture regulatory agencies, and corrupt officials that the failures are found. This is best studied as a historical–institutional process over time and involves loss of flexibility and the ability to reform outmoded practices under changed conditions. In the case of the Asian countries, special emphasis on failures in the financial system rather than in production and industrial competitiveness need to be stressed as well. Thus there are A/B divisions that are important and allow contrasting views of how trade policy and practices are to be understood and evaluated.

Normative preferences are also important. Comparative advantage of many poorer countries can be heightened by child labor and anti-labor policies by dictatorial states in which strikers are beaten, union organizers jailed and killed. Neoclassical economists do not ask the sources of different national labor relations regimes. They take them as given. Anne Krueger, for example, has prominently argued that the case for free trade based on comparative advantage 'is independent of why there might be cost differences' between countries (Krueger 1990). Markets are presumed to work freely in the countries in question. From an institutionalist B mode perspective, this is unlikely. As Werner Sengenberger and Frank Wilkinson argue:

> The case for labor standards – universally applied equitable terms and conditions of employment – rests on the recognition that labour markets are deeply segmented by power relationships so, in the absence of countervailing regulation, labour is undervalued to varying degrees. Far from determining equal pay for work of equal value . . . the institutions on the supply and demand side of the labour market operate so as to discriminate between claimants in the allocation of job opportunities and in doing so generate wage inequalities which bear little or no relationship to the value contribution of individual workers.
>
> (Sengenberger and Wilkinson 1995, cited in Milberg and Elmslie 1997)

That Michael Jordan, the basketball star, is reputed to be paid more by Nike, the athletic shoe manufacturer, to promote their shoes than the 25,000 Indonesian workers who make shoes for Nike, Adidas, LA Gear, and the other shoe companies producing in the country are paid a year, and the policy of the Indonesian dictatorship to prevent unions should give pause to the automatic assumption that it is all a matter of free markets. Philip Knight, Nike's chairman and chief executive (and the sixth richest person in America with a personal fortune of over $5 billion), in the summer of 1998, understanding that there was more than given costs and given factors of production, bowed to pressure from critics by promising to limit his labor supply and further shifting his cost curve by paying his workers closer to what his critics considered a living wage. Even the 'given' technology might change, as he accepted outside inspectors to evaluate health and safety in Nike supplier plants. It was time to intervene in such markets. The reasoning was straightforward. He said: 'The Nike product has become synonymous with slave wages, forced overtime and arbitrary abuse. I truly believe that the American consumer does not want to buy products made in abusive conditions' (Cushman 1998: D1). The company had been hurt by falling stock prices and weak sales, as it had been 'pummeled in the public relations arena' by labor rights activists.

The notion of fairness in trade is not as vacuous as many economists think. The citizenry, through the democratic process, after all has a right to restrict trade when it undermines domestic arrangements supported by widely held norms within the society. There are other values that count beside the economists' understanding of efficiency (Rodrik 1997: 80). At a practical political level, it is unlikely that successful NIC exporters would lose their markets if they paid somewhat higher wages so that their workers could subsist at a level of basic necessities and dignity, banned child labor, and experienced somewhat less extremes between their elites and masses. Similarly, demands that taxes and public services be cut to increase competitiveness can be refused by citizens, and alternatives involving sacrifices by the rich and powerful contemplated instead. It is also not clear that economists' efficiency arguments are always based on irrefutable 'scientific judgment,' as is often claimed. If some versions of endogenous growth theory are correct, there would not be a negative relationship between increased trade and public spending.

As many political economists have argued, one would expect that the greater the power of the left and organized labor, the more likely government would be to pursue the new growth path in competing in global markets: 'high public spending, highly skilled workers, high value added and high quality production – because these policies also favor workers and the poor' (Garrett 1996: 90). Thus many of the issues that in the 1970s and 1980s were fought out in the language of macroeconomic modeling, by the mid-1990s came to be discussed in terms of alternative conceptions of new growth theory and the advantages of high road strategies. Such arguments are also related to observation of persistent differences in innovation and initiative capacities across nations.

The institutionalist case that technological change is path dependent and cumulative is increasingly accepted. Understanding the process of learning and of modifying organizational form replaces scarcity and the efficient use of given resources as the categories of choice in contemporary analysis (Dosi *et al.* 1990). Had economists been more attuned to the B side of classical economics, they might have retained the understanding that development capacity is cumulative and that 'The superiority of one country over another in a branch of production often arises only from having begun it sooner. There may be no inherent advantage,' as John Stuart Mill explained in his *Principles*, 'but only a present superiority of acquired skill and experience' (Mill 1848: 922). Mill (and, as noted earlier, Ricardo) understood dynamic comparative advantage as well as the more restrictive, static comparative advantage framework. In the closing decade of the twentieth century, the competitive advantage of nations was seen increasingly in such terms.

In the wealthy countries like the United States, the skill premium and income inequality grow as a result of capital and labor migration as factor prices converge. It is the mobility of factors of production, a violation of the presumption of the pure trade theorists that factors of production are internationally immobile, that explains what is going on. Jeffrey Williamson, for example, in his 1995 presidential address to the Economic History Association, makes such an argument based on a comparison of late nineteenth-century convergence, twentieth century interwar period divergence and the late twentieth-century convergence experiences (Williamson 1995). Just how important openness of an economy is and how important trade-related factors are in explaining both national growth and income trends within and among nations has become a major growth field not only for economic historians but for trade theorists and labor economists.

Policy working and the statistics of persuasion

Paul Krugman, a major contributor to what is known as the new trade theory, has provocatively criticized those who extend the implications of new trade theory in ways he finds unsound.[9] He contends that economists such as his MIT colleague Lester Thurow and policy makers such as President Clinton's first term Secretary of Labor Robert Reich in their best sellers show a shocking lack of capacity to do simple arithmetic. Krugman writes:

> The key point is that total U.S. employment is well over 100 million workers. Suppose that a million workers were forced from manufacturing into services and as a result lost the 30 percent manufacturing wage premium. Since these workers are less than 1 percent of the U.S. labor force, this would reduce the average U.S. wage rate by less than 1/100 of 30 percent – that is, by less than 0.3 percent.
>
> (Krugman 1994b)

His critics, who think the global economy impacts on American workers in any meaningful sense, must, Krugman says, be 'careless' in their arithmetic; and if one accepts the terms of his formulation then perhaps such a calculation proves his case. His interlocutors differ not perhaps in their mathematical abilities, however, but in the methodology they consider appropriate to the analysis. Krugman's critics point out that the impact of trade directly affects over half the US economy. It is not simply exports and imports (which together are currently 21 per cent of GNP) but the threat of foreign competition that impact on pricing and wage setting more broadly, and induce labor replacing innovations in higher labor cost nations facing greater import competition.

Blackboard economies may quickly return to equilibrium, but the real world is in a perpetual state of disequilibrium, and as Krugman is well aware, people displaced in one sector do not find jobs instantly or perhaps at all elsewhere, and fear can be a powerful factor in wage bargaining for other workers. The general forcing down of wages in trade-exposed, labor-intensive industries also encourages a pattern and a change of labor relations climate that impacts more broadly. Technological rents can be renewed by staying ahead of competitors, and in the advanced higher wage economies, technology will be increasingly labor displacing as a competitive strategy response to globalization pressures. The changes in technology, difficult to isolate from the enlarging market, demand far greater adaptability from workers than in the past, and younger, better trained workers can be hired for less in a labor surplus economy. The spread of part-time work and two-tier compensation structures rolls outward from trade-impacted industries. Welfare State protections are less generous as increasingly mobile capital can minimize its contribution and workers rebel from tax increases needed to finance government. These factors surely impact on more than '0.3 per cent' of the nation's economic wellbeing. The static calculation with which Krugman and others have beaten down those who appreciate the alternative channels through which trade impacts on growth are themselves highly suspect, because of the limitation of the partial framework they use.

The back-of-the-envelope calculation offered by Krugman may be supplemented by some numbers provided by Adrian Wood, a scholar who once preached, indeed authored, World Bank orthodoxy, rejecting the idea that low wages in the south posed any threat to wage workers in the north. Conventionally,[10] economists suggest that trade with the south increases labor productivity in the north because of the change in output mix to more capital-intensive products and technologies. Wood estimates labor quality content in a model in which the differences in productivity that have positive impact on the demand for unskilled labour in the south appear to be about five times as large as the conventional calculations suggest, and the negative impact on unskilled labour in the north about ten times as large (Wood 1994: 10).

Wood concludes that to 1990 the changes in trade with the south had reduced the demand for unskilled relative to skilled labor in the north as a whole by something like 20 per cent (ibid.: 11). His estimate is for an occurrence over three decades. In his view, 'expansion of trade with the South was an important cause of the deindustrialization of employment in the North over the past few decades (ibid.: 13). His estimates have been criticized as being too large (Burtless 1995 and Freeman 1995a). The debate goes on and, over time, moves in the direction of greater realism of assumptions and specifications of capital and labor inputs and to alternative stories based on competing stylized 'facts,' as economists sort out the labor impacts of technological change and their relation to globalization.

Trade tends to make the skilled/unskilled wage ratios in the north and south more similar, to narrow the wage gap for unskilled workers (they fall in the north and rise in the south), and to widen the absolute north–south gap in skilled wages (Borjas and Ramey 1994a). We get specialization, but move only part way toward factor price equalization. As the knowledge basis of increased productivity has become central (in ways Marx and Marshall suggested), there is reason to believe that without social intervention many working people in the new climate will not receive much of the increased output. The growing inequality that accompanies the higher income of the symbolic analyst class (to use Robert Reich's useful descriptor) dramatically increases the return to the designers and presenters of globally available products. Trade does seem to be implicated in the rising inequalities the United States has been experiencing; as Richard Freeman and Lawrence Katz summarize the econometric evidence, it suggests that the increased supply of less educated workers arising from the US trade deficit accounted for perhaps 15 per cent of the increase in the college–high school wage differential from the late 1970s to the mid-1980s (Freeman and Katz 1994: 46). Economists have recognized the upside of this growing inequality – the superstar effects of globalization that increase inequality of return within professional groups, as well as between strata – as the size of the market increases (Frank and Cook 1995). The polemic over 'obscene wealth,' on the one hand, and 'reasonable' reward to innovation given the value created by such activity, on the other, has become part of the core political debate of the era concerning the trajectory of the global economy and its differential impacts.

Similar debates over whether an activist state can improve development prospects through active export promoting policies reveals another aspect of the globalization–free trade question. Jeffrey Sachs and Andrew Warner suggest a generalized trade optimism that obviates the need for, and suggests the ineffectiveness of, statist intervention. They argue that 'convergence can be achieved by *all* countries, even those with low initial levels of skills, as long as they are open and integrated in the world economy' (Sachs and Warner 1995: 41). Their paper is an argument for an A mode approach in which the same forces work the same way in all socio-economic formations and in which allowing unimpeded markets to function produces optimal results. It is an affirmation of the applicability of the neoclassical general equilibrium framework for explaining why statist intervention reduces efficiency. Their statistical work would seem to offer impressive confirmation of such a conclusion. Yet Sachs–Warner findings depend crucially on the categorizations that are the foundation for their statistical work and on the way they divide nations into 'open' and 'closed.'

Japan, South Korea, and Taiwan in the postwar years are declared 'open' economies on such grounds as, in the case of Japan, the achievement of full currency convertibility and a low average tariff. Rather than testing whether state-led development promoted growth in such countries, Sachs and Warner declare instead that they are 'open' economies and attribute their remarkable performance to an acceptance of free trade, privatization, and the usual neoliberal policy package. This conclusion is in stark contrast with the findings of economists who have studied the actual experience of these nations and who have framed their developmentalist regimes quite differently to Sachs and Warner, seeing the departure from the neoclassical model as the essence of their historical success.[11] By the late 1990s, as these East Asian miracle economies became mired in financial crisis and slower growth, the consensus view in the mainstream was that the 'crony capitalism' of these regimes needed to be replaced by a more free market approach along the lines of an 'American model.' Yet such a conclusion was far from obvious to institution-oriented students of the region, who saw liberalization of financial markets in the institutional context of the debt ratios normal in the region as the problem, and saw the neoliberal solutions on offer as likely to do harm to the long-term prospects of the nations involved (Wade 1998). There are vast literatures in each of these areas, but the commonalities are impressive. On the one side are those believing that markets work along neoclassical lines, and on the other are those who approach the issues from institutional–historical perspectives. Whilst progress is made within each of the research programs, the fundamental divisions are not reconciled.

There are immense difficulties of moving to policy conclusions from the various theories and models of growth that win wide approval. The diversity of historical experience is difficult to capture in such econometric testing or through arguments from theoretical premises extended to unique social formations and historical contexts. For example, even if we consider the theory of strategic trade to be sound, in practice, under conditions prevailing in this country, pork barrel proclivities would dominate over rational nation building. Yet, at the same time, the social cost of policy inaction based on such policy pessimism can be substantial. It is worth investigating what kind of institutional reforms, political programs, and larger analytic frameworks could help change the state of things, given the substantial cost of existing arrangements for millions and negative spillovers for all of us, even those who are privileged in the existing scheme of things. More important than the squabbling over competitiveness is what I take to be the larger point that the measures at hand to improve America's competitiveness are steps that should be taken in their own right to raise domestic productivity (addressing unacceptable increases in inequality that are a product of the uneven reward structures of the contemporary economy). More importantly perhaps, as the world moves toward the new millennium, alternative macro frameworks acknowledge deflation and over-investment as theoretical problems that, under emerging conditions, could have real-world importance.

Endogenous growth

Endogenous growth theory (see e.g. Krugman 1990; see also Helpman 1989) is a broad catch-all conceptualization of the development process that suggests that dynamic sources of growth can come from departures from the more rigid neoclassical rules and assumptions. Endogenous technical progress is substituted for the exogenous technology of the standard neoclassical model. Theories of adaptation replace assumptions of instantaneously available (at no cost) state of the arts capacities. By modeling imitation and taking into account the receiving country's economic environment, its tax laws, regulations, and so on, more realism can be added to such models.

Endogenous growth theory has become an important current in the literature because it uses more believable assumptions – doing away with the requirement of diminishing returns to capital (indeed, highlighting the importance of increasing returns to capital invested in knowledge production), permitting increasing returns to scale of production, and giving place to a host of externalities.[12] It suggests, for example, that the simple dichotomy between private and public goods does not hold in the case of research that allows non-rivalry. The theory accepts the possibility that because applied research is not an ordinary public good, policy makers would do well to consider the funding of critical technologies out of taxpayer funds. Such innovative suggestions, because they are presented with rigor at the level of high theory, give permission to economists 'to reconsider some of the most basic propositions in economics' (Romer 1994: 19).

Writers comfortable with the neoclassical approach have attempted to expand their tradition's representation of factors of production, so that ideas being developed by the endogenous growth theorists fall within their framework. It would seem to be an unwarranted claim, however, to assert that this is simply a version of neoclassical economics. By interpreting the role of capital more broadly, considering knowledge as a type of capital, N. Gregory Mankiw, for example, has suggested that endogenous growth is a limiting case of the neoclassical model and so can claim that the neoclassical growth theory is still the most useful one we have (Mankiw 1995). The heroic stretches of such neoclassical assumptions as considering technology a public good available everywhere in the world, however, means that Mankiw's revitalized neoclassicism ignores the reality that a key source of relative growth is different access to knowledge and ability to put it to productive uses – the very heart of the growth process (Romer 1995). Further, as Richard Nelson has written, 'these "new" neoclassical models are "mechanical" in the same sense as the old ones' (Nelson, R. R. 1995: 68). They do not 'explain' in the meaning of the term important to evolutionary economists.

What is clear from contemporary discussions is that they hinge on what kind of stories economists find convincing, what generalizations they embrace, and what simplifications they find acceptable. What is particularly refreshing about the best . of the endogenous growth theorists is that they are aware, as Paul Romer has said, that their project is 'the scholarly equivalent of creating myths, simple stories that economists tell themselves and each other to give meaning and structure to their current research efforts' (Romer 1994: 3). Wherever we come down on such matters, the undisputed achievement of endogenous growth theory (like the new trade theory) is to show that what happens in reality is also capable of occurring in theory (Lucas 1990).

The concept of social knowledge and the idea of increasing returns are no doubt important. They are part of what David Hume, that most brilliant of early

political economists, in a consideration of what has been rediscovered as endogenous growth theory, called 'the art of world-making.' These stories are not new and
can be found in the B side tradition in the history of economic thought, but are
rarely cited in this literature.[13] What tends to be new is the formalism of presentation.

Social capability and flexibility

The matter of rigor in the formulation and presentation of economic models is one
of the issues over which debates range. Many important ideas seem inherently
imprecise. Consider the ideas of social capacity and flexibility. These concepts
emerge as important to economists studying the dynamics of economic growth; but
can they be made operational? Social capacity, Moses Abramovitz suggests,

> is a vague complex of matters, few of which can be clearly defined and sub-
> jected to measurement. It includes personal attitudes, notably levels of
> education, an attribute that is subject to measurement however imperfectly.
> But it also refers to such things as competitiveness, honesty, and the extent to
> which people feel able to trust the honesty of others. And it also pertains to a
> variety of political and economic institutions. It includes the stability of gov-
> ernments and their effectiveness in defining and enforcing the rules of
> economic life in supporting growth.
>
> (Abramovitz 1994: 88)

Nonetheless, indices of social capability can be constructed out of the ahistorical
stories and case studies economists find convincing. We can expect, therefore, various versions of social capability to meet the preferences of competing pre-analytic
visions. The case is the same for the even more popular concept of 'flexibility,'
which is the notion that the economy performs better if all factors of production
can quickly adjust from one use to another as relative costs change and new opportunities emerge. Flexibility can be, and frequently is, used to mean accommodating
or reacting to events – not shaping them. This use of flexibility, as the requirement
of smoothly functioning markets, was what the neoclassical model assumes as
always true. Perhaps for this reason 'flexibility' was not discussed in the textbook
neoclassical models.[14]

In my view, total flexibility of the type presumed in the neoclassical model
would be a frightening prospect for most people. Instantaneous movement would
prove devastatingly chaotic. Indeed, the reason that institutions are so important is
that they impart a regularity and consistency of expectations over time.[15] Would
greater flexibility in many realms not also cause serious problems? Indeed, considering the speed with which many people must adjust to painful dislocations,
would it not be better if more of our attention were turned from 'maladaptability
to the costs of hyperflexibility'? For if the level of uncertainty and lack of security
presumed by a neoclassical level of flexibility were to exist, it would make the
foreseeable future 'a boiling metabolism' (Jones 1995: 97).

When institutions work well they provide what, in the context of the Japanese postwar system, Ronald Dore calls 'flexible rigidities.' This tension between coherence of institutions (and the larger social structure of accumulation in which they are embedded) and the quick response to opportunity (as well as the creation of opportunity) is at the heart of the new economic sociology that was discussed in Chapter 7, and it provides a focus for the evolutionary discourse concerning the nature and causes of the wealth of nations in our time. The flexibility of successful late industrializers comes in creating comparative advantage, anticipating change, and strategically selecting intervention strategies rather than responding after the fact. Especially with the recognition of the East Asian NIEs' successes, such understanding of flexibility and social capacity is more frequently stressed. (That such relational interdependencies can become corrupting to the point of provoking a crisis for the developmentalist state is also true, of course.)

Rather than production being the black box in which factors of production are combined in some optimal ratio, new organization theorizing is about building an optimally flexible rigidity.[16] Organizational forms that best share information draw on the competence of many individuals. They require rigidities. With limited abilities to absorb and process information, bounded rationality requires rules to cope with complexity. Path dependency – the awareness that the choices made today guide and constrain those that will be made tomorrow – is a concept associated with optimal flexibility. The favored story here is Paul David's instant 1985 classic explaining the continued dominance of the QWERTY keyboard (originally developed because it was inefficient – it slowed down typists to prevent the keys from sticking on the early typewriters). Once in place, it became the standard and proved impossible to replace, even after the mechanical problems were overcome and a faster design would have been a more efficient layout.

Economists and economic historians find that many such locked-in patternings in technological adaptation impart surprisingly persistent rigidities. These are created by situations in which obtaining short-run optimality reduces the prospect of a more desirable outcome in the long run. Where once economists saw only perfect competition (and departures from perfect competition as undesirable and to be quickly rectified), they are now more inclined to see complexities of overshooting and underadjusting, networking and bandwagon effects (Arthur 1989). Understanding the history of an economic relation or a specific arrangement (such as the standard keyboard) enables us to ask what the cost and benefits of making non-marginal changes will be, where it would otherwise not be easy to reverse path dependent development. Such ideas have not gone unchallenged, and specific cases keep the economic historians busy looking for facts, in many cases those that seem to provide evidence for the theoretical slant to which they incline.[17]

Transaction cost theory moves economists in the direction of jettisoning the idea of perfect and costless coordination, courtesy of the invisible hand or the imaginary auctioneer. The market is demoted to one mechanism among others for coordination, and markets themselves are increasingly seen to be organized by the state and the wider cultural economy.[18] The tenacious hold of the neoclassical mode of thinking on many transaction cost theorists and other new institutional-ists requires passing comment. It has been noticed that the individualism presumed of economic man comes with a psychology unconducive to successful networking. In discussing the growing importance of strategic alliances and relational con-tracting among successful cutting edge firms, if we assume guile and such motivations of distrust, it is hard to develop competitor–cooperator modes of mutually advantageous dealing. We know such relational contracting is especially important in cases with unknown (and unknowable) parameters. Further, high transaction costs may be a good thing. They can reflect investment in mutual monitoring and in trust creating experience as activities shift in unpredicted but possibly profitable directions.

Some analysts have gone further and returned to a political economy perspec-tive in which the frame for economic analysis is the societal structure in which market and non-market decisions are made. Some economic cultures may under-write more effective, faster, more complex, and efficient networking. By focusing on static allocative efficiency of given resources among given ends, the neoclassical mind-set misses the sources of dynamic efficiency that are proving so important in a fast moving, knowledge-based, globalized market. In Alfred Chandler's terms, neoclassical economics is about structure and not strategy.[19] The administrative decisions relevant to transformative economics are the strategic ones. They deal with long-run allocation and the development of new resources that will result in successful growth over an extended time horizon. Neoclassical questions are tacti-cal. They are directed to the efficient use – in a static sense – of current resources. Once we move away from the precision possible with neoclassical assumptions, out-comes become indeterminate and theory conceptually inexplicit.

There are a number of ways such ideas can be grouped, and where one makes demarcations between schools and approaches is a matter of preference and has not yet hardened into generally accepted categorizations. For example, Chandler is often grouped with Oliver Williamson and others in the new institutionalist eco-nomics (Williamson 1985), but this is a mistake. Chandler makes the distinction between coordination and transactions, arguing that 'The savings resulting from such coordination [more effective scheduling of flows to achieve a more intensive use of facilities and personnel employed in the process of production] were much greater than those resulting from lower information and transactions costs' (Chandler 1977: 7). Transaction cost theory focuses on an important aspect of eco-nomics, but cannot provide an alternative from a B perspective. Chandler offers us an organizational perspective as contrasted to the exchange frame favored by A mode economists, who use transactional analysis whilst remaining within the basic neoclassical model. There is agency involved in the Chandler approach, which places his work clearly in the B mode. Chandler's argument that 'the strategic and organization choices made by managers, choices not necessarily dictated by mar-kets and technologies – shape if not determine both firm level and national economic performance.'

The idea that it is both business organizations and socio-political institutions that configure markets has important implications for economic analysis. Indeed, as

David Teece (1993: 199) suggests, its implication 'is that much of what is in the textbooks in mainstream microeconomics, industrial organization, and possibly growth and development ought to be revised, in some cases relegated to the appendices,' that is, if economic analysis is to come to terms with the essence of productivity improvement and of wealth generation in advanced industrial economies. It is a small step from such a discussion of the firm in the socially constructed marketplace to the framework of economic society. At the societal level, social custom and the broader construct 'culture' are finding their way into the literature in unfamiliar ways related to a broader institutionalism.[20] Culture becomes an important economic category for analysts who suggest that communities that lack certain desirable attributes can encourage their emergence by strengthening certain collective practices and discouraging others. Economists and others are finding ways to talk about the learned patterns of flexibility and institutional effectiveness found in different national contexts and historic conjunctures.[21]

As we have reviewed various studies, the interplay between efficiency creating strategies and distributional issues constantly recurs. It is not enough to replace factor input models with institutional studies that look inside the black box of production to see how organization and social relations impact on efficiency. Issues of inclusion and exclusion, of opportunity and appropriation of surplus, are also important to a social economics. The structure of work and the way technologies are incorporated are thus central concerns not just from a competitiveness perspective but to income distribution and quality of life issues. Because of political pressure to address such aspects of growth patterns, economists are being drawn into questions of not only social organization of production and distribution, but how production is linked to other aspects of societal functioning. One way political economists have come to think about such questions is in terms of regulation or regime theory.

Regulatory regimes

The assemblage of social and political conditions that have a continuing (although over extended periods not unchanging) influence on individuals may be thought of as 'regimes.' Regimes are 'sets of explicit or implicit principles, norms, rules and decision-making procedures around which actors' expectations converge' and 'create the conditions for orderly multilateral negotiations, legitimate and delegitimate different types of state action' (Krasner 1983: 2). Regimes lower transaction costs because they foster continuing interaction 'on a common wave length.' What may be thought of as forum stability and common discourse, increase the payoff from cooperation and reduce the incentive to cheat on agreements in the face of well-understood and mutually agreed rules. Regimes exhibit agreements on contract enforcement and property rights that, to work well, have to be perceived as fair, or at least acceptable, by enough members of the society to provide stability.

The power of such middle-range theorizing is that it explains specific conjunctural regularities in ways that do not rely on the unchanging determinants of a mode of production, as in an orthodox Marxism that tries to use unmediated abstractions to explain historically specific situations or assumes an ahistoric set of economic laws applied in the same fashion in all times and places, as neoclassical economics does. To both the French regulation school and the social structure of accumulation analysts in the US, the regime is grounded in the historical specificity of an environment in which the capitalist accumulation process is organized.[22] It is this framework that is almost totally absent from the mainstream discussion of what is happening in the macroeconomy and allows us to characterize these approaches as strongly B mode in orientation.

These discourses represent another return to institution-focused mesoeconomics, in which the historically specific placement of decision makers is a dominant consideration. They provide a vocabulary and grammar to interrogate the period in which we live using categories that Max Weber and Joseph Schumpeter might applaud. They furnish a frame for discussing social facts using categories that are both descriptive and analytically situated between the fixed forms of traditional economic variables and the less permanent categories of workaday sociology,[23] and offer the middle range re-presentation that will be employed in the next chapter as we sort through the features of the present conjuncture that I believe most germane to understanding where we are in economic history.

By definition, *social structure of accumulation* is the specific institutional environment within which the accumulation process is organized. Such accumulation occurs within concrete historical structures. Firms buy inputs in one set of markets, producing goods and services, and sell those outputs in other markets. They are surrounded by other structures that are part of the capital accumulation process: the monetary and credit system, the state, and class relations. This set of institutions is the social structure of accumulation (Gordon *et al.* 1982: 9).

The French regulation school version employs a somewhat different, though not unrelated, construct, *a regime of accumulation*, which describes the fairly long-term stabilization of the allocation of social production between consumption and accumulation. This frame implies a correspondence between the transformation of the conditions of production and the transformation of the conditions of the reproduction of labor, and between certain of the 'modalities in which capitalism is articulated with other modes of production within a national economic formation, and between the social and economic formation under consideration and its outside world' (Aglietta 1976: 14).

Such categories allow reexamination of our historical conjuncture and offer a language in which to discuss the hows and whys by which the accommodations of the postwar period came to an end. When the material base of old patterns eroded, it was not simply that the reproductive mechanisms of the mode of regulation grew arthritic. The established social structures of accumulation were undermined by such changes. The postwar regulatory regime was undermined by a complex of processes that have been linked under the label globalization.[24] The new industries that emerged based on the microchip, the decline in the importance of Fordist basic industry in the advanced economies, the redeployment of economic assets over space, the creation of commodity webs spanning national borders (which undercut the nation-state-based accommodations), the rise of new centers of accumulation in East Asia and elsewhere, and the intensification of competitive pressures in the older centers of accumulation destroyed postwar stability and rendered the accords of the era obsolete.

Economists who have written on social structures of accumulation presume that they come to an end because regulative mechanisms or accommodations cease to operate effectively. It is perhaps closer to the mark to suggest that accords which are mutually beneficial under one set of circumstances become less rewarding to powerful participants under new conditions. The challenge comes from larger, systematic imbalances that arise in a process of combined and uneven growth. They set a framework in which the particularistic regulatory mechanisms are embedded. Thus in the case of the end of the postwar regulatory regime, trade imbalances, overcapacity, and overaccumulation resulting from developments in the forces of production (technological innovations and managerial responses to new possibilities) strengthened the bargaining position of internationalized capital at the expense of their locally resident 'partners.'

Both the regulation school and the social structure of accumulation analysts stress labor militancy as a major cause of economic slowdown and, in that sense, 'blame' the workers for the difficulties of regime reproduction.[25] Increased competitiveness at the world scale made producers unable to sustain profit rates. This caused a decline in investment and contributed to the crisis of the welfare state. There is thus a correspondence with labor market theories discussed in the last chapter which draw on a version of transaction cost theory that stresses the guile of workers and their tendency to shirk, the cost of properly motivating workers, and the unemployment that ensues because employees are 'overpaid.' The policy implication of the models discussed here is, however, that more worker-friendly social relations in production would increase productivity.

Social structure of accumulation theorists argue that the decrease in corporate profitability can be explained by the decline in the power of the United States capitalist class to deal with not simply the growing challenges from the domestic working class, but also 'the domestic citizenry, and foreign suppliers and buyers' (Lipietz 1986: 157). The mechanistic inevitability of these explanations raises important questions about causation. What precipitates these challenges? Why did they succeed when they did? As importantly, since European capitalists in a variety of state formations experienced similar difficulties in the 1970s and 1980s, when slow growth and profit squeeze became the general order of the day, how are the specifics of a nationally rooted social structure of accumulation related to wider developments? Are nation-specific answers the whole story or even the major story? There is the presumption that it is the breakdown of the structural accommodations, between labor and capital, the citizens and the state, and so forth that brings the era to an end; but it is changes in the material base of the economy, its technological and organizational development, that undermine these accommodations.

It is the economic base and not primary superstructural accommodations (especially the changing relations of production within the larger structure of the world system), rather than the seemingly autonomous collapse of postwar national accommodations that these analysts stress, that is central (Arsen 1991 and Magdoff 1992; see also Cox 1987 and Chase-Dunn 1989). There is also the question as to whether the key institutions of the social structure of accumulation theorists were not in place until well *after* the period of vigorous accumulation they are alleged to have caused had begun (Kotz 1987). A fuller B mode analysis would have to specify the relation of structure and agency involved in the choices made by individuals, businesses, and state actors. What the framework does do is bring economic analysis a large measure of the way toward the sort of social economic analysis Weber and Schumpeter had in mind.

The dramatic changes in the accumulation process, on the one hand, mean greater pressure for institutional standardization and enforcement mechanisms across borders as globalization forces take hold. The political fallout cannot be predicted if growth slows or if too many are excluded from the potential benefits of the international reorganization of production. The consensus view is that twenty-first-century factor mobility means governments can no longer support the institutional arrangements they have had in the past. The difficulty many working people have in accepting that social adaptability is necessary to restructure institutions, as the nature of the accumulation process changes, makes the political side of these developments more important. If large numbers of people are unwilling or able to adapt and be absorbed into the regime struggling to emerge, social costs grow and political resistance builds, which economists may argue is 'wrong' and 'counterproductive' but which nonetheless will shape economic outcomes. A social analysis needs such a broader political economy framework to analyze transformational periods in which old regimes are decomposing and there is contestation surrounding new ones struggling to emerge.

As we have seen, it is not easy to form a consensus view on events long past. Contemporary concerns and philosophies stimulate rereads and revisions of past understandings. The sort of basic questions societies face at the dawn of the twenty-first century concerning globalization, the instability of the financial system, and income polarization and impacts of technological change, whilst not without historical parallel in some senses, are of course unique to the contemporary moment in economic history. There are conflicting views as to whether globalization makes social spending less affordable due the greater mobility of capital than of labor, and on such questions as whether downsizing of the redistributive functions of the state are inevitable, whether individuals and particular social groups are being asked to pay too high a price, and whether destabilizing social decay is worth the price. Different people and different interests would respond from distinctive perspectives. In any event, these are not questions economists have any particular professional capacity to address. However, there is relevant research they do that helps to put the issues in perspective.

One of the interesting lines of research popularized within the social sciences in the mid-1980s was prompted by the work of Peter Katzenstein. Katzenstein, a political scientist, had long had an interest in the management of international economic interdependence, holding the view that the distinction between state and society 'connotes a gap between the public and the private sector which exists today [he was speaking in 1976] which exists in no advanced industrial state' (Katzenstein 1978: 17). In the mid-1980s he reported that small, open economies in Europe had large government sectors to provide social research so that their citizens would accept liberalism in trade matters (Katzenstein 1984, 1985). The flexibility of these economies, and their success in international markets, came from a highly successful version of embedded liberalism. A decade or so later, Dani Rodrik, using both time series and cross-sectional data, found 'a surprisingly robust' positive association between the degree of exposure to trade and the importance of government in a country's economy, concluding that the social welfare state had been the 'flip side' of the open economy (Rodrik 1996). In Asia, many of the more successful economies have been those with strong development states, protecting economic actors by limiting possible disruptions while speeding adaptation. In Latin America, after costly financial crises in the early 1980s, Chile adapted controls on short-term capital inflows that insulated its economy to a substantial degree from the speculative inflow–dramatic capital flight problems that plagued other more open emerging markets, demonstrating that commitment to markets was best tempered by such measures. Such examples fit, in the broad sense, the statistic evidence of the relationship between government spending and openness in Europe and North America.

There is also evidence, however, that within the larger context of an international order, in which powerful forces are demanding liberalization of domestic economies and restricting the capacity of nation-states to set their own economic policies, there is increased difficulty in insulating national economies. Rodrik, looking at more recent data from the OECD nations on the relationship between government spending and openness, concludes that 'while countries that are exposed to significant amounts of external risk traditionally have had government playing a more substantial role in the provision of social insurance, it becomes increasingly difficult to discharge this role as economic integration advances' (Rodrik 1997: 63). The question is why? Is it that nations individually and collectively cannot exercise more independent national policies, or has the politics changed so that these nations do not develop a regime that would enable continued regulatory capacity?

In the next and concluding chapter we further explore this topic of theorizing the contemporary conjuncture against the background of the history of thinking about economics we have discussed earlier. It will be suggested that a version of regulation theory will provide the box within which the pieces of a historical, institutional, and comparative growth discourse can usefully be organized.

11 From equilibrium into history

> Since the very beginning, the study of economics has served two purposes, though economists are not always conscious of this duality. One concerns the problem of how in a de-centralised, 'undirected' market economy, scarce resources are allocated among different uses in the right proportions. . . . The second object has been to explore the determinants of economic progress – what are the critical factors which make for continued growth.
>
> (Kaldor 1984: 3)

> Once we admit an economy exists in time, history goes one way, from the irrevocable past into the unknowable future, the concept of equilibrium based on the mechanical analogy of a pendulum swinging to and fro in space becomes untenable. The whole of traditional economics needs to be thought out afresh.
>
> (Robinson 1973: 5)

In contrast to most discussions of the history of economic thought which, in Whig fashion, stress the progress of the profession in understanding and presumably better theorizing the economy, I have been concerned to show how profoundly similar issues concern economists over the centuries and also how the particulars of the historic conjuncture in which they live, and their own pre-analytic vision, shape the particular questions and outlook they bring to their inquiries. Technological revolutions and political upheavals condition economic possibilities, which then become the givens for sustained periods of seeming stability in which regulatory regimes designed for the conditions of the social structure of accumulation of the era lend a semblance of orderly progress. These institutional forms, appropriate to one stage of development, become a drag on the development of new forces and emergent relations of production. The vitality of market forces create in their wake social problems which, when they become severe enough, need to be addressed through spirited struggle out of which new rules, regulations, and institutions form. It has always been thus and it would be unlikely that the world has changed in this regard.

Legacies

Classical political economy from Smith to Marx, despite important differences among its practitioners, dealt with historical change in the basic institutions of production and reproduction. Its B side privileged class relations grounded in conflicting cultural and material locations, in a manner shedding light on the dynamics of social change and the transforming nature of the economic growth process for nations and class fractions. I think less appreciated are the tensions between this mainline of classical political economy and the A mode laws of the classical model, which are stressed especially in the Senior–Say–Bastiat contributions and privilege the automaticity of markets which, without the folly of human intervention, would be a well-functioning allocative machine. Both ways of looking at economics have been present since Adam Smith, and indeed antedate the publication of his foundational text.

The mainline classical economists' concern for class, in their own time the contestation between landowners and capitalists struggling to control the state and the ends to which its laws would be directed, remains relevant. Today the recomposition of distance and the politics of location suggest that the fault line now runs between those who see themselves benefiting from the globalization process, on the one side, and those who find themselves in less advantageous relation to the international economy, on the other. The anger of those who retain loyalties rooted in older accommodations to nation, social identity, and place-based cultures is surely understandable. A social economics for our time needs to explore the bases of combined and uneven development in the latest stage of capitalist development and to theorize an economics of technological and political–economic change.

In the present period, as in earlier eras, interpretation of the labor market's basic functioning and the international and the national contexts of wage and income determination represent the crucial axis of policy debate. The fallout from economic displacement is the stuff of human history, if not of mainstream theorizing. Just as J.B. Say could believe in a model of automatic market equilibrium, even as he bemoaned the pain of sustained depression in the aftermath of the Napoleonic Wars, so today economists teach the long-term benefits of technological progress and the more desirable equilibrium toward which the system tends. If the system is moving toward a new equilibrium in which factors will be distributed efficiently in relation to new price and technological possibilities, then it is reasonable to worry that efforts to slow down the transition through governmental pursuit of justice concerns can make the economy poorer in the end. Such an analysis is not only the legacy of Say's Law and of 1870s neoclassical economics, but is influentially argued by the dominant mainstream interpretations found in various forms of real business cycle theory and rational expectations models.

A historical parallel and evolution of debate can be seen between the *Methodenstreit* in Germany at the turn of the twentieth century and more recent discussion of economics, political economy, and economic sociology. The path Schmoller and Weber encouraged, and which Schumpeter embraced as useful for economists – 'the study of institutional factors which are treated as noneconomic givens in economic theory, and thus attempt to approach socio-cultural development as a whole' (Shionoya 1991: 193) – is present in much of the growth theory that we discussed in the last chapter. Weber's critique is relevant in the contemporary context in which Menger's descendants derive objective, ahistoric, stylized facts and laws. The emergent economic sociology (and economic-sociology) and international political economy within political science, to take two important instances, suggest a cross-disciplinary ferment pulling at the subject claims of economics that has not been seen for a hundred years.[1]

What Keynes called classical economics (basically all the economics that came before him) rested on three pillars: Say's Law, the Quantity Theory of Money, and versions of the Iron Law of Wages. The three were used to explain how product prices, wages, and the price level were determined. Keynes is given credit for what at the time seemed an effective repudiation of Say's Law and a successful escape from the quantity theory. His concept of aggregate demand stimulation appeared to displace the neoclassical wage theory which insisted on an exclusive micro determination of wages. Modern theory, in its textbook mainstream version, has gone a considerable distance toward the successful restoration of these pillars of orthodoxy.

These changes were well underway before Keynes' death. Indeed, it was the 1940s when the transfer of dominance passed from Great Britain to the United States in terms of both political–economic power and as the intellectual center of the economics profession. Paul Samuelson was the central figure in this transition. As Paul Krugman observed at a celebration of the golden jubilee celebration of the Stolper–Samuelson theorem, circa 1940, John R. Commons was widely regarded as 'a, perhaps the, leading American economist' and yet it was within a very few years that the 'modelers,' led by Samuelson, had completely routed the institutionalists (Krugman 1944a: 275). Critics of neoliberalism, who claim it erodes the ability of governments to provide public services, protect workers and the environment today, ironically, invoke the central themes of John R. Commons (De Martino 1996: 22).

There has also been renewed, as well as continued, interest in Keynes by those who think later-day Keynesians took economics away from the promising openings Keynes' work pioneered, and that there is much that is of contemporary relevance in Keynes' approach to his subject. The question is in what ways can his method formulated within a particular historic context be applied to a different historical conjuncture? Keynes, rejecting a self-regulating economy, turned economics upside down so that it could better see the world of the 1930s. He insisted that if we are to study the causes and cures of high levels of unemployment, we should not start with a model that *a priori* assumes the impossibility of involuntary unemployment. That unemployment is a waste of resources meant to him that the promotion of full employment is good, market speculation is capable of great destruction, and that competent activism was possible and necessary on efficiency and equity grounds; these are the messages of the Keynesian Revolution. Keynes believed that government could increase the size of the pie, produce jobs, higher income for workers, and greater profits for capitalists. Today economists are less sure. Many doubt that government can make a positive difference. They doubt that the goals Keynes championed can be achieved. Other economists think they can in the very different conditions of the more globalized capitalism of the twenty-first century, if only we have the iconoclastic courage Keynes exemplifies.

Global neoclassical economics imparts a new rationale for the automaticity of markets by suggesting that the law of one price now makes government efforts to pursue independent policies counterproductive. New Keynesians in different ways, and with distinct emphases, have taken up these issues. Their general retreat from the more radical elements of Keynes' thinking came not in a vacuum, but in the context of postwar growth. Whilst Post Keynesians have certainly developed alternatives to mainstream theory across a wide area of topics central to the discipline, they, along with other critics, remain marginal to the mainstream consensus. It is the new classical economics that has been the dominant school for perhaps two decades – dominant not on the basis of the number of its adherents but in its ability to set the agenda for economic theory debate.

The important achievements of the expectations revolution were first to dethrone the presumption central to Keynesian macro models that economic actors, in setting wages and prices, do not react rationally to the expected future state of the economy. Second is the demolishing of the presumed stable trade-off between unemployment and inflation embodied in the Phillips Curve, and privileged in the account of the macroeconomic core as expostulated by Samuelson and Solow, which influenced millions through the version of this view, which was the centerpiece of Samuelson's best selling introductory text. Third is its dismissal of existing models used for policy evaluation and formulation, which ignored the fact that market participants had access to the same models and so could take policy makers' expected actions into account in formulating their own, so that the consequences of policy were unlikely to be what the models predicted. When policy makers choose new policies or are expected to do so, people's expectations, and so behavior, change, frustrating models that ignore such feedback effects. This 'Lucas Critique' has had a profound impact and is a key intellectual component of the dramatic downsized role of macroeconomic intervention policies. It has also been integral in the development of rational expectations macroeconomics (Chari 1988).

The policy presumptions of most macromodeling in the 1980s and 1990s suggested that economic growth would be stimulated if wages could be kept down (both nominal wages with respect to the money supply and, in the NAIRU framework, by holding down real wages so that labor markets will clear). In an open economy in which higher wages produce larger trade deficits, interest rates need to be increased to stem these rising deficits, thus cutting off growth. Devaluation of the currency, the traditional answer, can induce inflationary expectations. Whether in European social democracies or in debtor Third World nations under IMF tutelage, the policy prescription was the same: contractionary policies must be pursued to lower wages and government spending. We are back to pre-Keynesian orthodoxy in which excess capacity does not signal the possibility that there are arrangements that could provide for non-inflationary expansion. Competitive pressure requires austerity measures. With the acceptance of the policy ineffec-tiveness proposition, which asserts the inability of conscious government intervention to improve the macro economy's performance, the postwar Keynesian project is overturned.

This also, in effect, signals the end of macroeconomics. Having lost its *raison d'être*, macroeconomics as a different approach from microeconomics makes little sense. Markets are presumed rational and efficient allocators. It is best not to tamper with them. Efficient markets theory concludes that one must look to exoge-nous factors to explain any instability, since there exists some future state of the world that acts as an expectational 'center of gravity' toward which individual actors converge and on this shared probabilistic understanding create an optimal future – if not the best of all possible worlds – the best that is logically possible. Whether this is a sign of high intellectual achievement independent of the anti-government politics of the era, and whether its policy recommendations for privatization and deregulation are the academic reflex of the public philosophy of the era, is a question that greater historical perspective may answer (see Hoover 1988).

Beside the focus on rational expectations and their consequences, the result of greater market freedom is a dramatic redistribution of income and wealth. The upper 1 per cent of the US income distribution received the lion's share of income growth since the end of the 1970s, and the top 10 per cent received almost all of it. As to wealth, in the 1980s the top 1 per cent of wealth holders enjoyed two-thirds of all increase in financial wealth (Wolff 1996). The question of whether continued perverse income and wealth distribution, rising inequality, and growing poverty will succeed 'in the long run' in improving the economic situation of those who bear the great burden of the experiment, cannot of course be known, although it is promised. The flexibility the new paradigm creates lowers costs, but realization problems grow as a result of the deflationary bias that the new orthodoxy builds into the system. Competitive austerity creates global underconsumptionist tendencies that show up in the slower growth of the world economy. The seriousness of what has been happening is to some extent obscured by first growth in the Pacific Rim and then financial crises in the region, and also by the expansion of money and stock markets fed by income distribution trends and restructuring growth.

The focus on fighting inflation would seem to compound an incorrect diagno-sis with an iatronic prescription. Textbook macroeconomics in America continues to focus on wage-led inflation through decades of stagnating real wages which dra-matically have lagged productivity growth in the United States; meanwhile, deunionization and the growth of contingent work have forced down wage shares. They also ignore the redistribution of GNP to the financial sector as the rise in real interest rates slows growth. On a global level, the emphasis on opening markets and intensified export competition has produced overcapacity and severe deflationary pressures. The difference between mild deflation caused by productivity growth, which increases real living standards, and severe deflation produced by overca-pacity and competitive devaluations, at the time of writing goes unappreciated and may turn out to be of consequence.

Paradigm shifting

Whilst macroeconomics seems slow to respond to these developments, the new growth theory highlights concepts that economic historians and new institutionalists, looking inside the black box of technology and to theories of firm/market relational contracting and organization, have found important in explaining economic development. By the mid-1990s it could be observed that economists were placing increased emphasis on how 'the rules of economic and social interaction determine economic outcomes,' as economic historian Claudia Goldin said, 'more than the stock of resources and the level of technology' (Goldin 1995: 201).

Most of these ideas have been around in the B side literature for some time and among the major figures in the history of economic thought there has been awareness of their importance. Not only the relation of social organization to economic development but endogenous growth theories that focus on increasing returns to shared knowledge are part of 'the art of world-making' discussed by Adam Smith's friend David Hume (1980: 36), which were the givens for the early political economists. Alfred Marshall's insights concerning the efficiency gains from geographic clustering of industries, the importance of knowledge spillovers from locational proximity, and other ideas about modeling the spatial dimension of innovation are now receiving a wide hearing (Audretsch and Feldman 1996).[2] Whilst the old Cambridge saw 'that it is all in Marshall' may be overdone, he demonstrated (in Appendix H of *The Principles*) that under conditions of increasing returns, which he saw as the normal case for firms continually introducing new technologies, no single stable equilibrium exists. Under what are really more plausible assumptions for conditions of modern industry, both demand and supply curves can be shown to slope downward and to be not independent of each other. Marshall believed that the part humans played in production showed increasing returns, both from internal economies of scale resulting from the improved organization of the firm (much of which these days is discussed in terms of transaction costs) and from external economies gained as a function of output and pricing decisions of other firms (and what today would be called the wider institutional framework and governance regime). Sraffa, beginning in the 1920s, also noted that increasing returns are important in modern industry and that cost curves are therefore probably negatively sloped, concluding that the constant cost assumption needed in mainstream price theory is misleading. Young's work on the way 'change becomes progressive and propagates itself in a cumulative way,' Joan Robinson's writing on competition in the 1930s, and Kaldor's conclusion that 'once however we allow for increasing returns, the forces making for continuous change are endogenous,' all give pause at the declared originality attributed to recently 'discovered' ways of thinking about such matters. Expanding on this approach allows for consideration of misallocation, underutilization, and unemployment as outcomes of production choices. Once we realize that because of specificity, production cannot be costlessly reshuffled, we are back to a Cambridge capital theoretic framework within which committing a production factor in such a relationship is a form of specific sunk investment that has a technological as well as institutional origin (Caballero and Hammour 1996: 181).

One can note both the continuities and departures in emphasis, but it cannot be known which of the contemporary theorizations will have lasting impact. Within the mainstream seeking to advance an A mode science, the new classical economics returns to pre-Keynesian verities. Among opposition currents, the Post Walrasian, characterized by models allowing multiple equilibria and complexity (in the modern physics sense), bounded rationality, and non-price coordinating mechanisms, is an effort to use sophisticated tools such as chaos theory and non-linear dynamics, which can be presented in sophisticated mathematical language, along with B mode assumptions concerning behavior and giving an important role to institutions (Colander 1996).[3] We cannot do justice to the various contenders.

History, and so intellectual history as well, is constantly being rewritten as the concerns and attitudes of new generations are imposed upon the past. If, for example, the European Union becomes a major world power (let us go further, this is only a 'for instance' exercise), and a united Europe under French–German dominance becomes the global hegemon of the twenty-first century, we could entertain a rewriting of the history of economic thought under such conditions in which English economists no longer dominated the field's advances, and the classical economists are found in Paris, Vienna, and Lausanne. Ricardo is demoted and Say promoted. Future historians of economic thought might look with great favor on George Stigler's view that 'Say's approach was fundamentally much more modern than that of his English contemporaries' (Stigler 1965: 304). 'Walras's true predecessors' as Schumpeter (1954: 828) called them, Cornot, Thunen, and Condillac, would become the founders of the mainstream neoclassical view. Bohm-Bawerk and Wieser would be given their due and Mill becomes a dead-end vestigial footnote. Menger, unlike the Englishman Jevons, did not even think he needed to mention the cost-of-production theories that dominated our telling of the history of economic thought. Hutchison tells us that Hermann in 1832 had 'demolished' the wage-fund theory and it never had significant support in German language scholarship. Walras drew on French language theory and also emphasized the role of utility and scarcity rather than the labor theory of value in the work that preceded his own (Hutchison 1972). All of this and far more could become central in the textbooks of the future. If the twenty-first century came to be dominated by Asia, the rewriting could be more interesting still. Just as the past will be rewritten, our current understanding of likely futures will meet with unexpected surprises. At the level of paradigm innovation, what is convincing depends on context. There would be no Keynesian Revolution without a deep crisis of capitalism. Marxism loses force without revolutionary movements. It is hard to think of a new departure without a radical disjuncture in the organization of the economy and so in social reproduction.

I believe a serious paradigm shift is underway in the present historical era. Its function is convincingly to theorize the globalization process and the far reaching economic transformations it brings, especially as related to employment and income trends among nations and regions, industries and classes of workers. What was transpiring as the world reached another *fin de siècle*, and indeed a millennial milestone, was as close to what had been known as the postwar period, the years from the termination of the Second World War to the fall of the Soviet Union. The institutional environment within which its accumulation dynamic had been organized in those years had become increasingly dysfunctional over time. As is often the case in such transformations, innovations in technology (prominently in communication and transportation) brought into being new industries that offered dynamism to a new period of accumulation and contributed substantially to the reorganization of older sectors and the recomposition of distance. The process was first experienced in the 1970s as 'deindustrialization' of the traditional industrial base. In the 1980s, labor replacing information technologies and the global resiting of production, generalized downsizing (doing away with levels of middle management), and then a search for core competencies by flexible management team organizations, produced new commodity webs and patterns of financial flows. These corresponded to a Schumpeterian break in which innovations in technology and modes of organization unleashed new growth patterns based on flexible specialization. Growth models are increasingly Schumpeterian in inspiration, dynamic, contingent, and less likely to be neoclassical in form. The process of creative destruction produced the dis-ease spawned by loss of security engendered by the emergent high-risk society, the specter of growing wealth and increasingly visible poverty, along with broken social contracts, regressive tax cuts, and a scaling back of welfare state supports.

Whilst much of the mainstream took a rather Panglossian stance toward such inevitable developments – they resulted, it was said, from market forces which after all were promoting greater efficiency – others asked what was 'natural' about the ensuing suffering such restructuring produced. Economists have become aware of the extent to which the rules of economic and social interaction determine economic outcomes more than their traditional variables – the stock of resources and the level of technology taken as given at each point in time. They are increasingly in agreement that the large differences in per capita income across countries cannot be exclusively explained by such traditional causes as the ratio of population to land or natural resources or different access to capital, but rather to a great extent by the quality of their institutions and economic policies which are decisive for economic performance.

The most widely accepted, long-standing theoretical frameworks such as the comparative advantage theoretical framework, which focuses on the abundance of factor endowment, seems a dull tool when one observes, for example, that the Silicon Valley is not important for the manufacture of computers because of deposits of silicon (Olson 1996: 13). The particularities of location, the importance of local institutions, governance regimes, and economic policies are decisive to economic achievement. In addition, the efficiency costs of departing from perfect markets are not quite what the pure theory suggests. Trade theorists are not all in agreement, but as Paul Krugman notes, there is 'a dirty little secret in international trade analysis. The measurable costs of protectionist policies – the reduction in real income that can be attributed to tariffs and import quotas – are not all that large.'

But if 'the empirical evidence for huge gains from free trade policies is, at best, fuzzy,' as Krugman says (1995: 31–2), then the question is, why the incredible pressure for market opening and unfettered markets? Why the creation of a climate in which no cost is considered too high for European nations to adopt a single currency? These are questions that need to be considered within a political economy framework, and are more likely to be pursued in the emergent field of international political economy on the political science side, another indication of the division of the social sciences and the consequence of the surrender of important questions in political economy by economists.

Flexibility and the dynamics of growth

Post-fordist flexible techniques, niche marketing, and time-responsive appropriation of social knowledge transformed production and consumption patterns. Theories of endogenous growth offer an explanatory frame in place of the traditional mainstream story. Theorists working in the new paradigm see growth arising from the discovery of 'new recipes and the transformation of things from low to high value configurations' (Romer 1996: 204). If such theorists are right, that the residual is due to the advance of knowledge, then intellectual resources can profitably be shifted to consideration of how technological and organizational knowledge are to be produced in greater abundance. The development of new products and production processes and of more efficient governance frameworks, and of organizational relations in the face of uncertainty of outcome, becomes the basis for a new development paradigm.

The Lionel Robbins' definition – allocation of known and fixed quantities of scarce resources recombined in response to price signals impacting on known technological possibilities – recedes from the center of economics to supporting role status. Technology and social organization become subjects of intense scrutiny, and Clapham's boxes are given substantially new content. Growth becomes a process of perpetual hybridization of what is known and found. Economic development is seen as path dependent, and branching iterations lead scholars to a 'combinatoric' approach to innovation that is antithetical to neoclassical theory's claims precisely because of the centrality of uncertainty in the new growth formulations. In such a world, there is a rigorous sense in which the state of present technology depends increasingly over time on 'the random history that determined which parent technologies happened to have been chosen in the past' (Weitzman 1996: 212; see also Young 1993).

Globalization has led economists to think about market size with renewed interest. They model stagnant equilibriums in which a market too small for the expected costs of invention to be worthwhile inhibits growth. From such a perspective, it is possible to reread the historical record and examine how micro inventions build up following technological shocks. Such models can mimic Japanese *kanban*, or constant improvement techniques, and follow the historical progress of the steam engine from Watt's breakthrough. Perhaps in response to the intellectual climate created by appreciation of East Asian economic growth in the postwar era, historians of the First Industrial Revolution tell us that Britain had an unusual proficiency in importing ideas and improving upon them (Crafts 1996: 199). Economic historians and development economists tell us it is important to consider a country's 'social capacity' for growth – the impact of institutions and policy decisions upon total factor productivity. Endogenous growth theory (broadly conceived) allows a reconceptualizing of the nature and causes of the wealth of nations in a manner more consistent with the founding classical tradition in political economy. Individual rationality does not, through spontaneous bargaining of the sort presumed in Coase-like models, produce social rationality. Economists are increasingly open to the idea that aggregate growth modeling needs to be supplemented by a variety of concepts and models from political economy, trade theory, location theory, development economics, and economic history (Findlay 1996: 47). Globalization, by its obvious complexity and interrelated aspects, invited just such discussions, and many economists are ready to engage full heartedly in such a departure from received practice.[4]

The very presumption of economies naturally allocating resources efficiently comes to be interrogated. The social context of individual choice is subject to more sophisticated investigation, and a host of economists asked in different ways whether the economy is normally at, or even close to, its potential. Globalization processes produce natural experiments that suggest that government policies matter greatly in stimulating or inhibiting growth. In many countries, rational utility maximizing women and men, working hard, barely eke out a living. Their collective actions do not produce outcomes remotely resembling social efficient ones, because of the structure of incentives they face as a result of legal systems, political structures, and the manner in which contracts are and are not carried out. Capital, theoretically obtainable, is not forthcoming because of such disincentives. In different ways, economists have demonstrated that it is quite possible that the countries of the world are nowhere near the frontier of their aggregate production functions, and that something like a free lunch is possible with proper institutional reforms (Lucas 1990 and Olson 1996).

Looking at the elephant from a somewhat different angle, some economists and some among the broader public are what may be called techo-optimists, and others global pessimists. The techno-optimists are modernist to the core, pointing out that it was decades before the larger impacts of the breakthroughs of Edison and Ford impacted to transform the larger political economy so dramatically. It may be decades before the full benefits of the computer-driven revolution will have its more far reaching impacts, not only in lowering costs and increasing output but in replacing jobs and raising living standards. Progress should not be resisted, the techno-optimists say, no matter how heartfelt the petitions to the king by candle makers against the injuries done them by the sun. The global pessimists recoil at a world in which the law of one price means a leveling down of wages and employment conditions. Many among the working class in the advanced nations see their jobs destroyed by technological innovation and out sourcing to lower wage venues around the world. They are joined by those displaced from secure fordist employment who see themselves as unlikely to find the better jobs in the new knowledge-based, high wage occupations. There are also free market optimists and pessimists with regard to *laissez-faire*.

Economists privileging free market allocative efficiency tend to blame government welfare state programs and attitudes they engender for our troubles. The loss of efficiency is said to be due to increased regulation and expenditure for social welfare. Economists of this persuasion argue that the opportunity costs of the social safety net are large and counterproductively affect the people they are supposed to protect. Thinkers including Assar Lindbeck, Jagdish Bhagwati, and Anne Krueger have maintained that institutional hysteresis constrains choices by market participants, promotes rent seeking by special interests, creates economic inflexibilities, and explains the slow growth of the era (Bhagwati 1982; Olson 1982; Lindbeck 1983). A very different interpretation is also possible in which instead of focusing on the inability of institutions and factors of production to be flexible, one can see the new pattern of accumulation as a process of redistributive growth in which past accommodations functional to social stability are undermined by a lack of social reregulation.

Again, history matters. The Golden Age of the postwar National Keynesian welfare state stimulated private accumulation. It was only with the breakdown of its regulatory regime that governmental fiscal crisis developed. In the globalized economy there are strong incentives for corporations to downplay or even discard national loyalties in developing competitive strategies. In those nations such as the United States, where statist protections were weak, real wages dramatically lag the gains that transnational corporations have enjoyed.[5]

When conditions change, presumptions of continuity can be dashed. Those with claims under the old structures and understandings whose place has been devalued in the restructuring that has occurred, find the old social contract broken. In terms of their implicit analysis of the political economy, many large corporations abandoned National Keynesianism and its strategic orientation of increasing domestic spending through government and higher wages, preferring in the context of globalization low taxes and wages, and a defunding of government programs. That this was possible was a political outcome of the power relations in the wider political economy, and the incapacity of democratic governance to formulate an alternative regulatory governance framework at the level of the international economy.

Such an interpretation suggests to some that what is needed are new rules that share costs and benefits more broadly and do not impose transition costs so exclusively on the victims of this transformation. For others, it is a good thing that global neoclassicism repeals the old rules and offers a very different regime of accumulation in which capital markets discipline national governments, forcing them to get their fiscal houses in order. A mode economists tend to take this change as both natural and desirable. They tend to be techno-optimists and believers in economic liberalism. B mode economists see the new conjuncture as socially created and tend to approve of conscious political intervention through the democratic process to produce outcomes consistent with a social efficiency perspective. They are not so much techno-pessimists as advocates of social interventions to produce shared gains and minimize dislocation costs from such developments.

We cannot know, of course, how future generations of historians of economic thought will describe what they come to see as the great divisions that characterize late twentieth- and early twenty-first century economics. To what extent will they see parallels between an organization of the discipline in divisions such as those between feudal social relations and a political economy of an emergent market society, or the struggle between landlords and a rising capitalist class, or the emergence of a new historical actor, the working class, as being the focal point of economic theorizing? I think it is possible that the present era will come to be characterized in terms of an emergent and contested new constitutionalism as a global governance framework. This development is best understood within a political economy framework. It seeks to separate economic policy from broad political accountability, to redefine the relationship between the market and the postwar era state governance regulatory model. New constitutionalism, for those on the political side of political economy, is understood as the legal–regulatory dimension of what has been called disciplinary neoliberalism. It involves class recomposition in which internationally imbricated rentier interests – bond traders, bankers, embryonic international state formation institutions such as the International Monetary Fund and millions of wage and salary earners who have increasing investments in share ownership – favor a new regulatory framework. The strategy assumes an economic order dominated by knowledge-intensive, internationally mobile capital in which a new type of 'Platonic monetary Guardian,' effectively removed from electoral control, manages the most important aspects of national and international economic policy (Gill 1998).[6]

Whilst moving from a rereading of the history of economic thought to a consideration of the alternative future paths that might be taken conjures up more issues than can satisfactorily be resolved in this chapter, in terms of the issues emphasized in this book there are three areas that I see as important to a reconstitution of political economy or social economy. First, a Keynes-inspired discussion of speculation and international capital mobility may be an important feature of the wider effort to theorize the post-postwar era. A study of capital markets and financial governance regimes can usefully be undertaken from such a perspective. A second area is the impact of technological change and globalization on domestic labor markets. Further comparative research on specifics of national labor market practices are likely to offer further insight into institutional factors that condition employment possibilities.

A third focus, which will not be discussed, is worth identifying. It is one that will also shape economics. This is the more difficult matter of the extent to which economics will come to see broader issues of institutional change, human agency, and social choice as part of its larger framework, and the articulation and more explicit examination of questions of vision. This last concern goes beyond the importance of social knowledge and institutional efficiency to issues of building an inclusive social order in which there is greater social peace because there is a shared sense of greater social justice. It is not one about which economists can claim special expertise, but it is important nevertheless because pre-analytic vision influences choice of research assumptions and cannot but influence what economists choose to do and how they work. This is why, as Mill, Marshall, and Keynes emphasized, economics is a moral science. Yet such matters go undiscussed for the most part by economists who thus abrogate responsibility as public intellectuals, a role they once accepted.

Expectations and financial markets

Policy makers at the time of Bretton Woods accepted a National Keynesian model in which rapid accumulation and redistributive liberalism required the ascendancy of state actors and democratic governance over market forces. In those days, a US Secretary of the Treasury (Henry Morganthau) could assert that our goal (and the purpose of the Bretton Woods Agreement) was to drive the usurious moneylenders from the temple of international finance. At that stage of world capitalist development, a liberal trading system was seen to require stable exchange rates. This requirement meant that free finance had to be sacrificed for a stable economic environment. Political elites endorsed what John Ruggie has called an embedded liberal order, which restricted capital's freedom for the purpose of defending the policy autonomy of the welfare state. The architects of the postwar economic regime constructed a decidedly non-liberal financial order in which the use of capital controls was strongly endorsed (Ruggie 1982).[7] Since those days, market developments, technological innovation, and political choices have promoted international capital movement on an undreamed of scale, raising concerns that are grist for many analytically heterodox interpretations of the postwar period.

The instantaneously adjusting market of neoclassical economics is today approximated in the financial arena. Yet deregulation of finance and floating exchange rates led to greater volatility, where most mainstream economists expected greater stability to result. The social costs resulting from relatively unimpeded capital mobility in cases of poor economic judgment by banks and by governments, and where rumor produces sudden and ultimately unwarranted shifts, can be extremely high. Portfolio allocation to particular countries is very responsive to small changes in perception of expected return. Investors rearranging their portfolios can cause markets to move suddenly, to dramatic effects. Even unsupported suspicion can trigger massive capital flows that are seemingly inconsistent with a country's fundamentals (Calvo and Mendoza 1996). Such developments reinforce Keynes' message concerning destabilizing impacts of international financial speculation and the need, as Hyman Minsky has argued, to give up some market efficiency or even a bit of aggregate income in order to contain 'democracy-threatening uncertainty' (Minsky 1996: 364).

Some economists are attracted to the benefits of throwing some sand in the wheels of speculative finance and of establishing a regime of global financial governance that puts politics in command again, despite the potential for abuse by short-sighted and rent seeking states (Crotty and Epstein 1996; see also Goodman and Pauly 1993 and Eichengreen *et al.* 1995). James Crotty and Gerald Epstein argue that it was the system of capital controls and credit allocation put in place after the Second World War that made possible the Golden Age (the expansion phase of the postwar era), that the unraveling of these controls contributed substantially to the Golden Age's subsequent demise, that the enlarged power of money and capital markets have made progressive domestic policies difficult if not impossible, and that today controls are both feasible and necessary. International agreements on environmental and labor standards, taxation of transnationals and other leveling up strategies are also possible (Crotty *et al.* 1998).

In a Keynes–Minsky perspective there is no 'true' model of the world held by participants, as presumed in many rational expectations models. Episodes of optimism and pessimism alternate to produce market outcomes. Political consciousness develops, leading to demands for new types of government policies that change the incentives of market participants. Speculative forces, rather than bringing about efficient, rational outcomes, are often wrong because the future is unknowable and investor psychology unstable. The herd instinct is strong. Periods of turbulence exhibit hair-trigger behavior that can turn slight tendencies into self-reinforcing panics in which the only 'new information' concerns subjective market mood, for example an increase in fear of being trampled as others rush to the door, or on the upswing to be left in the dust of a stampede to buy. The institutional setting is important to how such events are played out, and responsible stabilizing measures can create greater stability at little cost to long-term economic efficiency (Wolfson 1995).

The imperative of financial markets' credibility has imposed a broadly deflationary macroeconomic strategy in place of the expansionary impulse of the era of National Keynesianism. Greater wage flexibility in a situation in which nations attempt to cut social spending and discipline labor, while defending their currencies from speculative attack, produces insufficient aggregate demand unable to create anything approaching full employment. Further, the ratcheting up of real interest rates has slowed global growth in this period of neoclassical globalism's dominance. From a Keynes–Joan Robinson framework, speculation may well be an important factor driving the overall global economy toward a low-growth, high-unemployment equilibrium. Whilst the managed international financial framework of the 1960s encouraged expansionary full employment policies, floating exchange rates with their speculative swings, higher real interest rates, and pressure to attain credibility in the eyes of financial markets, produce slower growth and higher unemployment (Eatwell 1996: 21).

Speculative capital and transnational producers resist any regulatory regime that would limit their freedom, but if the social cost of such freedom becomes evident, the need for a new global governance structure to regulate finance comes to be widely appreciated. Such reconsideration of the cost of 'free' markets recurs cyclically. Their appearance is related to the erosion of a formerly functional, regulatory regime when, as at the present moment, the emergence of a new pattern of accumulation revalues older accommodations.[8]

The assertion that the bond market, because it can override democratic governance, provides a more efficient and so desirable outcome is not a new claim. We are again being asked to accept, as Keynes wrote in his *Tract on Monetary Reform*, 'the advise of a parliament of banks.' Many economists today celebrate the development of financial market control and its ability to enforce cuts in government welfare state spending, despite rising levels of unemployment. These are the very forces and the logic that Keynes so ardently decried; but this is not Keynes' historical conjuncture and the National Keynesian welfare state is seen as a spent model. The issue becomes what is the best regulatory framework under these new conditions, using 'best' to mean both possible and desirable? The two most striking aspects of the present period are the dynamism of technological change and organizational innovation accompanying more flexible manufacturing systems and customized production of goods and services, on the one side, and the social dislocations of rapid economic change, on the other. Economists have generally paid more attention to the former, yet the latter is also part of the period's economic transformation and should not be left to the other social sciences.

Technology and labor market flexibility

The fascination with post-fordist reorganization of production – lean production, just-in-time production, flexible production – and the spatial reorderings – commodity webs, relational contracting, multi-local governance structures – gives descriptive content to the claim that there is a new time–space compression that reorganizes our political economy. At the heart of such discussions is the information revolution and the claim that a new stage of 'Friction-Free Capitalism,' to use Bill Gates' term, is coming into being in which perfect information becomes the basis for the perfection of the market (Gates 1995; see Dawson and Foster 1996). The attraction of mass customization, the selling to individuals based on detailed knowledge of their preferences (from records of past credit card purchases and from interactive computer choice screen responses), promise a virtual marketplace in which goods can be accessed by the internet and the company selling may be large, small, or merely virtual, subcontracting most functions and indirectly employing workers they will never see or know exist. Adam Smith's invisible hand takes the form of clicking mouses producing the virtual perfect market.

The possibilities of technology in the present era are also celebrated in the promise of non-hierarchical, creative flexibility, in which continuous learning with unpredictable outcomes result, and management of the learning process is key to corporate success. The promised triumph of decentralized control by small-scale producers may not, however, be quite the sure thing some of those who stress a new industrial divide claim (Piori and Sabel 1984), for the changing landscape of corporate power in the age of flexibility is beginning to show some familiar patterns (Harrison 1994). The scope of technological possibilities for the independence of small-scale creative innovators seems to fade with the inevitability of product cycle maturity and corporate reconcentration. The very industries that are said to represent the new dispensation – computers, software, media, and telecommunications – are experiencing intense merger and convergence and offer bimodal compensation patterns. Social democratic and corporatist national governance traditions also show different configurations to the Anglo-American experience. The speed of technological change and the extent of corporate restructuring matter for social stability and cohesion.

Flexibility strategies reorganize labor. How they do so depends on a larger context. They may restore labor market efficiency by multi-skilling workers and taking advantage of their knowledge and creativity. In a period of trade union weakness and excess labor supply, however, the form such reregulation of the labor market takes differs according to the bargaining power of different classes of employees and the options of employers. Some firms have pursued a 'defensive flexibility' associated with deregulation and job insecurity, others an 'offensive flexibility' associated with training schemes and long-term employability agreements. It may be a bit early, however, to count out old style understandings of labor, capital, and class relations which, whilst they may take new form, also demonstrate underlying stability. The nature of work relations for most workers continues fundamentally unchanged. Indeed, it is more difficult to retain long-term employment when corporations dramatically reinvent themselves and continually restructure (Peck 1996: ch. 5). These are issues that will be resolved by history and then clarified by theory.

During the Great Depression, Joan Robinson wrote that except under peculiar conditions, a decline in effective demand will not lead to unemployment in the sense of complete idleness, but will rather drive workers into a number of inferior occupations (her examples ranged from selling matchbooks in the Strand to cutting brushwood in the jungle). Her point was that a decline in one sort of employment leads to an increase in another sort. At first sight a decline in effective demand would not seem to create unemployment at all, but, she pointed out, the new employment is less productive. She describes the adoption of inferior occupations by dismissed workers as *disguised unemployment* (Robinson 1937).

John Eatwell, following Robinson, says that disguised unemployment (defined as employment in very low productivity sectors) has grown in the United States far more than anywhere else since the mid-1970s, the years in which income inequality has also grown substantially in the United States. He does an interesting calculation. Based on assumptions within this Robinson framework, he presents figures for G7 countries, adding disguised unemployment to published unemployment figures to give what he calls the 'true' unemployment rate. When this is done, the supposed superiority of US labor market patterns immediately disappears. The much-maligned, high-wage German economy is the most efficient in the G7 group. They could, by eliminating their unemployment benefits or lowering them to US levels, reduce their measured unemployment or even eradicate it entirely, but this would reduce the performance of the German economy. Japan too has a great deal of disguised unemployment (in distribution, retailing, and agriculture especially), but its more egalitarian wage structure and productivity growth has been able, even in the aftermath of the collapse of the bubble economy's overheated speculative excesses, to pay relatively high wages to secondary workers compared to the US and to fund the disguised unemployment at livable income levels.

The extent of 'bad' jobs (low productivity, low pay), which are the sponge absorbing workers in the United States, impacts on the character of American society, and the Europeans and Japanese have not been eager to follow the American pattern. Richard Freeman has argued that despite the superficial appeal to US-style wage flexibility, the response of European labor markets may prove the better choice. Put crudely, Freeman notes that wage flexibility produces 'a free fall' in pay at the bottom of the earnings distribution (Freeman 1995b: 65). Because of the high social costs of crime and imprisonment as a result of the weak job market for the less skilled and the spill-over effects of the high degree of inequality in the American pattern, US labor markets are hardly the envy of the civilized world that some have claimed.

Alfred Marshall noted long ago that high wages increase 'the efficiency not only of those who received them, but also of their children and grand-children.' He believed that parents would spend higher pay on improving their children and 'an increase in wages, unless earned under unwholesome conditions, almost always increases the strength, physical, mental and even moral of the coming generation' (Marshall 1895: 1135). Remembering such alternative stories of what we may call social hysteresis is an important part of the struggle to maintain social and economic cohesion in a period in which we are told that market forces will force wages to their natural level and that intensified global competition requires greater flexibility, meaning downward adjustment of wages and social wages in the advanced economies.[9] Normative political economy dependent on vision is important to the work economists carry out in this and other policy areas.

It also depends on the larger framework of the historical evolution of real-world capitalism. Further work on unemployment trends in Europe, as compared to the United States, would do well to combine careful consideration of institutional change with traditional macroeconomic and microeconomic explanations, so that the impact of the Maastricht Treaty requirements for those countries wishing to join the single currency unit are taken into account. Because of the separation of specialist literatures, it is easily forgotten when it comes to discussions of labor markets that European governments have consciously followed deflationary (and unemployment creating) strategies in order to meet requirements as to the size of their budget deficits and rates of inflation.

One expects there will be continued basic clashes in the stylized facts considered relevant, given political sympathies and theoretical starting points. If 'progress in economic thinking means getting better and better abstract, analogue models, not better verbal observations about the world,' as Robert Lucas maintains, then such discussions based on analysis of data that is fitted into a larger effort to interpret the economics of a world swiftly changing should give way to greater refinement of Walrasian-style thinking. For those who think it is important that the Walrasian auctioneer does not really exist and that 'as if' stories provide comfortable fictions about make-believe worlds, however, we cannot study problems of wage and price coordination, as Bruce Greenwald and Joseph Stiglitz (1993: 42) have written, 'in the context of a macroeconomy consisting of an aggregated representative agent, like Robinson Crusoe.' The stories we tell matter: they affect the way economists are socialized and how they make the world in their models and color their policy presumptions.

A view of human beings as unsocialized, autonomous economic actors, the starting point for mainstream theory, means that individuals pursuing their own ends, free of constraint, will benefit society and produce social harmony. Equilibrium is produced by non-coerced exchange which is both efficient and can be seen to be 'good.' Joan Robinson, writing in the mainline tradition, objects, arguing that 'The moral problem is concerned with the conflict between the individual interests and the interests of society. And since the doctrine tells us that there is no conflict, we can all pursue our self-interest with a good conscience' (Robinson 1978: 45). We are back to the mainstream understanding of the invisible hand that was subject to critical scrutiny in Chapter 3, which ignores Smith's theories of moral sentiment.

Albert Hirschman has described the period we have entered as the third reactionary wave. He has evaluated the contemporary critique of the welfare state and attempts to role back or 'reform' many of its major provisions and to annul commitments based on its philosophy of governance in terms of historically familiar reactive–reactionary theses (Hirschman 1991). Positive claims are also being made, however, that go beyond the moment of denunciation of the perversity, futility, and jeopardy created by Keynesian welfare state activities. The values of individual responsibility, the contention that individuals know what is best for them, and certainly know better than governments, that decisions made as close to the local level where effects of policy are felt are best, that high taxes have disincentive effects and lower taxes unleash entrepreneurial zeal and work effort, that free exchange between consenting parties produces mutual gains – all of these are widely shared sociopolitical values. The question is: what are the results of the policies that flow from such beliefs in the present conjuncture? There can be little question that the economics of the free market and a rejection of government has been a major political reality in the United States of recent decades. It is less clear that it represents a more workable alternative to Keynesian welfare state liberalism. Some form of regulation and governance are needed for economies, which are political by nature, to function.

There are two points to be made concerning the stress on efficient market theory at the start of the twenty-first century. The first is with regard to self-interest and social cohesion. Adam Smith, it has been noted, exemplified a complex liberal tradition in his understanding of self-interest and the common good. Leon Walras, by contrast, 'defined the pure science to which he aspired as the study of the relationships among *things*, not *people* and sought, with notable success to eliminate human relationships from his purview.' Samuel Bowles and Herbert Gintis call the device he used to accomplish this *Walras' fiction*, the idea introduced in Chapter 1 that interrelations among economic agents 'might be represented *as if* they were relationships among inputs and outputs' (Bowles and Gintis 1993: 84). Walras, who saw the pure theory of economics as resembling 'the physico-mathematical sciences in every respect,' would surely have agreed with characterization of his work as an effort to develop a social *science*, the purist A mode version possible.

Critics in the B mode *social* science approach would side with Bowles and Gintis in their suggestion that exchange is always contested. Not only should *Homo economicus* be characterized, as Oliver Williamson suggests, to include 'the full set of *ex ante* and *ex post* efforts to lie, cheat, steal, mislead, disguise, obfuscate, feign, distort and confuse,' but it needs to enforce contracts, an undertaking that is never costless. If we understand the market to be contested in the older political economy sense, the benefits parties derive from a transaction depend on their capacity to enforce competing claims. Only some of these conflicts can be understood in terms of competition among independent and isolated individual actors. These claims are enforced within a set of institutions and asymmetric social relations, as Smith to Marx understood and made central to their thinking. Conflict over means and ends involves power and class conflict, as the classical political philosophers and economists knew.

Rousseau, for example, viewed preferences, such as the desire to accumulate property, not as universal postulates on which a scientific theory could be founded, but as the products of society. Law and custom, norms, and institutions shape preferences, he thought. The kind of natural inequalities of a given society produce outcomes that emerge not from some presocial state but from a historically contingent social order. The structure of political opportunities within that social formation will shape the strategies of organized groups and their beliefs in what is possible and which political actions are most efficacious. As Bowles' work stresses, this is a recursive process since institutional forms shape political attitudes, and indeed personalities, which then influence political choices that individuals and groups think it appropriate to make.

Public choice theory, in which social welfare functions are presumed to be simple aggregates of individual preferences, allows for tractability and solid micro foundations, but will not do within the older conception of political economy favored here. Mechanisms for aggregating interests do not, in fact, sum but reshape interests. New ideas develop in the process of reaching decisions and discussing issues. They are not there beforehand, accessible equally to all participants (Immergut 1998). People redefine their preferences in the process of selecting which issues they want to vote on and how choices are framed. There may be no clear cut consensus initially, and mechanisms of collective decision making act to reach agreement in ways very different from those the individual choice models suggest. That is, political economy is not solely an economic process, and is inherently a political process. In addition, the forms of decision making will differ even across polities. Among democracies, institutional rules for opinion articulation and policy formation differ. There can be no identical natural equilibrium of preferences among the various decision systems.

The second point about social decision making on economic issues is that despite all of the talk about globalization and the 'new economy,' the essential issues are the same as they were when Adam Smith wrote. Also, despite the seeming newness of the rapidity of technological changes and challenges to statist programs of reform and redistribution, we might remember that what Marx and Mill had to say in 1848 also marked the beginning of a century and more in which the clash between the imperatives of efficiency, in a competitive private enterprise system of changing technologies, and the imperatives of human welfare, rooted in western culture and its religions, dominate the agenda of political economy and politics.

(Rostow 1990: 94)

The issues that have been important to the political economists of the mainline tradition remain remarkably similar.

A new classical situation?

The possible relationships between pre-analytic vision, descriptions of reality, estimation of trends, alternative futures, and outcomes advocated are complex. Yet there have been periods in the history of economic thought when certain perspectives have been hegemonic, providing a widely shared understanding of the economy and how economists should go about their work. Robert Heilbroner and William Milberg, building on a concept introduced by Schumpeter, refer to *classic situations*, 'punctuated equilibria' in the development of economic thought – historic periods of statis and consolidation marked by widespread agreement as to the questions that doctrine addresses and the kinds of answers that it considers most acceptable. They see classic situations as attaining their importance not from a claim to truth in some presumed objective sense, superior accuracy, or even usefulness, but from wide acceptance of the defensibility of the world-view they offer, and importantly, because of a shared basis for judgments of the reasonableness of the social order presumed – that is, from a shared pre-analytic vision without which analysis, the deducing of consequences from initial conditions, could not proceed. Heilbroner and Milberg explore the breakdown of the Keynesian consensus, why no alternative has gained wide acceptance, and what a new consensus would require.

In my view, there has been a major challenger to the Keynesian mantle. In its various versions – monetarism, rational expectations, new classical economics, and other formulations – this newer orientation presents a possible successor model. It is one that returns economics to its pre-Keynesian basic understanding of the world. Indeed, this theoretical orientation, as we have suggested, has been hegemonic in recent decades. It may well be that future historians of economic thought will consider it as a classic situation in the same way that we can now speak of a first classical situation in the late eighteenth- and early nineteenth-century English economic society. Of course, it is also possible that it may not be consolidated into a long running consensus view. Providing a prolonged classic situation requires interpretation of where we are in economic history. My own perspective is that as the outlines of the restructured global economy become clearer and the consequence of accepting hypermobility of capital, and unrestricted market forces, becomes evident, a new regulatory regime will emerge and this period of renewed faith in unrestricted markets will pass. My contention is not made simply out of ideological conviction, although my pre-analytic vision is evident. My position will be convincing to the extent to which my story of where we are in history makes sense.

In 1993 Bob Jessop suggested that 'a tendential shift' was underway toward the establishment of what he called the Schumpeterian workfare state, which is in major respects the policy alternative of the new classical economics. He related this transition to both a shift from Fordism to post-Fordism in production and a hollowing out of the nation-states in the advanced capitalist economies in the realm of governance (Jessop 1993). Jessop is careful in the claim being made, for he sees tendencies and countertendencies in the new global economy, extensive improvisation, and trial and error involved in experimentation by policy entrepreneurs. Accepting his terminology, we can consider the difference between the two models in ways that are not spelled out this way by Jessop.

The Schumpeterian workfare state is in many ways a negation of the Keynesian welfare state. Rather than a guiding role of government in stabilizing the macroeconomy and encouraging growth through activist fiscal and monetary policy, as in the Keynesian welfare state, the Schumpeterian workfare state relies on individual initiative and market incentives. It sees guaranteeing income support as an inducement not to work, and advocates reversing state-induced dependency by ending the welfare state as we know it.

Whether the Schumpeterian workfare state becomes a successful regulatory regime and basis for a new classical situation is an open question. The very flexibility with which it responds to the structural rigidities of National Keynesianism presents a double moment in terms of system growth and reproduction. We can see this double moment in terms of the contradictory meanings of flexibility in the workfare state side. The workfare state element undoes the welfare state regime's institutional protections. This is its negative moment. The positive moment, if successful, would be in its establishment of an alternative regime based on individual incentives and efficient markets capable of productively absorbing those now dependent on the state. It is with regard to the viability of the positive moment's potential to produce stable reproduction that serious question must be raised. The problem is most obvious in the pairing of its two central elements: the reigning natural rate theory which tells us we must have 6 per cent or so unemployment to avoid higher inflation, and the demand to end welfare as we have known it. In the ardor to achieve the negative moment of dismantling and removing the cost burden to the state, no one seems to notice the problem created by a demand that everyone should be required to work, especially welfare recipients, in the face of the requirement that substantial unemployment is necessary to the health of the system.

The neoliberal labor market policies of a Schumpeterian workfare state regime are politically contentious. They call attention to the sharp divide between a neoclassical approach to labor as another factor of production and the B mode appreciation of the social character of labor which sets it apart and gives it special claims. From the latter perspective, it can be suggested that whilst the workfare state may be capable of undermining the rigidities by revoking the protections that have built up in the Keynesian welfare state model, it is at the same time not clear that such a model can provide a sustainable alternative. This is an empirical matter that will test the limits of labor market flexibility. The presumed need to maintain 6 per cent or so unemployment, which translates into far higher rates in America's inner cities, represents a conceptual switch from viewing the unemployed worker as a resource whose labor produces economic growth, to acceptance of the idea that unemployment and underemployment are the price of economic stability that persisted through the 1980s and 1990s and provided a weapon to hold down prices and smooth corporate restructuring at the expense of labor. If the Schumpeterian workfare state model proves internally crisis prone and therefore unstable, it is inappropriate to label it an emergent mode of production (Lipietz 1992; Peck and Tickell 1994: 294).

Given the openness of the period, any confident forecast as to the inevitability of any developmental tendency at this time must be questioned, yet some comments may be ventured with regard to a framework for understanding the present in history. These involve discussion of not only economics but also politics and normative political economy issues. In this context it would seem useful to entertain the possibility that we are experiencing what Antonio Gramsci called an organic crisis, in which the social alliance, the historical bloc – that complex of economic, political, and cultural institutions that permits relatively smooth social reproduction in the postwar period – has broken down. The characteristics of the postwar social structure of accumulation or mode of regulation have imploded. National Keynesianism cannot be sustained within a global marketplace of hyper-mobile capital. The protections borders once afforded to national governments to pursue independent macroeconomic policy are reduced, and technological innovations of the period in a context of liberalization have allowed radical reorganization that has tended to hollow out the nation-state in much of the world. In the United States, the bloc whose interest was served by the old alliance has been fractured by a change in the way technology and globalization reorganize production and cultural space. How might we characterize these changes in the larger political landscape?

The New Deal–National Keynesian liberal–labor coalition has decomposed and a new historic bloc has formed, a globalist free market alliance of international capitalism with its assertive modernism combined with elements drawn to traditional conservativism. Social issue conservatives and competitive sector capitalists join in opposing the welfare state. Internationally oriented, capital fearing, nation-state level restrictions benefit from and feed this broader anti-regulatory climate. Working-class elements whose living standards and status have fallen, vote for tax cuts and against social programs seen as helping the non-deserving poor, and so give bulk to this voter coalition. The Schumpeterian workfare state may be the resulting social structure of accumulation in this post-fordist, post-Keynesian era. How long such a consensus model will remain hegemonic is a matter of conjecture. Even the issue of whether it has been, or can be, successfully implemented, as we emphasize, remains contested.

Conclusion

John Maynard Keynes, during the Great Depression, addressing himself to the position that nothing could really be done, responded to such advice,

> the worst of it is, that we have one excellent excuse for doing nothing. To a large extent the cure lies outside our own power. The problem is an international one, and for a country which depends on foreign trade as much as we do there are narrow limits to what we can achieve by ourselves.
>
> (Keynes 1930a: 150–1)

It was just such pessimism that Keynes wrote to refute. There was much that England then, or America today, could do besides accepting a painful course of action for millions who are unlikely to benefit from their concessions and are being written off by those who will enjoy the fruits of these sacrifices.

There are, of course, important differences between the 1990s and the 1930s. In terms of thinking clearly about where we are in history and about policy alternatives, perhaps the most important of these is that in the 1930s the world was in crisis more or less together. Rich as well as poor were shaken by the Great Depression, and whilst Keynes and Roosevelt might have been considered dangerous socialists bent on destroying capitalism, it was clear to thinking people then, as it is even more obvious in retrospect, that they were formulating strategies to save the system from its crisis. In the 1990s an emergent global elite is benefiting from the dramatic restructuring of an increasingly internationalized economy, and many of us are happy consumers of the wonderful new products technology showers upon those who can afford them. Those who are suffering are largely sections of the traditional working class and beneficiaries of the welfare state constructed under the regime of National Keynesianism.

Periods of restructuring, with their disorienting dislocations, are not new to human experience. Change must have seemed just as bewildering to Adam Smith's contemporaries as they read *The Wealth of Nations* or those who, in the year of revolution, 1848, read Mill's *Principles* or perhaps the *Communist Manifesto*, or in 1890, as economic concentration and imperialism were reshaping economics at home and abroad, read Marshall's great text and of course in 1936, in the Great Depression, reading Keynes' *General Theory*. There was an abiding belief expressed by each of these economists of the mainline tradition that pessimism in the face of destabilizing developments is not the only possible response, and surely not the best one. Humans are capable of theorizing alternative futures and individuals of collective activity. There is much in such attitudes to inspire those who would do political economy in our time.

Notes

1 The two cultures in economics

1 The economists we characterize as part of the mainline tradition are routinely labeled as 'eclectics.' Jacob Viner calls Adam Smith '*the* great eclectic.' Landreth and Colander write that 'Mill's greatest strength, which was also the strength of the two most important post-Millian English economists, Marshall and Keynes was his *eclecticism* . . .' Emphases in originals. See Viner's 1927 essay 'Adam Smith and Laissez-faire,' and Landreth and Colander 1994: 155.

2 The emphasis on overly abstract modeling has produced dissatisfaction within the field and a self-study by some of the profession's leading practitioners on behalf of the American Economics Association: 'Report of the Commission on Graduate Education in Economics' (1991) *Journal of Economic Literature*, September.

3 Whilst Mill did much to shape economists' understanding of the motivations and character of economic man, his own views of human beings were far more complex. He saw economic man constrained in his choices by institutions that could be restructured through human agency in ways that could encourage making 'better' choices. See Persky (1995).

4 Critiques of the use of *Homo economicus* are like the grains of sand. See, for example, Hollis and Nell (1975).

5 On economics' long-standing bad press, see Jacob Viner (1963).

6 One of the more useful interventions demonstrating this point is Moore (1994).

7 A reader pointed out that the term 'feminist economist' is problematic since there can be economists who are feminists and mainstream neoclassical economists, game theorists, and so on. I accept that this is the case but that the term feminist economist still has a readily identifiable meaning as it is used here.

8 Support for such an embedded view of character formation is the norm in many other social sciences. See, for example, Cohen (1980).

9 The suggestion originated with Polly Hill (Mrs Humphreys), Keynes' niece who assisted Robinson in editing the *Economic Journal* under Keynes.

10 A good instance of the tone and mode of dismissal is found in a review of this book by Stephen Baker using the time-honored formula 'Other observers have covered much of this terrain . . . the MIT professor comes up short of solutions.' The dismissal that ideas are not new and that since an author cannot solve a serious problem (s)he has identified the work may reflect unwillingness to engage arguments one does not like. Stephen Baker (1996: 15).

11 Klamer writes on Samuelson's aesthetic: 'Keynes' text resembles an impressionistic painting whereas Samuelson's text appears to be drawn in the spirit of Piet Mandrian . . .' (Klamer 1995: 330). See also Klamer (1990).

12 The comment appears in the context of Samuelson's working through assumptions for a neo-Walrasian equilibrium analysis which start with his expressed preference for the

'rock bottom simplicity' of collective indifference curves 'of the Robinson Crusoe type,' which he suggests as working for 'all society.' Compare such usage with the assumptions about economics exhibited by Daniel Defoe's *Robinson Crusoe* in chapter 2.

13 Others with a similar outlook define political economy even more broadly so that it

> is not a fixed subject or discipline but a recurrent mode of conceptualizing social life. Its scope or field of vision has broadened and narrowed at different times as economic belief systems have alternatively displaced or rekindled interest in fundamental issues such as human equality and growth. Thus it tends to be rediscovered . . . when prevailing ideologies and thought patterns are called into question by events.
>
> (Vig 1985: 5–6)

2 Of dialogic debates and the uncertain embrace

1 Alfred Eichner has called our B group post-Keynesian, but as he says 'it could just as well be termed post-classical, or even post-Marxist, since it also picks up where the classical mode of analysis left off following the marginalist revolution in the 1870s. Indeed,' he goes on, 'institutionalist since an important characteristic of the theory is the prominent role it ascribes to the dominant institutions' of the economy (Eichner 1985: 3).

2 See for example the exchange between David Papineau (1998) and Steven Rose (1998).

3 The new physics is often compared to zen or the tao and even to suggest modes of motorcycle maintenance – all efforts to bring a different understanding of 'order.' See, for example, Chick (1995).

4 The essay will appear in John Cornwall (ed.) *Nature's Imagination: The Frontier of Scientific Vision.*

5 Throughout I shall use 'liberal' in its contemporary American usage. In the United States the term liberal was adopted after 'progressive' went into disfavor following Theodore Roosevelt's defeat on a Progressive third party ticket. Traditional liberals were not happy with the adaption of the label to mean what had been referred to previously as progressive. In the 1920s, the *New York Times* (then an organ of traditional not modern liberalism) complained of 'the expropriation of the time-honored word "liberal".' The *Times* wanted 'the Radical-Red school of thought' to hand it back to its original owners. Both Herbert Hoover and Franklin Roosevelt claimed to be liberals. FDR won and the rest is history. Roosevelt declared liberalism to be 'plain English for a changed concept of the duty and responsibility of government toward economic life.' There is some irony then that in recent years one can detect a renewal of the progressive self-descriptor among those who might not long ago have called themselves liberals, along with a growing number of conservatives who join Milton Friedman and others who had refused to give up the label 'liberal' for their free market ideas. I am endebted for the quotations above to Daniel Yergin and Joseph Stanislaw (1998: 15).

6 Calls for such moral regeneration are common enough historically. Their programmatic content, privatization of charity and so on, have not been successful in increasing self-reliance among the 'worthy' poor. See Ziliak (1996).

7 The passage appears in Joseph Schumpeter's 'Preface to the Japanese edition of *Theorie Der Wertschaftlichen Entwicklung*, 1937 as reprinted in Richard V. Clemence, 1951: 158; and quoted by Nathan Rosenberg (1994: 49).

8 On the distinction between logical time and historical time see Robinson (1980).

9 For another example see Colander (1995); also see Klamer and Leonard (1994).

10 Some economists may prefer Wiseman and Littlechild (1990).

11 The account from box of sugar to barrel of fine flour, from nails to grindstone, and of course from muskets, ball, and power to '3 very good Bibles,' are detailed. Defoe (1719: 53–60).

12 Marx notes that political economists are fond of Robinson Crusoe stories, which they

always use anachronistically. Marx, for example, chides Ricardo for having his primitive fisherman and hunters calculate the value of their implements in accordance with the annuity tables used on the London Stock Exchange in 1817. Marx (1867: 169, fn. 31).

13 Nor is this the whole story, for 'How many merchants and carriers, besides, must have been employed in transporting the materials from some of those workmen to others who often live in a distant part of the country!' Smith is only warming to his story at this point. On he goes to tell

> How much commerce and navigation in particular, how many ship-builders, sailers, sail-makers, rope-makers, must have been employed in order to bring together the different drugs made use of by the dyer, which often come from the remotest corners of the world.

He goes on to detail how the tools used were themselves made, the varieties of labor requisite to the builder of the furnace for smelting ore and on.

14 As Sanford Jacoby wrote in 1990, 'The standard modeling metaphor learned by graduate students in economics remains that of Robinson Crusoe, alone on his island without a community, a history, or even an employer' (Jacoby 1990: 333). Robert Barro and Xavier Sala-I-Martin explain the basic structure of simplified growth models: 'We can think of a composite unit — a household/producer like Robinson Crusoe — who owns the inputs and also manages the technology that transforms inputs into outputs' (Barro and Sala-I-Martin 1995: 14).

15 For Defoe's subtexts concerning the nature of capitalism and colonialism, interested readers are directed to Downie (1983); also see Novak (1962), Watt (1951), and Seidel (1991).

3 Contestation and canonicity

1 These canonical texts are unstable because as the emphases in a field change, a certain amount of intergenerational reinterpretation of foundational materials is essential, and contestation over meanings unavoidable. The Adam Smith problem has really been that acceptance of a narrowly functional marketeer's Adam Smith is inconsistent with Smith's moral philosophy. It is my task to convince you that a broader reading is not only more faithful, but more useful as well.

2 Marx bestows the title of 'father of political economy' on William Petty, and reading him we certainly come upon familiar material. Consider Petty's discussion of the division of labor in the manufacture of a watch from *Another Essay in Political Arithmetic*:

> if one man shall make the Wheels, another the Spring, another shall Engrave and Dialplate, and another shall make the cases, then the Watch will be better and cheaper, than if the whole Work be put upon by any one Man.

> (Rashid 1986)

3 On the Glasgow School, Smith's teacher Hutcheson, Smith and Smith's student John Millar (who was professor at Glasgow between 1761 and 1801), see Olson (1993). The leading figures of the Scottish Enlightenment wrote on a wide range of social, moral, and historical issues which today are considered early sociology. The manner in which late nineteenth-century economists demanded a separation of economics from the other disciplines would have been wholly alien to them. See Marshall (1994).

4 This view, against which Smith is reacting, was set forth in classic form in Sir James Steuart's 1767 *Inquiry into the Principles of Political Oeconomy*. It presumes the statesman directs rational strategies to improve competitiveness, that he is the master who sails his ship with the greatest dexterity. Smith, in the Scottish Enlightenment tradition, followed his teacher Adam Ferguson in understanding outcomes to be the *unintended* consequence of human activity and not the straightforward product of human design.

5 Appleby, Hunt, and Jacob, surveying his influence, write:

> The Newtonian universe acted as an imaginary backdrop on which to project pre-
> scriptions for order, stability, harmony, and freedom. Rising as it were on its own
> mathematically knowable forces, the *Principia* became a model for balanced govern-
> ments and self-regulated economics, for elections, constitutions, and free markets.
>
> (Appleby *et al.* 1994: 31)

6 William Shakespeare, *Macbeth*, Act III, Scene ii.

7 Indeed, she goes further, suggesting that 'Smith's three uses of the phrase have in
common that the individuals concerned are quite undignified; they are silly polytheists,
rapacious proprietors, disingenuous merchants' (Rothschild 1994: 320).

8 It must be said that Smith barely makes mention of actual class struggle, which in its
concrete manifestation was ever present through the period in which he was writing. As
Ashton in his classic book on the industrial revolution reports:

> from 1760 the coalfields, the ports, and the textile villages were often scenes of vio-
> lence. In 1765, the pitmen of the Tyne, on strike against the introduction of a
> leaving certificate, cut the winding ropes, smashed the engines, and set fire to the coal
> underground. In the later 'sixties jenny riots in Lancashire led to the destruction of
> machines and houses – and perhaps to the flight of Hargraves and Arkwright to
> Nottingham. In 1773 the sailors of Liverpool staged a pitched battle in which (as Mr.
> Wadsworth tells us) they hoisted the 'bloody flag', sacked the house of the shipown-
> ers and trained cannon on the Exchange.
>
> (Ashton 1948: 133)

9 There needs to be more discussion of the hold physiocratic thinking has on Adam
Smith and the contradiction between his domestic preference investment schema and
his endorsement of comparative advantage theory as a guide to policy. What is extra-
ordinary is that there seems to be little interest in how far the real Adam Smith fitted
these matters together.

10 As Hobsbawm explains:

> The country which succeeded in concentrating other people's export markets, or
> even in monopolizing the export markets of a large part of the world in a suffi-
> ciently brief period of time, could expand its export industries at a rate which made
> industrial revolution not only practicable for its entrepreneurs, but sometimes
> virtually compulsory. And this is what Britain succeeded in doing in the eighteenth
> century
>
> (Hobsbawm 1968: 48–9)

11 This is clearly a contestable point. Smith himself wrote that without mentioning
Steuart's book he had refuted 'every false principle in it.' Steuart has not lacked for critics both when he wrote or since. See Irwin (1996: esp. 41–2).

12 The internal punctuation here is his, its purpose to reject the widespread though incorrect use of the term.

13 For a distinction not unlike the one we are making, see Screpanti and Zamagni (1993:
62–4) on Adam Smith's 'two souls.'

4 The legacies of classical political economy

1 Nassau Senior once confessed himself guilty (in a letter to Malthus) of error in thinking
that Malthus had meant that a growing population pressing on the means of subsistence
was 'a more probable event' than the opposite; but since such a conclusion was incompatible with the facts that Malthus himself had shown (that the standard of living rises
over time), Malthus clearly must mean that there is the 'tendency' toward what we now
call a Malthusian population trap, but that it is offset by other tendencies (improvement
in productivity) that make it not the governing 'tendency' of real-world events. Malthus'

reply did nothing to separate the two meanings of the word 'tendency,' and so perpetuated a misunderstanding that has lasted to this very day.

2   Almost as soon as Ricardo's *Principles* was off the press, criticism of his A type economics appeared. Richard Jones, for example, objected that economics was not a field in which 'premeditated experiments' were possible, and he denounced 'the too hasty creation of whole systems' based on 'a frail thirst for a premature exposition of commanding generalities.' Jones wanted an economics concerned with 'things as they exist in the world,' with 'institutions,' and with 'history,' among other matters of B type relevance. See Jones (1831: xx) in Sowell (1994: 144).

3   Blaug writes:

> His gift for heroic abstractions produced one of the most impressive models, judged by its scope and practical import, in the entire history of economic theory: seizing hold of a wide range of significant problems with a simple analytical model involving only a few strategic variables, he produced dramatic conclusions oriented to policy action.
>
> (Blaug 1985: 136)

4   Ricardo, because he was the most rigorous theorist among the classical economists, and his style of abstract, deductive model building dominates economic theorizing still, gets credit for all sorts of ideas that he may have presented more precisely but which he was not the first to discover. This is a case in point. Ricardo himself acknowledged Malthus' prior formulation.

5   Of course, Malthus' economics here is not unrelated to his class sympathies, although as usual in such matters the argument is couched in terms of the public interest. Retaining wealth and power for the landowning class was good for all Englishmen, Malthus argued:

> It is an historical truth which cannot for a moment be disputed, that the first formation and subsequent preservation and improvement, of our present constitution, and of the liberties and privileges which have so long distinguished Englishmen, are mainly due to the landed aristocracy.
>
> (Malthus 1836: 380)

6   These are contained in the rest of Chapter 7 of his text and in his 'Essay on the Influence of a Low Price of Corn Upon the Profits of Stock.' See Findlay (1984, Vol. I: 186); also see Maneschi (1992).

7   Rostow remarks on Stigler's judgement: 'Even if there were not more good logic in Malthus's position than Stigler is willing to grant, his *bon mote* is rather more a stricture on modern mainstream economics than on Malthus' (Rostow 1990: 65).

8   It should be said that there is not any more comfortable agreement about what Darwinism 'really means' than about any of the 'isms' in economics that we take up for consideration. See, for example, the accessible treatment in Eldredge (1995).

9   A very useful graduate seminar could be taught considering the meanings of Say's Law or laws and the consequence of each interpretation's acceptance for macro theorizing. A number of interpretive contributions to this discussion are available. See, for example, Clower and Leijonhufvud (1973), reprinted as the concluding essay in Leijonhufvud's *Information and Coordination: Essays in Macroeconomic Theory* (New York: Oxford University Press); and Baumol (1977).

10   His response was essentially along Keynesian lines and implies an accelerator–multiplier understanding of the investment–consumption relationship. He envisioned the possibility of sticky wages and a decline in demand leading not to lower real wages but to unemployment. Malthus anticipated Marx's proportionality argument (in the latter's two sector reproduction schema) and the post-Keynesian stock-adjustment model. There is a lot that is tantalizingly suggestive in Malthus's writings. To take another example, in his chapter 'Of the Modes of correcting the Prevalent Opinions on Population,' Malthus comes close to foreshadowing the possibility of a demographic transition that would offer another solution to the Malthusian problem.

11 Matters are, as usual, far more complicated, and economists have argued for over 200 years about what Say's Law really means, what it meant to Say and others (see note 9 above). See as well Kates (1997). The consensus view is that Say's Law, properly understood, does not rule out recessions and unemployment but denies that deficient demand or generalized overproduction are possible.

12 This account is drawn from Sowell (1994).

13 He thus formalized utilitarian thinking beyond the presentation of earlier ethicists such as David Hume, who offered a utilitarian outlook well before Bentham. Bentham's *Introduction to the Principles of Morals and Legislation* is read more by philosophers than economists, yet his theory of human nature and how wellbeing might be improved made a great impression on contemporary economists, especially James Mill and his son John Stuart Mill, of whom more a little later.

14 Utilitarianism also had its radical edge. Institutions or practices that failed to meet the test of utility could be swept into the dustbin of history based on its broad criterion. It stayed for the most part a liberal doctrine, however, because by the mid-eighteeth century working-class socialism was a viable competitor and held more stirring rationales for sweeping aside the old order.

15 Modern economists, in a more secular age, often claim that they begin by assuming the existing distribution of income, either because they do not wish to enter into making value judgments or because marginal productivity theory states that each has been rewarded according to the resources they contribute. Whether the secularization of Bastiat's faith in the god-given status quo is an improvement is an open question.

16 I am aware that on so many of the points that I make there are extensive debates and discussions. I therefore feel a constant temptation to address historians of thought in the audience, but this chapter is not for them. Nonetheless, here are a citation or two on this matter of the 'recantation,' since it stirs up so many feelings among such scholars: Forget (1992) and Donoghue (1997).

17 Comte initially called his science of society 'social physics' and only later, sociology. It was a science of the social whole and included economics, psychology, anthropology, and history. It also embraced the study of humanity, the science of man. From Comte, Mill accepted the view that political economy has to be intertwined with other branches of social philosophy. As Mill pointed out, there was nothing new in such a perspective, and Adam Smith had known this as well, he said. It is this holism of political economy that waned within the mainstream.

18 Mill's is an odd formulation even if his problem is understandable. He wants to keep a strict economics as science, but also to admit contingency and human agency. He wants his 'A' cake and to have a theory that relates to the real life of men, women, and society. 'The laws and conditions of the Production of wealth partake of the character of physical truths,' but as Leo Rogin summarizes the other side of Mill's position, distribution 'is contingent on the type of institutions which happen to prevail; not on nature, but on culture, man-made and subject to historical change and reform' (Rogin 1956: 281, fn. 4).

19 For Marx, such reformist 'nonsense' represented 'a shallow syncretism,' an attempt 'to reconcile irreconcilable,' as he wrote in the Preface to the 1873 edition of *Capital*.

20 J.S. Mill

> gave only a very qualified adherence to laissez faire. It was for him only a rule of expediency, always subordinate to the principles of utility and never a dogma. The dogmatic exponents of laissez faire of the time were the Manchester School and Mill – like Torrens before him and Cairnes, Jevons, Sedgwick, Marshall, Edgeworth and others after him – denied repeatedly, and forcefully almost to the point of blasphemy, that the Cobdenites had either authority or logic to support them when they invoked the 'Laws of Political Economy' to stop government from coming to the relief of distress.
>
> (Viner 1949: 175)

21 Some would extend that distinction on Marx, who is so substantially in the classical tradition that it would seem wrong to deny him this status.
22 In a famous passage penned in 1852, he writes that if

> the choice were to be made between communism . . . and the present state of society with all its sufferings and injustice; if the institutions of private property necessarily carried with it a consequence, that the produce of labor should be apportioned as we now see it, almost in an inverse to the labour . . . if this or communism were the alternative, all the difficulties, great or small of Communism would be but dust in the balance.

But, he said, it was not an either/or choice. Reformism, support of trade unions, rejection of wage fund thinking and other modern liberal ideas offered a middle way.

5 Marx and the long run

1 The comment is not meant to deprecate the importance of Hegel. For assistance see Likikijsomboon (1992).
2 Actually still more is involved. Marx's goal is to lay bare the economic laws of motion of modern society. In attempting to establish how capitalism works, the 26-year-old Marx wrote (in the preface to what we know as the *Economic and Philosophical Manuscripts of 1844*) that he would publish a

> critique of law, ethics, politics, etc., in a series of distinct, independent pamphlets, and afterwards try in a special work to present them again as a connected whole showing the interrelationships of the separate parts, together with a critique of the speculative elaboration of that material.

> (Marx 1844: 63)

There are a number of places where Marx lays out his plan of work. At the start of the Preface to *A Contribution to the Critique of Political Economy* (1859), he writes that he will 'consider the system of bourgeois economy in the following order: *Capital, landed property, wage labor, state, foreign trade, world market.*' But of course there was no systematic treatment of state, foreign trade, or the world market. The plan presented in the *Grundrisse* makes what we know as *Capital* (the first three volumes) merely a quarter of his planned work *Capital*. Further, the whole of his planned *Capital* was only one of six books he intended to write. *Capital*, as we know it, is then one twenty-fourth of his project on political economy.
3 Engels makes the same point in his 'Preface' to Volume III of *Capital*.
4 The classic explanation of his method is in 'Introduction to the Critique of Political Economy,' which is reprinted in almost any selection from his writings.
5 And that is:

> by the relationship of the different classes to one another and by their respective positions, namely, and first, through the relationship of total surplus value to wages, and secondly, through the relationship of the different parts into which the surplus is divided (profit, interest, rent, taxes, etc.); and so here again it is shown that nothing can be explained on the basis of supply and demand until the basis which that relationship itself reflects is made clear.

> (Marx 1894: 191)

6 As Marx wrote in another context: 'Without competition, the fire of growth would burn out.' The compulsion for capital to grow through technological development is central to his model of the dynamics of the system (Vol. II: 368, Penguin edition).
7 In recent years many more economists have come to Marx's position on institutions, even though most implicitly presume that they are either 'natural,' created by market forces, or imposed by governments, and so illegitimate artificial interferences. Marx has the following to say about the way he thought the economists of his time tended to think about institutions, if they considered them when doing technical economics:

The economists go to work in a strange manner. It appears as if for them there are only two kinds of institutions, the artificial and the natural . . . . In this manner, the economists are like theologians who also distinguish two kinds of religion. Every religion that is not their own they characterize as a human invention, while their own religion is a revelation from God.

(Marx 1867: 96)

8 The passage is from *The Poverty of Philosophy* and is quoted by Colletti (1977: 464).
9 As Marx writes in *Capital*:

Within the capitalist system all methods for raising the social productiveness of labor are brought about at the cost of the individual laborer; all means for the development of production transform themselves into means of domination over, and exploitation of, the producers; they mutilate the laborer into a fragment of a man, degrade him to the level of an appendage of a machine, destroy every remnant of charm in his work and turn it into a hated toil; they estrange from him the intellectual potentialities of the labor process in the same proportion as science is incorporated in it as an independent power.

(Marx 1894, Vol. 1: 708)

10 Hence exploration of all of nature in order to discover new, useful qualities in things; universal exchange of the products of all alien climates and lands; new (artificial) preparation of natural objects, by which they are given new use values. The exploration of the earth in all directions, to discover new things of use as well as new useful qualities in the old; such as new qualities of them as raw materials, etc.; the development, hence, of the natural sciences to their highest point; likewise the discovery, creation and satisfaction of new needs arising from society itself.

(Marx 1857: 408–9)

11 Marshall distinguishes between internal economies, those enjoyed within the particular firm, and external economies, those outside the firm but internal to the industry. Social externalities or social economies can be defined as those available to all enterprises functioning within a social formation that enjoys a particular supportive social order. This extends to the education and trained capacities, attitudes toward work, physical and social infrastructure, public safety and social harmony.

12 Forces of production and social relations – two different sides of the development of the social individual – appear to capital as mere means, and are merely means for it to produce on its limited foundation. In fact, however, they are the material conditions to blow this foundation sky-high.

(Marx 1857: 706)

13 Marx and Engels were clear that communism 'presupposes the universal development of productive forces and the world intercourse bound up with them. . . . The proletariat can thus only exist world-historically, just as communism, its activity, can only have a "world-historical" existence' (Marx and Engels 186: 49).
14 Maurice Dobb has written that:

it is hardly surprising that one does not find in Marx any simple demonstration that crises are due to a single cause, or any clear cut model to show the sequence of events by which crises always and inevitably arise. Such would have been too mechanical a procedure to have been congenial to the method of Marx.

(Dobb 1955: 196)

15 Ernest Mandel writes

the question to know whether the crisis 'centres' on the sphere of production or the sphere of circulation is largely meaningless. The crisis is a *disturbance* (interruption) of the process of enlarged *reproduction* and accordingly to Marx, the process of reproduction is precisely a (contradictory) unity of production and circulation.

(Mandel 1990: 31–2)

16   See the responses to Brewer following his essay.

6 The neoclassical (counter) revolution

1   The birth date of neoclassical economics is given as 1870. Cornot, Dupuit, Goshen, and von Thunen, among others earlier in the century, had prior claims to central elements of marginalism and utility theory, as the more careful treatments of neoclassical economics detail.

2   See Aspromourgos (1986). The need for a separation between Marshall and the three other founders of neoclassical economics is not always made clear but, as shall be seen, is important. The larger issue of what economics is to be considered neoclassical (or neo-classical) remains contested. The usage in this chapter may be considered overly broad. Also see Hodgson (1986) .

3   The lack of continuity with classical economics is argued as well by Kenneth Arrow in his 1972 Nobel Prize speech, where he says 'none of the classical economists had a true general equilibrium theory.' This was, for Arrow, because none had an explicit role for demand conditions: it was all supply. One might comment that neoclassical general equilibrium returns the favor. It has no production-only exchange. The point, however, is that Arrow, one of the modern masters of general equilibrium thinking, recognizes the disjuncture. See Arrow (1983).

4   Roger Backhouse, for example, has written

> By the 1960s it became clear that the project of basing economics on ever more general foundations was going to get nowhere. Existence of equilibrium had been proved, but only in a model which described no conceivable real-world economy (it had, for example, no role for money), and it became clear that once the model's assumptions were relaxed, it would prove impossible to obtain such general results. More important, it became clear, as a result of work in the late 1950s and 1960s, that it would *never* be possible to provide general proofs of stability; it was shown that in the general case anything could happen.

(Backhouse 1994: 217)

5   Screpanti and Zamagni explain this perspective:

> In order that the criticisms of socialism, and of marxism in particular, should not seem too ideological, it was necessary to focus on their scientific foundations. But these were the same as those of the classical economic theory. It was necessary, therefore, to 're-invent' economic science, reconstructing it on a foundation which would allow the deletion of the concepts themselves of 'social class', 'labour power', 'capitalism', 'exploitation', etc. from the body of the science. The theory of marginal utility provided the solution. Moreover, it seemed that it would permit the demonstration that an almost perfect kind of social organization would be realized in a competitive economy; a kind of organization in which the market rules would allow an optimum allocation to be reached and, with it, the harmony of interests and the maximization of individual objectives.

Screpanti and Zamagni 1993: 154)

6   Marx would have loved the religious symbolism of Clark's concept. ('Capital,' John Bates Clark wrote, 'lives, as it were, by transmigration, taking itself out of one set of bodies and putting itself into another again and again.') This is more than metaphor. To Clark, God really does work through marginal productivity:

> To get a glimpse of what it can do and what man can help it do is to get a vision of the kingdoms of the earth, and the glory of them – a glory that may come from a

moral redemption of the economic system. . . . A new Jerusalem may actually arise out of the fierce contentions of the modern market. The wrath of men may praise God and his Kingdom may come, not in spite of, but by means of the contests of the economic sphere.

(Clark 1914: 35–6 and 47)

7   The similarity of the tone of Jevons's social observations with certain great passages in *Capital* and with Frederich Engels' *The Condition of the Working Classes in England*, is so striking that one could sandwich a passage from Jevons between a couple of those of Marx and Engels without any sharp change of feeling or style being obvious.

(Walsh and Graham 1980: 125)

8   The problem is that the language of reform is not the language of mathematical regularities. Mirowski and Cook, writing of Walras' *Economics and Mechanics*, offer an epigraph from Goethe: 'Mathematicians are like Frenchmen: whatever you say to them, they translate into their own language, and forthwith it is something entirely different' (Mirowski and Cook 1990: 189).

9   Also see Thurow (1975). For a perhaps surprising and not totally dissimilar critique, see Marshall (1890: 519).

10 Later economists were able to draw different conclusions by modifying these unrealistic assumptions, for example the Hotelling–Lerner proposition. With increasing returns (or decreasing costs), the long-run marginal cost curve lies below the long-run average cost curve, *and therefore government intervention is desirable*. This is because, under the modified assumptions, marginal cost pricing in all industries operating with a falling supply price requires subsidies. This sort of thing continues to entertain economists and is not without its impact on the political debate.

11 'Microsoft's Long March,' *Business Week*, June 24, 1996. Microsoft attempted to enter China on free market terms and was told to study the last 500 years of Chinese history. After some intensive study, the firm decided to share its design codes with Chinese ministries, invest heavily in assisting Chinese taxation administrators and people's banks, as well as training Chinese in computer architecture and client serving applications. It has adopted an inside cooperation strategy in the world's biggest emerging software market because that is the way the Chinese bureaucrats and politicians insisted they operate. At the level of theory, realist and Marxist perspectives explain the behavior of Mr. Murdoch and the decisions his media empire have made better than the liberalism. It is on the political science side of political economy that the more interesting discussions of such theorizing is to be found. (See Stubbs and Underhill 1994 and Gill and Law 1988.)

12 When the London School of Economics in 1933 republished Menger, the first edition was chosen. In his introduction, Hayek helped to remove the posthumous Menger from the consciousness of economists by passing over the manuscript, calling it 'fragmentary and disordered.' One may also examine the 1950 edition with an introduction by Frank Knight, throughout which the term *wirtschaftend* (literally 'engaged in economic activity') is translated as 'economizing,' although Menger had himself used a different term to make the distinction between the two clear. See Polanyi (1971).

13 As Tobin writes,

Many of the ablest minds attracted into professional economics find their exposure to general equilibrium theory the most exciting intellectual experience of their lives. Elegant, rigorous, mathematically powerful, the theory reaches far from obvious results. It gives economics a theoretical core that 'softer' social sciences lack and often envy. It 'is the only game in town' . . . .The patent and admitted unrealism of assumptions does not matter.

(Tobin 1985: 105)

14 The lack of realism of such projects has led others to ask if we should not just banish neoclassical economics from the field of study since it is an obstacle to proper understanding. Of course, who the 'we' would be that could do this is generally not discussed. In Hodgson's opinion:

> Unlike the attitude of many economists in the mainstream toward institutional economics, the right of neoclassical theorists to work and publish as economists should be defended as we defend free thought itself. But there should be no false leniency toward the propositions of neoclassical theory that are incompatible with our conceptions and theories of the real world.
>
> (Hodgson 1992a: 761)

15 And see discussion in Kaldor's Second Mattioli Lecture in Kaldor (1984).

16 Viner captures Marshall's view when he writes:

> That non-symbolic language and simple statistical methods alone had the elasticity to deal with the infinite detail and variability of concrete economic phenomena; that resort to mathematics, unless confined to a preliminary stage of investigation, involved a greater degree of surrender of this elasticity than it was wise to accept; and that only the relatively simple propositions in economics could be expressed in mathematical form, and even then only at the cost of artificial and often serious further simplification.
>
> (Viner 1941:124)

This is hardly too strong an interpretation. In a 1901 letter to A.L. Bowley, Marshall wrote that 'a good mathematical theory dealing with economic hypotheses was very unlikely to be good economics.' The reason was that

> every economic fact, whether or not it is of such a nature that it can be expressed in numbers, stands in relation as cause and effect to many other facts; and since it *never* happens that all of them can be expressed in numbers, the application of exact mathematical methods of those that can is nearly always a waste of time, while in the large majority of cases it is particularly misleading, and the world would have been further on its way forward if the work had never been done at all.
>
> (Letter to A.L. Bowley 1901, quoted in Pigou 1925: 774, and cited by, among others, Kaldor 1984: 21)

17 Mirowski has called attention to the passage in the preface to the 8th edition of the *Principles*, which shows Marshall's admiration for the use of differential calculus in physics and its applicability to economics. One would not want to suggest that Marshall did not think using mathematics useful, only that clear thinking and presentation of ideas is not to be rivaled by formalism. See Mirowski (1984).

18 See McWilliams-Tullberg (1975).

19 'In all economic questions, considerations of the higher ethics will always assert themselves, however much we try to limit our inquiry for an immediate practical purpose' (Marshall 1887: xxvi, cited in Coats 1990: 153).

20 In Appendix H of the *Principles*, we are shown that under conditions of increasing returns (a normal occurrence for today's corporations), no single stable equilibrium exists for output and price and that even a 'casual disturbance,' Marshall explains, can result in a substantial increase in capacity and output. A cessation of that disturbance would not result in a return to the initial position. Irreversible shifts take place in, among other things, consumer tastes. Supply and demand curves are not independent of one another.

21 Indeed, it has been suggested that Marshall had a sociology, and there is a literature discussing sociological aspects of the British economic thought of his era. See Parsons (1932) and Coats (1967).

22 This is yet another of the many parallels we find between Alfred Marshall and John Stuart Mill. Mill, who had so inspired Marshall's choice of subject matter, was also concerned with what he called ethology, the study of character formation which Mill

thought might possibly constitute the foundation for a general study of society. Part of this interest, for both Mill and Marshall, was in the importance for the irrational on economic behavior. In their discussion of business cycles, for example, Marshall and Mill saw an important role for irrational expectations in affecting the behavior of investors and capital markets.

7 Heterodoxy and holism

1 This connection is too often missed. As Geoffrey Hodgson has written: 'It was with institutionalism as a midwife that Keynesian macroeconomics was born' (Hodgson 1994: 68).
2 List's work and the state-led development it promoted has become part of the late industrializer policy debate. His work was known in the Japan of the Meiji Revolution, and translated into Japanese. In the contemporary period, a parallel can be drawn to the East Asian developmentalist state strategies. If, as certainly seems possible, a new paradigm is shown to have emerged in the economic practice of such countries, the position of the historical school may prove more central, even mainstream, but this is a matter of conjecture to be resolved by history.
3 Marx designated Roscher 'Wilhelm Thucidides' (a reference to Roscher's immodest reference to himself and the great historian in the preface of one of the good professor's books). 'Thucidides Roscher,' Marx thought, did not know his history and was taken to task for crudely distorting both economic conditions of the past he discussed as well as in the history of economic thought his work encompassed (Marx 1850–60: 123).
4 It would be improbable and an occasion for raised eyebrows among some colleagues if a young, untenured economist today were to publish in such a venue on such a topic. Yet these were the questions the young German trained rebels were raising in the context of the broader social struggles of the period. See Fine (1956: Ch. 6).
5 For example:

> The hedonistic conception of man is that of a lightening calculator of pleasures and pains, who oscillates like a homogeneous globule of desire of happiness under the impulse of stimuli that shift him about the area, but leave him intact. He has neither antecedent nor consequence. He is an isolated, definite human datum in a stable equilibrium except for the buffets of the impinging forces that displace him in one direction or another. Self-imposed in elemental space, he spins symmetrically about his own spiritual axis until the parallelograms of forces bear down upon him, whereupon he follows the line of the resultant. When the force of the impact is spent, he comes to rest, a self-contained globule of desire as before.
>
> (Veblen 1919: 232–3)

After one has read Veblen, it is difficult to read utilitarian and neoclassical discourse without thinking of these self-contained globules spinning symmetrically about their spiritual axes, and smiling a big smile inside.
6 Rutherford (1994); Ramstad (1996); and for the modern political economy approach, Banks and Hanushek (1995).
7 Talcott Parsons, whose structural-functionalism stresses integrative norms and pattern maintenance, dominated American sociology in the postwar years, at least until the 1970s, when the 1960s generation who came of age in the era of the civil rights, anti-war and women's movements saw an ideological justification for the status quo as characterizing his work. In the 1980s, in a different intellectual climate within academia, a Parsonian revival stressed the usefulness of his theorizing systems of coordination and took exception to earlier criticism which was seen as conflated analytic order and empirical stability. See Munch (1987).
8 Such views are easy to caricature. For a more sophisticated and so perhaps quite different presentation, see Becker (1957) and Friedman (1962: ch. 7).

9 Paul Samuelson, addressing a conference on economic education, told his audience how a fellow Nobel Prize winner, the father of public choice theory, had told him that 'as a matter of principle he refused to go beyond Pareto optimality.' Samuelson noted that 'Pareto efficiency is today all the rage. Since it is not easy to say things uncontroversial about distributional equity, let equity go hang' (Samuelson 1987: 109).

10 In his Marshall Lectures in the early 1950s, Parsons was very explicit about his opinion that within its own domain, neoclassical economics was quite adequate. In *Economy and Society*, 'Parsons and Smelser say that economic theory is not only adequate, but a *model* for the other social sciences to follow. The whole argument of *Economy and Society*,' Mark Granovetter suggests, 'was that it was a remarkable thing that you could take economic theory and fit it into Parsonian categories. According to Parsons–Smelser, this somehow validated the Parsonian categories.' See his interview with Swedberg (1990: 107).

11 For such economists the important text in the field is more likely Nelson and Winter's *An Evolutionary Theory of Economic Growth*. Langlois and Everett tell us that 'Present-day efforts in evolutionary economics almost all take their cues from Nelson and Winter.' This is an indication of their importance, but such an embracing conclusion is surely overdrawn. *The Journal of Economic Issues*, published by the Association for Evolutionary Economics and closely identified with the older institutionalists, surely lays claim to the evolutionary economics mantle, and one would rarely encounter a reference to the Nelson–Winter book in its pages. This is because what Nelson and Winter provide us with are search-and-select models that reach many of the same conclusions as marginalist theory whilst allowing more complex and believable stories of reactions in the face of market and other changed conditions. See Nelson and Winter (1982). Nelson is represented in the Smelser–Swedberg collection. Also see Winter (1992) and Langlois and Everett (1994: 22).

12 What Schumpeter especially admired in Schmoller's work was its exemplary broad vision of the economic processes and Schmoller's attempt to explain this totality in an innovative and scientific manner. Schmoller, Schumpeter said, looked at everything that economic theorists tended to ignore, namely the concrete economic circumstances of a people, its natural possibilities, its capacities, its international economic relations, its social structure, its figures of production, the size and distribution of its social product, and its social and political constitution.

(Swedberg 1991: 86)

13 Schumpeter's 1909 *Habilitation* lecture was on 'The Verification of Abstract Theorems by Statistics.' In 1930, he helped found the Econometric Society in the United States. When Schumpeter came to Harvard, a department in which historical economics had traditionally dominated, and in which sociology was also taught (there was no separate department for that subject), Schumpeter was brought in to introduce mathematics. He taught the first course in mathematical economics at Harvard. With what he considered the over-mathematization of the field, he distanced himself from mathematical economics.

14 Schumpeter wrote:

Since what we are trying to understand is economic change in historical time, there is little exaggeration in saying that the ultimate goal is simply a reasoned (= conceptual clarified) history, not of crises only, nor of cycles or waves, but of the economic process in all its aspects and bearings to which theory merely supplies some tools and schemata, and statistics merely part of the material. It is obvious that only detailed historical knowledge can definitively answer most of the questions of individual causation and mechanism and that without it the study of time series must remain inconclusive, and theoretical analysis empty.

(Schumpeter 1939: 220)

15 William Fellner makes the parallel, quoting a bit of the *Communist Manifesto*:

> The bourgeoisie cannot exist without constantly revolutionizing the instruments of production, and with them the whole relations of society. Conservation of the old mode of production in unaltered form was, on the contrary, the first condition of existence for all earlier classes.

He then notes that 'Except for the language used, this sounds like the expression of the Schumpeterian vision of the role of innovation in the capitalist process' (Fellner 1981: 53).

16 The fiscal history of a people is above all an essential part of its general history. An enormous influence on the fate of nations emanates from the economic bleeding which the needs of the state necessitate, and from the use to which its results are put . . . .Fiscal measures have created and destroyed industries, industrial forms, and industrial regions even where that was not their intent and have, in this manner, contributed directly to the construction (and distortion) of the edifice of the modern economy.

(Schumpeter 1918: 6)

17 Thus the same economic process that undermines the position of the bourgeoisie by decreasing the importance of the functions of entrepreneurs and capitalists, by breaking up protective strata and institutions, by creating an atmosphere of hostility, also decomposes the motor forces of capitalism from within. Nothing else shows so well that the capitalist order not only rests on props made of extra-capitalist material but also derives its energy from extra-capitalist patterns of behavior which at the same time it is bound to destroy.

(Schumpeter 1942: 161–2)

18 An influential intervention is Nelson and Winter (1974). Also see Hodgson (1993).

8 Keynes and the world turned upside down

1 On Keynes' views on probability and the idealistic strain that has such a large influence in Keynes' work, see O'Donnell (1991) and Fitzgibbons (1988).
2 Sheila Dow suggests that Keynes' method might be characterized as Babylonian. She tells us that 'Babylonian mathematics combined the notion of an organic whole with the practice of reasoning from a variety of premises depending on the practical problem at hand.' I wouldn't know about how Babylonians do, or used to do, math, but as a description of Keynes' flexibility of intellect, the description seems *a propos*. Dow in O'Donnell (1991: 154).
3 As is so frequently the case, the ideas are not original to the great man who gets the credit for having originated them, and secondly, these ideas were unlikely to have come together at another time. On these points let us interject the comments of Roger Backhouse and Sir John Hicks. First Backhouse:

> Given the central ideas of the *General Theory*, in particular the multiplier, were ideas which in some form had been around for many years, and given the unprecedented nature of the economic crisis for which a remedy had to be found, it was hardly surprising that similar ideas should emerge in so many places at the same time.

(Backhouse 1994: 18?)

Hicks writes:

> There can be no doubt at all that Keynes wrote as he did because of the times in which he was living. There was little general economics of which he made use that had not been long in existence; yet can one imagine the *General Theory of Employment* being written, by the greatest genius in 1900?

(Hicks 1975: 233)

4 Joan Robinson has argued that there is no question that Kalecki got there first in all the

essentials, pointing to the paper he gave to the Econometric Society in October 1933 on 'A Macro-dynamic Theory of the Business Cycle' which contains the basic elements of the theory of saving, investment and employment. At the same date, Robinson writes,

> I published a piece on 'The Theory of Money and the Analysis of Output' which was a kind of interim report on how far the Keynesians had got by that time and it is now evident that Kalecki had got much further.
>
> (Robinson 1979: 187)

5 Myrdal, in *Monetary Equilibrium*, argued that investment decisions depend on the entrepreneur's expectations with regard to profit and (introducing the terminology for the first time in the literature), that this *ex ante* investment need not equal *ex ante* savings which was a matter of how much individuals chose to save. Wicksell, in his writings on monetary economics, had shown that banks could create credit independently of savings and that monetary expansion propels demand for real goods. The implication, as Wicksell also pointed out, was that inflation could result in violation of Say's Law. Erik Lindahl had the rudiments of the multiplier in 1929 even if, as noted above in the text, it was Kahn who independently helped Keynes in this regard. The point is that the rudiments of 'Keynesian' economics were developed by the Stockholm School. See Hansen (1981).

6 This idea was also prominent in Keynes' 1930 *Treatise on Money*.

7 John Vaizey is not alone in thinking that 'Kahn, more than anyone else, was responsible for the *General Theory*, by explaining that an economy could be in equilibrium and still have massive unemployment' (Schumpeter 1954: 1172); see also Harcourt (1994) and Vaizey (1977).

8 Business and many traditional economists did fear an expanding role for government. Many loudly proclaimed rising public debt a grave threat. They claimed that the economy, left alone, would heal itself (in good time). It might be added, that things a half century later had gotten back to this same orthodoxy – with the addition that rising unemployment is now blamed on Keynes and Keynesian policies.

9 Cited in Backhouse (1994), where a discussion of opinion of the period appears.

10 Keynes' early writings, his unpublished essays on moral and political philosophy (written over the period 1904–14) have a parallel to Marx's early writings and Smith's lectures on *Rhetoric* and *Belles Lettres*. See Fitzgibbons (1992).

11 Phillips began his career as an engineer, and the legacy of his training is evident in the hydraulic diagrams he developed showing consumption curves attached to pictorial representations of consumption flows, and (in the same diagram) a demand curve for stocks showing the level of stock with production flows in and consumption flows out and what look like pressure gages relating price to production.

12 John Buridan was a fourteenth-century French philosopher famed for his alleged consideration of the fate of an ass equidistant between two bales of hay. He died (the donkey, not the philosopher). 'Buridanitis', in which the sufferer finds himself or herself confronting two options between which he or she has no conscious preference and so cannot or will not select or act, was not a condition recognized by economists until fairly recently. Delving into transaction costs, some realized that there is a cost to making choices and so if differences are small, Buridanitis may be more common than they had thought. Custom, habit, and other social norms may be quite influential as well, as Keynes stressed. Thus B side thinking makes progress into the mainstream belief system. The term Buridanitis is not yet in usage among economists, but see George (1995). On Keynes' contribution:

> In making a decision we have before us a large number of alternatives, none of which is demonstrably more 'rational' than the others, in the sense that we can arrange in order of merit the sum aggregate of the benefits obtainable from the complete consequence of each. To avoid being in the position of Buridan's ass, we

fall back, therefore, and necessarily do so, on the motives of another kind, which are not 'rational' in the sense of being concerned with the evaluation of consequences, but are decided by habit, instinct, preference, desire, will, etc.

(Keynes 1971 Vol. XXIX: 294)

13 On modern approaches to asset volatility based on extreme sensitivity to new information leading to frenzies and crashes, see Bulow and Klemperer (1994); and on noise trader models of over and undervaluation of assets based on self-amplifying reactions of speculators to small deviations from 'equilibrium,' see Lux (1995). I am not sure one really learns more from such models than one already knows from Keynes. The difference is in the effort to place such behavior and the large volume responses in a 'rational' framework. At the same time, the literature on learning behavior and macroeconomics can be seen as closer to Keynes than perfect foresight and extrapolated expectations 'Keynesian' models of a decade or two or three ago. See, for example, Sargent (1993).

14 The topic of Keynes, mathematics, and statistics is a complicated one. See O'Donnell (1990).

15 'The underlying vision of equilibrium economics is atomistic, certain and determinate. As a Cambridge rationalist, Keynes was drawn to the polar opposite view of the world as holistic, uncertain and indeterminate' (Hillard 1992: 75).

16 Again, see Klamer and Colander (1990), Table 2.1 and accompanying text, including comments by students interviewed at the leading graduate economics programs on the pretentious uses of mathematics and ignorance of the real economy (two of which were quoted in Chapter 1). Another student, in describing one workshop, told the interviewer: 'All of us go, week after week, and come back and just laugh at their big reputations. What they do is usually very complicated and very implausible' (p. 19).

17 There is a powerful parallel in dichotomies made by Keynes between speculation and enterprise (rentier vs. entrepreneur) and Veblen's (captains of industry, captains of finance) and Marx's money capital and industrial capital (recall his comments on the swindlers of finance and the capitalist driven to innovate). See Niggle (1986).

18 As Keynes wrote:

The state of long-term expectations, upon which our decisions are based, does not solely depend, therefore, on the most probable forecast we can make. It also depends on the confidence with which we make this forecast – on how highly we rate the likelihood of our best forecast turning out to be quite wrong. If we expect large changes but are very uncertain as to what precise form these changes will take, than our confidence will be weak.

(Keynes 1936: 148)

19 Mainstream economists disagree profoundly with this assessment, as has been noted. Keynes, however, made his personal fortune and quite handsomely built up Cambridge University's endowment on the market as a speculator. He and Ricardo shared a certain understanding of the irrationalities of decision making in the face of uncertainty denied by many theorists who act 'irrationally' by not putting their money where their mouth is and risk their fortunes to confirm their intellectual findings.

20 This is an important reason for later monetarists working so hard marshaling evidence that the prolonged Depression was caused by government error – primarily for the United States an overly restrictive monetary policy by the Federal Reserve. Whether their efforts should be interpreted as adequate explanation of the worldwide depression, the onset of which preceded Fed errors, or whether the more restricted claim that the prolongation of the depression in the United States is best understood in terms of government failure, is a longer discussion.

21 Blinder criticizes efforts by Lucas and others to tie up these 'loose ends' with 'sunspot theories' (Blinder 1987a: 130). The sunspot reference is to our friend Jevons' pioneering statistical testing of a business cycle theory. The unfortunate man found a high corre-

lation between business cycles and the occurrence of sunspots. Later economics laughed at this obvious error of assuming causation from observed correlation. It was not that dumb. Given the state of knowledge of the time, he hypothesized that sunspots affected crops, agriculture being the core of the economy, and so caused the cycle. It may prove the case that future historians of economic thought may find Blinder's characterization of rational expectations on the generous side.

22 It is difficult to emphasize enough the degree to which Keynes' critics (including many 'Keynesians') just don't get it. As Shackle clarifies what is at issue:

> Keynes in the *General Theory* attempted a rational theory of a field of conduct which by the nature of its terms could only be semi-rational. But sober economists gravely upholding a faith in the calculability of human affairs could not bring themselves to acknowledge that this could be his purpose. They sought to interpret the *General Theory* as just one more manual of political arithmetic. In so far as it failed this test, they found it wrong, or obscure, or perverse.
>
> (Shackle 1967: 129)

23 'If human nature felt no temptation to take a chance, no satisfaction (profit apart) in constructing a factory, a mine or a farm, there might not be much investment merely as a result of cold calculation.'

24 Similar statements have been made by Kaldor (1983) and others.

25 For a very different interpretation, see Patinkin (1976).

26 As Asimakopulos comments on the post-*GT* writings on this topic:

> These papers on finance were part of an exchange with Ohlin, Robertson and Hawtrey in which Keynes was determined not to allow the determination of the rate of interest to be seen as the outcome of the equilibrium adjustment of saving and investment, dressed up in the guise of the supply and demand for loanable funds.
>
> (Asimakopulos 1991: 87)

27 His first economic study was *Indian Currency and Finance* (1913). He had written a *Tract on Monetary Reform* in 1923 and *A Treatise on Money* (1930), which in many respects is of greater contemporary relevance than the *GT*.

28 Black, along with Myron Scholes, developed the basic asset pricing model upon which modern financial theory is built. See Black and Scholes (1972).

29 In August 1924, for example, Keynes had written in *The Nation and the Athenaeum* on 'Foreign Investment and National Advantage.' He urged his readers to understand the lessons of past colonialism. The expense and sacrifice of the many for the benefit of the few was hardly in the nation's interest.

30 Hans Singer writes, describing Keynes' situation,

> D-Day was only a short while ago, VE day and VJ Day still on the far horizon. Keynes had to defend his bold ideas with one arm, or rather both arms, tied behind his back. His overriding instructions were to do nothing that could endanger the Lease–Lend Agreement, a big, big loan then under negotiation, and other forms of literally vital American support. No wonder then that the final result of the Conference bore more resemblance to what was acceptable in Washington rather than the pre-Bretton Woods visionaries. In the circumstances, it was a tribute to Keynes's negotiating skill and his high prestige that so much of the original vision survived.
>
> (Singer 1994: 3)

31 It would take us too far afield to review earlier debates. The nineteenth-century Currency School held what today is the monetarist position that the level of production is determined from the supply side by the availability of resources, in debates with the Banking School, which argued that the level of real output can be stimulated by credit expansion. Keynes is in the second camp. Credit money allows profit generation, which is used to pay back funds used for investment.

32 Skidelsky writes, 'His most profound and poetical pages on economics have to do with the encroachment of money values on exchange values, the triumph of making money over making things' (Skidelsky 1994: xxiv).

33 There is a multitude of real assets in the world which constitute our capital wealth – buildings, stocks of commodities, goods in the course of manufacture and of transport, and so forth. The nominal owners of these assets, however, have not infrequently borrowed *money* in order to become possessed of them. To a corresponding extent the actual owners of wealth have claims, not on real assets, but on money. A considerable part of this 'financing' takes place through the banking system which interposes its guarantee between depositors who lend it money, and its borrowing customers to whom it loans money wherewith to finance the purchase of real assets. The interposition of this veil of money between the real asset and the wealth owner is a specially marked characteristic of the modern world.

(Keynes 1931: 151)

34 Keynes in the *GT* presupposes an exogenous money stock. Post-Keynesians argue that he was wrong to do so. See Cottrell (1994).

35 Keynes' view of the internal connectedness of the elements of his system in which the whole is more than the sum of its parts is reminiscent of Marx. As Anna Carabelli describes this dialectical connectedness,

For Keynes, a monetary macroeconomy is a system characterized by 'complexity', possessing attributes such as organic interdependence among variables, non-homogeneity through time and space, non-numerical measurability, physical heterogeneity, openness, incompleteness, indivisibility, secondary qualities, contingency and change.

(Carabelli 1992: 3–4)

9 The last half-century in the mainstream

1 This view has been popular since the contribution of Milton Friedman and Anna Schwartz to the monetary history of the period. However, as Robert Gordon and James Wilcox have shown, the monetarist explanation has weaknesses and key aspects of the traditional Keynesian explanation are supported by the data. The Crash reduced wealth and lowered consumer and corporate confidence, producing a downward spiral of consumption and investment. Ben Bernanke has argued that the non-monetary effects of the financial crisis (bank failures not monetary policy) restricted funds available to finance investment in the 1930s. Any story that relies primarily on monetary causes of the Great Depression is another fable that needs considerable editing, if not a total rewrite, as Charles Calomiris' work suggests. As for monetary policy prolonging the depression and so being 'government's fault,' a close look at how bankers used the Fed in these years offers a different political spin. See Epstein and Ferguson (1995); Friedman and Schwartz (1963); Gordon and Wilcox (1981); Bernanke (1983); and Calomiris (1993).

2 Sraffa is usually considered a neo-Ricardian. He saw himself as a marxist. It can be suggested that Sraffa's very abstract model succeeds by taking seriously Marx's treatment of value as a social phenomenon, and by placing class conflict at the core of the explanation of the production process. Sraffa offers, as the subtitle of his book (Sraffa 1960) promises, a *Prelude to a Critique of Economic Theory*, in the same spirit that *Capital* does, in its subtitle, *A Critique of Political Economy* (suggesting that it can be read 'just like a first chapter of *Capital* which Marx would have written if he had been a little less Ricardian and a little more Marxist' (see Screpanti and Zamagni 1993: 409).

3 The key collection of essays is the *Quarterly Journal of Economics* of November 1966, with contributions by many of the key participants and reviews of the issues. It includes a

concessionary summing up or strategic retreat from Paul Samuelson. For a Cambridge England telling of the story, see Harcourt (1969).

4 Keynes hated inflation, seeing it as a way in which consumption was increased at the expense of savers, confiscating wealth. Inflation provided windfall gains and allowed the community to live beyond its means, consume capital and could, he thought, lead to collapse. This is not the theme of the *General Theory*, which is written for a different historical moment. Those who want to know what Keynes thought about the dangers of inflation need to read his *Tract on Monetary Reform* (1923), *Treatise on Money* (1930), and his voluminous other writings on money. Keynes saw that during the First World War governments learned to manufacture money as a form of hidden taxation, and in the postwar period he saw that the 'unendurable fact' was that the European standard of living would have to come down.

5 With this chapter, if not earlier, the vastness of the literature and the ongoing divisions and branching of approaches becomes close to unmanageable. Let me offer three references to aspects of the since Keynes debates: Kaldor (1983) and in numerous other writings offers spirited critique of many of the developments in mainstream economics that I also find problematic. The very idea of equilibrium turns out to be far more difficult than most students of macroeconomics have been led to believe. See Weintraub (1991) if further doubt remains that the text of the *GT* 'remains unstable, contested, and problematic' (p. 27). For what he calls 'the 4,827th reexamination of Keynes's system,' see Weintraub (1979). Finally, anyone who thinks empirical research can sort out the relative usefulness of the various models discussed in this chapter is referred to an essay by Larry Summers, where he discusses empirical research on real business cycles, the efficient market hypothesis, and a number of other research programs discussed in this chapter. His title, like another useful article by Edward Leamer (1983) referring to 'taking the "con" out of econometrics,' conveys the message; see also Summers (1991). Both question whether any conclusions reached in empirical macroeconomics do or should have any influence on serious thinking about substantive questions.

6 The same criticism can be extended to the use of aggregate demand and supply curves. The economy is subject to change of the sort that makes these textbook curves suspect. There is no unique stable equilibrium. These demand and supply curves both slope downward and are not independent of each other. As Colander writes, 'In the aggregate, the price incentive signals are overwhelmed by supply and demand interdependencies of aggregate supply and demand. The normal supply and demand curves are partial equilibrium concepts and are not useful in analyzing macro issues' (Colander 1992: 156).

7 This is another of those important issues we simply cannot take the space to go into here, but see the list of such questions offered in the trenchant paper by Brenner (1992a: 132 and answers 141); comments by Keynes (1971, Vol. 14: 79); Hicks (1973: 157) and (1976: 141). Also, for the discussion of Hicks' views on equilibrium and those of other important participants in the debate, see Weintraub (1991, especially chapter 5.)

8 Commenting on the New Classical Economics, which seemed to suggest such reasoning, and on its position of influence within the mainstream, Backhouse has written that:

> the new classical macroeconomics appeared to be based on rigorous microeconomic foundations, but its models were implausible, whilst Keynesian macroeconomics had no satisfactory microeconomic foundations. Keynesian models mostly assumed fixed, or at least sticky, prices and wages, failing to provide any formal explanation of why prices and wages failed to change in response to unemployment.
>
> (Backhouse 1994: 189)

9 For some of these concessions see essays in Barro (1989).

10 These included market imperfections, stochastic variability in demands and supplies, the cost of gathering information about job vacancies and labor availabilities, the costs of mobility, and so on. See, for example, Barro (1989: 178).

11 I say began its modern career because we may date the idea to Fisher (1926). I encountered this essay as Irving Fisher, 'I Discovered the Phillips Curve,' a reprinting of the essay in *Journal of Political Economy*, March/April, 1973.
12 For some interesting historical parallels, see Maloney (1985).
13 There are many versions of rational expectations theory, some of which are accepted by non-new classical theorists. A more nuanced picture of the discourse can be found in Hoover (1988). The major contributions in the developing of the New Classical Economics are reprinted in Hoover (1992). Volume III, Part I of this collection includes the key contributions surrounding the Lucas Critique, which will shortly be mentioned, and Part II of Volume II of this collection includes the now standard articles on growth theory with increasing returns, which are discussed in the next chapter where we consider endogenous growth theory. There is also another set of essays on growth theory in the Elgar series, which includes coverage of major schools of thought and literatures of interest within economics.
14   The choice between alternative theories of the business cycle – in particular, between real business cycle theory and new Keynesian theory – is partly a choice between internal consistency and external consistency. Real business cycle theory extends the Walrasian paradigm, the most widely understood and taught model in economics, and provides a unified explanation for economic growth and economic fluctuations. New Keynesian theory, in its attempt to mimic the world more accurately, relies on nominal rigidities that are observed but only little understood. Indeed, new Keynesians sometimes suggest that to understand the business cycle, it may be necessary to reject the axiom of rational optimizing individuals, an act that for economists would be the ultimate abandonment of internal consistency.

(Mankiw 1989: 89)

15 Barbara Bergmann, for example, has written:

The profession has been uncritical of the low quality of thought about expectations. You can say almost anything if you use the word 'expectations,' and woe to those who leave out the magic word. The Lucas and Rapping paper is one example of expectations-garbage. They make ridiculous assumptions about *which* expectations are formed, and about *how* expectations are used.

(Bergmann 1987: 198)

16 Gordon (1976: 5). Gordon is a leader in the rival New Keynesian School; see Gordon (1990).
17 In one of the few studies using a data set allowing the separation of supply and demand side explanations of unemployment, Osberg, Apostle, and Clairmont conclude that

individual unemployment, at a point in time, is largely determined by the demand side of the labour market and that estimates of the probabilities and duration of individual unemployment which omits data on employer characteristics suffer from omitted variable bias. We therefore argue that the economic analysis of unemployment should emphasise the incentives forced by firms to lay off and hire particular workers rather than the incentives faced by workers to accept or decline employment.

(Osberg *et al.* 1986: 14)

18   Real business cycle models concern Robinson Crusoe economies. A single representative individual is making choices for the whole economy. This simplification enables the model-builder to derive behavior explicitly from rational optimization subject only to constraints of resource availabilities and technology.

(Tobin 1992a: 127)

19 Klein and Goldberger (1955). This was the basis for Michigan, Wharton and MIT–Penn–Social Science Research Council models, which were to run into prediction problems in the early 1970s and were intellectually devastated by the Lucas Critique discussed in the text. On this important history see Epstein (1987) and Redman (1991: 8).

20 One may consult a contemporary graduate macro theory text written to present the state of current thinking on the exposition. For example, Blanchard and Fisher (1989).

21 Phelps' work constantly vents this view of working people and the security they purportedly enjoy thanks to the all-encompassing welfare state. Readers will have to judge for themselves whether such characterizations are empirically valid or ideologically laden to the point of gross distortion. Consider, for example, Phelps' treatment of worker resistance to downward labor market mobility circa mid-1990s:

> If I own my house and a car and what-not, I am more likely to be an independent sort with a high propensity to quit or shirk or strike or be absent from my job. If the welfare state will provide me free or nearly free of charge with my apartment, hospitalization, education, and so forth, my dependence on steady employment in my job or in my future ones is considerably reduced of course, if in addition there is a means test, so that with little or no earnings I will receive unemployment benefits, food stamps, and other assistance not otherwise made available, I have even less reason to preserve my employment.
>
> (Phelps 1995: 230)

22 The passage just quoted about the 'plump cushions' enjoyed by the workers is fast followed by an invocation of Keynes' famous call for the 'euthanasia of the rentier class.' I must confess to not knowing what to make of such a reading. Keynes condemns the unproductive hereditary English ruling elite, the 1 per cent, the filthy rich of England's class-bound society who lived off the labor of others. Is Phelps presuming that working people are getting huge amounts of unearned income? It appears to be the case that he thinks that the workers as individual recipients are the holders of the national debt, and that when government deficits increase, these workers have more coupons to clip, that their incomes go up significantly. Phelps' model is consistent with a larger literature which sees workers and government (because it extends perverse incentives) as being to blame for current economic problems.

23 I single out this particular contribution because it is representative of an approach to class that I find more broadly present in the contemporary literature, or at least certain segments of that literature. Phelps is also so major a figure that to single him out for critical comment hardly does him damage whilst allowing the broader point to be made.

24 On the trends in earnings and a review of explanatory alternatives, see Levy and Murnane (1992). The evidence does not show a relationship between labor supply and welfare state taxes and transfers. This is true both for the United States and Europe, where labor supply elasticities (for males at least) are close to zero. See Atkinson and Mogensen (1993); Pencavel (1986); and Danziger et al. (1981).'

25 For a more positive view on the state of modern macroeconomics and a helpful exposition of the major schools of thought, discussed all too briefly here, see Snowdon et al. (1994).

10 Theorizing economic growth

1 This work, written at the dawn of the Keynesian Revolution, like so many in its gatekeeper tradition, begins by observing: 'The efforts of economists during the last hundred and fifty years has resulted in the establishment of a body of generalizations whose substantial accuracy and importance are open to question only by the ignorant and the perverse' (Robbins 1932: 1).

2 For the original theoretical statement and review of growth theory, see Blanchard and Fisher (1989).

3 This is not the universal point of view. For a model supporting the Solow approach, see Mankiw *et al.* (1992); also Mankiw (1995). Charles Plosser, reviewing the literature in the early 1990s, concludes that the Solow–Denison approach does not offer a basis for explaining extreme and persistent differences in living standards and growth rates across countries (Plosser 1992). Two decades later, he echoes Hahn's and Mathews' conclusions, writing that many economists 'came to view growth theory as a rather sterile and uninteresting branch of economic thought through most of the 1960s and 1970s' (p. 57).

4 Perhaps Marshall's most underestimated contribution to growth theory is found in a previously overlooked lecture he gave at Yale in 1891, which has recently been recovered (Wall 1995).

5 Richard Nelson observed, in introducing a summary of such developments: 'Evolutionary or developmental language is used quite widely by economists to describe how the structures of an economy, or an industry, or technology, or the law, changes over time' (Nelson 1995: 49).

6 Those who have questioned free trade have, as a result, been (at least until fairly recently) been pilloried in the profession. John Culbertson, a University of Wisconsin professor who in the mid-1980s had the temerity to suggest that American workers were being hurt by the workings of international trade, was denounced on the front page of the *Wall Street Journal*. Paul Krugman, the featured criticizer for the piece and who has made something of a second career as a denouncer of heterodoxy and peddlers of what he considers policy nonsense, likened Culbertson's claim to 'someone talking about the psychic power of plants getting the same attention as people doing research on recombinant DNA' (Blustein 1987: 1). This article, like many that were to follow in the media attacking dissenters from orthodoxy, was based on strong denunciations by Krugman.

7 His first chapter is a good summary of basic trade theorems. The consideration of production processes in this book emphasizes the problems of properly identifying the various components of 'capital' and forming them into a single composite – a task the mainstream theory has generally taken as non-problematic, obvious and trivial but which is at the heart of understanding not only trade questions but the nature of economic growth, as shall be further argued.

8 This is perhaps the best single introduction and evaluation of this literature by some of the key contributors to the debate.

9 For an insightful evaluation of Krugman, see Friedman (1994).

10 Given the mobility of financial and industrial capital across national borders, some economists suggest that there is less reason to think the north should be considered inherently to have a comparative advantage in capital-intensive products, unless production requires technologically complementary inputs and such technological–professional–managerial labor is not available at comparable cost in the south.

11 On Taiwan, South Korea, and Japan see Wade (1990); Amsden (1989); and Tabb (1995).

12 For a review of the history of growth theory, see Stern (1991).

13 Sorting through the origin of 'new' ideas, as we repeatedly find, is a difficult and controversial process. Endogenous growth theorizing, of course, goes back at least to Adam Smith (the division of labor) and Karl Marx (the rising organic composition of capital). Modern treatments by Nicholas Kaldor tend to be ignored in the US in favor of Kenneth Arrow. See Kaldor (1957); Arrow (1962); and the literature review in Jong-Il You (1994). This last article highlights the important contributions of Michael Kalecki to Marx-derived endogenous growth thinking.

14 That is, 'flexibility is unimportant because it is total' (Basu 1995: 64).

15 Among economists, the term 'institution' is taken to mean 'an arrangement between economic units that defines and specifies the ways in which these units can co-operate and compete' (North and Thomas 1973: 5). The entry point for contemporary economists has been transaction cost theory and the analysis of information. Oliver Williamson has been the key contributor. For our purposes here, see Stiglitz (1988).

16 As Ha-Joon Chang writes:

> Without certain rigidities, no complex system inhabited by agents with bounded rationality can run efficiently, or at all. Therefore, certain degrees of rigidities are a prerequisite for the existence of a complex modern economy. The kind of flexibility assumed to be ideal in the neo-liberal model may not be able to sustain anything more than an economy made up, to borrow Coase's analogy, of lone individuals exchanging nuts and berries on the edge of a forest.
>
> (Chang 1995: 202)

17 One discussion of this approach suggests not only that such occurrences are rare in practice, but that this, in David's paradigmatic case, 'Alas, almost every element of this tale is false' (Liebowitz and Margolis 1994: 147). See their fuller argument in Liebowitz and Margolis (1990).

18 On the usage of cultural economy, see Tabb (1995: 286–7 and 293–4).

19 'Structure has been the design for integrating the enterprise's existing resources to current demand; strategy has been the plan for the allocation of resources to anticipated demand' (Chandler, Jr. 1986: 476).

20 See, for example, a study of the Prato district showing the importance of trust and lived linkages among subcontractors, creditors and others: (Ottati 1994).

21 Much of what we consider as 'culture' and beyond the scope of economic analysis may have a substantial impact on the environment in which individual consciousness is formed and choices made. There has been, for example, a modest boomlet in the sub-literature of institutional–historical studies of numerous references by such economists to a book by Robert Putnam on the longevity and viability of regional performance differences in Italy, in which Putnam suggests the importance of 'civic community' (or trust and social cooperation), and the distribution of civic community in present-day Italy was already clearly evident as long ago as the thirteenth century (Putnam *et al.* 1993).

22 For a comparison on the two, see 'A Comparative Analysis of the Theory of Regulation and the Social Structure of Accumulation Theory' in Kotz *et al.* (1994).

23 On the issue of the originality of these theorists, Alain Noel is particularly helpful in demonstrating the crucial points that regulationists borrow from Schumpeter, Keynes, and Kalecki. (Noel 1987; esp. 313 and esp. fn 46).

24 This postwar accommodation, as formulated by Bowles, Gordon, and Weiskopf includes a number of elements. There is a presumed accord between labor and capital in which government would stimulate the economy to produce jobs and continued corporate prosperity, in which labor granted management unquestioned dominance of the workplace in exchange for job security and rising compensation. There is a citizen–state accord featuring government benefits, to retirees (social security), the temporarily jobless (unemployed compensation), income support to indigent mothers and their children (AFDC) and so on, which are extended in exchange for acceptance of a centrist, two-party governance which excludes any independent labor or socialist parties as were prominent elsewhere in the advanced capitalist nations in contesting for political power. Finally there was the Pax Americana, the shared understanding on foreign policy that the US would be the world's sheriff. In a web of military and economic alliances, NATO, SEATO, and so on, under US command, would police the world for communist aggression and internal subversion. Some B mode economists suggest that it is the breakdown in these accommodations that brought the postwar social structure of accumulation to an end.

25 Alain Lipietz sums up his understanding of the importance of the decline in the Fordist regime of accumulation in the following terms:

> Toward the end of the sixties this order [the Fordist Regime] came apart as the Taylorist organization of labor, in which the producers were allowed no say in the organization and improvement of the processes of production, revealed itself to be increasingly irrational. Against a background of mounting rank-and-file protest,

engineers and technicians could not halt a decline in the rate of productivity growth except through even more costly investments. The result was a fall in profit rates which, in turn, caused a decline in investment, growth of unemployment and a crisis of the welfare state.

(Lipietz 1979: 38)

11 From equilibrium into history

1 The important text is Smelser and Swedberg (1995).
2 One sees fewer references in the American literature to Nicholas Kaldor's work on increasing returns, perhaps because such discussions by him are usually accompanied by lectures on the uselessness of the Walrasian framework. For example: Kaldor (1972) and (1984).
3 Colander has struck at two powerful pressure points. To say that economists are doing low-level mathematics is a wonderful attention getter in a profession that prides itself on the sophistication of its math. His point is that to make its models tractable, Walrasians oversimplify dynamics which can in fact be handled by giving up the simple world and embracing a more complex and real one. Policy makers find the abstract world of the Walrasians so unreasonable and the policy advice they draw from their models so inadequate that economics has gained a bad reputation among those who deal with less abstract problems. As of yet, however, the Post Walrasians have offered only a suggestive research program.
4 These discussions have also begun to take place across disciplinary borders. See, for example, Piori and Sabel (1984); Chase-Dunn (1989) and Axford (1995).
5 The significance to the average American worker who, in 1993, earning what the average American worker had earned in 1973, twenty years earlier (whilst producing 25 per cent more) is that if the gains from increased productivity had been shared equally between labor and capital, their real incomes would have been approximately 25 per cent higher. (Calculation is more complicated since capital investment is paid for out of borrowed funds and retained earnings and the returns to both are affected by broader market considerations. On the other side, the figure probably underestimates productivity gains.) The frequently heard policy demand of holding down US wages to regain competitiveness cannot be the right story. More must be involved, since American real wages arc not rising. Indeed, holding the line on wages seems to go hand in hand with growing income inequality and stagnant living conditions for working people.
6 The reference to Platonic monetary guardians is from Cooper (1994: 70).
7 The discussion here follows Helleiner (1994), from which the Ruggie reference is drawn.
8 Craig Murphy has made the observation that liberal fundamentalists thrive in the early years of the world order crises when the power of private investors is at its peak (Murphy 1994: 37).
9 With regard to Europe, consideration of the Social Charter continues to be a complex, multi-sided discussion over commitment to a social market economy, with continuation of a serious welfare state and civilized industrial relations and the terms of 'flexibility' to be negotiated around such concerns. As George Ross has argued: 'In spite of the limitations of EC social policy making to date, it is quite misleading to claim that these represent an ineluctable triumph of the market over state-building' (Ross 1993: 65).

References

Aaron, H.J. (1994) 'Public Policy, Values, and Consciousness,' *Journal of Economic Perspectives* Spring.

Abraham, K.G. and Houseman, S.N. (1993) *Job Security in America: Lessons from Germany*,Washington, D.C.: Brookings Institution.

Abramovitz, M. (1994) 'Catch-up and Convergence in the Postwar Growth Boom and After,' in W. J. Baumol, R. R. Nelson, and E. N. Wolff (eds) *Convergence of Productivity: Cross-National Studies and Historical Evidence*, New York: Oxford University Press.

Adams, H.C. (1891) 'An Interpretation of the Social Movements of our Time,' *International Journal of Ethics* II, October.

Ades, A. and Di Tella, R. (1997) 'National Champions and Corruption: Some Unpleasant Interventionist Arithmetic,' *Economic Journal* July.

Aglietta, M. (1976) *A Theory of Capitalist Development: The US Experience*, London: Verso, 1987.

Akyuk, Y. (1995) 'Taming International Finance,' in J. Michie and J. Grieve Smith (eds) *Managing the Global Economy*, Oxford: Oxford University Press.

Allais, M. (1992) 'The General Theory of Surplus as a Formalization of the Underlying Theoretical Thought of Adam Smith, His Predecessors and His Contemporaries,' in M. Fry (ed.) *Adam Smith's Legacy: His Place in the Development of Modern Economics*, London: Routledge.

Amsden, A.H. (1989) *Asia's Next Giant: South Korea and Late Industrialization*, New York: Oxford University Press.

Anderson, W.H.L. and Thompson, F.W. (1988) 'Neoclassical Marxism,' *Science and Society* Summer.

Appleby, J., Hunt, L., and Jacob, M. (1994) *Telling the Truth About History*, New York: W.W. Norton, 1995.

Arestis, P. (1992) *The Post-Keynesian Approach to Economics: An Alternative Analysis of Economic Theory and Policy*, Aldershot: Edward Elgar.

Arestis, P. and Bain, K. (1995) 'The Independence of Central Banks: A Nonconventional Perspective,' *Journal of Economic Issues* March.

Arrow, K. (1962) 'The Economic Implications of Learning by Doing,' *Review of Economic Studies* June.

— (1983) 'General Economic Equilibrium: Purpose, Analytic Techniques, Collective Choice,' *Collected Papers, Volume 2: General Equilibrium*, Cambridge, Mass.: Belknap Press.

— (1986) 'History: The View from Economics,' in W.N. Parker (ed.) *Economic History and the Economist*, Oxford: Basil Blackwell.

Arsen, D.D. (1991) 'International and Domestic Forces in the Postwar Golden Age,' *Review of Radical Political Economics* Spring and Summer.

Arthur, W.B. (1989) 'Competing Technologies, Increasing Returns, and Locked-In by Historical Events,' *Economic Journal* August.

— (1990) 'Positive Feedbacks in the Economy,' *Scientific American* February.

Ashton, T.S. (1948) *The Industrial Revolution, 1760–1830*, London: Oxford University Press.

Asimakopulos, A. (1991) *The General Theory of Employment in Keynes's General Theory and Accumulation*, Cambridge: Cambridge University Press.

Aspromourgos, T. (1986) 'On the origin of the term "neo-classical",' *Cambridge Journal of Economics* September.

Atkinson, A.B. and Mogensen, G.V. (eds) (1993) *Welfare and Work Incentives: A North European Perspective*, New York: Oxford University Press.

Attewell, P. (1984) *Radical Political Economy Since the Sixties: A Sociology of Knowledge Analysis*, New Brunswick, NJ: Rutgers University Press.

Audretsch, D.B. and Feldman, M.P. (1996) 'R&D Spillovers and the Geography of Innovation and Production,' *American Economic Review* June.

Axford, B. (1995) *The Global System: Economics, Politics, Culture*, New York: St Martin's Press.

Backhouse, R.E. (1993) 'The Debate over Milton Friedman's Theoretical Framework: An Economist's View,' in R. Backhouse, T. Dudley-Evans, and W. Henderson (eds) *Economics and Language*, London: Routledge.

— (1994) *Economists and the Economy: The Evolution of Economic Ideas*, New Brunswick, NJ: Transaction Publishers.

Baker, D. and Weisbrot, M. (1994) 'The Logic of Contested Exchange,' *Journal of Economic Issues* December.

Baker, G. and Holstrom, B. (1995) 'Internal Labor Markets: Too Many Theories, Too Few Facts,' *American Economic Review* May.

Baker, S. (1996) 'Is Capitalism Headed for a New Dark Age?' *Business Week* March 11.

Baldwin, R.E. (1992) 'Are Economists' Traditional Trade Policy Views Still Valid?' *Journal of Economic Literature* June.

Balogh, T. (1982) *The Irrelevance of Conventional Economics*, New York: Liveright Publishing Corporation.

Banks, J.S. and Hanushek, E.A. (eds) (1995) *Modern Political Economy: Old Topics, New Directions*, Cambridge: Cambridge University Press.

Banuri, T. and Schor, J.B. (eds) (1992) *Financial Openness and National Autonomy: Opportunities and Constraints*, Oxford: Clarendon Press.

Barber, W.J. (1987) 'Should the American Economics Association Have Toasted Simon Newcomb at its 100th Birthday Party?' *Journal of Economic Perspectives* Summer.

Baron, J.N. and Hannan, M.T. (1994) 'The Impact of Economics on Contemporary Sociology,' *Journal of Economic Literature* September.

Barro, R.J. (1974) 'Are Government Bonds Net Wealth?' *Journal of Political Economy* November/December.

— (1989) 'The Neoclassical Approach to Fiscal Policy,' in R.J. Barro (ed.) *Modern Business Cycle Theory*, Cambridge, Mass.: Harvard University Press.

— (1992) 'Human Capital and Economic Growth,' in *Politics of Long-Run Economic Growth*, Kansas City: Federal Reserve Bank of Kansas City.

Barro, R.J. and Sala-I-Martin, X. (1992) 'Convergence,' *Journal of Political Economy* April.

— (1995) *Economic Growth*, New York: McGraw-Hill.

Barro, R.J., Mankiw, N.G,. and Sala-I-Martin, X. (1995) 'Capital Mobility in Neoclassical Models of Growth,' *American Economic Review* March.

Bartlett, R.L. (1995) 'Attracting "Otherwise Bright Students" to Economics 101,' *American Economic Association* May.

Basu, K. (1995) 'Flexibility in Economic Theory,' in T. Killick (ed.) *The Flexible Economy: Causes and Consequences of the Adaptability of National Economies*, London: Routledge.

Baumol, W.J. (1977) 'Say's (at least) Eight Laws, or What Say and James Mill May Really Have Meant,' *Economica* May.

— (1985) 'On Methods in US Economics a Century Earlier,' *American Economic Association* December.

— (1988) 'Economic Education and the Critics of Mainstream Economics,' *Journal of Economic Education* Fall.

— (1994) 'Multivariate Growth Patterns: Contagion and Common Forces as Possible Sources of Convergence,' in W. J. Baumol, R. R. Nelson, and E. N. Wolff (eds) *Convergence of Productivity: Cross-National Studies and Historical Evidence*, New York: Oxford University Press.

Baumol, W.J., Blackman, S.A.B. and Wolff, E.N. (1989) *Productivity and American Leadership: The Long View*, Cambridge, Mass.: MIT Press.

Bean, C.R. (1994) 'European Unemployment: A Survey,' *Journal of Economic Literature* June.

Beaud, M. and Dostaler, G. (1995) *Economic Thought Since Keynes: A History and Dictionary of Major Economists*, London: Routledge.

Becker, G.S. (1957) *The Economics of Discrimination*, Chicago: University of Chicago Press.

— (1976) *The Economic Approach to Human Behavior*, Chicago: University of Chicago Press.

Begg, D.K.H. (1982) *The Rational Expectations Revolution in Macroeconomics: Theories and Evidence*, Oxford: Philip Allan Publishers.

Benassy, J.-P. (1993) Nonclearing Markets: Macroeconomic Concepts and Macroeconomic Applications,' *Journal of Economic Literature* June.

Bennett, A. (1994) 'Along With Its High Honor, Nobel Award In Economics Influences Future Research,' *Wall Street Journal* October 11.

Bergmann, B.R. (1987) '"Measurement" or Finding Things Out in Economics,' *Journal of Economic Perspectives* Spring.

Bernanke, B. (1983) 'Non-Monetary Effects of the Financial Crisis in the Propagation of the Great Depression,' *American Economic Review* June.

Bernstein, P.L. (1992) *Capital Ideas: The Improbable Origins of Modern Wall Street*, New York: Free Press.

Bhagwati, J.N. (1982) 'Directly Unproductive, Profit-seeking (DUP) Activities,' *Journal of Political Economy* October.

Black, F. and Scholes M.S. (1972) 'The Valuation of Option Contracts and a Test of Market Efficiency,' *Journal of Finance* May.

— (1973) 'The Pricing of Options and Corporate Liabilities,' *Journal of Political Economy* May/June.

Blackburn, M.L., Bloom, D.E., and Freeman, R.B. (1990–91) 'An Era of Falling Earnings and Rising Inequality?' *Brookings Review* Winter.

Blanchard, O.J. and Fisher, S. (1989) *Lectures on Macroeconomics*, Cambridge, Mass.: MIT Press.

Blank, R. (1994) 'Does a Larger Social Safety Net Mean Less Economic Flexibility?' in R.B. Freeman (ed.) *Working Under Different Rules*, New York: Russell Sage.

Blaug, M. (1972) 'Was There a Marginalist Revolution?' *History of Political Economy* Fall.

— (1976) 'Kuhn versus Lakatos or Paradigms versus Research Programmes in the History of Economics,' in S.J. Latsis (ed.) *Methods and Appraisal in Economics*, Cambridge: Cambridge University Press.

— (1980) *The Methodology of Economics*, Cambridge: Cambridge University Press.

— (1985) *Economic Theory in Retrospect*, Fourth Edition, Cambridge: Cambridge University Press.

Blinder, A.S. (1987a) *Hard Heads, Soft Hearts*, Reading, Mass.: Addison-Wesley.

— (1987b) 'Keynes, Lucas, and Scientific Progress,' *American Economic Association* May.

— (1994) 'On Sticky Prices: Academic Theories Meet the Real World,' in N.G. Mankiw (ed.) *Monetary Policy*, Chicago: University of Chicago Press.

Block, F.L. (1977) *The Origins of International Economic Disorder: A Study of United States International Monetary Policy from World War II to the Present*, Berkeley: University of California Press.

Block, F.L. and Somers, M.R. (1984) 'Beyond the Economistic Fallacy: The Holistic Social Science of Karl Polanyi,' in T. Skocpol (ed.) *Vision and Method in Historical Sociology*, New York: Cambridge University Press.

Bloom, D.E. and Freeman, R.B. (1992) 'The Fall in Private Pension Coverage in the United States,' *American Economic Review* May.

Blustein, P. (1987) 'Protectionist Views Win Respect, Friends for John Culbertson; But Then He Needs Them; Most Fellow Economists Condemn Him as a Heretic,' *Wall Street Journal* April 2.

Boitani, A. and Salanti, A. (1994) 'The Multifarious Role of Theories in Economics: The Case of Different Keynesianisms,' in P.A. Klein (ed.) *The Role of Economic Theory*, Boston: Kluwer.

Boland, L.A. (1979) 'A Critique of Friedman's Critics,' *Journal of Economic Literature* June.

— (1982) *The Foundations of Economic Method*, London: George Allen & Unwin.

Borjas, G. and Ramey, V.A. (1994a) 'The Relationship Between Wage Inequality and International Trade,' in J.H. Bergstrand, T.F. Cosimano, J.W. Houck, and R.G. Sheehan (eds) *The Changing Distribution of Income in an Open US Economy*, New York: North-Holland.

— (1994b) 'Rising Inequality in the United States: Causes and Consequences,' *American Economic Review* May.

Borjas, G., Freeman, R., and Katz, L. (1992) 'On the Labor Market Effects of Immigration and Trade,' in G. Borjas and R. Freeman (eds) *Immigration and the Work Force*, Chicago: University of Chicago Press.

Bostaph, S. (1978) 'The Methodological Debate Between Carl Menger and the German Historicists,' *Atlantic Economic Journal* September.

Boulding, K.E. (1950) *A Reconstruction of Economics*, New York: John Wiley.

— (1969) 'Economics as a Moral Science,' *American Economic Review* March.

— (1971) 'After Samuelson, Who Needs Adam Smith?' *History of Political Economy* Fall.

— (1992) 'Kenneth Boulding,' in P. Arestis and M. Sawyer (eds) *A Dictionary of Dissenting Economists*, Aldershot: Edward Elgar.

Bound, J. and Johnson, G. (1992) 'Changes in the Structure of Wages in the 1980s: An Evaluation of Alternative Explanations,' *American Economic Review* June.

Bowles, S. (1998) 'Endogenous Preferences: The Cultural Consequences of Markets and Other Economic Institutions,' *Journal of Economic Literature* March.

Bowles, S. and Gintis, H. (1976) *Schooling in Capitalist America: Educational Reform and the Contradictions of Economic Life*, New York: Basic Books.

— (1993) 'The Revenge of Homo Economicus: Contested Exchange and the Revival of Political Economy,' *Journal of Economic Perspectives* winter.

Bowles, S., Gintis, H., and Gustafsson, B. (eds) (1993) *Markets and Democracy: Participation, Accountability and Efficiency*, Cambridge, Mass.: Cambridge University Press.

Boyer, R. (1993) 'Introduction to Part II, The Models Revolution, Cumulative Learning, Irreversibility and Diversity of Trajectories,' in D. Foray and C. Freeman (eds) *Technology and Wealth of Nations: The Dynamics of Constructed Advantage*, London: Pinter.

Bradford, Jr., C.I. (1994) *From Trade-Driven Growth to Growth-Driven Trade: Reappraising the East Asian Development Experience*, Paris: Organization for Economic Cooperation and Development.

Brander, J.A. (1986) 'Rationales for Strategic Trade and Industrial Policy,' in P. R. Krugman (ed.) *Strategic Trade Policy and the New International Economics*, Cambridge, Mass.: MIT Press.

Braudel, F. (1972) 'History and Social Sciences,' in P. Burke (ed.) *Economy and Society in Early Modern Europe*, London: Routledge & Kegan Paul.

— (1981–84) *Civilization and Capitalism, 15th–18th Century*, Three Volumes, New York: Harper & Row.

— (1982) *The Wheels of Commerce*, New York: Harper & Row.

Brenner, R. (1992a) 'Macroeconomics: The Masks of Science and Myths of Good Policies,' in D. Colander and R. Brenner (eds) *Educating Economists*, Ann Arbor: University of Michigan Press.

— (1992b) 'Truth In Teaching Microeconomics,' in D. Colander and R. Brenner (eds) *Educating Economists*, Ann Arbor: University of Michigan Press.

Brenner, R. and Glick, M. (1991) 'The History of the Regulation Approach: Theory and History,' *New Left Review* July/August.

Brewer, A. (1995) 'A Minor Post-Ricardian? Marx as an Economist,' *History of Political Economy*, spring.

Bronfenbrenner, M. (1971) '"The Structure of Revolutions" in Economic Thought,' *History of Political Economy* Spring.

— (1985) 'Early American Leaders – Institutional and Critical Traditions,' *American Economic Review* December.

Brown, A. (1992) 'Keynes and the Quantity Theory of Money,' in B. Gerrard and J. Hillard (eds) *The Philosophy and Economics of J.M. Keynes*, Brookfield, Vt.: Edward Elgar.

Brown. C. (1995) *American Standards of Living*, Cambridge, Mass.: Blackwell.

Brown, V. (1994a) *Adam Smith's Discourse: Canonicity, Commerce and Conscience*, London: Routledge.

— (1994b) 'The Economy as Text,' in R.E. Backhouse (ed.) *New Directions in Economic Methodology*, London: Routledge.

Buchanan, J.M. and Tullock, G. (1962) *The Calculus of Consent: Legal Foundations of Constitutional Democracy*, Ann Arbor: University of Michigan Press.

Buchele, R. and Christiansen, J. (1993) 'Industrial Relations and Relative Income Shares in the United States,' *Industrial Relations* Winter.

Buiter, W.H. (1980) 'The Macroeconomics of Dr. Pangloss: A Critical Survey of New Classical Macroeconomics,' *Economic Journal* March.

Bulow, J. and Klemperer, P. (1994) 'Rational Frenzies and Crashes,' *Journal of Political Economy* February.

Burawoy, M. (1998) 'Critical Sociology: A Dialogue Between Two Sciences,' *Contemporary Sociology* January.

Burtless, G. (1991) 'The Tattered Safety Net,' *Brookings Review* Spring.

— (1995) 'International Trade and the Rise in Earnings Inequality,' *Journal of Economic Literature* June.

Butterfield, H. (1959) *The Whig Interpretation of History*, London: G. Bell & Sons.

Caballero, R.J. and Hammour, M.L. (1996) 'The "Fundamental Transformation" in Macroeconomics,' *American Economic Association* May.

Caldwell, B.J. (1982) 'Friedman's Methodological Instrumentalism,' in *Beyond Positivism: Economic Methodology in the Twentieth Century*, London: George Allen & Unwin.

— (ed.) (1984) *Appraisal and Criticism in Economics: A Book of Readings*, Boston: Allen & Unwin.

— (1990) 'Woo's *What's Wrong with Formalization in Economics?* An Epistemological Critique,' in W.J. Samuels (ed.) *Research in the History of Economic Thought and Methodology*, Volume 7, Greenwich, Conn.: JAI Press.

Caldwell, B.J. and Coats, A.W. (1984) 'The Rhetoric of Economists: A Comment on McCloskey,' *Journal of Economic Literature* January.

Calomiris, C.W. (1993) 'Financial Factors in the Great Depression,' *Journal of Economic Perspectives* spring.

Calvo, G.A. and Mendoza, E.G. (1996) 'Petty Crime and Cruel Punishment: Lessons from the Mexican Debacle,' *American Economic Review* May.

Cannan, E. (ed.) (1896) *Lectures of Adam Smith,* Oxford: Clarendon Press.

Carabelli, A. (1992) 'Organic Interdependence and Keynes's Choice of Units in the *General Theory,*' in B. Gerrard and J. Hillard (eds) *The Philosophy and Economics of J.M. Keynes,* Aldershot: Edward Elgar.

Cardoso, E. and Helwege, A. (1991) 'Populism, Profligacy, and Redistribution,' in R. Dornbush and S. Edwards (eds) *The Macroeconomics of Populism in Latin America,* Chicago: University of Chicago Press.

Carmichael, A.M. (1987) 'The Control of Export Credit Subsidies and Its Welfare Consequences,' *Journal of International Economics* August.

Chandler, Jr., A.D. (1977) *The Visible Hand: The Managerial Revolution in American Business,* Cambridge, Mass.: Belknap Press of Harvard University Press.

— (1986) *Strategy and Structure: Chapters in the History of Industrial Enterprise,* Garden City, NY: Anchor Books.

Chang, H.-J. (1995) 'Explaining "Flexible Rigidities" in East Asia,' in T. Killick (ed.) *The Flexible Economy: Causes and Consequences of the Adaptability of National Economies,* London: Routledge.

Chari, V.V. (1998) 'Nobel Laureate Robert E. Lucas, Jr.: Architect of Modern Macroeconomics,' *Journal of Economic Perspectives* Winter.

Chase-Dunn, C. (1989) *Global Formation: Structures of the World-Economy,* Cambridge, Mass.: Basil Blackwell.

Chenery, H. and Srinivasan, T.N. (eds) (1988) *Handbook of Development Economics,* Volume I, Amsterdam: North-Holland.

Chick, V. (1981) 'The Nature of the Keynesian Revolution: A Reassessment,' in V. Chick *On Money, Method and Keynes; Selected Essays,* P. Arestis and S. C. Dow (eds), New York: St Martin's Press, 1992.

— (1995) '"Order out of Chaos" in Economics,' in S. Dow and J. Hillard (eds) *Keynes, Knowledge and Uncertainty,* Aldershot: Edward Elgar.

Clark, B. (1991) *Political Economy: A Comparative Approach,* Westport, Conn.: Praeger.

Clark, J.B. (1899) *The Distribution of Wealth,* New York: Augustus M. Kelley, 1965.

Clark, J.M. (1936) *Social Economics,* New York: Farrar & Rinehart.

Clemence, R.V. (ed.) (1951) *Essays of J.A. Schumpeter,* Cambridge: Addison-Wesley.

Cline, W.R. (1997) *Trade and Wage Inequality,* Washington, D.C.: Institute for International Economics.

Clower, R. and Leijonhufvud, A. (1973) 'Say's Principle, What It Means and Doesn't Mean,' *Intermountain Economic Review* Fall, in A. Leijonhufvud *Information and Coordination: Essays in Macroeconomic Theory,* New York: Oxford University Press.

Coase, R. (1974) 'The Lighthouse in Economics,' *Journal of Law and Economics* October.

— (1977) 'The Wealth of Nations,' *Economic Inquiry* July.

— (1992) 'The Institutional Structure of Production,' *American Economic Review* September.

Coats, A.W. (1967) 'Sociological Aspects of British Thought,' *Journal of Political Economy* October.

— (1984) 'The Sociology of Knowledge and History of Economics,' in W. J. Samuels (ed.) *Research in the History of Economic Thought and Method,* Volume 2, Greenwich, Conn.: JAI Press.

— (1988) 'Economic Rhetoric: The Social and Historical Context,' in A. Klamer, D.N.

McCloskey, and R.N. Solow (eds) *The Consequences of Economic Rhetoric*, Cambridge, Mass.: Cambridge University Press.

— (1990) 'Marshall and Ethics,' in R. McWilliams Tullberg (ed.) *Alfred Marshall in Retrospect*, Brookfield, Vt.: Edward Elgar.

Coddington, A. (1975) 'The Rationale of General Equilibrium Theory,' *Economic Inquiry* December.

— (1976) 'Keynesian Economics: The Search for First Principles,' *Journal of Economic Literature* December.

Coe, R.D. and Wilbur, C.K. (1985) 'Schumpeter Revisited,' in R.D. Coe and C.K. Wilbur (eds) *Capitalism and Democracy: Schumpeter Revisited*, South Bend: University of Notre Dame Press.

Coffee, Jr., J.C. (1986) 'Shareholders Versus Managers: The Strain in the Corporate Web,' *Michigan Law Review* October.

Cohen, B.J. (1991) 'What Ever Happened to the LDC Debt Crisis?' *Challenge* May/June.

Cohen, B.S. (1980) 'History and Anthropology: The State of Play,' *Society and History* April.

Colander, D. (1984) 'Was Keynes a Keynesian or a Lernerian?' *Journal of Economic Literature* December.

— (1992) 'Truth in Teaching Macroeconomics,' in D. Colander and R. Brenner (eds) *Educating Economists*, Ann Arbor: University of Michigan Press.

— (1995) 'The Stories We Tell: A Reconsideration of AS/AD Analysis,' *Journal of Economic Perspectives* Summer.

— (1996) 'Beyond New Keynesian Macroeconomics: Post Walrasian Macroeconomics,' in R. Rotheim (ed.) *Post Keynesian Perspectives on New Keynesian Macroeconomics*, Aldershot: Edward Elgar.

Colletti, L. (1977) 'Some Comments on Marx's Theory of Value,' in J. Schwartz (ed.) *The Subtle Anatomy of Capitalism*, Santa Monica, Calif.: Goodyear Publishing Company.

Collins, S.M. and Bosworth, B.P. (1996) 'Economic Growth in East Asia: Accumulation versus Assimilation,' *Brookings Papers on Economic Activity* 2.

Commons, J.R. (1924) *Legal Foundations of Capitalism*, Madison: University of Wisconsin Press.

Cooper, R. (1994) 'Yes to European Monetary Unification, but No to the Maastricht Treaty,' in A. Steinherr (ed.) *Thirty Years of European Monetary Integration*, London: Longman.

Corbridge, S. (1994) 'Plausible Worlds: Friedman, Keynes and the Geography of Inflation,' in S. Corbridge, N. Thrift, and R. Martin (eds) *Money, Power and Space*, Oxford: Blackwell.

Corbridge, S., Thrift, N., and Martin, R. (1994) *Money, Power and Space*, Oxford: Blackwell.

Cornwall, J. (1994) *Economic Breakdown and Recovery: Theory and Policy*, Armonk, NY: M.E. Sharpe.

Cort, J.C. (1988) *Christian Socialism: An Informal History*, Maryknoll, NY: Orbis Books.

Cottrell, A. (1994) 'Post-Keynesian Monetary Economics,' *Cambridge Journal of Economics* December.

Cox, R.W. (1987) *Production, Power, and World Order: Social Forces in the Making of History*, New York: Columbia University Press.

Crafts, N.F.R. (1996) 'The First Industrial Revolution: A Guided Tour for Growth Economists,' *American Economic Review* May.

Crotty, J. (1983) 'Keynes on Capital Flight,' *Journal of Economic Literature* March.

Crotty, J. and Epstein, G. (1996) 'In Defense of Capital Controls,' Working Paper, Department of Economics, University of Massachusetts, Amherst.

Crotty, J., Epstein, G., and Kelly, P. (1998) 'Multinational Corporations in the Neo-Liberal regime,' in Dean Baker, Gerald Epstein and Robert Pollin (eds) *Globalization and Progressive Economic Policy*, New York: Cambridge University Press.

Cushman Jr, J.H. (1998) 'Nike Pledges to End Child Labor and Apply US Rules Abroad,' *New York Times*, May 13, p. D1.

Cutler, D.M. and Katz, L.F. (1992) 'Untouched by the Rising Tide,' *The Brookings Review* Winter.

Danziger, S., Haveman, R. and Plotnick, R. (1981) 'How Income Transfer Programs Affect Work, Savings, and Income Distribution: A Critical Review,' *Journal of Economic Literature* September.

David, P. (1985) 'Clio and the Economics of QWERTY,' *American Economic Association* May.

Davidson, P. (1989) 'Keynes and Money,' in R. Hill (ed.) *Keynes, Money and Monetarism*, Houndsmill, England: Macmillan.

— (1996) ' What Revolution? The Legacy of Keynes,' *Journal of Post Keynesian Economics* Fall.

Davis, D.E. (1989) 'Divided Over Democracy: The Embeddedness of State and Class Conflict in Contemporary Mexico,' *Politics and Society* 3.

Dawes, R.M. and Thaler, R.H. (1988) 'Anomalies: Cooperation,' *Journal of Economic Perspectives* Summer.

Dawson, M. and Foster, J.B. (1996) 'Virtual Capitalism: The Political Economy of the Information Highway,' *Monthly Review* July/August.

Deane, P. (1989) *The State and the Economic System*, Oxford: Oxford University Press.

de Cecco, M. (1977) 'The Last of the Romans,' in R. Skidelsky (ed.) *The End of the Keynesian Era: Essays on the Disintegration of the Keynesian Political Economy*, New York: Holmes & Meier.

Defoe, D. (1719) *Robinson Crusoe*, London: Penguin Books, 1994.

DeMarchi, N. and Blaug, M. (eds) (1991) *Appraising Economic Theories: Studies in the Methodology of Research Programmes*, Aldershott: Edward Elgar.

De Martino, G. (1996) 'Against Global Neo-Liberalism: Normative Principles and Policy Alternatives,' *New Political Science* 35.

Demsetz, H. (1991) 'The Theory of the Firm Revisited,' in O.E. Williamson and S.G. Winter (eds) *The Nature of the Firm: Origins, Evolution, and Development*, New York: Oxford University Press.

Denison, E.F. (1979) *Accounting for Slower Economic Growth: The United States in the 1970s*, Washington, DC: Brookings Institution.

Dertouzos, M.L., Lester, R.K., Solow, R.M., and the MIT Commission on Industrial Productivity (1989) *Made in America: Regaining the Productive Edge*, Cambridge, Mass.: MIT Press.

Dixit, A. (1984) 'International Trade Policy for Oligopolistic Industries,' *Economic Journal* Supplement.

Dobb, M. (1937) 'Imperialism,' in M. Dobb *Political Economy and Capitalism*, London: George Routledge & Sons.

— (1955) *On Economic Theory and Socialism*, London: Routledge & Kegan Paul.

Domar, E.D. (1947) 'Expansion and Employment,' *American Economic Review* March.

— (1957) *Essays in the Theory of Economic Growth*, New York: Oxford University Press.

Donoghue, M. (1997) 'Mill's Affirmation of the Classical Wage Fund Doctrine,' *Scottish Journal of Political Economy* February.

Dooley, P.C. (1990) 'Value,' in J. Creedy (ed.) *Foundations of Economic Thought*, Oxford: Basil Blackwell.

Dornbusch, R. and Edwards, S. (1991) 'The Macroeconomics of Populism,' in R. Dornbusch and S. Edwards (eds) *The Macroeconomics of Populism in Latin America*, Chicago: University of Chicago Press.

Dosi, G., Pavitt, K. and Soete, L. (1990) *The Economics of Technological Change and International Trade*, New York: New York University Press.

Dow, A., Dow, S., Hutton, A., and Keaney, M. (1998) 'Tradition in Thought: The Case of Scottish Political Economy,' *New Political Economy* March.

Dow, S.C. (1985) *Macroeconomic Thought: A Methodological Approach*, Oxford: Basil Blackwell.

— (1987) 'The Scottish Political Economy Tradition,' *Scottish Journal of Political Economy* November.

— (1997) 'Mainstream Economic Methodology: Critical Survey,' *Cambridge Journal of Economics* January.

Downie, J.A. (1983) 'Defoe, Imperialism, and the Travel Books Reconsidered,' in G.K. Hunter and C.J. Rawson (eds) *The Yearbook of English Studies*, Volume 13 'Colonial and Imperial Themes' Special Number, London: Modern Humanities Research Association.

Drucker, P.F. (1994) 'The Age of Social Transformation,' *Atlantic Monthly* November.

Dugger, W.M. (1979) 'Methodological Differences between Institutional and Neoclassical Economics,' *Journal of Economic Issues* December.

Dyson, F. (1995) 'The Scientist as Rebel,' *New York Review of Books* May 25.

Eatwell, J. (1995) 'Disguised Unemployment: The G7 Experience,' Cambridge, Mass.: Trinity College, Cambridge University, August.

— (1996) 'Unemployment on a World Scale,' in J. Eatwell (ed.) *Global Unemployment in the '90s*, Armonk, NY: M.E. Sharpe.

Eatwell, J., Milgate, M., and Newman, P. (eds) (1990) 'Preface', *The New Palgrave: Marxian Economics*, New York: W.W. Norton.

Edwards, S. (1998) 'Openness, Productivity and Growth: What Do We Really Know?' *Economic Journal* March.

Eggertsson, T. (1995) 'On the Economics of Economics,' *Kyklos* Volume 48, Fasc. 2.

Eichengreen, B. (1984) 'Keynes and Protectionism,' *Journal of Economic History* June.

Eichengreen, B., Tobin, J., and Wyplosz, C. (1995) 'Two Cases for Sand in the Wheels of International Finance,' *Economic Journal* January.

Eichner, A.S. (1985) *Toward a New Economics: Essays in Post-Keynesian and Institutional Theory*, Armonk, NY: M.E. Sharpe.

Ekelund, Jr., R.B. and Hebert, R.F. (1990) *A History of Economic Thought and Method*, New York: McGraw-Hill.

Eldredge, N. (1995) *Reinventing Darwin: The Great Debate at the High Table of Evolutionary Theory*, New York: John Wiley & Sons.

Elster, J. (ed.) (1986) *Analytical Marxism*, Cambridge, Mass.: Cambridge University Press.

Ely, R. T. (1893) *Outline of Economics*, New York: Macmillan, 1937.

Epstein, G. and Ferguson, T. (1995) 'Monetary Policy, Loan Liquidation, and Industrial Conflict: The Federal Reserve and the Open Market Operations of 1932,' in T. Ferguson *Golden Rule: The Investment Theory of Party Competition and the Logic of Money-Driven Political Systems*, Chicago: University of Chicago Press.

Epstein, R.J. (1987) *A History of Econometrics*, Amsterdam: North-Holland.

Evensky, J. (1992) 'Ethics and the Classical Liberal Tradition in Economics,' *History of Political Economy* Spring.

Feenstra, R.C. and Hanson, G.H. (1996) 'Globalization, Outsourcing, and Wage Inequality,' *American Economic Review* May.

Feiner, S. and Roberts, B. (1995) 'Using Alternative Paradigms to Teach About Race and Gender: A Critical Thinking Approach to Introductory Economics,' *American Economic Association* May.

Feiwel, G.R. (1975) *The Intellectual Capital of Michael Kalecki: A Study in Economic Theory and Policy*, Oxville: University of Tennessee Press .

Felix, D. (1994) 'Debt Crisis Adjustment in Latin America: Have the Hardships Been Necessary?' in G. Dymsky and R. Pollin (eds) *New Perspectives on Monetary Macroeconomics: Explorations in the Tradition of Hyman P. Minsky*, Ann Arbor: University of Michigan Press.

Fellner, W. (1981) 'March Into Socialism, or Viable Postwar Stage of Capitalism,' in A. Heertje (ed.) *Schumpeter's Vision*, New York: Praeger.

Ferguson, C.E. (1969) *The Neoclassical Theory of Production and Distribution*, Cambridge, Mass.: Cambridge University Press.

Ferris, T. (1995) 'Minds and Matter,' *New Yorker* May 15.

Field, A.J. (1994) Review of *Adam Smith in His Time and Ours: Designing the Decent Society* by Jerry Z. Muller, *Journal of Economic Literature* June.

Findlay, R. (1984) 'Growth and Development in Trade Models,' in R.W. Jones and P.B. Kenen (eds) *Handbook of International Economics*, Volume I, Amsterdam: North-Holland.

— (1996) 'Modeling Global Interdependence: Centers, Peripheries, and Frontiers,' *American Economic Review* May.

Fine, S. (1956) *Laissez Faire and the General-Welfare State: A Study of Conflict in American Thought 1865–1901*, Ann Arbor: University of Michigan Press, 1964.

Fisher, I. (1926) 'A Statistical Relation between Unemployment and Price Changes,' *International Labor Review* June. Reprinted as Irving Fisher, 'I Discovered the Phillips Curve,' *Journal of Political Economy*, March/April 1973.

Fishlow, A., Gwin, C., Haggard, S., Rodrik, D., and Wade, R. (1994) *Miracle or Design? Lessons from the East Asian Experience*, Washington, DC: Overseas Development Council.

Fitoussi, J.-P. (1994) 'Wage Distribution and Unemployment: The French Experience,' *American Economic Review* May.

Fitzgibbons, A. (1988) *Keynes's Vision, A New Political Economy*, Oxford: Clarendon Press.

— (1992) 'The Political Economy of the New Keynesian Fundamentalism,' in Bill Gerrard and John Hillard (eds) *The Philosophy and Economics of J.M. Keynes*, Aldershot: Edward Elgar.

Folbre, N. (1995) *The New Field Guide to the US Economy*, New York: New Press.

Forget, E.L. (1992) 'J.S. Mill and the Tory School: The Rhetorical Value of the Recantation,' *History of Political Economy* Spring.

Foster, J. (1987) *Evolutionary Macroeconomics*, London: Allen & Unwin.

Foster, J.B. (1990) 'Liberal Practicality and the US Left,' in R. Miliband, L. Panitch, and J. Saville (eds) *Socialist Register 1990*, London: Merlin.

Frank, R.H. (1992) 'Melding Sociology and Economics: James Coleman's *Foundations of Social Theory*,' *Journal of Economic Literature* March.

Frank, R.H. and Cook, P.J. (1995) *The Winner-Take-All Society*, New York: Free Press.

Freeman, R.B. (1992) 'How Much Has De-Unionization Contributed to the Rise in Male Earnings Inequaliy?' in S. Danziger and P. Gottschalk (eds) *Uneven Tides: Rising Inequality in America*, New York: Russelll Sage Foundation.

— (1994) 'How Labor Fares in Advanced Economies,' in R.B. Freeman (ed.) *Working Under Different Rules*, New York: Russell Sage Foundation.

— (1995a) 'Are Your Wages Set in Beijing?' *Journal of Economic Perspectives* Summer.

— (1995b) 'The Limits of Wage Flexibility to Curing Unemployment,' *Oxford Review of Economic Policy* Spring.

Freeman, R.B. and Katz, L.F. (1994) 'Rising Wage Inequality: The United States vs. Other Advanced Countries,' in R.B. Freeman (ed.) *Working Under Different Rules*, New York: Russell Sage Foundation.

Frey, B.S. and Eichenberger, R (1993) 'American and European Economics and Economists,' *Journal of Economic Perspectives* Fall.

Friedman, B.M. (1994) 'Must We Compete?' *New York Review of Books* October 20.

Friedman, M. (1953a) 'The Methodology of Positive Economics,' in *Essays in Positive Economics*, Chicago: University of Chicago Press.

— (1953b) 'The Case for Flexible Exchange Rates,' in *Essays in Positive Economics*, Chicago: University of Chicago Press.

— (1962) *Capitalism and Freedom*, Chicago: University of Chicago Press.

— (1968) 'The Role of Monetary Policy,' *American Economic Review* March.

Friedman, M. and Friedman, R. (1980) *Free to Choose*, New York: Harcourt Brace Jovanovich.

Friedman, M. and Schwartz, A. (1963) *A Monetary History of the United States, 1867–1960*, Princeton: Princeton University Press.

Frisby, D. (1969) 'Introduction to the English Translation,' *The Postwar Dispute in German Sociology*, London: Heinemann.

Galbraith, James K. (1997) 'Testing the Limit,' *The American Prospect* September–October.

Galbraith, John K. (1955) *Economics and the Art of Controversy*, New York: Vintage.

Garnsey, E. (1981) 'The Rediscovery of the Division of Labor,' *Theory and Society* May.

Garrett, G. (1996) 'Capital Mobility, Trade, and Domestic Politics of Economic Policy,' in R.O. Keohane and H.V. Milnar (eds) *Internationalization and Domestic Politics*, Cambridge, Mass.: Cambridge University Press.

Gates, B. (1995) *The Road Ahead*, New York: Viking.

Gellner, E. (1982) *Nations and Nationalism*, Ithaca: Cornell University Press.

George, A. (1995) 'Indecision: Some Abandoned Reflections,' *Raritan* Fall.

Gereffi, G. and Korzeniewicz, M. (1994) *Commodity Chains and Global Capitalism*, Westport, Conn.: Greenwood Press.

Giersch, H. (1984) 'The Age of Schumpeter,' *Papers and Proceedings of the American Economics Association* May.

Gilder, G. (1981) *Wealth and Poverty*, New York: Basic Books.

Gill, S. (1998) 'European Governance and New Constitutionalism: Economic and Monetary Union and Alternatives to Disciplinary Neoliberalism,' *New Political Economy* March.

Gill, S. and Law, D. (1988) *The Global Political Economy: Perspectives, Problems and Policies*, Baltimore: Johns Hopkins Press.

Glyn, A. (1995) 'The Assessment: Unemployment and Inequality,' *Oxford Review of Economic Policy* Spring.

Glyn, A., Hughes, A., Lipietz, A., and Singh, A. (1991) 'The Rise and Fall of the Golden Age,' in S.A. Marglin and J.B. Schor (eds) *The Golden Age of Capitalism: Reinterpreting the Postwar Experience*, Oxford: Clarendon Press.

Goldin, C. (1995) 'Cliometrics and the Nobel,' *Journal of Economic Perspectives* Spring.

Gonce, R.A. (1996) 'The Social Gospel, Ely, and Commons' Initial Stage of Thought,' *Journal of Economic Issues* September.

Goodfriend, M. and McDermott, J. (1995) 'Early Development,' *American Economic Association* March.

Goodman, J.B. and Pauly, L. (1993) 'The Obsolescence of Capital Controls? Economic Management in an Age of Global Markets,' *World Politics* October.

Gordon, D.M. (1988) 'The Un-natural Rate of Unemployment: An Econometric Critique of the NAIRU Hypothesis,' *American Economic Review* May.

— (1996a) 'Wageless Recovery, Wageless Growth? Prospects for U. S. Workers in the 1990s,' in J. Eatwell (ed.) *Global Unemployment: Loss of Jobs in the '90s*, Armonk, NY: M.E. Sharpe.

— (1996b) 'Growth, Distribution and the Rules of the Game: Social Structuralist Macro-Foundations for a Democratic Economic Policy,' in G. Epstein and H. Gintis (eds) *The Political Economy of Investment, Saving and Finance: A Global Perspective*, New York: Cambridge University Press.

Gordon, D.M., Edwards, R., and Reich, M. (1982) *Segmented Work, Divided Workers: The Historical Transformation of Labor in the United States*, Cambridge, Mass.: Cambridge University Press.

Gordon, R.A. (1976) 'Rigor and Relevance in a Changing Institutional Setting,' *American Economic Review, Papers and Proceedings* May.

— (1990) 'What is New Keynesian Economics?' *Journal of Economic Literature* September.

Gordon, R.A. and Wilcox, J.A. (1981) 'Monetarist Interpretations of the Great Depression: An Evaluation and Critique,' in K. Brunner, (ed.) *Contemporary Views of the Great Depression*, Hingham, Mass.: Martinus Nijhoff.

Gordon, W. (1980) *Institutional Economics: The Changing System*, Austin: University of Texas Press.

Gottschalk, P. and Moffitt, R. (1994) 'The Growth of Earnings Instability in the US Labor Market,' *Brookings Papers on Economic Activity* 2.

Grapard, U. (1995) 'The Quintessential Economic Man?' *Feminist Economics* Spring.

Gray, A. (1976) 'Adam Smith,' *Scottish Journal of Political Economy* June.

Greenwald, B. and Stiglitz, J. (1993) 'New and Old Keynesians,' *Journal of Economic Perspectives* Winter.

Greif, A. (1998) 'Historical and Comparative Institutional Analysis,' *American Economic Review* May.

Grouchy, A. (1947) *Modern Economic Thought: The American Contribution*, Englewood Cliffs, NJ: Prentice-Hall.

Gunderson, M. (1994) Review of *Small Differences that Matter: Labor Markets and Income Maintenance in Canada and the United States*, D. Card and R. B. Freeman (eds), University of Chicago Press, 1993, *Journal of Economic Literature*, June.

Haggard, S. (1994) 'Politics and Institutions in the World Bank's East Asia,' in *Miracle or Design? Lessons From the East Asian Experience*, Washington, DC: Overseas Development Council.

Hahn, F. (1984) 'Reflections on the Invisible Hand,' in *Equilibrium and Macroeconomics*, Oxford: Basil Blackwell; from *Lloyds Bank Review* April 1982.

— (1991) 'The Next Hundred Years,' *Economic Journal* January.

Hahn, F. and Matthews, R.C.O. (1965) 'The Theory of Growth: A Survey,' in American Economic Association and the Royal Economic Society, *Surveys of Economic Growth: Growth and Development*, New York: St. Martin's Press, 1967.

Hansen, B. (1981) 'Unemployment, Keynes and the Stockholm School,' *History of Political Economy* Summer.

Harcourt, G.C. (1969) *Some Cambridge Controversies in the Theory of Capital*, Cambridge, Mass.: Cambridge University Press.

— (1994) 'Kahn and Keynes and the making of *The General Theory*,' *Cambridge Journal of Economics*, February.

Harding, S. (1995) 'Can Feminst Thought Make Economics More Objective?' *Feminist Economics* Spring.

Harris, D. (1975) 'The Theory of Economic Growth: A Critique and Reformulation,' *American Economic Review*, May.

— (1980) 'A Post-Mortem on the Neoclassical "Parable",' in E.J. Nell (ed.) *Growth, Profit and Property*, New York: Cambridge University Press.

Harrison, B. (1994) *Lean and Mean: The Changing Landscape of Corporate Power in the Age of Flexibility*, New York: Basic Books.

Harrod, R. (1948) *Towards a Dynamic Economy: Some Recent Developments of Economic Theory and Their Application to Policy*, London: Macmillan.

— (1969) *Money*, London: Macmillan.

Hartlyn, J. and Morley, S.A. (1986) 'Introduction,' in J. Hartlyn and S.A. Morley (eds) *Latin American Political Economy: Financial Crisis and Political Change*, Boulder: Westview.

Hausman, D.M. (1992) *The Inexact and Separate Science of Economics*, Cambridge, Mass.: Cambridge University Press.

Hausman, D. M. and McPherson, M.S. (1993) 'Taking Ethics Seriously: Economics and Contemporary Moral Philosophy,' *Journal of Economic Literature* June.

Hayek, F.A. von (1945) 'The Uses of Knowledge in Society,' *American Economic Review* September.

— (1966) 'The Principles of a Liberal Social Order,' *Il Politico*, December; reprinted in C. Nishiyama and K.R. Leube (eds) *The Essence of Hayek*, Stanford: Hoover Institute Press, 1984.

— (1973) 'The Place of Menger's *Grundsatze* in the History of Economic Thought,' in J.R. Hicks and W. Weber (eds) *Carl Menger and the Austrian School of Economics*, Oxford: Oxford University Press.

Hayes, R.H. and Abernathy, W.J. (1980) 'Managing Our Way to Economic Decline,' *Harvard Business Review* July–August.

Heidenheimer, A.J., Heclo, H., and Teich Adams, C. (1990) *Comparative Public Policy: The Politics of Social Choice in America, Europe, and Japan*, New York: St Martin's Press.

Heilbroner, R. (1996) 'Reflections on a Sad State of Affairs,' in J. Eatwell (ed.) *Global Unemployment: Loss of Jobs in the '90s*, Armonk, NY: M.E. Sharpe.

Heilbroner, R. and Milberg, W. (1996) *The Crisis of Vision in Modern Economic Thought*, New York: Cambridge University Press.

Helleiner, E. (1994) *States and the Reemergence of Global Finance: From Bretton Woods to the 1990s*, Ithaca: Cornell University Press.

Helpman, E. (1989) 'The Non-Competitive Theory of International Trade and Trade Policy,' *Proceedings of the World Bank Annual Conference on Development Economics*.

Hennis, W. (1987) 'A Science of Man: Max Weber and the Political Economy of the German Historical School,' in W.J. Mommsen and J. Osterhammel (eds) *Max Weber and His Contemporaries*, London: Unwin Hyman.

Hicks, J.R. (1973) 'Recollections and Documents,' *Economica* February.

— (1975) 'The Scope and Status of Welfare Economics,' *Oxford Economic Papers*, reprinted in *Wealth and Welfare: Collected Essays on Economic Theory*, Vol. 1, Oxford: Basil Blackwell, 1981.

— (1976) 'Some Questions of Time in Economics,' in A. Tang, F.W. Westfield, and J.S. Worley (eds) *Evolution, Welfare, and Time in Economics: Essays in Honor of Nickolas Georescu-Roegen*, Lexington: Lexington Books, D. C. Heath.

— (1977) *Economic Perspectives*, Oxford: Oxford University Press.

Hillard, J. (1992) 'Keynes, Orthodoxy and Uncertainty,' in B. Gerrard and J. Hillard (eds) *The Philosophy and Economics of J. M. Keynes*, Aldershot: Edward Elgar.

Hillard, M. and McIntyre, R. (1994) 'Is There a New Institutional Consensus in Labor Economics?' *Journal of Economic Issues* June.

Hillard, M. and Misukiewicz, C. (1988) 'Marxism in America: the *Monthly Review* Experience,' An Interview, *Rethinking Marxism* Spring.

Hillier, B. (1991) *The Macroeconomic Debate: Models of the Closed and Open Economy*, Oxford: Basil Blackwell.

Himmelfarb, G. (1995) *The De-Moralization of Society: From Victorian Virtue to Modern Values*, New York: Alfred A. Knopf.

Hirschman, A.O. (1984) 'Against Parsimony: Three Easy Ways of Complicating Some Categories of Economic Discourse,' in *Rival Views of Market Society and Other Recent Essays*, Cambridge, Mass.: Harvard University Press, 1992.

— (1991) *The Rhetoric of Reaction: Perversity, Futility, Jeopardy*, Cambridge, Mass.: Harvard University Press.

Hobsbawm, E.J. (1968) *Industry and Empire*, Baltimore: Penguin Books, 1969.

— (1987) *The Age of Empire 1875–1914*, New York: Vintage, 1989.

— (1994) *The Age of Extremes; A History of the World, 1914–1994*, New York: Pantheon Books.

Hodgson, G.M. (1986) 'Beyond Methodological Individualism,' *Cambridge Journal of Economics* September.

— (1992a) 'The Reconstruction of Economics: Is There Still a Place for Neoclassical Theory?' *Journal of Economic Issues* September.

— (1992b) 'Thorstein Veblen and Post-Darwinian Economics,' *Cambridge Journal of Economics*, September.

— (1993) *Economics and Evolution: Bringing Life Back into Economics*, Cambridge, Mass.: Polity Press.

— (1994) 'The Return of Institutional Economics,' in N.J. Smelser and R. Swedberg (eds) *The Handbook of Economic Sociology*, Princeton: Princeton University Press.

— (1998) 'The Approach of Institutional Economics,' *Journal of Economic Literature* March.

Hoffman, E., McCabe, K., and Smith, V.L. (1996) 'Social Distance and Other-Regarding Behavior in Dictatorship Games,' *American Economic Review* June.

Hofstadter, R. (1944) *Social Darwinism in American Thought*, Boston: Beacon Press, revised edition 1955.

Hollis, M. and Nell, E.J. (1975) *Rational Economic Man: A Philosophical Critique of Neo-Classical Economics*, Cambridge: Cambridge University Press.

Hoover, K.D. (1988) *The New Classical Macroeconomics: A Skeptical Inquiry*, Oxford: Basil Blackwell.

— (1992) *The New Classical Macro-Economics*, Three Volumes, Elgar Reference Collection, Aldershot: Edward Elgar.

— (1995) 'Why Does Methodology Matter for Economics?' *Economic Journal* May.

Hopkins, T.K. and Wallerstein, I. (1986) 'Commodity Chains in the World-Economy Prior to 1800,' *Review* 10:1.

Howard, M.C. (1995) 'Comment on Brewer' *History of Political Economy* Spring.

Hudson, M. (1992) *Trade, Development and Foreign Debt: A History of Theories of Polarisation and Convergence in the International Economy*, London: Pluto Press.

Hume, D. (1980) *Dialogues Concerning Natural Religion and the Posthumous Essays*, Indianapolis: Hackett Publishing.

Hunt, E.K. (1992) *History of Economic Thought; A Critical Perspective* Second Edition, New York: HarperCollins.

Hutchison, T.W. (1969) 'Economists and Economic Policy in Britain After 1870,' *History of Political Economy* Fall.

— (1972) 'The Marginalist Revolution and the Decline and Fall of English Classical Political Economy,' *History of Political Economy* Fall.

Hutton. W. (1995) 'A Postscript,' in J. Michie and J. Grieve Smith (eds) *Managing the Global Economy*, Oxford: Oxford University Press.

Hymer, S. (1971) 'Robinson Crusoe and the Secret of Primitive Accumulation,' *Monthly Review* September.

— (1972) 'The Internationalization of Capital,' *Journal of Economic Issues* March.

Immergut, E.M. (1998) 'The Theoretical Core of the New Institutionalism,' *Politics and Society* March.

Ingram, G. (1994) 'States and Markets in the Production of World Money,' in S. Corbridge, N. Thrift, and R. Martin (eds) *Money, Power and Space*, Oxford: Basil Blackwell.

Ingrao, B. and Israel, G. (1990) *The Invisible Hand: Economic Equilibrium in the History of Science*, Cambridge, Mass.: MIT Press.

Irwin, D.A. (1996) *Against the Tide: An Intellectual History of Free Trade*, Princeton: Princeton University Press.

Jacoby, S. (1990) 'The New Institutionalism: What Can It Learn from the Old?' *Industrial Relations* Spring.

Jessop, B. (1993) 'Towards a Schumpeterian Workfare State? Preliminary Remarks on Post-Fordist Political Economy,' *Studies in Political Economy* 40.

Jevons, W.S. (1871) *The Theory of Political Economy*, London: Macmillan.

—— (1879) *The Theory of Political Economy*, Second Edition, London: Macmillan.

Jones, E.L. (1995) 'Economic Adaptability in the Long Run,' in T. Killick (ed.) *The Flexible Economy: Causes and Consequences of the Adaptability of National Economies*. London: Routledge.

Jones, R. (1831) *An Essay on the Distribution of Wealth*, London: John Murray.

Kaldor, N. (1957) 'A Model of Economic Growth,' *Economic Journal* December.

—— (1972) 'The irrelevance of Equilibrium Economics,' *Economic Journal* December.

—— (1981) 'The Role of Increasing Returns, Technical Progress and Cumulative Causation in the Theory of International Trade and Economic Growth,' in F. Targeti and A.P. Thirlwall (eds) *Further Essays on Economic Theory and Policy*, London: Duckworth, 1989.

—— (1982) *The Scourge of Monetarism*, Oxford: Oxford University Press.

—— (1983) 'Keynesian Economics After Fifty Years,' in F. Targetti and A.P. Thirlwall (eds) *Further Essays on Economic Theory and Policy*, London: Duckworth, 1989.

—— (1984) *Causes of Growth and Stagnation in the World Economy*, Cambridge: Cambridge University Press, 1996.

Kalecki, M. (1952) *The Theory of Economic Dynamics: An Essay on Cyclical and Long-Run Changes in Capitalist Economy*, New York: Monthly Review Press, 1968.

Kahneman, D., Knetsch, J., and Thaler, R.H. (1991) 'Anomolies: The Endowment Effect, Loss Aversion, and Status Quo Bias,' *Journal of Economic Perspectives* Winter.

Kanter, R.M. (1995) 'Cosmopolitans: The Power of Networks,' *World Class: Thriving Locally in the Global Economy*, New York: Simon & Schuster.

Kates, S. (1997) 'On the True Meaning of Say's Law,' *Eastern Economic Journal* Spring.

Katz, L.F., Loneman, G.W., and Blanchflower, D.G. (1995) 'A Comparison of Changes in the Structure of Wages in Four OECD Countries,' in R.B. Freeman and L.F. Katz (eds) *Differences and Changes in Wage Structures*, Chicago: University of Chicago Press.

Katz, L.F. and Murphy, K.M. (1992) 'Changes in Relative Wages: 1963–1987; Supply and Demand Factors,' *Quarterly Journal of Economics* February.

Katzenstein, P.J. (1978) 'Introduction: Domestic and International Forces and Strategies of Foreign Economic Policy,' in P.J. Katzenstein (ed.) *Between Power and Plenty: Foreign Economic Policies of Advanced Industrial States*, Madison: University of Wisconsin Press.

—— (1984) *Corporatism and Change: Austria, Switzerland, and the Politics of Industry*, Ithaca: Cornell University Press.

—— (1985) *Small States in World Markets: Industrial Policy in Europe*, Ithaca: Cornell University Press.

Kauder, E. (1953) 'Genesis of Marginal Utility Theory,' *Economic Journal* September.

Kaufman, R.R. and Stallings, B. (1991) 'The Political Economy of Latin American Populism,' in R. Dornbusch and S. Edwards (eds) *The Macroeconomics of Populism in Latin America*, Chicago: University of Chicago Press.

Kelley, M.R. and Harrison, B. (1992) 'Unions, Technology, and Labor-Management Cooperation,' in L. Mischel and P. Voos (eds) *Unions and Competitiveness*, Armonk, NY: M.E. Sharpe.

Kenen, P. (1994) *The International Economy*, Third Edition, Cambridge: Cambridge University Press.

Keynes, J.M. (1923) 'Robert Malthus,' *Essays and Sketches in Biography*, New York: Meridian Books, 1956.

— (1926a) 'Am I a Liberal?' reprinted in *Essays in Persuasion*, New York: W.W. Norton, 1963.

— (1926b) 'The End of Laissez Faire,' reprinted in *Essays in Persuasion*, New York: W.W. Norton, 1963.

— (1926c) 'Liberalism and Labour,' reprinted in *Essays in Persuasion*, New York: W.W. Norton, 1963.

— (1930a) 'The Great Slump of 1930,' reprinted in *Essays in Persuasion*, New York: W.W. Norton, 1963.

— (1930b) 'Economic Possibilities for our Grandchildren,' reprinted in *Essays in Persuasion*, New York: W.W. Norton, 1963.

— (1931) 'Consequences to Banks,' reprinted in *Essays in Persuasion*, New York: W.W. Norton, 1963.

— (1936) *The General Theory of Employment, Interest, and Money*, New York: Harcourt Brace and Company.

— (1937) 'The General Theory of Employment,' *Quarterly Journal of Economics* February.

— (1971) *The Collected Writings of John Maynard Keynes*, London: Macmillan.

Keynes, J.N. (1890) *The Scope and Method of Political Economy*, Fourth Editon 1917, New York: Augustus M. Kelley, Bookseller, 1965.

Khalil, E.L. (1995) 'Has Economics Progressed? Rectilinear, Historicist, Universal, and Evolutionary Historiographies,' *History of Political Economy* Spring.

Kindleberger, C.P. (1969) *American Business Abroad*, New Haven: Yale University Press.

Kirman, A. (1989) 'The Intrinsic Limits of Modern Economic Theory: The Emperor Has No Clothing,' *Economic Journal* Supplement.

Kirzner, I.M. (1997) 'Entrepreneurial discovery and the competitive market process: an Austrian approach,' *Journal of Economic Literature*, March.

Klamer, A. (1984a) *Conversations with Economists: New Classical Economists and Opponents Speak Out on the Current Controversy in Macroeconomics*, Totowa, NJ: Rowman and Allanheld.

— (1984b) 'Levels of Discourse in New Classical Economics,' *History of Political Economy* Summer.

— (1990) 'The Textbook Presentation of Economic Discourse,' in W.J. Samuels (ed.) *Economics as Discourse*.

— (1995) 'The Conception of Modernism in Economics: Samuelson, Keynes and Harrod,' in S. Dow and J. Hilliard (eds) *Keynes, Knowledge and Uncertainty*, Aldershot: Edward Elgar.

Klamer, A. and Colander D. (1990) *The Making of an Economist*, Boulder: Westview.

Klamer, A. and Leonard, T.C. (1994) 'So What's an Economic Metaphor,' in P. Mirowski (ed.) *Natural Images in Economic Thought*, New York: Cambridge University Press.

Klamer, A. and McCloskey, D.N. (1988) 'Economics in the human conversation,' in A. Klamer, D.N. McCloskey, and R.M. Solow (eds) *The Consequences of Economic Rhetoric*, Cambridge: Cambridge University Press.

Klein, L. and Goldberger, A. (1955) *An Econometric Model of the United States: 1929–51*, New York: John Wiley.

Klein, P.A. (1988) 'Of Paradigms and Politics,' *Journal of Economic Issues* June.

Knight, F. (1921) *Risk, Uncertainty and Profit*, Chicago: University of Chicago Press.

Kolko, G. (1963) *The Triumph of Conservatism: A Reinterpretation of American History, 1900–1916*, Chicago: Quadrangle Books, 1967.

Kotz, D.M. (1987) 'Long Waves and Social Structures of Accumulation: A Critique and Reinterpretation,' *Review of Radical Political Economics*, Winter.

Kotz, D.M., McDonough, T., and Reich, M. (1994) 'Introduction,' in D.M. Kotz, T. McDonough and M. Reich (eds) *Social Structures of Accumulation: The Political Economy of Growth and Crisis*, New York: Cambridge University Press.

Krasner, S. (1983) 'Structural Causes and Regime Consequences: Regimes as Intervening Variables,' in S. Krasner (ed.) *International Regimes*, Ithaca, NY: Cornell University Press.

Kregel, J. A. (1976) 'Economic Methodology in the Face of Uncertainty: The Modeling Methods of Keynes and the post Keynesians,' *Economic Journal* June.

Krueger, A.B. (1993) 'How Have Computers Changed the Wage Structure? Evidence from Micro Data,' *Quarterly Journal of Economics* February.

Krueger, A.O. (1990) 'Free Trade is the Best Policy,' in R.Z. Lawrence and C.L. Schultz (eds) *An American Trade Strategy: Options for the 1990s*, Washington, DC: Brookings Institution.

Krugman, P. (1990) 'Endogenous Innovation, International Trade and Growth,' in P. Krugman (ed.) *Rethinking International Trade*, Cambridge, Mass.: MIT Press.

— (1991) *Geography and Trade*, Cambridge, Mass.: MIT Press, 1993.

— (1994a) 'Stolper–Samuelson and the Victory of Formal Economics,' in A.V. Deardorff and R. M. Stern (eds) *The Stolper–Samuelson Theorem: A Golden Jubilee*, Ann Arbor: University of Michigan Press.

— (1994b) 'Competitiveness: A Dangerous Obsession,' *Foreign Affairs* March/April.

— (1995) 'Dutch Tulips and Emerging Markets,' *Foreign Affairs* July/August.

Krugman, P. and Lawrence, R. (1993) 'Trade, Jobs, and Wages,' National Bureau of Economic Research Working Paper No. 4478.

Lall, S. (1995) 'Industrial Adaptation and Technological Capabilities in Developing Countries,' in T. Killick (ed.) *The Flexible Economy: Courses and Consequences of the Adaptability of National Economies*, London: Routledge.

Landes, D.S. (1998) *The Wealth and Poverty of Nations: Why Some Are Rich and Some Are Poor*, New York: W.W. Norton.

Landreth, H. and Colander, D. C. (1994) *History of Economic Thought*, Boston: Houghton Mifflin.

Lange, O. (1963) 'The Method of Political Economy,' in *Political Economy*, Volume I, 'General Problems,' New York: The Macmillan Company.

Langlois, R.N. and Everett, M.J. (1994) 'What is Evolutionary Economics?' in Lars Magnusson (ed.) *Evolutionary and Neo-Schumpeterian Approaches to Economics*, Dordrecht: Kluwer.

Lave, D. (1993) 'Artificial Worlds and Economics,' *Journal of Evolutionary Economics*

Lawson, T. (1995) 'A Realist Perspective on Contemporary "Economic Theory",' *Journal of Economic Issues* March.

Leamer, E.E. (1983) 'Let's Take the Con out of Econometrics,' *American Economic Review* March.

— (1984) *Sources of International Comparative Advantage: Theory and Evidence*, Cambridge, Mass.: MIT Press.

— (1996) 'Wage Inequality from International Competition and Technological Change: Theory and Country Experience,' *American Economic Review* May.

Lebowitz, M.A. (1976) 'Marx's Falling Rate of Profit: A Dialectical View,' *Canadian Journal of Economics* May.

— (1994) 'Analytical Marxism and the Marxian Theory of Crisis,' *Cambridge Journal of Economics* April.

Leeson, R. (1997) 'The Political Economy of the Inflation–Unemployment Trade-Off,' *History of Political Economy* Spring.

Leijonhufvud, A. (1968) *On Keynesian Economics and the Economics of Keynes: A Study in Monetary Theory*, New York: Oxford University Press.

— (1973) 'Life Among the Econ,' in *Information and Coordination: Essays in Macroeconomic Theory*, New York: Oxford University Press, 1981.

Lerner, M. (ed.) (1948) *The Portable Veblen*, New York: Viking Press.

Levitt, T. (1976) 'Alfred Marshall: Victorian relevance for modern economics,' *Quarterly Journal of Economics*, August.

Levy, F. and Murane, R.J. (1992) 'U.S. Earnings Levels and Earnings Inequality: A Review of Recent Trends and Proposed Explanations,' *Journal of Economic Literature* September.

Lewis, W.A. (1954) 'Economic Development with Unlimited Supplies of Labour,' *Manchester School of Economics and Social Studies* May.

Lie, J. (1993) 'Visualizing the Invisible Hand: The Social Origins of "Market Society" in England, 1550–1750,' *Politics and Society* September.

Liebowitz, S.J. and Margolis, S.E. (1990) 'The fable of the keys,' *Journal of Law and Economics*, April.

— (1994) 'Network Externality: An Uncommon Tragedy,' *Journal of Economic Perspectives*, Spring.

Likikijsomboon, P. (1992) 'The Hegelian dialectic and Marx's *Capital*,' *Cambridge Journal of Economics* December.

Lindbeck, A. (1983) 'The Recent Slowdown of Productivity,' *Economic Journal* March.

— (1994) 'The Welfare State and the Employment Problem,' *American Economics Review* May

Lipietz, A. (1979) 'The Debt Problem, European Integration and the New Phase of World Crisis,' *New Left Review* November–December.

— (1986) 'Behind the Crisis: The Exhaustion of a Regime of Accumulation. A regulation school perspective on some French empirical work,' *Review of Radical Political Economy* Spring and Summer.

— (1992) 'The Regulationist Approach and Capitalist Crisis: an Alternative Compromise for the 1990s,' in M. Dunford and G. Kafkalas (eds) *Cities in the New Europe: The Global/Local Interplay and Spatial Development Strategies*, London: Belhaven.

Lipsey, R.E. and Kravis, I.B. (1985) 'The Competitive Position of US Manufacturing Firms,' *Banco Nazionale del Lavorno Quarterly Review* June.

Loasby, B.J. (1991) *Equilibrium and Evolution: An Exploration of Connecting Principles in Economics*, Manchester: Manchester University Press.

Lucas, Jr., R.E. (1973) 'Some International Evidence on Output–Inflation Tradeoffs,' *American Economic Review* June.

— (1980) 'Methods and Problems in Business Cycle Theory,' *Journal of Money Credit and Banking* pt 2.

— (1990) 'Why Doesn't Capital Flow from Rich to Poor Countries?' *American Economics Associations Papers and Proceedings* May.

Lucas, Jr., R.E. and Sargent, T. (1989) 'Rational Expectations and Economic Practice,' in R.J. Barro (ed.) *Modern Business Cycle Theory*, Cambridge, Mass.: Harvard University Press.

Lux, T. (1995) 'Herd Behaviour, Bubbles and Crashes,' *Economic Journal*, July.

McCloskey, D.N. (1985) *The Rhetoric of Economics*, Madison: University of Wisconsin Press.

— (1993) 'Some Consequences of a Conjective Economics,' in M.A. Ferber and J.A. Nelson (eds) *Beyond Economic Man: Feminist Theory in Economics*, Chicago: University of Chicago Press.

— (1997) 'Other Things Equal: One Small Step for Gary,' *Eastern Economic Journal* Winter.

McCollum, B.T. (1979) 'The Current State of the Policy Ineffectiveness Proposition,' *American Economic Association* May.

— (1986) 'The Development of Keynesian Macroeconomics,' *Papers and Proceedings of the American Economic Association* May.

Machlup, F. (1955) 'The Problem of Verification in Economics,' *Southern Economic Journal* (22).

— (1983) 'The Rationality of "Rational Expectations",' *Kredit und Kapital* 16: 2.

— (1991) '"Truth" and "Discourse" in the Social Construction of Economic Reality: An Essay on the Relation of Knowledge to Socioeconomic Policy,' *Journal of Post Keynesian Economics*,

McPherson, M. (1984) 'Limits to Self-Seeking: The Role of Morality in Economic Life,' in D.C. Colander (ed.) *Neoclassical Political Economy: The Analysis of Rent-Seeking and DUP Activities*, Cambridge: Ballinger.

McWilliams-Tullberg, R. (1975) 'Marshall's "tendency to socialism",' *History of Political Economy* Spring.

Maddison, A. (1987) 'Growth and Slowdown in Advanced Capitalist Economies: Techniques of Quantitative Assessment,' *Journal of Economic Literature* June.

— (1994) 'Explaining the Economic Performance of Nations, 1820–1989,' in W.J. Baumol, R.R. Nelson, and E.N. Wolfe (eds) *Convergence of Productivity: Cross-national Studies and Historical Evidence*, New York: Oxford University Press.

Magdoff, H. (1992) 'Globalization – To What End?' Part II *Monthly Review* March.

Maloney, J. (1985) *Marshall, Orthodoxy and the Profession of Economics*, Cambridge: Cambridge University Press.

Malthus, T.R. (1798) *An Essay on the Principle of Population, as it Affects the Future Improvement of Society, with Remarks on the Speculations of Mr. Godwin, M. Condorcet, and other Writers* in *An Essay on the Principle of Population and a Summary View of the Principles of Population*, A. Flew (ed.) Baltimore: Penguin.

— (1836) *Principles of Political Economy* New York: Augustus M. Kelley, 1964.

Mandel, E. (1990) 'Karl Marx,' in J. Eatwell, M. Milgate and P. Newman (eds) *The New Palgrave: Marxian Economics*, New York: W.W. Norton.

Maneschi, A. (1992) 'Ricardo's international trade theory: beyond the comparative cost example,' *Cambridge Journal of Economics* December.

Mankiw, N.G. (1985) 'Small Menu Changes and Large Business Cycles: A Macroeconomic Model,' *Quarterly Journal of Economics*, May.

— (1989) 'Real Business Cycles: A New Keynesian Perspective,' *Journal of Economic Perspectives* Summer.

— (1995) 'The Growth of Nations,' *Brooking Papers on Economic Activity* 1.

Mankiw, N.G., Romer, D., (eds) (1991a) *New Keynesian Economics*, Two Volumes, Cambridge, Mass.: MIT Press.

Mankiw, N.G. and Romer, D. (1991b) 'Introduction,' to N.G. Mankiw and D. Romer, Volume 1, *Coordination Failures and Real Rigidities*, Cambridge, Mass.: MIT Press.

Mankiw, N.G., Romer, D., and Weil, D. (1992) 'A Contribution to the Empirics of Economic Growth,' *Quarterly Journal of Economics* May.

Markusen, J.R. (1995) 'The Boundaries of Multinational Enterprises and the Theory of International Trade,' *Journal of Economic Perspectives* Spring.

Marshall, A. (1873) 'The Future of the Working Classes,' in A.C. Pigou (ed.) *Memorials of Alfred Marshall*, London: Macmillan 1925.

— (1887) 'Preface,' in *Industrial Peace: Its Advantages, Methods and Difficulties*.

— (1890) *Principles of Economics*, Eighth Edition, London: Macmillan, 1920.

— (1895) *Principles of Economics*, Third Edition, London: Macmillan.

— (1919) *Industry and Trade: A Study of Industrial Technique and Business Organization*, London: Macmillan.

Marshall, G. (1994) 'Political Economy,' *The Concise Oxford Dictionary of Sociology*, Oxford: Oxford University Press.

Marshall, R.F. (1987) *Unheard Voices*, New York: Basic Books.

— (1993) 'Commons, Veblen and Other Economists,' *Journal of Economic Issues* June.

Martin, R. (1994) 'Stateless Monies, Global Financial Integration and National Economic Autonomy: The End of Geography?' in S. Corbridge, N. Thrift, and R. Martin (eds) *Money, Power and Space*, Oxford: Blackwell.

Marx, K. (1844) *Economic and Philosophical Manuscripts of 1844*, New York: International Publishers, 1967.

— (1846–7) *The Poverty of Philosophy*, New York: International Publishers, 1973.

— (1850–60) *Theories of Surplus Value* Part II, Moscow: Progress Publishers, 1968.

— (1857) *Grundrisse, Foundation of the Critique of Political Economy*, London: Penguin Books, 1973.

— (1859) *A Contribution to the Critique of Political Economy*, London: Lawrence and Wishart, 1971.

— (1867) *Capital: A Critique of Political Economy; Volume I*, New York: Vintage Books, 1977.

— (1894) *Capital: A Critique of Political Economy; Volume III*, Moscow: Progress Publishers.

Marx, K. and Engels, F. (1846) *The German Ideology*, New York: International Publishers, 1970.

Mayer, T. (1993) *Truth versus Precision in Economics*, Aldershot: Edward Elgar.

— (1994) 'Monetarism and Its Rhetoric,' in P.A. Klein (ed.) *The Role of Economic Theory*, Boston: Kluwer.

Mayhew, A. (1987) 'The Beginnings of Institutionalism,' *Journal of Economic Issues* September.

Meek, R.L. (1967) 'The Scottish Contribution to Marxist Sociology,' in *Economics and Ideology and Other Essays: Studies in the Development of Economic Thought*, London: Chapman & Hall.

— (1972) 'Marginalism and Marxism,' *History of Political Economy* Fall

— (1973) *Studies in the Labour Theory of Value*, Second Edition, London: Lawrence & Wishart.

— (1974) 'Value in the History of Economic Thought,' *History of Political Economy* Fall.

Meek, D., Raphael, D.D., and Stein, P.G. (eds) (1978) 'Introduction,' Adam Smith *Lectures on Jurisprudence*, Oxford: Clarendon Press.

Melton, J.V.H. (1991) 'The Emergence of "Society" in Eighteenth- and Nineteenth-Century Germany,' in P. J. Corfield (ed.) *Language, History and Class*, Oxford: Blackwell.

Mendell. M. (1990) 'Karl Polanyi and Feasible Socialism,' in K. Polanyi-Levitt (ed.) *The Life and Work of Karl Polanyi*, Montreal: Black Rose Books.

Michel, L. and Voos, P.B. (1992) 'Unions and American Economic Competitiveness,' in L. Michel and P.B. Voos (eds) *Unions and Competitiveness*, Armonk, NY: M.E. Sharpe.

Michie, J. and Wilkinson, F. (1994) 'The Growth of Unemployment in the 1980s,' in J. Michie and J. Grieve Smith (eds) *Unemployment in Europe*, London: Academic Press.

Milberg, W. and Elmslie, B. (1997) 'Free Trade and International Labor Standards,' *New Labor Forum* Fall.

Milgate, M. (1982) *Capital and Employment: A Study of Keynes's Economics*, London: Academic Press.

Mill, J.S. (1836) 'On the Definition of Political Economy; and on the Method of Investigation Proper to It,' *London and Westminster Review* October.

— (1848) *Principles of Political Economy*, W.J. Ashley (ed.) New York: Longmans Green and Co., 1923.

Minsky, H.P. (1975) *John Maynard Keynes*, New York: Columbia University Press.

— (1986) *Stabilizing an Unstable Economy*, New Haven: Yale University Press.

— (1996) 'Uncertainty, and the Institutional Structure of Capitalist Economies,' *Journal of Economic Issues* June.

Mirowski, P. (1984) 'Physics and the "marginal revolution",' *Cambridge Journal of Economics* December.

— (1989) *More Heat than Light: Economics as Social Physics,* Cambridge: Cambridge University Press.

— (1994) 'Doing What Comes Naturally: Four Metanaratives on What Metaphors Are For,' in P. Mirowski (ed.) *Natural Images in Economic Thought: Markets Read in Tooth and Claw,* New York: Cambridge University Press.

Mirowski, P. and Cook, P. (1990) 'Walras' "Economics and Mechanics": Translation, Commentary, Context,' in W.J. Samuels (ed.) *Economics as Discourse: An Analysis of the Language of Economics,* Boston: Kluwer Academic Publishers.

Mitchell, W.C. (1913) *Business Cycles,* Berkeley: University of California Press.

Modigliani, F. (1977) 'The Monitarist Controversy or Should We Foresake Stabilization Policies?' *American Economic Review* March.

Moggridge, D.E. (1992) *Maynard Keynes: An Economist's Biography,* London: Routledge.

Moore, D.C. (1994) 'Feminist accounting theory as a critique of what's "natural" in economics,' in P. Mirowski (ed.) *Natural Images in Economic Thought: Markets Read in Tooth and Claw,* New York: Cambridge University Press.

Munch, R. (1987) 'Parsonian Theory Today: In Search of a New Synthesis,' in A. Giddens and J. H. Turner (eds) *Social Theory Today,* Stanford: Stanford University Press.

Murphy, C.N. (1994) *International Organization and Industrial Change: Global Governance since 1850,* New York: Oxford University Press.

Murrell, P. (1995) 'The Transition According to Cambridge, Mass.' *Journal of Economic Literature* March.

Mussa, M. (1974) 'Tariffs and the Distribution of Income: The Importance of Factor Specificity, Substitutability, and Intensity in the Short and Long Run,' *Journal of Political Economy* November.

Myrdal, G. (1939) *Monetary Equilibrium,* London: Hodge & Co.

Neary, J.P. (1978) 'Short-Run Capital Specificity and the Pure Theory of International Trade,' *Economic Journal* September.

Nelson, J.A. (1995) 'Feminism and Economics,' *Journal of Economic Perspectives* Spring.

Nelson, R.R. (1994) 'Evolutionary Theorizing about Economic Change,' in N.J. Smelser and R. Swedberg (eds) *The Handbook of Economic Sociology,* Princeton: Princeton University Press.

— (1995) 'Recent Evolutionary Theorizing About Economic Change,' *Journal of Economic Literature* March.

Nelson, R.R. and Winter, S.G. (1974) 'Neoclassical Versus Evolutionary Theories of Economic Growth: Critique and Perspective,' *Economic Journal,* December.

— (1982) *An Evolutionary Theory of Economic Change,* Cambridge: Harvard University Press.

Nelson, R.R. and Wright, G. (1992) 'The Rise and Fall of American Technological Leadership: The Postwar Era in Historical Perspective,' *Journal of Economic Literature* December.

Nickell, S. (1997) 'Unemployment and Labor Market Rigidities: Europe versus North America,' *Journal of Economic Perspectives* Summer.

Niggle, C.J. (1986) 'Financial Innovation and the Distinction Between Financial and Industrial Capital,' *Journal of Economic Issues* June.

Noel, A. (1987) 'Accumulation, Regulation and Social Change: An Essay on French Political Economy,' *International Organization* Spring.

North, D.C. (1981) *Structure and Change in Economic History*, New York: W.W. Norton.
— (1995a) 'Foreword,' in T. Killick (ed.) *The Flexible Economy: Causes and Consequences of the Adaptability of National Economies*, London: Routledge.
— (1995b) 'Review of Christina Bicchieri, *Rationality and Coordination*,' *Journal of Economic Literature* June.
North, D.C. and Thomas, R.P. (1973) *The Rise of the Western World*, Cambridge: Cambridge University Press.
Notermans, T. (1993) 'The Abdication from National Policy Autonomy: Why the Macroeconomic Policy Regime Has Been So Unfavorable to Labor,' *Politics & Society* June.
Novak, M.N. (1962) *Economics and the Fiction of Daniel Defoe*, Berkeley: University of California Press.
O'Brien, D.P. (1976) 'The Longevity of Adam Smith's Vision: Paradigms, Research Programmes, and Falsifiability in the History of Economic Thought,' *Scottish Journal of Political Economy* June.
Ocampo, J.A. (1986) 'New Developments in Trade Theory and LDCs,' *Journal of Development Economics* June.
O'Donnell, R.M. (1990) 'Keynes on Mathematics: Philosophical Foundations and Economic Applications,' *Cambridge Journal of Economics* March.
— (1991) *Keynes as Philosopher–Economist*, New York: St Martin's Press.
Ohlin, B. (1938) 'Economic Progress in Sweden,' *Annals of the American Academy of Political and Social Science* (197).
Okun, A.M. (1970) *The Political Economy of Prosperity*, Washington, DC: Brookings Institution.
Ollman, B. (1976) *Alienation: Marx's Conception of Man in Capitalist Society*, Second Edition, Cambridge: Cambridge University Press.
Olson, Jr., M. (1982) *The Rise and Decline of Nations*, New Haven: Yale University Press.
— (1996) 'Big Bills Left on the Sidewalk: Why Some Nations are Rich and Others Poor,' *Journal of Economic Perspectives* Spring.
Olson, R. (1993) *The Emergence of the Social Sciences 1642–1792*, New York: Twayne Publishers.
Ormerod, P. (1994) 'On Inflation and Unemployment,' in J. Michie and J. Grieve Smith (eds) *Unemployment in Europe*, London: Academic Press.
Osberg, L., Apostle, R., and Clairmont, D. (1986) 'The Incidence and Duration of Individual Unemployment: Supply Side or Demand Side?' *Cambridge Journal of Economics* March.
Osterman, P. (1994) 'How Common is Workplace Transformation and Who Adopts It?' *Industrial and Labor Relations Review* January.
Ottati, G.D. (1994) 'Trust, interlinking transactions and credit in the industrial district,' *Cambridge Journal of Economics* December.
Panic, M. (1995) 'The Bretton Woods System: Concept and Practice,' in J. Michie and J. Grieve Smith (eds) *Managing the Global Economy*, Oxford: Oxford University Press.
Papineau, D. (1998) 'Don't Know Much Biology,' *New York Times Book Review* January 18.
Parsons, T. (1932) 'Economics and Sociology: Marshall in Relation to the Thought of His Time,' *Quarterly Journal of Economics* February.
Passell, P. (1995) 'A Nobel Award to a University of Chicago Economist, Yet Again,' *New York Times*, October 11.
Patinkin, D. (1976) *Keynes' Monetary Thought: A Study of its Development*, Durham: Duke University Press.
Pearce, K.A. and Hoover, K.D. (1995) 'After the Revolution: Paul A. Samuelson and the Textbook Keynesian Model,' in A.F. Cottrell and M.S. Lawlor (eds) *New Perspectives on Keynes*, Durham: Duke University Press.
Peck, J. (1996) *Work Place: The Social Regulation of Labor Markets*, New York: Guilford Press.

Peck, J. and Tickell, A. (1994) 'Searching for a New Institutional Fix: The After Fordist Crisis and the Global–Local Disorder,' in A. Amin (ed.) *Post-Fordism: A Reader*, Oxford: Blackwell.

Pencavel, J. (1986) 'Labor Supply of Men: A Survey,' in O. Ashenfelter and R. Layard (eds) *Handbook of Labor Economics*.

Persky, J. (1995) 'The Ethology of *Homo Economicus*,' *Journal of Economic Perspectives* Spring.

Peterson, W.C. (1994) *Silent Depression*, New York: W.W. Norton.

Phelps, E.S. (1967) 'Phillips Curves, Expectations of Inflation and Optimal Unemployment over Time,' *Economica* August.

— (1970) *Macroeconomic Foundations of Employment and Inflation Theory*, New York: Norton.

— (1994) 'Low Wage Employment Subsidies versus the Welfare State,' *American Economic Association* May.

— (1995) 'The Structuralist Theory of Unemployment,' *American Economic Association* May.

Phelps, E.S. in collaboration with Hoon, H.T., Kanaginis, G., and Zoega, G. (1994) *Structural Slumps: The Modern Equilibrium Theory of Unemployment, Interest and Assets*, Cambridge, Mass.:x Harvard University Press.

Phillips, A.W.H. (1950) 'Mechanical Models in Economic Dynamics,' *Economica* August.

— (1958) 'The Relation Between Unemployment and the Rate of Change of Money Wages in the United Kingdom, 1861–1957,' *Economica* November.

Pigou, A.C. (ed.) (1925) *Memorials of Alfred Marshall*, London: Macmillan.

Piori, M.J. and Sabel, C.F. (1984) *The Second Industrial Divide: Possibilities for Prosperity*, New York: Basic Books.

Plosser, C.I. (1992) 'The Search for Growth,' *Policies for Long-Run Economic Growth*, Kansas City: Federal Reserve Bank of Kansas City.

Polanyi, K. (1944) *The Great Transformation: The Political and Economic Origins of Our Time*, Boston: Beacon Press.

— (1971) 'Carl Menger's Two Meanings of "Economic",' in G. Dalton (ed.) *Studies in Economic Anthropology*, Washington, DC: American Anthropological Association.

— (1977) *The Livelihood of Man* edited by H.E. Pearson, New York: Academic Press.

Polanyi-Levitt, K. (1990) *The Life and Work of Karl Polanyi*, Montreal: Black Rose Books.

Porter, M.E. (1990) *The Competitiveness of Nations*, New York: Free Press.

Putnam, R.D. with Leonard, R., and Nanetti, R.Y. (1993) *Making Democracy Work: Civic Traditions in Modern Italy*, Princeton: Princeton University Press.

Putterman, L. (ed.) (1986) *The Economic Nature of the Firm: A Reader*, Cambridge: Cambridge University Press.

Rabin, M. (1998) 'Pyschology and Economics,' *Journal of Economic Literature* March.

Radice, H. (1988) 'Keynes and the Policy of Practical Protection,' in J. Hillard (ed.) *J.M. Keynes in Retrospect: The Legacy of the Keynesian Revolution*, Aldershot: Edward Elgar.

Ramstad, Y. (1996) 'Is a Transaction a Transaction?' *Journal of Economic Issues* June.

Rashid, S. (1986) 'Adam Smith and the Division of Labour: A Historical View,' *Scottish Journal of Political Economy* August.

Rasmussen, L. (1993) *Moral Fragments and Moral Community*, Minneapolis: Fortress Press.

Rebitzer, J.B. (1993) 'Radical Political Economy and the Economics of Labor Markets,' *Journal of Economic Literature* September.

Reder, M.W. (1982) 'Chicago Economics: Permanence and Change,' *Journal of Economic Literature* March.

Redman, D.A. (1989) *Economic Methodology; A Bibliography with Reference to Works in the Philosophy of Science, 1860–1988*, New York: Greenwood Press.

— (1991) *Economics and the Philosophy of Science*, New York: Oxford University Press.

— (1992) *A Reader's Guide to Rational Expectations, a Survey and Comprehensive Annotated Bibliography*, Aldershot: Edward Elgar.

Reynolds, L.G. (1951) *The Structure of Labor Markets: Wages and Labor Mobility in Theory and Practice*, New York: Harper.

Ricardo, D. (1817) *The Principles of Political Economy and Taxation*, London: Dent, 1962.

Richardson, J.D. (1995) 'Income Inequality and Trade: How to Think and What to Conclude,' *Journal of Economic Perspectives* Summer.

Rima, I.H. (1986) *Development of Economic Analysis*, Homewood, Ill.: Irwin.

— (ed.) (1991) *The Joan Robinson Legacy* Armonk, NY: M.E. Sharpe.

Robertson, D. (1949) *Banking Policy and the Price Level*, New York: Augustus Kelley.

Robertson, H.M. and Taylor, W.L. (1957) 'Adam Smith's Approach to the Theory of Value,' *Economic Journal* June.

Robins, L. (1932) *An Essay on the Nature and Significance of Economic Science*, New York: St. Martin's Press, 1962.

— (1952) *The Theory of Economic Policy in English Classical Political Economy*, London: Macmillan.

— (1979) 'On Latsis's method and appraisal in economics: a review essay,' *Journal of Economic Literature* September.

— (1981) 'Economics and Political Economy,' *American Economic Association* May.

Robinson, E.A.G. (1946) 'John Maynard Keynes 1883–1946,' in R. Lekachman (ed.) *Keynes' General Theory: Report of Three Decades*, New York: St Martin's Press.

— (1964) 'Could There Have Been a "General Theory" Without Keynes?' in R. Lekachman (ed.) *Keynes' General Theory: Report of Three Decades*, New York: St. Martin's Press.

Robinson, J. (1937) 'Disguised Unemployment,' in *Essays in the Theory of Unemployment*, London: Macmillan.

— (1962) *Economic Philosophy*, London: Pelican Books, 1964.

— (1967) *Economics: An Awkward Corner*, New York: Pantheon Books.

— (1973) 'What has become of the Keynesian Revolution,' in J. Robinson (ed.) *After Keynes*, Oxford: Basil Blackwell.

— (1976) 'Michael Kalecki: A Neglected Prophet,' *The New York Review of Books* March 4.

— (1977) 'What Are the Questions?' *Journal of Economic Literature* December

— (1978) 'Morality and Economics,' *Challenge* March/April.

— (1979) *Collected Papers*, Volume V, Oxford: Basil Blackwell.

— (1980) 'Time in Economic Theory,' *Kyklos*, 33; in M.C. Sawyers (ed.) *Post-Keynesian Economics*, Aldershot: Edward Elgar, 1988.

Rodrik, D. (1994) 'King Kong Meets Godzilla: The World Bank and *The East Asian Miracle*,' in *Miracle or Design? Lessons From the East Asian Experience*, Washington, DC: Overseas Development Council.

— (1996) 'Why do More Open Economies Have Bigger Governments?' National Bureau of Economic Research, Working Paper 5537.

— (1997) *Has Globalization Gone too Far?*, Washington, DC: Institute for International Economics.

Roemer, J. (1986) *Value, Exploitation, and Class*, New York: Harwood Academic Publishers.

— (1988) *Free to Lose: An Introduction to Marxist Economic Philosophy*, Cambridge: Harvard University Press.

Rogers, C. (1989) *Money, Interest and Capital: A Study in the Foundations of Monetary Theory*, Cambridge: Cambridge University Press.

Rogin, L. (1956) *The Meaning and Validity of Economic Theory: A Historical Approach*, New York: Harper.

Romer, P.M. (1986) 'Increasing Returns and Long Run Growth,' *Journal of Political Economy* October.
— (1987) 'Growth Based on Increasing Returns Due to Specialization,' *American Economic Association, Papers and Proceedings* May.
— (1994) 'The Origins of Endogenous Growth,' *Journal of Economic Perspectives* Winter.
— (1995) 'Comments,' *Brookings Papers on Economic Activity* 1.
— (1996) 'Why, Indeed, in America? Theory, History, and the Origins of Modern Economic Growth,' *American Economic Review* May.
Rose, S. (1998) 'Armchair Philosophers,' Letters, *New York Times Book Review* February 15.
Rosen, S. (1997) 'Austrian and Neoclassical Economics: Any Gains From Trade?' *Journal of Economic Perspectives* Fall.
Rosenberg, N. (1960) 'Some Institutional Aspects of the *Wealth of Nations*,' *Journal of Political Economy* December.
— (1979) 'Adam Smith and Laissez-Faire Revisited,' in G. O'Driscoll (ed.) *Adam Smith and Modern Political Economy*, Ames, Iowa: Iowa State University Press.
— (1994) 'Joseph Schumpeter: Radical Economist,' *Exploring the Black Box: Technology, Economics, and History*, Cambridge: Cambridge University Press.
Ross, D. (1991) *The Origins of American Social Science*, Cambridge: Cambridge University Press.
Ross, G. (1993) 'The European Community and Social Policy: Regional Blocs and a Humane Social Order,' *Studies in Political Economy* Spring.
Rostow, W.W. (1990) *Theorists of Economic Growth from David Hume to the Present*, New York: Oxford University Press.
Roth, A.E. (1995) 'Bargaining Experiments,' in J.H. Kagel and A. Roth (eds) *The Handbook of Experimental Economics*, Princeton: Princeton University Press.
Rothschild, E. (1992) 'Adam Smith and conservative economics,' *Economic History Review* February.
— (1994) 'Adam Smith and the Invisible Hand,' *Papers and Proceedings of the American Economic Association* May.
Routh, G. (1959) 'The Relation Between Unemployment and the Rate of Change of Money Wages: A Comment,' *Economica* November.
Roxborough, I. (1984) 'Unity and Diversity in Latin American History,' *Journal of Latin American Studies* May.
Ruggie, J. (1982) 'International Regimes, Transactions, and Change: Embedded Liberalism in the Postwar Economic Order,' *International Organization* 36.
Rutherford, M. (1994) *Institutions in Economics: The Old and the New Institutionalism*, Cambridge: Cambridge University Press.
Sachs, J.D. and Shatz, H.J. (1994) 'Trade and Jobs in US Manufacturing,' *Brookings Papers on Economic Activity* 1.
Sachs, J.D. and Warner, A. (1995) 'Economic Reform and the Process of Global Integration,' *Brookings Papers on Economic Analysis* 1.
Samuels, W.J. (1972) 'The Scope of Economics Historically Considered,' *Land Economics* August.
— (1974) *Pareto on Policy*, Amsterdam: Elsevier Scientific Publishing Company.
— (1980) 'Economics as a Science and its Relation to Policy: The Example of Free Trade,' *Journal of Economic Issues* March.
— (1985) 'A Critique of *Capitalism, Socialism and Democracy*,' in R.D. Coe and C.K. Wilbur (eds) *Capitalism and Democracy: Schumpeter Revisited*, South Bend: University of Notre Dame Press.
— (1992) 'Machlup on Knowledge: Science, Subjectivism and the Social Nature of Knowledge,' *Essays on Methodology and Discourse in Economics*, Houndsmills, England: Macmillan Press.

— (1997) 'The Work of Historians of Economic Thought,' *Research in the History of Economic Thought and Methodology*, Volume 15.

Samuelson, P.A. (1962) 'Parable and Realism in Capital Theory: The Surrogate Production Function,' *Review of Economic Studies*, June.

—(1966) 'A Summing Up,' *Quarterly Journal of Economics* November.

— (1967) *Economics*, New York: McGraw-Hill.

— (1969) 'Classical and Neoclassical Theory,' in R.W. Clower (ed.) *Monetary Theory*, Harmondsworth: Penguin.

— (1978) 'The Canonical Classical Model of Political Economy,' *Journal of Economic Literature* December.

— (1981) 'Schumpeter's *Capitalism, Socialism and Democracy*,' in A. Heertje (ed.) *Schumpeter's Vision*, New York: Praeger.

— (1987) 'How Economics Has Changed,' *Journal of Economic Education* Spring.

— (1988) 'Out of the Closet: A Program for the Whig History of Science,' *History of Economics Society Bulletin*; in N. DeMarchi and M. Blaug (eds) *Appraising Economic Theories: Studies in the Methodology of Research Programmes* Aldershot: Edward Elgar, 1991.

— (1992) 'The Overdue Recovery of Adam Smith's Reputation as an Economic Theorist,' in M. Fry (ed.) *Adam Smith's Legacy: His Place in the Development of Modern Economics*, London: Routledge.

— (1993) 'My Life Philosophy: Policy Credos and Working Ways,' in M. Szenberg (ed.) *Eminent Economists: Their Live Philosophies*, Cambridge: Cambridge University Press.

— (1994) 'The Classical Classical Fallacy,' *Journal of Economic Literature* June.

Samuelson, P.A. and Solow, R.M. (1960) 'Analytical Aspects of Anti-Inflationary Policy,' *American Economic Review, Papers and Proceedings* May.

Sardoni, C. (1992) 'Interpretations of Kalecki,' paper presented at the conference on 'Employment, Distribution and Markets,' Jerome Levy Institute, September.

Sargent, T.J. (1976) 'Rational Expectations and the Theory of Economic Policy,' *Journal of Monetary Economics* April.

— (1979) *Macroeconomic Theory*, New York: Academic Press.

— (1993) *Bounded Rationality in Macroeconomics*, Oxford: Clarendon Press.

Sargent, T.J. and Wallace, N. (1976) 'Rational Expectations and the Theory of Economic Policy,' *Journal of Monetary Economics* April.

Sattinger, M. (1993) 'What the dump truck brings,' *Journal of Economic Literature* June.

Say, J.B. (1821) *A Treatise on Political Economy of the Production, Distribution, and Consumption of Wealth*, trans. from the 4th ed. (Lippincott, 1857).

Sayer, A. (1995) *Radical Political Economy: A Critique*, Oxford: Blackwell.

Schor, J. (1992) 'Introduction,' in T. Banuri and J.B. Schor (eds) *Financial Openness and National Autonomy; Opportunities and Constraints*, Oxford: Clarendon Press.

Schumpeter, J. (1918) 'The crisis of the tax state,' in A Peacock (ed.) *International Economic Papers*, New York: Macmillan.

— (1939) *Business Cycles: A Theoretical–Historical and Statistical Analysis of the Capitalist Process*, , Volume I, New York: McGraw-Hill.

— (1942) *Capitalism, Socialism, and Democracy*, New York: Harper & Brothers.

— (1947) 'John Maynard Keynes, 1883–1946,' reprinted in S.E. Harris (ed.) *The New Economics: Keynes' Influence on Theory and Public Policy*, New York: Alfred A. Knopf.

— (1954) *History of Economic Analysis*, New York: Oxford University Press.

— (1961) *The Theory of Economic Development*, Oxford: Oxford University Press.

— (1962) *Capitalism, Socialism and Democracy*, Third Edition, New York: Harper & Row.

— (1965) *Ten Great Economists; from Marx to Keynes*, New York: Oxford University Press.

— (1991) *The Economics and Sociology of Capitalism* edited by Richard Swedberg, Princeton: Princeton University Press.

Schwartz, J. (1977) 'Introduction,' in *The Subtle Anatomy of Capitalism*, Santa Monica, Calif.: Goodyear Publishing Company.

Scott, A.J. (1988) *New Industrial Spaces: Flexible Production Organization and Regional Development in North America and Western Europe*, London: Pion.

Screpanti, E. and Zamagni, S. (1993) *An Outline of the History of Economic Thought*, Oxford: Clarendon Press.

Seidel, M. (1991) *Robinson Crusoe: Island Myths and the Novel*, Boston: Thayne Publishers.

Sen, A. (1977) 'Rational Fools: A Critique of the Behavioral Foundations of Economic Theory,' *Philosophy and Public Affairs*, in *Choice, Welfare and Measurement*, Cambridge, Mass.: MIT Press, 1982.

— (1995) 'Rationality and Social Choice,' *American Economic Review* March.

Sengenberger, W. and Wilkinson, F. (1995) 'Globalization and Labour Standards,' in J. Michie and J. Grieve Smith (eds) *Managing the Global Economy*, Oxford: Oxford University Press.

Shackle, G.L.S. (1967) *The Years of High Theory: Invention and Tradition in Economic Thought 1926–1939*, Cambridge: Cambridge University Press.

Shionoya, Y. (1991) 'Schumpeter on Schmoller and Weber: A Methodology of Economic Sociology,' *History of Political Economy* Summer.

Shleifer, A. and Summers, L.H. (1987) 'Breach of Trust in Hostile Takeovers,' National Bureau of Economic Research, Working Paper #2342, August.

Shleifer, A. and Vishny, R.W. (1987) 'Management Buyouts as a Response to Market Pressure,' in A.J. Auerbach (ed.) *Mergers and Acquisitions*, Chicago: University of Chicago Press.

Shove, G.F. (1942) 'Marshall's *Principles* in Economic Theory,' *Economic Journal* December.

Simon, H.A. (1984) 'On the Behavioral and Rational Foundations of Economic Dynamics,' *Journal of Economic Behavior and Organization* (5).

Singer, H.W. (1994) 'Rethinking Bretton Woods – From a Historical Perspective,' Institute for Development Studies, University of Sussex, August.

Skidelsky, R. (1983) *John Maynard Keynes; Volume I; Hopes Betrayed, 1883–1920*, New York: Elizabeth Sifton Books, Viking, 1986.

— (1991) 'Keynes's Philosophy of Practice and Economic Policy,' in R.M. O'Donnell (ed.) *Keynes as Philosopher–Economist*, New York: St Martin's Press.

— (1994) *John Maynard Keynes: Volume Two: The Economist as Saviour, 1920–1937*, New York: Allen Lane, Penguin Press.

Sklar, M.J. (1988) *The Corporate Restructuring of American Capitalism, 1890–1916: The Market, the Law, and Politics*, New York: Cambridge University Press.

Small, A.W. (1972) 'Preface,' in *Adam Smith and Modern Sociology: A Study of the Methodology of the Social Sciences*, Clifton, NJ: Augustus M. Kelley.

Smelser, N.J. and Swedberg, R. (eds) (1994) *The Handbook of Economic Sociology*, Princeton: Princeton University Press.

Smith, A. (1748–51) *Lectures on Rhetoric and Belles Lettres*, J.C. Bryce (ed.), Oxford: Clarendon Press, 1985.

— (1759) *The Theory of Moral Sentiments*, D.D. Raphael and A.L. Macfie (eds), Indianapolis, Ind.: Liberty Classics, 1982.

— (1762–63) *Lectures on Jurisprudence*, R.L. Meek, D.D. Raphael and P.G. Stein (eds), Oxford: Clarendon Press, 1978.

— (1776) *An Inquiry into the Nature and Causes of the Wealth of Nations*, Edwin Cannan (ed.), New York: Random House, 1937.

— (1795) *Essays on Philosophical Subjects*, W.P.D. Wightman and J.C. Bryce (eds), Oxford: Clarendon Press, 1980.

— (1976) *The Theory of Moral Sentiments*, D.D. Raphael and A.L. Macfie (eds), Oxford: Clardendon Press.

Snow, C.P. (1959) *The Two Cultures: And a Second Look; An Expanded Version of the Two Cultures and the Scientific Revolution*, London: Cambridge University Press.

Snowdon, B., Vane, H., and Wynarczyk, P. (1994) *A Modern Guide to Macroeconomics: An Introduction to Competing Schools of Thought*, Aldershot: Edward Elgar.

So, A.Y. (1990) *Social Change and Development: Modernization, Dependency, and World-Systems Theories*, Newbury Park: Sage.

Solow, R.M. (1956) 'A Contribution to the Theory of Economic Growth,' *Quarterly Journal of Economics* February.

— (1986) 'What is a Nice Girl Like You Doing in a Place Like This: Macroeconomics after Fifty Years,' *Eastern Economic Journal* No. 3, p. 191.

— (1990) *The Labor Market as a Social Institution*, Cambridge, Mass.: Basil Blackwell.

Somers, M.R. (1990) 'Karl Polanyi's Intellectual Legacy,' in K. Polanyi-Levitt (ed.) *The Life and Work of Karl Polanyi*, Montreal: Black Rose Books.

Sowell, T. (1994) *Classical Economics Reconsidered*, Princeton: Princeton University Press.

Sraffa, P. (1960) *Production of Commodities by Means of Commodities: Prelude to a Critique of Economic Theory*, Cambridge: Cambridge University Press.

Srinivasan, T.N. (1989) 'Recent Theories of Imperfect Competition and International Trade: Any Implications for Development Strategy?' *Indian Economic Review* January–June.

Stabile, D.R. (1995) 'Pigou's Influence on Clark: Work and Welfare,' *Journal of Economic Issues* December.

Stadler, G.W. (1994) 'Real Business Cycles,' *Journal of Economic Literature* December.

Staiger, D., Stock, J.H., and Watson, M.V. (1997) 'The NAIRU, Unemployment and Monetary Policy,' *Journal of Economic Perspectives* Winter.

Stark, W. (1994) *History and Historians of Political Economy*, C.M.A. Clark (ed.), New Brunswick: Transaction Publications.

Stern, M. (1991) 'The Determinants of Growth,' *Economic Journal* January.

Stigler, G.J. (1941) *Production and Distribution Theories*, New York: Macmillan.

— (1965) *Essays in the History of Economics*, Chicago: University of Chicago Press.

— (1966) *The Theory of Price*, New York: Macmillan.

— (1971) 'Smith's Travels on the Ship of State, *History of Political Economy* Fall.

— (1976) 'The Success and Failures of Professor Smith,' *Journal of Political Economy* December.

— (1992) 'Law or Economics,' *Journal of Law and Economics* October.

Stiglitz, J.E. (1988) 'Economics of Organization, Information, and Development,' in H. Chenery and T.N. Srinivasan (eds) *Handbook of Development Economics*, Volume I, Amsterdam: North-Holland.

Stolper, W. (1997) 'Evolutionary Economics,' *The Economist* January 11.

Storper, M. (1990) 'Industrialization and the Regional Question in the Third World: Lessons of Post-imperialism; Prospects of Post-Fordism,' *International Journal of Urban and Regional Research* September.

Strober, M.H. (1994) 'Rethinking Economics Through a Feminist Lens,' *Papers and Proceedings of the American Economic Association* May

Stubbs, R. and Underhill, G.R.D. (eds) (1994) *Political Economy and the Global Order*, Toronto: McClellan & Stewart.

Summers, L. (1991) 'The Scientific Illusion in Empirical Macroeconomics,' *Scandinavian Journal of Economics* (93:2).

Swan, T.W. (1956) 'Economic Growth and Capital Accumulation,' *Economic Record* November.

Swedberg, R. (1990) *Economics and Sociology; Redefining their Boundaries: Conversations with Economists and Sociologists*, Princeton: Princeton University Press.

— (1991) *Schumpeter: A Biography*, Princeton: Princeton University Press.

Sweezy, P.M. (1956) *The Theory of Capitalist Development*, New York: Monthly Review Press.

Tabb, W.K. (1995) *The Postwar Japanese System: Cultural Economy and Economic Transformation*, New York: Oxford University Press.

Teece, D.J. (1993) 'The Dynamics of Industrial Capitalism: Perspectives on Alfred Chandler's *Scale and Scope*,' *Journal of Economic Literature* March.

Temin, P. (1982) 'The Impact of the Depression on Economic Thought,' in C. P. Kindleberger and G. di Tella (eds) *Economics in the Long View; Essays in Honor of W.W. Rostow, Volume I Models and Methods*, New York: New York University Press.

Thrift, N. (1994) 'On the Social and Cultural Determinants of International Financial Centres,' in S. Corbridge, N. Thrift, and R. Martin (eds) *Money, Power and Space*, Oxford: Basil Blackwell.

Thurow, L.C. (1970) *Investment in Human Capital*, Belmont, Cal.: Wadsworth.

— (1975) *Generating Inequality: Mechanisms of Distribution in the US Economy*, New York: Basic Books.

— (1994) 'Microchips, Not Potato Chips,' *Foreign Affairs* July/August.

— (1996) *The Future of Capitalism: How Today's Economic Forces Shape Tomorrow's World*, New York: Morrow.

Tilly, C. (1991) 'Individualism Askew,' *American Journal of Sociology* March.

Tobin, J. (1975) 'Keynesian Models of Recession and Depression,' *American Economic Review* May.

— (1985) 'Theoretical Issues in Macroeconomics,' in G.R. Feiwel (ed.) *Issues in Contemporary Macroeconomics and Distribution*, Albany: State University of New York Press.

— (1992a) 'The Invisible Hand in Modern Macroeconomics,' in M. Fry (ed.) *Adam Smith's Legacy: His Place in the Development of Modern Economics*, London: Routledge.

— (1992b) 'Keynesian Theory: Is It Still a Useful Tool in the Economic Reality of Today?' in M. Baldassarri (ed.) *Keynes and the Economic Policies of the 1980s*, New York: St Martin's Press.

Topel, R.H. (1994) 'Regional Labor Markets and the Determinants of Wage Inequality,' *American Economic Review* May.

Toporowski, J. (1995) 'The Contradictions of Market Socialism,' *Monthly Review* April.

Traxler, F. and Unger, B. (1994) 'Governance, Economic Restructuring, and International Competitiveness,' *Journal of Economic Issues* March.

Turner, L. (1992) 'Industrial Relations and the Reorganization of Work in West Germany: Unions for the US,' in L. Mishel and P. Voos (eds) *Unions and Economic Competition*, Armonk, NY: M.E. Sharpe.

Tversky, A. and Kahneman, D. (1991) 'Loss Adversion in Riskless Choice: A Reference Dependent Model,' *Quarterly Journal of Economics* November.

Vaizey, J. (1977) 'Keynes and Cambridge,' in R. Skidelsky (ed.) *The End of the Keynesian Era: Essays on the Disintegration of the Keynesian Political Economy*, New York: Holmes & Meier.

Veblen, T. (1919) 'Why is Economics Not an Evolutionary Science?' from *The Place of Science in Modern Civilization, and Other Essays* in M. Lerner (ed.) *The Portable Veblen*, New York: Viking Press, 1948.

— (1964) 'The Beginnings of Ownership,' *Essays in Our Changing Order*, New York: Augustus M. Kelley.

Vernon, R. (1971) *Sovereignty at Bay*, New York: Basic Books.

Verspagen, B. (1992) 'Endogenous Innovation in Neo-Classical Growth Models: A Survey,' *Journal of Macroeconomics* Fall.

Vig, N.J. (1985) 'Introduction: Political Science and Political Economy,' in N.J. Vig and S.E. Schier (eds) *Political Economy in Western Democracies*, New York: Holmes & Meier.

Vincent, D.R. (1995) 'Review of Stephen J. Brams' "Theory of moves",' *Journal of Economic Literature* June.

Viner, J. (1927) 'Adam Smith and Laissez-Faire,' *Journal of Political Economy*; in D.A. Irwin (ed.) *Essays on the Intellectual History of Economics*, Princeton: Princeton University Press, 1991.

— (1941) 'Marshall's Economics in Relation to the Man and His Time,' in D.A. Irwin (ed.) *Essays on the Intellectual History of Economics*, Princeton: Princeton University Press, 1991.

— (1949) 'Bentham and J.S. Mill: The Utilitarian Background,' *American Economic Review* March; reprinted in June 22, 1998 D.A. Irwin (ed.) *Essays on the Intellectual History of Economics*, Princeton: Princeton University Press, 1991.

— (1960) 'The intellectual history of laissez faire,' *Journal of Law and Economics* October.

— (1963) 'The Economist in History,' *American Economic Review* May.

Wade, R. (1990) *Governing the Market: Economic Theory and the Role of Government in East Asian Industrialization*, Princeton: Princeton University Press.

— (1994) 'Selected Industrial Policies in East Asia: Is *The East Asian Miracle* Right?' in *Miracle or Design? Lessons From the East Asian Experience*, Policy Essay No. 11, Washington, DC: Overseas Development Council.

— (1998) 'The Asian Debt-and-Development Crisis of 1997–9: Causes and Consequences,' *World Development* August.

Wall, H.J. (1995) 'Cricket v Baseball as an Engine of Economic Growth,' *Royal Economic Society Newsletter* July.

Wallerstein, I. (1974) *Capitalist Agriculture and the Origins of the European World-Economy in the Sixteenth Century: The Modern World System*, Volume I, New York: Cambridge University Press.

— (1979) 'The Rise and Future Demise of the World Capitalist System: Concepts for Comparative Analysis,' *The World Capitalist System*, Cambridge: Cambridge University Press.

Walsh, V. and Graham, H. (1980) *Classical and Neoclassical Theories of General Equilibrium: Historical Origins and Mathematical Structures*, New York: Oxford University Press.

Ward, B. (1972) *What's Wrong with Economics?* New York: Basic Books.

Warren, B. (1980) *Imperialism: Pioneer of Capitalism*, London: Verso.

Waterman, A.M.C. (1991) *Revolution, Economics and Religion; Christian Political Economy, 1798–1833*, Cambridge: Cambridge University Press.

Watt, I. (1951) 'Robinson Crusoe as a Myth,' *Essays in Criticism, The Rise of the Novel*, Berkeley: University of California Press, 1957.

Weintraub, E.R. (1979) *Microfoundations*, New York: Cambridge University Press.

— (1985) *General Equilibrium Analysis: Studies in Appraisal*, New York: Cambridge University Press.

— (1991) *Stabilizing Dynamics*, New York: Cambridge University Press.

Weiskopf, T.E. (1994) 'Alternative Structures of Accumulation Approaches to the Analysis of Capitalist Booms and Crises,' in D.M. Kotz, T. McDonough, and M. Reich (eds) *Social Structures of Accumulation: The Political Economy of Growth and Crisis*, New York: Cambridge University Press.

Weiskopf, T.E., Gordon, D.M., and Bowles, S. (1983) 'Hearts and Minds: A Social Model of US Productivity Growth,' *Brookings Papers on Economic Activity* 2.

Weitzman, M.L. (1996) 'Hybridizing Growth Theory,' *American Economic Review* May.

Weldes, J. (1989) 'Marxism and Methodological Individualism: A Critique,' *Theory and Society* May.

Werhane, P.H. (1991) *Adam Smith and His Legacy for Modern Capitalism*, New York: Oxford University Press.

Wightman, W.P.D. (1980) 'Introduction,' in W.P.D. Wightman and J.C. Brice (eds) Adam Smith *Essays on Philosophical Subjects*, Oxford: Clarendon Press.

Williamson, J.G. (1995) 'Globalization, Convergence, and History,' National Bureau of Economic Research, Working Paper 5259.

Williamson, O.E. (1985) *The Economic Institutions of Capitalism: Firms, Markets, Relational Contracting*, New York: Free Press.

Williamson, O.E. and Winter, S.G. (eds) (1991) *The Nature of the Firm: Origins, Evolution, and Development*, New York: Oxford University Press.

Winter, S.G. (1992) *Evolutionary Economics*, London: Edward Elgar.

Wiseman, J. and Littlechild, S.C. (1990) 'Crusoe's Kingdom: Cost, Choice and Political Economy,' in S. F. Frowen (ed.) *Unknowledge and Choice in Economics*, Houndsmills, England: Macmillan

Wolff, E.N. (1996) *Top Heavy*, New York: The New Press.

Wolfson, M. (1995) 'A Methodological Framework for Understanding Institutional Change in the Capitalist Financial System,' *Social Concept* July.

Wood, A. (1994) *North–South Trade, Employment and Inequality: Changing Fortunes in a Skill Driven World*, Oxford: Clarendon Press.

Wood, E.M. (1989) 'Rational Choice Marxism: Is the Game Worth the Candle?' *New Left Review* September/October.

Wood, R.E. (1986) *From Marshall Plan to Debt Crisis: Foreign Aid and Development Choices in the World Economy*, Berkeley: University of California Press.

Woodford, M. (1994) 'Review of '*Structural Slumps*,' *Journal of Economic Literature* December.

World Bank (1993) *The East Asian Miracle: Economic Growth and Public Policy*, New York: Oxford University Press.

— (1995) *World Development Report: Workers in an Integrated World*, New York: Oxford University Press.

Wright, E.O. (1989) 'What is Analytical Marxism? *Socialist Review* July–December.

Yergin, D. and Stanislaw, J. (1998) *The Commanding Heights: The Battle Between Government and the Marketplace that is Remaking the Modern World*, New York: Simon & Schuster.

You, J.-I. (1994) 'Macroeconomic structure, endogenous technical change and growth,' *Cambridge Journal of Economics* April.

Young, A. (1993) 'Invention and Bounded Learning by Doing,' *Journal of Political Economy* June.

— (1928) 'Increasing Returns and Economic Progress,' *Economic Journal* December.

Zevin, R. (1992) 'Are World Financial Markets More Open? If so Why and With What Effect?' in T. Banuri and J. Schor (eds) *Financial Openness and National Autonomy*, Oxford: Oxford University Press.

Ziliak, S.T. (1996) 'The End of Welfare and the Contradictions of Compassion,' *Independent Review* Spring.

Index